CADD Made Easy

CADD Made Easy

A Comprehensive Guide for Architects and Designers

Antony Radford

Garry Stevens

WITHDRAWN

McGraw-Hill Book Company

New York   St. Louis   San Francisco   Auckland   Bogotá
Hamburg   Johannesburg   London   Madrid   Mexico
Milan   Montreal   New Delhi   Panama
Paris   São Paulo   Singapore
Sydney   Tokyo   Toronto

Library of Congress Cataloging-in-Publication Data

Radford, Antony.
     CADD made easy.

     Bibliography: p.
     Includes index.
     1. Architectural design — Data processing.
     2. Architectural practice — Data processing.   3. Computer-
aided design.   I. Stevens, Garry.   II. Title.
     NA2728.R34   1987)   720'.28'5   86-18017
     ISBN 0-07-051094-6

1234567890   DOC/DOC   8932109876

ISBN 0-07-051094-6

*The editors for this book were Joan Zseleczky and Edward N. Huggins,
the designer was Naomi Auerbach, and the production
supervisor was Teresa F. Leaden. It was set in Century Schoolbook
by Digitype.*

Printed and bound by R. R. Donnelley & Sons Company.

Contents

Preface

The Book

The future of the design and construction industries will be closely linked to the developing use of computers and computer methods. The thesis of this book is that architects and designers need to know about both the theory and practice of computing in order to survive and prosper. This book provides in one place the information necessary to understand the background, principles, and practice of computer-aided drafting and design (CADD), the support of design through computer-aided management, and the new concepts of computer-aided knowledge. While addressed primarily to architects, the book will be of value to other designers and engineers.

The book is in three parts. The first part, *Context*, provides the background: a brief history of architectural computing, followed by discussions about the computer industry, how computers work, and the concepts of systems and mathematical models that lie behind computer programs. The second part, *Applications*, describes the range of computer applications in design practice, from office automation through drafting to design aids, and the notions that the computer itself can be a designer and source of knowledge. The third part, *Decisions*, looks at the risks, issues, and options involved in introducing and working with computers and speculates on the influence of computers and microprocessors on the future form and practice of architecture.

We have aimed in this book to bring together strands from design, systems theory, computer technology, and artificial intelligence. Information on the current state of hardware and software is combined with some ideas and directions derived from research activities. It is not a catalog of applications, although most significant areas of computers in architecture are mentioned in the course of discussion. The mood is optimistic but reasoned, with a discussion of some of the problems as well as advantages associated with computing in architecture. Our intention has been to explain the topic as clearly and succinctly as possible, avoiding hyperbole but displaying some of the enthusiasm we feel. We hope you enjoy and learn from the result.

How to Use This Book

Each chapter except the last is divided into "major" and "secondary" texts. The major text provides the essential information and develops the themes of the book. The secondary text provides background information (Chap. 1), technical detail (Chap. 2), extensions into further less central areas (Chaps. 3, 4, and 8), and detailed examples (Chaps. 5, 6, and 7).

As an *introduction to CADD and architectural computing*, read the major text for each chapter, plus any of the secondary text that interests you, or simply browse at will.

As a *textbook* for an introductory course in CADD and architectural computing, each chapter should parallel one or two lectures that discuss the topics introduced. Such a series of lectures would provide a sound foundation for higher-level courses exploring computer programming or particular application areas. There is a suggested bibliography for further reading in App. 1.

As a *reference book*, go straight to the chapter or section of interest. The major and secondary text for each chapter is designed to be self-contained and is cross-referenced to other parts of the book where necessary. Captions to all illustrations are complete without depending on the text for explanation. There is a comprehensive glossary of terms in App. 2.

Acknowledgments

A book such as this owes much to those in the computer and architecture industries who have shared their knowledge and experience, both in their earlier writings and in their personal discussions with the authors. We thank them all, and particularly our colleagues in the Architectural Computing Unit in the Faculty of Architecture at Sydney University, among others David Cornell, Richard Coyne, John Gero, John Mitchell, Zoltan Nemes-Nemeth, Michael Rosenman, Andrzej Sambura, and Fay Sudweeks. We must also thank Roy Hill of Cadcom (Australia) for help in producing the illustrations to the secondary text in Chap. 5. Any faults, of course, are all our own.

Tony Radford
Garry Stevens

Context

1

The Architect
and the Computer

1.1 Introduction

The extraordinary role of computing as the world's most dynamic industry derives from two circumstances: First, computers are actually useful, so people and firms have created a demand for them; second, computers are very cheap and becoming cheaper. Humans are very good at many things, such as language and tool making. Of all our tools, the most powerful is the computer, and we happen to be very good at designing and building computers. All this has led to their penetration into everyday life to a degree that would not have been thought possible 20 or even 10 years ago. For about the same price as a family car, an individual can buy computing power that whole governments could not have commanded in 1960. If we could get along quite well without such computing in 1960, why do we need it now? In particular, why do designers need computers? As with the laser, which at the time of its invention was a solution looking for a problem, the availability of personal computing allows us not only to do things better than they were done before but also to do things that we could not possibly have done before (Fig. 1.1).

Computers are one of the forces that will mold the future of the architectural profession. They are not the greatest of the currents felt in architecture, but their effect will still be considerable. They have the capacity to do both great harm and great good; which this shall be lies largely in the hands of architects. To prevent the one and encourage the other, and to survive in this new industrial revolution, architects and designers must acquire a solid grasp of computing and computer-aided design. Toward that goal we have written this book on computer-aided drafting and design (CADD).

The special subject area concerned with the use of computers in architecture goes by several names. The wider field of the use of computers in engineering, construction, and industry to design objects is called *com-*

puter-aided design, usually abbreviated *CAD* (pronounced either "cad" or "cee ay dee"). Sometimes the term *technical computing* is used to cover CAD in this sense as well as the more conventional data-processing uses of

Figure 1.1   Architecture is a late profession to embrace computing as an everyday tool. The attitude of most architects has only recently passed from indifference to wary acceptance, and the relationship between the two is still controversial. Those who have invested time and money into computer use have discovered that computers demand constant effort to use effectively but repay the attention in the form of better business practices and better building designs. It is often said that a user becomes "married" to his or her computer, and this encapsulates neatly the close ties that develop between humans and computers as the machines become as essential a tool as pens and T squares. *(Cartoon drawn with a computer by the authors; all diagrams in this book are drawn with a computer unless otherwise indicated.*

computers in design offices, construction, and engineering. The term *computer-aided architectural design (CAAD)* is usually used to mean CAD specifically in architecture. In this book we generally use the phrase *architectural computing* to include the use of computers in the design process (CAAD), their use in project and office management, and all the other things that architectural firms might want to do with computers.

In this first chapter we describe the field of architectural computing and discuss the relationship between architects and computers, the history of this relationship, and some of the problems that arise in making it work. In this chapter's secondary text we briefly describe the histories of computing and technology in architecture.

1.2   Why Computers Don't Make Life Easy

The modern computer is the most complex, sophisticated, and versatile tool devised by human minds. Tools like spanners and hammers are really simple, and correspondingly easy to use; a hammer can pretty well only be used to hit objects, a spanner to undo nuts, a pen to write and draw. Slightly more complex tools like lathes require at least reading an instruction manual, and moderately complex tools like cars oblige one to be trained. Computers are in another league altogether. A car can only ever do one thing: transport us from *A* to *B*. We will never be able to convert our car into a bulldozer, a minibus, a crane, a boat, or an airplane. Moreover, the car always works the same way: we only have to learn to drive once, for all the major control devices in the car (steering wheel, accelerator, brake, etc.) always have the same function and form.

A computer can do many different things, depending on the programs it is running. Each program may have a different mode of operation, so the use of each program must be learned afresh. Moreover, the more versatile a particular program is, the more things we must learn. This is familiar through pocket calculators, even for those who don't already own a computer. Anyone can use a four-function calculator, but the skill to use one of those programmable scientific jobs takes a couple of hours to learn.

Many of the difficulties stem from the fact that the industry still hasn't had much experience in designing computers that normal people can use. In the mid-1970s all computers were managed by professionals who had spent long years in acquiring the necessary expertise, so computer designers did not have to spend much effort accommodating these professionals. Since then, microcomputers and many minicomputers (both defined in Sec. 2.3) have usually been operated by people without this background. The industry has not yet adequately solved the problems that occur when naive users are confronted with computers, and it is unlikely that it ever will. The users and the industry will each have to travel part way along the road (Laurie, 1983).

Really to use a computer well, then, demands a certain commitment from the user. Machines do not work telepathically. A reasonably functional program, like a word processor or project manager, comes complete with a thick manual (perhaps 200 or so pages), which we at least have to skim through if we are going to use the program. If we want to be fluent and obtain the full benefit, there is just no alternative to reading and digesting a lot of material. So computers aren't magically going to make life effortless. Since computers are used not only to do some tasks better but also to do tasks never before attempted, most people find themselves putting in at least as much effort on a computer-assisted job as on the manual equivalent.

Word processing is a good example. This book was written completely on a word processor. It allowed us to compose as we wrote, very easily moving paragraphs around, rearranging text, changing the page width, correcting mistakes, and making sundry alterations. Right up to the moment we sent it to the publisher, we could make major changes. Had this been typed on a typewriter, even tiny changes would have meant retyping whole paragraphs or pages, and major alterations would have been laborious. However, the ability to make changes so easily encouraged us to tinker constantly with the book — and all this tinkering cost us more than than if we had let things be by having it typed manually.

Nonetheless, the excitement of computing doesn't come from doing things more quickly and easily than we could do them by hand. It comes, rather, from doing things we had never dreamed of doing before, things for which there is no parallel in manual methods. This is the challenge of computing.

1.3   The Discipline of Architectural Computing

The subject matter of architectural computing can be roughly divided into six areas (Fig. 1.2):

- Computer science
- Information processing
- Computer graphics
- Design theory
- Knowledge engineering
- Applications issues

Computer science is the whole field of computer study and development, a vastly greater field than architectural computing. For that matter, it is larger than architecture; there are many more computer scientists than architects. It has been noted that the term *science* is somewhat of a misnomer: *the art and craft of computing* might be more appropriate. From the many subfields of the discipline, architectural computing has concentrated on those most relevant to its needs. The more recondite mathematics is not

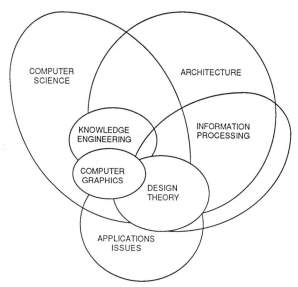

Figure 1.2 Architectural computing draws upon computer science for programming practices and techniques, and, being such a visual profession, particularly upon computer graphics. The more mundane commercial uses of computers involve the field of information processing and raise applications issues. A guiding set of methodologies is provided by design theory. Knowledge engineering is assuming greater importance as more and more intelligence is sought in drafting and expert systems. *(Diagram by the authors.)*

so much of interest as are the many tools and techniques accumulated over the years. A few languages (nowadays Pascal, C, and PROLOG), the techniques of good programming, the design of computer algorithms, computer systems analysis and design, computer communications, and database methodologies are perhaps the major parts, and we explain all these in Chaps. 2 and 3.

Information processing is the production of information by accessing and processing data on a computer, usually associated with the commercial applications of computers. *Data processing* is the more traditional name. It is discussed in Chap. 4.

Computer graphics is, strictly speaking, a subfield of both computer science and information processing, but it deserves its own place in the context of architectural computing. This area is concerned with the creation and manipulation of images, using a computer. At present, computer-aided drafting systems are the major preoccupations: how they work, how to design them, how to use them. More abstruse, but very interesting, problems arise in the generation of lifelike scenes and the exploration of form, color, shading, and texture. Computer graphics is discussed in Chap. 5.

Design theory in architectural computing is concerned with the use of computers as a design medium and is to a large degree the successor of the design methods movement. Partly by studying the design process itself, it attempts to construct coherent, systematic methods for building design. These methods may involve (1) the simulation of some properties and aspects of buildings in order to appraise different design solutions or (2) the actual generation of design solutions. Many of its techniques are borrowed from the field called *operations research,* which is concerned partly with the mathematics of simulation (predicting the future state of some system) and of optimization (finding the best way to arrive at some future state). Problems of allocation, scheduling, and routing come within its ambit. It is related to systems analysis (the analysis of complex systems) and to management science. Operations research techniques can be used to systematize decision making. Design theory is discussed in Chap. 6.

Knowledge engineering is a relatively new field, sprung from long-standing work in artificial intelligence, that is, the study of intelligence through computers. Knowledge engineering studies the ways that knowledge can be acquired and represented by a computer and utilized by people who do not themselves possess that knowledge. CAD systems are increasingly being viewed as primarily concerned with knowledge rather than with graphics and modeling. These matters are discussed in Chap. 7.

Applications issues are those matters arising from the selection and use of computers in the office and in buildings. These issues include training, finance, legal issues, the ergonomics of computing, methods of designing buildings to cope with computers, and the management of computer systems. We discuss applications issues in Chap. 8.

1.4   A History of Architectural Computing

1.4.1   Architectural computing yesterday

Architectural computing sprang from four sources. The first was the world of conventional data processing, in which computers were used to assist in office management and mundane business functions. This was commonplace by 1960 in government and large organizations. The second was the area of computer graphics and computer-aided design. Initial work was done in the early 1960s in the United States, and by the mid-1960s a few large firms were using computers to design automobiles, aircraft, electronic components, and lenses. The third source was operations research, a branch of applied mathematics developed during the Second World War to improve decision making by building mathematical models of simulations. The fourth was the design methods movement, which introduced the notion that design could be a systematic, analytical process.

Architectural computing appeared as an object of study in its own right in the late 1960s. Inspired by the success of computers in large engineering firms and the promise of the design methods movement, adventurous individuals in several schools of architecture (notably MIT in Boston and UCLA in Los Angeles in the United States; Edinburgh, Strathclyde, and Cambridge universities in the United Kingdom; and the University of Sydney in Australia) commenced projects involving the computerization of some aspect of the architectural function. They were very conscious of the pioneering nature of their work; after all, computers cost hundreds of thousands of dollars, hardly a reasonable purchase for most architectural firms. The very early conferences and books (Barnett, 1965; Milne, 1968; Campion, 1968; Harper, 1968) could produce only the results of tentative forays, yet they looked forward to an exciting future just around the corner. This millenarian fervor has been characteristic of writings on architectural computing. Articles from the 1960s read much the same as those of the 1980s in their expectation of great things "soon."

In the late 1960s the first computer-aided drafting systems were released on the market by American vendors, capitalizing on the advent of mini-computers and the (relatively) cheap new display devices of the Tektronix Corporation, which reduced the cost of systems from millions of dollars to a few hundred thousand. The Computervision Corporation released the first general-purpose computer-aided design system in 1969, and the firms Calma and Applicon developed systems intended for electronics firms (Albert, 1982). In the early 1970s Autotrol entered the AEC (architecture, engineering, and construction) market with a two-dimensional drafting system intended for plant design by large engineering firms. Skidmore, Owings, and Merrill in the United States and some large Japanese multi-disciplinary firms started work on their own drafting systems. With these rare exceptions, the architectural profession showed little interest in computing. In Britain, researchers at Cambridge commenced development on a system that was not simply a drafting tool, but a design aid. Umbrella organizations of CAD vendors, researchers, and users were formed in the United States [e.g., the Society for Computer Applications in Engineering, Planning, and Architecture (CEPA)], Britain [e.g., the Construction Industry Computing Association (CICA), then known as the Design Office Consortium], Australia [e.g., the Association for Computer-Aided Design (ACADS)], and other countries.

By the mid-1970s it became clear that CAD systems would have to develop some sort of intelligence far above and beyond being simple drawing systems. In the United States, M&S Intergraph developed a general CAD system particularly suited to mapping; it quickly captured that market and still dominates it today (Daratech, 1984). Intergraph also challenged Autotrol in the AEC field, and other vendors devoted their efforts toward penetrating the mechanical engineering market (Albert, 1982). These systems were still very expensive, and only quite large firms could contemplate investing the time and money necessary. Microcomputers had only just entered the marketplace and were mainly for (wealthy) hobbyists. Further, the promise of the design methods movement had dissipated before the realities of the fuzzy design process. The recession that began in 1974 effectively dampened the already limited enthusiasm of architectural and construction firms for CAD systems. Architectural firms, in particular, had the more serious concern of simple survival on their minds. The profession was dubious and skeptical, although their colleagues in engineering were finding the systems more and more useful.

Toward the end of the 1970s the great debate between the advocates and the critics became more strident. Possibly computers would be of no practical use in design (Bazjanac, 1975, p. 24):

> The promise that computers will improve the efficiency of the design process is absurd. Even if the use of machines allowed the designer to spend more time designing — and it does not — how can anyone claim that the designer would therefore produce better design solutions? The design process cannot be controlled by the manipulation of resources: adding resources will not necessarily speed up the design process or improve its quality.

If they did prove useful, then the social effects might be bad (Cross, 1977, p. 440):

> The more realistic threat of CAD is that computer power will equal design power: those who can afford the expensive computer systems will come to dominate the design process. This computer-strengthened design power will be centralised in large organisations, and the scope for the majority of private individuals to influence the design of the built environment will be greatly reduced.

Both sides agreed that things were going to change (Mitchell, 1977, p. xi):

> . . . the theory and practice have developed to the point where it can confidently be predicted that, during the 1980s, everyday use of CAD techniques will radically transform the practice of architecture. . . .

And maybe design would even improve (Maver, 1978, p. 104):

> The promise is of a wide range of readily accessible, easily usable and inexpensive design aids which will allow the design team . . . to explore the formal and functional attributes of a wide range of design alternatives in search for "that future state which most closely approximates to man[kind's] concept of the ideal."

Computer-aided drafting systems took off from the end of the 1970s. Their advantages were touted by the vendors, the technical press, and the government departments that could afford them. Aggressive competition between vendors ensured rapid improvements in utility and steady price reductions. Engineers found them fun (not an aspect to be despised), even if they could do little to justify proposals except rely on an intuition that the systems were beneficial. Most justifications were based on potential savings over employing draftspeople, based in the main on vendor-supplied information.

1.4.2 Architectural computing today

Architectural computing came of age in the 1980s. In the 1970s computer-aided architectural design was the fond dream and hope of academics and enthusiasts. In the 1980s the profession discovered what other professionals and businesspeople had known for years: Computers were realistic, practical tools that could ease a great many tedious, dreary tasks. In the United States, 30 percent of the 2500 most active architectural and engineering firms were involved in computing in 1976, leaping to 65 percent in 1981. Of course, "involvement" can mean many things; the most expensive and glamorous products, the computer-aided design and drafting systems, were owned by only 10 percent of the architectural firms ("Use of Computers Accelerates," 1982).

A 1985 survey (Wagner, 1985) illustrated the suddenness of the upsurge in computer use among architects: Fully 62 percent of the computer users had purchased their systems in the 2 years prior to the survey. This survey gave a picture of what architects were doing with their computers (Fig. 1.3). The most common function was office management — particularly word processing (93 percent of computer-using architects), specification writing (85 percent), and the use of spreadsheets (69 percent). Then came the area of project cost analysis and control, common tasks being project cost accounting (43 percent), job estimating (40 percent), job budgeting (36 percent), and job costing (35 percent). Project scheduling and management

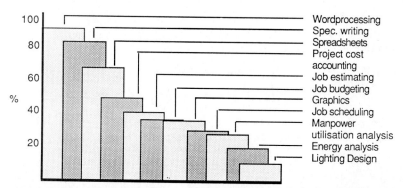

Figure 1.3 Percentage of computer-using respondents replying that they use computers in the displayed applications areas (Wagner, 1985). Although CAD systems are one of the most interesting areas, and certainly the most discussed area, of architectural computing, they are only used by a minority of computer users. The emphasis on word processing and spreadsheets is typical of any small business. While it is hoped that computers will allow architects to improve and expand their services, the small number using design aids indicates that this has not yet happened. *(Diagram by the authors.)*

tasks were the third most cited area, including job scheduling (25 percent) and manpower utilization analysis (22 percent). Architectural engineering functions were not a major interest of the respondents, only 19 percent using their computers for energy analysis and 9 percent for lighting design, for example. Some 33 percent were using computer graphics, although this figure did not differentiate between those architects who used everyday business graphics for the construction of charts and diagrams and those who used drawing and drafting systems.

As a snapshot of computing in the architect's office, the 1985 survey revealed a surprisingly conventional pattern of usage, not too dissimilar from any other business in its emphasis on mundane office management functions (Fig. 1.4). It would seem that architects had not yet truly taken up the challenge of computing and incorporated it as a standard tool in the architectural design process.

Research in architectural computing has been intense and widespread—probably one of the two or three most active research fields in architecture and building (Bedford and Groak, 1983). International cooperation has been consolidated with the establishment of an umbrella orga-

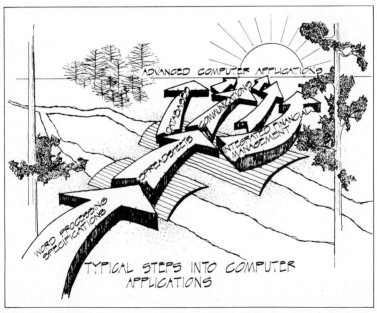

Figure 1.4 Almost all firms start off by computerizing their office management, commencing with word processing. Spreadsheets require both more effort and more imagination to use, and beyond them a whole cluster of applications areas opens up, including database management systems and communications to other computers for electronic mail and database access. Only after these paths have been explored do most offices progress to using design aids and CAD. *(Hand-drawn, used by permission of Architectural Technology.)*

nization called FACE (International Federation of Computer Users in Engineering, Architecture, and Related Fields). There has also been a growing interest in education in architectural computing. The first specialist postgraduate qualification in the discipline was offered in 1978 by the University of Sydney, and other tertiary institutions now offer postgraduate programs. Almost all schools provide undergraduate facilities (Doubilet, 1984), and relationships between instructors in the field have been strengthened by the establishment of the Association for Computer-Aided Design in Architecture (ACADIA) in the United States and eCAADe (Education in CAAD in Europe) on the continent.

1.5   Problems in Architectural Computing

1.5.1   Problems in the office

The advantages that computers are to bring to building design are threefold: saving time, reducing drudgery, and achieving the optimum. If computers do indeed confer these benefits, why have they been so slow to enter the architect's office, and why have they enjoyed such uneven acceptance? John Lansdown listed four reasons in 1980 that still apply (Lansdown, 1980).

First, practicing architects have been ignorant of the scope and potential of computers in architectural design. Much is still experimental or has only just come out of the research stage. Architecture is not a research-intensive field, and the profession is highly skeptical of architectural research as a whole (Bedford and Groak, 1983). The work of CAD researchers is almost invariably published in abstruse academic journals, which are not at all like the international glossies. Worse still, those articles which do appear in the popular architectural journals are often of the pretty picture sort, complete with "Isn't this amazing?" captions and text. Such articles tend to distance the architect from CAAD and give credence to the unfortunate belief that computing is a mysterious business (Lawson, 1978). People get tired of being told how glorious the future is going to be and how all the old fuddy-duddies had better smarten themselves up and buy one of these incredible machines.

Second, CAD has become associated with the design of standardized, or industrialized, buildings. It is true that some of the largest, most expensive, and most visible systems (such as the British modeling system BDS in its earlier incarnation as OXSYS) were developed for some standardized building system, but CAD encompasses a far greater field, and a misunderstanding of this has obscured the merits of CAD as a systematic approach to any rational building method.

Third, there is an understandable concern over the idea of using keyboards, screens, and mice (we shall explain these later) as opposed to drawing boards, paper, and pen. Some architects feel a great antipathy toward the mechanical quality of drawings generated by drafting systems.

Fourth, a large number of architects take the view that architectural design is so completely an intuitive and qualitative activity that mathematical and quantitative aids are totally inappropriate. A legacy of disillusionment from the failure of the highly touted design methods of the 1960s has contributed to this view (Goumain and Mallen, 1980).

In small firms, the directors control all or almost all the decisions and take the responsibility. They are in the business of designing buildings, not of computing. Their education did not include architectural computing (only now are graduates being turned out with some computing expertise) and, quite rightly, they are unwilling to entrust the management and use of computers to others. A computer has a major impact on the whole working of a firm, and directors who have no computing expertise lose personal control over important functions in their firm ("Roundtable," 1984). It is no surprise that computing is much more readily acceptable in medium to large firms, where the directors have already delegated the decision-making responsibilities.

1.5.2 Problems in the building industry

William Mitchell (1977, 1982) has identified other problem areas. The first and now the most enthusiastic users of CAD were the automobile, aerospace, and electronics industries, all of which are composed of a small number of large firms that have no difficulty investing in the very expensive equipment required for CAD. Any single product will have a design budget many times the cost of an individual item, and one design can serve as a template for hundreds or thousands of items. Moreover, most of these items (be they a chassis, wing, or computer board) are amenable to precise definition by numerical data and are designed within a well-defined problem paradigm.

Architectural firms, on the other hand, are small and numerous. In the United States 80 percent of the 13,000 or so architectural firms have less than 10 people, with 62 percent employing but a single architect, and in Britain the mean staff size of architectural firms is about 20. Engineering firms in Britain, which have a much greater acceptance of computing, have an average of 50 staff (Baxter, 1984; Witte, 1985b). Architectural firms traditionally possess little capital beyond the premises they occupy and their office furniture, if that. The installation of a sophisticated computer-aided drafting system thus represents a significant addition to the amount of capital owned, as compared to only a minor increase over current capital in the other industries. In 1985, seventy percent of nonusers gave excessive cost as their main reason for not having a computer; they believed that a first system would cost about $15,000 (Wagner, 1985). Such a sum would not be considered a very great capital cost in most businesses, and it is much less than the annual cost of a junior architect; nonetheless, architects worry about the consequences of incurring such a long-term debt. Even the rental of computer time from a firm can constitute a considerable expense for a small office. Since the design cost of a building can only be a small percentage of its total cost, it is difficult to amortize the cost of CAD over successive projects.

Yet another problem arises over the means of communication within the building industry, in which the central information channel is that from the architect to the main contractor. Under the standard forms of contract, all the design information must flow through this channel, and most of this information passes in the form of drawings or schedules. Unlike the industries that first used CAD, the building industry is fragmented: Mitchell (1977, 1985a) called it Balkanized. The specialists at both ends of the information channel are each independent firms working as temporary groups. Having completed one job, they will separate to form new groupings, and often they will be working on several jobs at once. This fragmentation is not conducive to the most effective use of computers.

1.5.3 Problems in the computer industry

Everybody has trouble with computers. The computer industry has not exactly gone out of its way to ensure that clients have successful installations. Marketing staff, from microcomputers to CAD systems, are frequently ignorant of the needs of architects and not even too hot on their own products (Mileaf, 1983b). Not that this is limited to architecture. A survey of Australian businesses using computers revealed enormous discontent (Davies, 1984). Only 5 percent were very satisfied with their installations, some 70 percent were dissatisfied in some way, and 10 percent had actually abandoned their systems completely. The main causes of complaints were faulty software, poor support, and misleading salespeople.

Computer-aided drafting systems, perhaps the most complex systems that architects have to deal with, have had more than their fair share of problems. Their use passes through three stages: from (1) installation and experiment to (2) inefficient use for production drawings, and finally, it is hoped, to (3) efficient generation of drawings. Organizations move from one stage to the other in variable time periods, depending on the degree of management success in organizing the process, on the presence or absence of industrial relations problems, and on the suppliers' failure to deliver the necessary software (Arnold and Senker, 1982). Only in the past few years has a methodology of CAD system management been formed (a methodology detailed in Chap. 8).

One of the problems encountered by architectural firms investing in computing has been the acute shortage of architecture-specific software.

Even for quite mundane accounting purposes, many firms have had difficulty acquiring suitable packages. This is partly because architects want to do quite peculiar things with computers and partly because the everyday sorts of things they want to do, they want to do in a peculiar way. Again, this situation has been alleviated only in the past few years, and the major problem today is not so much a lack of software as a lack of knowledge about the existence of that software. Fortunately, some major architectural periodicals are now disseminating information and publishing comprehensive lists (Fanning, 1983; "Guide to Computer Software," 1984; Krawczyk, 1984; Witte, 1985c).

1.5.4   Problems in the future

We should not be surprised by these problems: although real, they are a symptom of the tender youth of the relationship between a long-established building industry and the brash young computer industry with which it finds it needs to consort. The long-term solution will arise through adaptation on both sides to exploit the good while hopefully avoiding most of the bad. True, this adaptation process may not be easy and will leave us with some casualties and a very different construction industry from the one we know today. Meanwhile, the relationship can be made as smooth as possible by both sides being informed. Most of the problems in architectural computing, large and small, have arisen because of the natural human tendency to be wise only after the event. The major problem in the immediate future will be the continuation of a rapid rate of change, which means that there is no right answer — no stable paradigm that can be used as a model of a computer-integrated architectural practice.

1.6   Summary

Architectural computing as a discipline in its own right is very young. Its utility and place in architecture have been much debated, reflecting the older and wider debate of art versus science in architecture. In the early days critics attacked computers both as dangerous to the profession and practice of architecture and as of dubious use. Now that computers are everyday tools of even small businesses, the latter argument is not often heard. Still, there is much to criticize in architectural computing, and many architects worry that computers will profoundly change architecture for the worse. We agree that computers will transform architecture and even the conservative construction industry, but we are hopeful that it will be for the better.

Computers bring new abilities to all of us. Word processing simplifies document creation, for instance, and painting and drawing systems enable people with minimal artistic ability to produce graphics previously quite beyond their skill. Computers also promise greater creativity by removing tedious tasks and destroying monotonous assembly-line jobs. But computers will not necessarily be used in such constructive ways. Rather than making life more pleasant for all, they can be used for the exclusive benefit of elite minorities. Like most of the tools that humankind has created, the use of computers depends at least as much on the user as on the machine. We return to these themes in Chap. 9.

Some Further History

A1.1   A Brief History of Computing

Three strands lie behind the history of the earliest computers (Ralston and Meek, 1976). The first is that of calculating machines. John Napier's publication of the first tables of logarithms in 1614 spurred scientific exploration by reducing the enormous tedium of the working scientist and mathematician. In 1622 William Oughtred, who also invented the multiplication sign ($\times$), reduced the tedium further by devising the first slide rule. Blaise Pascal, the mathematical prodigy who, it was claimed, independently discovered the first 32 Euclidean theorems (in their correct order) before he was 16, invented the first true calculating machine in 1642; unreliable and expensive, the machine was never widely used, dashing his financial hopes. The first calculating machine to be produed on a commercial scale was not devised until 1820. Only at the very end of the nineteenth century were reasonably compact calculators available.

The second strand is that of *logical automatons,* that is, automatic (or self-controlled, self-regulating) devices. One of the significant inventions made toward the end of the eighteenth century was the power loom, invented by Edmund Cartwright in 1785; along with the steam engine and the spinning jenny, it ushered in the industrial revolution. Twenty years later Joseph Jacquard came up with a way of controlling a power loom by strings of cards to weave quite complex patterns. Displaying a foresight perhaps motivated by Napoleonic rivalry with Britain, the French government appropriated the loom and declared it public property (an early example of the practical dissemination of advanced technology), leaving Jacquard a handsome annuity.

These first two strands came together in the work of Charles Babbage (Laver, 1983). Babbage, having become dissatisfied with the accuracy of published mathematical tables and various astronomical data, applied himself to their correction. In 1822 he built a small machine that used the method of finite differences to generate successive values of simple algebraic functions. By 1834 he had become obsessed with a much grander project, his Analytical Engine: a machine which would be built of tens of thousands of intricately geared cylinders interlocked in complicated ways, which would be directed to work by means of punched cards, which would possess a memory to store partial results for later processing, and which would print out its results. In short, a true computer. At first Babbage was funded by the British government, but as both his obsession and his machine grew, the money dried up. His marked eccentricity, almost to the point of madness, did not help. (During his lifetime he was most renowned for a relentless campaign against organ grinders, who retaliated by serenading him at peculiar hours of the day and night.) Babbage devoted the remainder of his life and resources to the Analytical Engine. The engine captivated the daughter of the poet Byron, Augusta Ada, the Countess Lovelace, to whom we owe much of our knowledge of this extraordinary machine. She and Babbage were well aware of the potential of the engine: Lady Lovelace even imagined it composing and playing music. The Analytical Engine was never built. Babbage revised its plans repeatedly until his last version was to have been powered by two locomotive engines and occupy a space the size of London's St. Paul's Cathedral. With this engine, Babbage, one of the truly magnificent failures of all time, was the grandfather of modern computing. He also, it is said, established a lasting tradition of computer projects going over budget and over time.

Fifty years later, in 1930, the American mathematician Vannevar Bush built a machine for solving differential equations. Later still, Harvard University and the IBM corporation collaborated on the first general-purpose calculator, an electromechanical contraption made in 1944. The mathematician Norbert Wiener laid the theoretical foundations for computers with his book *Cybernetics; or Control and Communication, the Animal and the Machine,* published in 1948. In February 1946 the first electronic computer, called ENIAC, was developed at the University of Pennsylvania. The most complex piece of electronic equipment constructed up to its time, ENIAC incorporated 19,000 vacuum tubes and consumed 20 kW of power. It was about as powerful as a modern pocket calculator.

The third strand of the skein is the need for statistical data. The Founding Fathers of the United States laid down in the Constitution that a census should be held every 10 years. During the preparations for the 1890 census it was found that the results of the 1880 census were still being tabulated. Things, it seemed, would have to be done quicker. A competition for a tabulating device was won by Herman Hollerith, and the census figures were compiled with his machines. Other countries used them to gather the data required by the developing welfare state. In the United States they were vital in implementing the New Deal, whose Social Security Act required tabulating the employment records of 26 million people.

The Soviet Union used them to collate the information needed for the economic vision of the First Five-Year Plan.

The strands merged in the Remington Rand Corporation's development of the first production computer, Univac, which was installed at the U.S. Bureau of the Census in 1951. By 1953 thirteen companies were making computers. It was thought at the time, by those in the know, that as many as 50 firms might eventually use them.

These very early machines employed a ponderous technology of vacuum-tube and magnetic core memory and are known as first-generation machines. The second generation (from about 1959) used transistors, improving speed by a factor of about 10, and resulted in huge computers about as powerful as today's microcomputers, at about 1000 times the cost. Transistors are more reliable, use less power, and generate less heat than vacuum tubes. First-generation computers were heavy, power-hungry machines tended constantly by technicians striving to prevent or correct failures. By increasing the reliability of a computer and substantially reducing its support systems, transistors made computers more viable for smaller organizations.

The third generation (after about 1964) used integrated circuits, in which a few hundred transistors could be fitted onto a single microchip. The fourth generation (from about 1970) uses the technology of very densely packed integrated circuitry called very large scale integration (VLSI), which routinely packs 100,000 transistors onto a chip. The price of a chip in relation to its power falls by about 35 percent each year (Reinecke, 1982), and the power of microchips increases tenfold each decade.

As recently as 1974, the Altair company marketed the first microcomputer, using a new sort of chip that contained the workings of an entire computer processor, the heart of a computer. Until that time microchips had been components of computer processors, not the entire processor itself. Nowadays these microprocessors are common, and more and more powerful computers-on-a-chip are in continual development. That first microprocessor cost $200 when released; at its demise in the early 1980s it sold for about $2. In 1980 the United States exported $13 billion worth of computer equipment; by 1983 the figure had grown to $27 billion, about equivalent to the gross domestic product of Australia.

A1.2 A Brief History of Technology in Architecture

Computers are the most recent and aggressive technology to intrude into architecture and the practice of architecture. Architectural technology sits uneasily between engineering and architecture, in that area usually called "architectural engineering" in the United States and "architectural science" or "building science" in the British Commonwealth. Its history contains repeated instances of daring innovation by engineers or other outsiders followed belatedly by architects. While nineteenth-century architects were arguing the superiority of neo-gothic over neoclassicism, a gardener designed the Crystal Palace. How did this happen?

The word "architect" first appeared in the English language in John Shute's *The First and Chief Groundes of Architecture* in 1563. In this work can be seen the beginnings of the slow separation of the roles of building designer and building constructor. Previously, in medieval England the word "mason" had comprehended both the master who designed a structure and the artisan who constructed it. These roles (designer and constructor) have always lain uneasily together through the centuries, sometimes fused in one individual and sometimes not.

John Shute's architect was the Renaissance man versed in literature, history, and astronomy as well as in the expected drawing, surveying, and geometry. This is evident in the fact that the great politicians, civil servants, and courtiers of Elizabethan England who constructed great country houses to show their wealth and status, their position in England and in the world, often coordinated their own building activities; here is the start of the architect as gifted amateur. At the same time surveyors emerged as individuals taking an active part in the design and construction of houses. Many of these came from the Royal Office of Works. With the appointment of Inigo Jones as Surveyor of the King's Works in 1615, we see the architect as known today: someone who can draw, who knows about building construction, and who is in control of the design process. His technology of drawing board and T square is still in use.

Out of the new technology of the early industrial revolution came new professions. The same individuals who constructed railways and bridges with iron had of necessity to take an interest in its manufacture and distribution. An interest in the more sophisticated ways of working with newly developed metals led individuals across occupations. John Smeaton, for instance, started life as an instrument maker in the 1750s and experimented with various mechanical apparatuses. His interests turned to engineering and he became one of the first professional engineers.

The engineers who worked with the new technology were very conscious of the sheer power at their disposal, the power to manipulate nature and to fashion society (Fig. A1.1). How vastly stronger than laborers, horses, or oxen were their steam engines and their locomotives, their mills and looms! When the land itself could not be molded and sculpted for the convenience of society with dams and canals, it could be tamed with bridges and aqueducts. An excited sense of the ability to command great forces permeates their work. In 1818 they formed the Institution of Civil Engineers. Its charter boldly arrogated the rank of *profession* — previously used for the law, medicine, and the clergy — to the engineer, defining the engineer's skill as "being the art of directing the Great Sources of Power in Nature for the use and convenience of man."

Figure A1.1 The engineering tradition: The Eiffel Tower in Paris (1887–1889), the best-known work of the engineer Gustave Eiffel, was built for the 1889 Paris Exhibition. Steel was used for bridges from the early nineteenth century and had become a standard and important engineering material by midcentury. Moreover, engineers such as Eiffel were also quite capable of developing an aesthetic with their materials. *(Generated by a computer program written by Steve Gregorio, Graduate School of Architecture and Urban Planning, University of California, Los Angeles.)*

The British Museum, built in the 1830s, was the first building on which bills of quantities were provided. The specialist discipline of quantity surveyor grew up to handle the calculation of costs as the complexity of buildings increased. General contractors such as Thomas Cubitt organized draftsmen on a permanent basis, removing a link between architects and the artisans under their direction. As architects chose to use the materials of the new technology, they were also obliged to use people who knew these materials best — the structural engineers. New machines could heat and ventilate buildings previously laboring under constraints of form and fabric, but to know how to do this the architect had to bring in the expertise of mechanical engineers (Fig. A1.2). Reyner Banham (1984, pp. 9, 10, and 268) chronicled the history of environmental engineering with melancholy and frustration:

> The idea that architecture belongs in one place and technology in another is comparatively new in history, and its effect on architecture, which should be the most complete of the arts, has been crippling. . . . Because of this failure of the architectural profession to — almost literally — keep its house in order, it fell to another body of men to assume responsibility for the maintenance of decent environmental conditions: everybody from plumbers to consulting

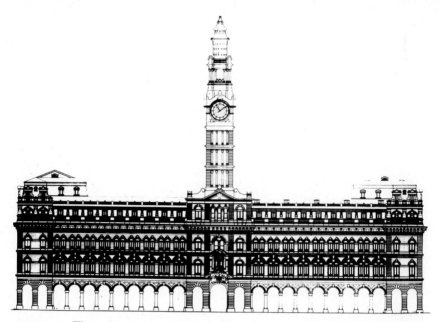

Figure A1.2   The architectural tradition: the General Post Office (1865–1887), Sydney, by the architect James Barnet. Masonry and timber remained the most important parts of the architect's vocabulary until the early twentieth century. Although Louis Sullivan saw the potential of such an unconventional material as steel, architects did not fully appreciate it until the Futurists and the Modern Movement. This computer drawing was produced for use in the restoration of the building, where each stone of the facade was to be individually identified and numbered. *(Reproduced courtesy of Jackson Teece Chesterman Willis and Partners Pty. Ltd.; drawn using GDS by Applied Research of Cambridge, a McDonnell Douglas company.)*

engineers. They represented "another culture," so alien that most architects held it beneath contempt, and still do. . . .

[The] profession has been ponderously slow to change its mind or reformulate its attitudes; it has tended to believe itself in the throes of major revolutions when confronted with technical innovations that other crafts and disciplines have taken in their strides.

As we shall see, computers are affecting the practice of architecture in a multitude of ways. For the first time, a new technology is directly acting on the ways that architects think and work in the office, and a whole new set of design tools is being developed. It is not a technology that can be handed over to yet another new profession — dismissed as the province of engineers — so that architects can get on with the *real* architecture. It is a technology that spans the diversified professions, for the same CAD system used to develop initial architectural proposals may also be used in the documentation of environmental conditions and in the generation of bills of quantities and cost estimates. With computers there is the real prospect of reintegrating the design (aesthetic and drawing-board) and the calculation (performance and number-based) traditions in construction (Fig. A1.3).

Figure A1.3   Although computers have been adopted without fuss by myriad firms and all the professions, they are still a source of contention within architecture. Some architects see them as a direct threat to their artistic integrity. Engineering students have used computers in their schools for decades, but they have only recently been introduced to architectural education. The consequence is that only a tiny number of architects at middle- and high-level management have computer expertise and experience. *(Cartoon hand-drawn by Simon Stern, used by permission.)*

Chapter

2

Computers

2.1 Introduction

This chapter discusses the computer industry and its most visible product, computer hardware. We introduce the several worlds of the computing industry and then provide an overview of computer systems and their components. In the secondary text we provide detailed information on computer hardware, including communications networks, and conclude with a look at the future development of computers.

2.2 The World of Computing

Computing covers two quite distinct cultures. The first consists of professional computerists and the second of what we shall call tribalists.

Before the invention of minicomputers and microcomputers, there were only a few thousand computers in the world and correspondingly few people interested in them. These professional computerists formed a buffer between the people who wanted the computers to do things (management) and the computers themselves. Managers gave requests to the computerists to produce a report, and in a few days or weeks they received back large folders of computer printout. The managers had little interest in how these reports were generated, as long as they got them.

This commercial *data processing (DP)* culture is concerned with large computers, the COBOL language, and applications such as order processing, sales ledgers, payroll, customer accounting, and stock control. It is still by far the largest component of the computer world and exists mainly in those medium to large businesses and government organizations which have their own data processing departments and in the plush offices of computer consultants and manufacturers. The culture likes to exercise firm control over computing resources, and the literature it reads contains articles on the latest IBM price changes, big sales contracts, and new accounting systems. It holds microcomputers in healthy contempt, regarding them by and large to be useless (except as ways to access bigger computers) and wondering why end-users would want to use a computer themselves anyway.

The second culture doesn't have a name. It is a collection of tribes — small groups of innovative users in technical organizations and universities. These groups use minicomputers and microcomputers from Silicon Valley, concern themselves with the C language and Unix, and watch developments in artificial intelligence. They are enthusiasts and get as much excitement out of computing as others might get from fast cars, music, or architecture. The tribal computerists have brought computing directly to the users. It is only a young culture, but the needs of architectural computing lie closer to these tribalists than to the DP professionals. Like the tribalists, architects want to do all sorts of peculiar things with their computers. Only a tiny fraction of the world's architectural firms (the very largest, including government organizations) can afford their own separate data processing departments, and even if they could afford them, architectural firms are not used to having and don't want to create quasi-independent bureaucracies functioning within themselves.

Traditionally, the DP professionals have not got on well with the tribalists. They have viewed the containment of microcomputing as a major job that they must take on to save management from itself. The precious data in their machines must be safeguarded from corruption by well-meaning amateurs who might access it from microcomputers. While reluctantly conceding that they cannot control individual microcomputers, they have firmly believed that only under their benevolent guidance can organizations acquire and intelligently use computers.

Computer consultants, unfortunately, often originate from the data processing legacy and are consequently used to implementing accounting and records systems on minicomputers or mainframes, although a few can handle the needs of design professionals and realize that they do not do much stocktaking or inventory control. The industry uses the term *independent consultant* in a funny way, meaning not necessarily an impartial, objective person who will help without fear or favor, but anyone not actually on the payroll of a manufacturer. He or she will often have a tie-in with a couple of manufacturers and be pushing their products and may also be the local agent for software packages. Consultants make their money by advising clients (for a fee) to buy certain machines and programs (from which they often receive a commission).

2.3 Types of Computers

Until recently all computers were big computers, sitting in the guarded air-conditioned rooms of banks and large companies. These *mainframe computers* are very very fast and can store enormous quantities of information. Mainframes (including their supporting equipment) occupy whole floors in office buildings, typically covering an area 2 or 3 times that of an average house. They can support dozens or hundreds of users simultaneously and are managed by the professionals of the data processing department. Mainframes are used primarily for large-scale commercial number crunching and for research and military purposes. Of more interest to designers, computer graphics is another application of mainframes and of their even bigger cousins, the rare *supercomputers* (Fig. 2.1). With some supercomputers, the price includes an engineer or two who will live with the machine and provide ongoing maintenance.

A rung below these are the *minicomputers* (Fig. 2.2), machines about the size of a washing machine or a fridge. Minicomputers can also support several users at once, although many fewer than a mainframe. They were born in the first phase of miniaturization in computer technology and allowed medium-size companies and individual university departments to run a computer without a full-time professional operating staff. Apart from the way they are physically structured and the form of the subsidiary equipment necessary *(system architecture),* the difference between main-

Figure 2.1   The Cray 2 supercomputer. In the foreground is the central processing unit. The compact nature and very high density of electronics necessitate a liquid cooling system, the components of which are in the background. The coolant is, of all things, an artificial blood plasma substitute. A computer like this would support numerous hard-disk drives and other peripherals, none of which is shown here. Although the basic cost of a supercomputer is comparatively low, the total cost is substantially increased when peripherals and hardware and software maintenance are included. Supercomputers are used for complex computer graphics. *(Courtesy of Cray Research Inc.)*

Figure 2.2   A Prime 5000 minicomputer. Minicomputers are extensively used in medium to large CAD systems and can support several users. Since the early 1980s such CAD systems have been challenged by supermicrocomputer-based systems, reflecting the overall trend in the computer industry away from large, centralized computer installations to ones consisting of several microcomputers connected in a local-area network. *(Courtesy of Prime Computers Inc.)*

frames and minicomputers lies mainly in speed and memory size, minicomputers being about an order of magnitude inferior to mainframes. Minicomputers have become very popular for the usual boring accounting purposes, and they are also used in most computer-aided drafting systems.

At the bottom of the heap are the *microcomputers* (Fig. 2.3). It is worthwhile remembering that the first microcomputer appeared (as a hobby kit) as recently as 1974. Ten years later they accounted for the majority of computers sold, both in numbers and dollar value. Many microcomputers can support only a single user at a time, but this is changing. Some time ago they joined other consumer goods in advertisements on television and have proved popular as toys, hobbies, and business tools. They have been very successful in small and medium firms because they are (relatively) cheap and easy to use and maintain.

There is much confusion in the labeling of the different sorts of computers (Fig. 2.4). For example, the word "mainframe" is sometimes used to mean a central computer (of any size) that runs peripheral equipment. With the increasing processing and memory capacities of small computers, the traditional boundaries are breaking down. For our purposes, if a computer (and its associated peripherals, such as plotters) requires several full-time professional computerists to maintain it, fills more than a small

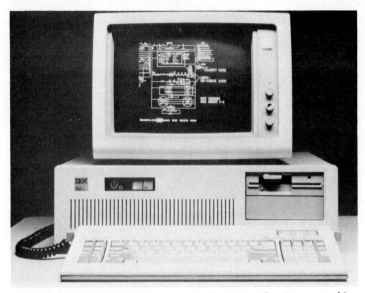

Figure 2.3   An IBM PC AT microcomputer displaying a drawing accessed from an Auto-trol Technology graphics workstation. With the PC, IBM legitimated microcomputers as worthwhile tools and, in the eyes of the commercial data processing community, elevated them from their status as trifling toys. Auto-trol is one of the larger vendors of minicomputer-based CAD systems. The spread of microcomputers challenged all the established CAD vendors to maintain cost-effectiveness in the face of these much-cheaper machines. *(Courtesy of Auto-trol Technology Inc.)*

room, and we wouldn't dream of moving it, we shall call it a mainframe. If it occupies a room and needs special equipment to move it, we shall call it a minicomputer. If one or two people can pick it up and carry it, we shall call it a microcomputer. This classification is a little unorthodox but is probably as good as any other system.

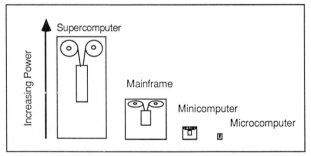

Figure 2.4   Comparing the different classes of machine is difficult at best. In terms of internal and external memory capacity, speed, and number of users, each is about a factor of 10 superior to the one below. *(Diagram by the authors.)*

2.4   Overview of Computer Hardware

Hardware is the term used to describe the physical parts of the computer system, as distinct from the sets of instructions known as *software* that control the operations to be carried out by the system (see Chap. 3). The hardware consists of individual components which each perform specific functions and which are linked together into a coherent whole. This section describes the form and function of these components and some of the characteristics that determine their performance in a working environment. It includes some discussion of the way in which computers store, transfer, and process information.

2.4.1   Hardware components

A complete computer system consists of four components:

1. Input and output devices.   For input, computers always have at least a *keyboard,* and often a pointing device like a *mouse* or (less often) a *light pen* or *touch screen.* A mouse fits in the palm of the hand and is moved over a flat surface to cause a relative movement of a pointer on a screen. A light pen is a penlike pointer that is held against the screen, and a touch screen requires only a finger against the screen to indicate position. A *display screen* must also be provided as the primary output device. A less common input device is the *digitizer;* it consists of a large flat tablet and pen and is used to enter graphical data accurately. All these devices allow people to

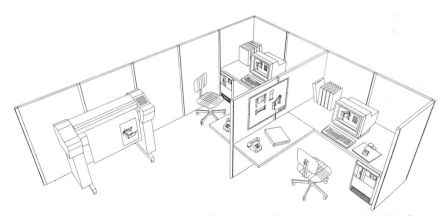

Figure 2.5   A typical CAD workstation. The drawing shows two workstations linked to a single plotter. In the front work space can be seen the major components of a CAD workstation: screen, keyboard, and digitizing tablet. Underneath the desk is the central processor and disk drive. The area consumed by all this is rather more than a draftsperson and his or her drawing board would use. *(Drawn by Geoff Carse with Eagle software at Cadcom Pty. Ltd., Australia.)*

interact directly with computers. Taken together, they are often referred to as a *workstation* (Fig. 2.5). Microcomputers package the whole lot with the computer proper. Sometimes it is possible to use a different screen, but not always. In larger systems the workstations are completely independent pieces of equipment, bought separately from the computer itself.

For permanent output, the computer system must also have a *printer* for textual output and a *plotter* for drawings and other graphics. For all sizes of computers, it is up to the computer owner to acquire a printer or plotter.

Since input-output devices are not part of the computing function of the computer, they are called *peripherals*.

2. Central processor. Inside the computer are many black rectangles mounted on fiberglass boards and connected by circuit lines. In microcomputers, one of these (often the largest) is the microprocessor, or *central processing unit (CPU),* which is the heart of the computer and controls everything else. Minicomputers and mainframes have several microprocessors. There will also be other chips playing supporting roles. Typically there is a *clock chip*, which does nothing but emit a tick or tock several thousand times a second. All the computer's operations are synchronized by the clock chip. There are also chips called *direct memory access processors* (which send data to and from the disk drives) and others that run the keyboard, the screen, and other functions of the computer, all orchestrated by the CPU. The quality of a CPU is a factor of its speed and of the number and sophistication of the basic operations it can carry out.

3. Internal memory. Also called *main memory* or sometimes *core memory*, the internal memory holds all the data and programming with which the microprocessors are immediately concerned. In a sense, the only memory that the central processor has direct access to is internal memory. Apart from the programs and their data, the internal memory holds a great deal of information needed to run the computer, such as memory allocated to the display. In a living brain the thinking function and memory storage are unified in the one entity, whereas computers use the CPU to calculate and the internal memory to store things. The more memory, the better.

4. Mass storage. Also called *external memory* or *secondary memory*, mass storage provides for permanent storage of data on magnetic media, either floppy or hard disks or magnetic tapes. A *floppy disk* is a single flexible magnetic disk $3\frac{1}{2}$, $5\frac{1}{4}$, or 8 in. in diameter, used as a medium for storing information. A *hard disk* is actually a set of disks stacked in layers as a removable or fixed disk pack. A mass storage unit consists of the driving device, analogous to a record player, and the storage media, analogous to records. Their capacity is many times greater than that of the internal memory. One can never have enough mass storage capacity.

In minicomputers and mainframes these four components occupy separate large cabinets linked by cables, which are usually hidden under special raised flooring. Microcomputers may instead have them integrated into the one case or connected by short cables.

To use a computer, we need a program of instructions for its operation. Perhaps we want to use a word processing program on a microcomputer. First we locate the floppy disk (see Sec. A2.4) that holds a permanent copy of the program and another disk that will be used to hold the permanent copy of the text we are writing. Each disk is placed into a mass storage device called a *disk drive.* We start the execution of the program at the keyboard, probably by typing its name. The computer then uses the disk drive to retrieve a copy of the word processing program from the disk and load the whole thing into its internal memory. When loaded, the computer runs the program and behold: instant word processor. The key concept here is that a computer can operate only on programs and data that exist in its internal memory. The floppy disk is used only for long-term permanent storage of data and programs.

2.4.2 Bits, bytes, and words

The fundamental unit of information is the *bit.* Each bit can have one of two values, represented by either 1 or 0, on or off, true or false, or any other binary system. This is a very small unit for most purposes, but it has the disadvantage that it does not relate well to what humans regard as the fundamental unit of information, namely, the *character.* Most talk concerning information uses a larger unit called a *byte,* which contains precisely 8 bits. Although it is partly through historical accident that bytes are as they are, they have the happy property of being just the right size to represent one single character.

A byte can be used to store a character or a number. Since it has 8 bits, a byte can store any number from 0 to 255 (being $2^8 - 1$). Or it can store one character from a total set of 256 characters if there is an agreed-upon system whereby the value of a byte is interpreted as a particular character. There is such a system, universally accepted by microcomputer manufacturers, most minicomputer makers, and some mainframe manufacturers, called the American Standard Code for Information Interchange (ASCII) code. For example, the number 33 (00100001 as a pattern of 8 bits) is the ASCII code for !, the exclamation mark. Full ASCII code charts can be found in many microcomputer books. There are 128 defined ASCII characters, some of which do not display as letters or numbers on the screen but cause some action to take place. The character called cr (short for carriage return) will, if sent to the screen, put the cursor (which marks the position where the next character will be printed) back to the beginning of the line. The character called bs (backspace) moves the cursor backward one character. There are 30 such characters, called *control characters.*

Although a byte could cater for 256 characters, the ASCII set contains only 128, which means that one bit of the byte is never used. This was done partly to release this bit for a use known as *parity checking*. When characters are transmitted, there is always the possibility of corruption, the chance that one or more bits might be sent incorrectly. The unused bit of the byte can be used as a check bit for data transmission. Before transmission, the computer examines the value of the byte to be sent: and if even, sets it to 0; and if odd, changes the reserve bit to a 1. Thus, all bytes are even in value. The receiving computer thus knows that something untoward has happened if it receives an odd-valued byte.

On modern machines there is a demand for more extensive character sets. Many manufacturers now supply character sets that utilize the full byte to provide 256 characters. However, the form of these extra characters is completely up to the maker.

In computing, a *word* is the amount of information a computer can handle as one entity. A word may vary from 8 bits on a small microcomputer to 64 bits or more on a large mainframe (Fig. 2.6). Bigger word lengths mean faster operation and more precision in calculations. Before 1980 almost all microcomputers were 8-bit machines and minicomputers were 16-bit machines. By the mid-1980s a 32-bit word size was common for both types.

Computer memory is organized into bytes, and microprocessors deal with bytes or multiples of bytes. Sometimes it is handy to regard a byte as made up of two 4-bit halves, and these too have a name, the nibble. When speaking of memory sizes, the byte is much too small for ease of use. The standard measure used for this purpose is the kilobyte, usually called just K, which is 1024 (2^{10}) bytes (Fig. 2.7). Larger sizes are referred to as megabytes (1M = 1024K) and gigabytes (1G = 1024M).

2.5   Multitasking and Multiuser Computers

The majority of computers in the world today are microcomputers designed as *single-user single-tasking* machines and are connected to nothing other than a printer and the power supply. Much of the utility of computers stems from their ability to carry out concurrent tasks, to serve several people concurrently, and to communicate with each other, as distinct from their innate processing powers. In this section we look briefly at multitasking and multiuser computers, leaving the much bigger topic of computer communications and networking to the secondary text.

2.5.1   Multitasking computers

In a single-tasking computer the user must go about his or her business in a serial (or sequential) fashion, completing one task before starting another. He or she must finish word-processing a specification before doing the

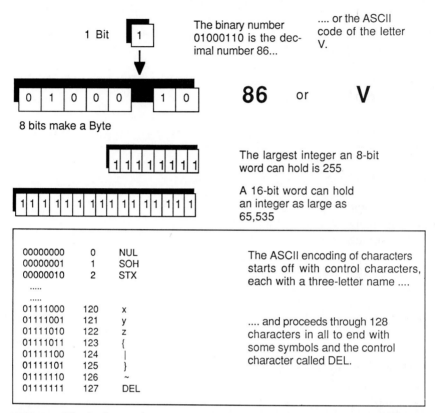

1 Bit

The binary number 01000110 is the decimal number 86...

.... or the ASCII code of the letter V.

| 0 | 1 | 0 | 0 | 0 | | 1 | 0 |

86   or   **V**

8 bits make a Byte

| 1 | 1 | 1 | 1 | 1 | 1 | 1 |

The largest integer an 8-bit word can hold is 255

| 1 | 1 | 1 | 1 | 1 | 1 | 1 | 1 | 1 | 1 | 1 | 1 | 1 | 1 | 1 |

A 16-bit word can hold an integer as large as 65,535

00000000	0	NUL
00000001	1	SOH
00000010	2	STX
.....		
.....		
01111000	120	x
01111001	121	y
01111010	122	z
01111011	123	{
01111100	124		
01111101	125	}
01111110	126	~
01111111	127	DEL

The ASCII encoding of characters starts off with control characters, each with a three-letter name ....

.... and proceeds through 128 characters in all to end with some symbols and the control character called DEL.

Figure 2.6   The fundamental storage unit of microcomputers and many minicomputers is the byte, which is made up of 8 bits. Each bit stores one of only two values, usually represented as either a 1 or a 0. The pattern of 1s and 0s in a byte must be interpreted by the computer appropriately. It could be a number, a single character, or even a machine-code instruction. Almost all computers do not manipulate single bytes, but chunks of them, called words. In general, the larger the word size, the more powerful the computer. *(Diagram by the authors.)*

week's time sheets, and must complete those before starting something new. This is just as bothersome as having too small a desk and having to tidy up constantly to make room for new papers.

Most of the 16- and 32-bit microcomputers on the market are capable of overcoming this irritation by a technique called *multitasking,* or *concurrent processing,* in which a task in progress may be suspended, some other job taken care of, and the original task resumed. To accomplish multitasking, a computer must remember all the details of the interrupted task before it starts a new one. There is only one place to remember them, and that is mass storage. All or part of the internal memory must be transferred to disk, freeing space for the new job. To implement multitasking effectively, one needs a hard-disk drive combined with a fast, powerful microprocessor.

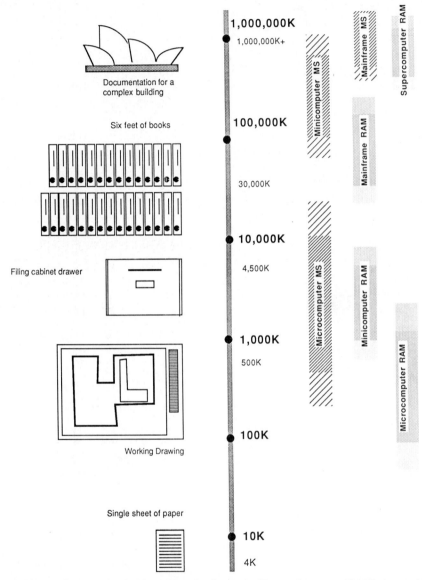

Documentation for a
complex building

Six feet of books

Filing cabinet drawer

Working Drawing

Single sheet of paper

Figure 2.7 Comparative memory sizes, showing typical internal memory (RAM) sizes and typical mass storage sizes of the various types of computers. *(Diagram by the authors.)*

2.5.2 Multiuser computers

Some computers can support several users at once, each with his or her own terminal or workstation. A computer that can do this is called a *multiuser* system. Few microcomputers are multiuser systems, but all mainframes and minicomputers are. Such systems operate by giving each user a small portion of the CPU's time a few hundred or thousand times a second.

Mainframes and minicomputers have ample speed to cope with time-sharing. Their fast CPUs can carry tasks so quickly, and humans are so slow, that although every user only gets a small fraction of the CPU's time, it appears to each that they have its undivided attention. Multiuser systems are usually set up as centralized systems, also known as *star networks* (Fig. 2.8). Users have *dumb terminals* (meaning that they have no processing capability of their own) separately connected by cable to the central host computer. Centralized systems have a substantial advantage in that they provide excellent security; all the operations of the system can be monitored from the computer, and access can be granted or denied by the computer supervisor. They also provide uniform procedures and can serve as controlled access points to other external systems.

Centralized systems have some handicaps, though. First, if the computer fails, the whole system is incapacitated. Second, each terminal must have its own communication line back to the computer. The cost of the communications lines, which are only used for part of the time, is considerable. Third, they also remove from the user direct control over his or her working environment. What the computer supervisor says, goes. If you want to buy a certain program, you must convince the supervising authority first. One of the major trends in recent years has been a decentralization of systems

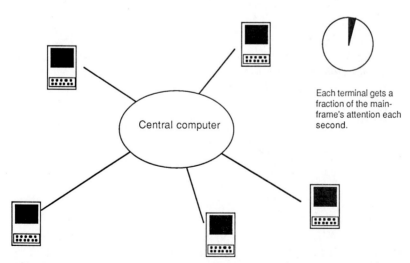

Each terminal gets a fraction of the main-frame's attention each second.

Figure 2.8 Star networks are most often used to connect several terminals or workstations to a central mainframe or minicomputer. They provide excellent security and require little intelligence in the outlying terminals. However, they are expensive to install and poorly suited to electronic mail. Performance will fall off quickly beyond a certain threshold number of terminals that the central unit can serve. *(Diagram by the authors.)*

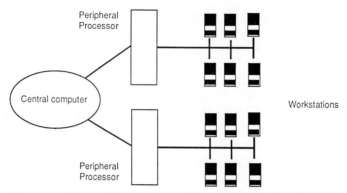

Figure 2.9 Most mainframes do not talk to the individual workstations directly but route communications through smaller computers called peripheral processors. These do some basic housekeeping tasks and remove some of the load from the central computer. *(Diagram by the authors.)*

as users demand more and more control over their own computers, a concept known as *user sovereignty.*

On most mainframe and some minicomputer systems, users do not communicate directly with the central computer but go through auxiliary computers called *peripheral processors* (Fig. 2.9). These take care of some of the more mundane tasks, thereby relieving the central computer of some of the load and improving performance. A variant of this scheme, a *multiprocessor system,* provides a multiuser ability on some microcomputer systems. Users still have dumb terminals in front of them, but the central computer contains one microprocessor for each person. Each CPU accesses a hard disk through another CPU which does nothing but handle mass storage operations. This scheme is not very common today, for many microprocessors are capable of handling several users comfortably. Systems that have several processors typically devote them to specialized functions instead, such as managing the screen or the output mechanisms, thus improving the performance of the whole.

2.6   The Computer Industry

There are four major groups of firms within the computer industry:

1. *Computer manufacturers.* These range from IBM — the most successful company (in any field) in the history of the world, and overwhelmingly the dominant computer manufacturer — to small firms making obscure microcomputers in equally obscure corners of the world.

2. *Original equipment manufacturers (OEMs).* These are firms who purchase computers from the manufacturers (at huge discounts), add on other peripherals and their own software, and then sell the whole package either to dealers or directly to end-users.

3. *Software houses.* The main concern of these firms is the development and selling of software for existing machines. Software houses range from large multinational concerns employing hundreds of people to one or two programmers working on a microcomputer in their living room.

4. *Dealers and distributors.* A distributor is roughly equivalent to a wholesaler. Distributors, fuzzily distinguished from OEMs, are responsible for the distribution, marketing, and support of computers within some large region, often a whole country. Most mainframe and minicomputer manufacturers are their own distributors, but microcomputers are rarely distributed by their manufacturer. Dealers are those who buy from distributors to sell directly to end-users and are a phenomenon unique to the microcomputer market.

2.6.1 Mainframes and minicomputers

At the pinnacle of the computer industry sit the manufacturers responsible for the couple of hundred supercomputers in the world. The Cray Research Corporation has always prided itself on producing the very fastest and biggest supercomputers in the world. Together with its main rivals, the Control Data Corporation (CDC), Fujitsu, and Hitachi, Cray Research caters to a very select market that requires only a handful of machines each year.

International Business Machines (IBM) has about 50 percent of the world market in computers. This dominance has been achieved not so much through technical innovation as through superb selling techniques, excellent support and service, and a safe, comfortable, pinstripe image ("No one was ever fired for recommending IBM" is an old industry adage). A major part of the mainframe market consists of vendors selling IBM *plug compatibles,* computers compatible with IBM computers but priced lower. Until 1981 IBM sold primarily mainframes, having been pipped in the minicomputer market by the Digital Equipment Corporation (DEC), the world's second-largest computing company. In that year IBM introduced its Personal Computer (or PC as it is known), which quickly became the biggest selling microcomputer in the United States. The other major mainframe manufacturers are Sperry (in its original incarnation as Sperry-Univac, the very first computer company), Honeywell, Siemens, International Computers Limited (ICL), Control Data, Burroughs, National Cash Register (NCR), and National Advanced Systems (NAS).

Other than IBM, who makes almost everything, the major minicomputer manufacturers are DEC, Data General, and Prime. Several architectural drafting packages are implemented on minicomputers made by these manufacturers, and there is a great deal of software available for them. Minicomputer manufacturers also stress office automation (partly a response to market pressures generated by microcomputers) involving the complete computerization of an office and the removal of paper in favor of electronic means of communication and information storage (see Chap. 4).

At the sales end of the industry, the mainframe and minicomputer market consists mainly of OEMs and the manufacturers themselves. Minicomputers and mainframes are big business; hundreds of thousands or millions of dollars are at stake. Manufacturers provide significant, ongoing support and service, and program customization is often not charged as a separate item. When a malfunction occurs, an engineer will be present in a few hours. Salesmen in white business shirts will conduct discreet negotiations and assemble wordy, tender documents. The mainframe business is conducted with respectable propriety, while the minicomputer industry is rather more hectic.

An interesting facet of the computer market is the price of software or programs. The price of software is dependent on three factors: the abilities of the program, the size of machine it is intended for, and the size of the potential market. Of these, the first is probably the least important. The more expensive the machine, the more a program costs, regardless of its abilities. Architectural programs, targeted at a tiny market, tend to be very pricey for what they can do. We look at software in the next four chapters.

2.6.2 The microcomputer business

Of all the markets, the microcomputer market is the most fragmented, occupied by hundreds of manufacturers. The large, established computer firms, seeing the microcomputer as a contemptible toy (A layman wants to use a computer? Ridiculous!), waited several years before taking microcomputers seriously, thereby allowing firms such as Apple, Tandy, and Commodore to establish themselves as major microcomputer makers. In the late 1970s and early 1980s IBM, DEC, ICL, and other large computer firms released their own systems, followed by a host of competitors, often from firms who had never before made a computer in their corporate lives.

The microcomputer business is chaotic. It is structured in quite a different way from the markets for minicomputers and mainframes, just as the market for bicycles differs in important ways from that of cars. The microcomputer market is similar to that for consumer goods: we shop around among suppliers (who often have street-front shops), choose our computer and some software, and a few days or weeks later it is delivered to our site. Support in the form of general advice and assistance is pretty minimal, and usually the vendor doesn't want to know us after he has cashed the check. Software problems are often difficult to rectify because the vendor doesn't know much about the programs he sells.

The big bugbear of the microcomputer market is the enormous number

of different manufacturers around and the consequent lack of interma-
chine compatibility. A major incompatibility is in the physical means of
storing data. Since minicomputers and mainframes invariably have one
or more tape drives onto which data may be saved or loaded and since the
tapes they use have their data stored in a common, well-defined format,
transporting a program from one machine to another is usually not much
of a problem. So far so good. On the other hand, since a typical microcomputer costs much less than a single tape drive unit, they are never used
together. Instead, the common mass storage medium for microcomputers
is the floppy disk, and over the years manufacturers have developed dozens
of different ways of physically storing data on these disks. The result is that
most microcomputers cannot use their floppies with any other brand of
machine. Software vendors are obliged to distribute many different versions of the one program. There are other ways of transporting programs
between machines, but these are clumsy or expensive to implement with
microcomputers.

The market is now intensely competitive. From the invention of microcomputers to the coming of IBM, Apple and Tandy had dominated the
business trade, and their 8-bit machines pioneered popular, or personal,
computing. Now in the computer business, if you don't keep up with the
latest, you're dead. This generates a justifiable and healthy paranoia
throughout the industry. While 8-bit computers remained strong in the
hobby market, by the mid-1980s the 16- and 32-bit microcomputer had
become dominated by IBM, with some competition from Apple, followed
by a much larger collection of offerings from both small independent and
large multinational organizations. This superabundance of microcomputer manufacturers will eventually disappear in the same way that the
hundreds of car manufacturers that existed from 1910 to 1940 were swal-
lowed up or went bankrupt. Which manufacturers will predominate by
then is quite impossible to predict, but this rationalization is largely being
forced by IBM and we can expect it to bring a greater compatibility between machines, as IBM's dominance of other markets has done.

Many of the traditional mainframe and minicomputer manufacturers
who entered the microcomputer market in the 1970s have since withdrawn, badly stung. They were not equipped for the frenetic nature of the
microcomputer market and the drain of having to support thousands of
end-users directly. Those who remain in the market are still not comfortable with it and are trying to mold it to fit their own ideas of what computing is about. In this they have the full support of the data processing
community. Architectural firms epitomize the very sort of thing they
dread: small, independent, idiosyncratic organizations with eccentric
computing requirements and no computer professionals on the staff.
Nothing like banks at all.

2.7 Summary

The computer industry has its own definite views on the nature of computing; it likes to deal with computer professionals who manage large computers. Architects prefer to use small computers and to run them themselves. One of the important issues over the next decade or so will be
whether (1) the architectural profession will make the computer industry
understand its needs or (2) the industry will force the profession to accept
its image of computing.

The most visible product of the computer industry is hardware. Architects often become preoccupied with this aspect, ignoring other important
issues about software and management. While a good knowledge of hardware matters is invaluable for the day-to-day running of a computer system, one should remember that there are other concerns. We examine
these in the following chapters.

SECONDARY TEXT

Computer Hardware

A2.1 Input-Output Devices

Input-output (I/O) devices are the means by which a user communicates
with and receives information from the computer. Such devices include
keyboards, screens displaying text and drawings, and printers of various
kinds. Most microcomputers also allow one to use plotters (for printing
drawings) and digitizers (for describing drawings to the computer). The
major issues in the selection and use of I/O devices concern their resolution, accuracy, and repeatability (Orr, 1985).

Resolution is a measure of the fineness of the device. All devices divide
the plane into a fixed number of points, and the closeness of these points
gives the device's resolution, which is usually measured in points per inch
or points per millimeter. *Accuracy* is important for those input devices
(such as flatbed digitizers) which are used to place old drawings into the
system and for output devices that produce working drawings. If one digi-
tizes a line precisely 12 in (300 mm) long, then an accurate device will input
it as exactly that length. *Repeatability* is a measure of accuracy over time. If
the same point is repeatedly entered on an input device, it should always
end up with the same coordinates.

A2.1.1 Keyboard

Most communication between people and machines takes place these days
via a keyboard and a *visual-display unit (VDU)*, also called a *monitor* or
screen. Microcomputers tend to have the VDU and keyboard integral to

the system; that is, they are part of the package. Minicomputers and mainframes require separate terminals. A *terminal* is simply a unit consisting of a keyboard and a VDU. A microcomputer could also itself be used as a terminal for a larger machine.

A computer keyboard is divided into groups of keys called pads (Fig. A2.1). The main one is called the *QWERTY pad* and more or less follows the traditional typewriter layout. Alternative keyboards, such as the Dvorak or the extraordinary Maltron (which has keys in arcs laid out for the human hand and looks like a design by Dali), have not caught on. Apart from the symbols found on typewriters, the keyboard will have symbols common in computing, such as $<$ and $>$, and several sorts of bracket, such as [ ] and { }. Around the periphery of the pad are the shift and shift lock keys and the carriage return key, which are also found on typewriters, plus some odd keys called ESCAPE, CONTROL, DELETE, and ALTERNATE. The control and alternate keys work like the shift key: They are depressed simultaneously with another key. Each key on a typewriter can emit two characters (usually lower and upper case); on a computer, however, the presence of control and perhaps of alternate allows a key to emit three or four different characters.

One of the problems of moving from one microcomputer to another or from one terminal to another is that the positioning of all these nontypewriter keys may be different. Typewriter keyboards follow a de facto stan-

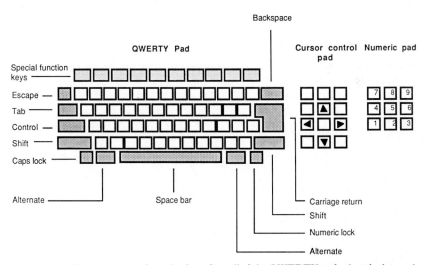

Figure A2.1 The main keypad on a keyboard is called the QWERTY pad, after the letters in the second row. Most keyboards also have two other pads: a numeric pad and a control pad. The last contains arrow keys and others that control various functions of the screen. A set of special function keys is free for use by programs (and programmers) for any necessary purpose. *(Diagram by the authors.)*

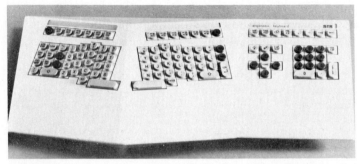

Figure A2.2   An innovative ergonomic keyboard by STR, capitalizing on the natural inward-turning of the hands. A few companies make such keyboards, and there are also alternative key arrangements of conventional keyboards, the most well-known being the Dvorak layout. Although making ergonomic sense, none has proved popular, largely because typists are trained on conventional keyboards and often use several different machines in their job. This means swapping between ergonomic keyboards and conventional ones, with the resultant confusion. Another factor is the failure of IBM, whose Selectric typewriter keyboard is the de facto standard, to adopt new arrangements. *(Courtesy of Standard Telephon und Radio AG.)*

dard laid down by the IBM Selectric series, but computer keyboards are still very much evolving (Fig. A2.2).

Most keyboards also have a separate numeric pad for speedy entry of numeric data, and a group of keys labeled with arrows to move the cursor around on the screen (Fig. A2.1). The best layout for these arrow keys is a Greek cross, followed by a T shape. A final pad consists of special function keys, each usually labeled just with a number. These keys can be used by individual programs for special purposes; for instance, a word processing program might use the computer's special function key 1 to mean "Store this document on disk," while a drafting system program might use the same key to mean "Display a grid on the screen."

A2.1.2   Visual-display unit (screen)

The VDU, or screen, will be a *cathode-ray tube (CRT)* using a technology either of *raster display,* in which the image is made up of large numbers of dots, as in an ordinary television, or (less likely these days) of *vector display,* in which the image is drawn with true lines, or vectors. Some portable computers use liquid-crystal displays (LCDs).

A screen is essential; we need it to monitor what the computer is doing, to check our actions in typing or drawing, and to view the multitude of ephemeral information that we need to look at briefly in the course of computing but do not want to keep or store. The *aspect ratio* of the screen is the ratio of its width to its height. A screen that is higher than it is wide is said to be in *portrait format,* and one that is wider than it is tall is in *landscape format.*

Raster display.   In a raster display the image is composed of a matrix of dots called *pixels* (picture elements, sometimes called pictels), and the electron beam in the display unit scans across the screen in a raster of parallel lines, as in a television. At pixels lying on characters or lines in the image, the electron beam is turned on and off again by its control circuitry. Since any image is reduced to dots on a retangular grid, we get a characteristic staircase effect (called jaggies) if we try to draw diagonal lines across the grid. Obviously, more dots means a better image quality (Fig. A2.3). The *resolution* of a screen is the number of discrete dots that can be displayed. A screen with 1000 by 1000 dots is of higher resolution than one with 600 by 600 dots. Early raster displays had very poor (or coarse) resolution, making them unsuitable for the display of line drawings. For comparison, a television displays about 500 by 500 (250,000) pixels, and the human retina contains in effect about 3 million pixels (Laurie, 1983).

Each dot needs one bit of memory (either on or off); thus, a screen

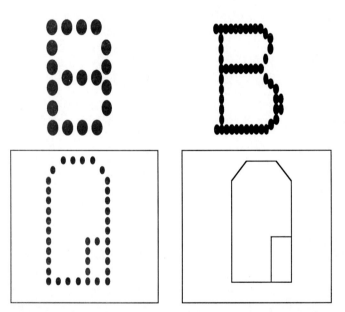

Figure A2.3 One of the most important characteristics of any graphics device (input or output) is its resolution, the number of points per unit length or area in an image. In raster devices (including screens, dot-matrix printers, laser printers, and electrostatic plotters) the image is formed from a matrix of dots. High resolution means high quality. The upper-left diagram shows the letter B on a low- to medium-resolution device; the upper-right diagram shows the same letter on a high-resolution device. The lower-left diagram shows a shape displayed on a raster device; the lines are actually made of dots. The lower-right diagram shows a vector device, in which the lines are true lines between given endpoints. Even in this case, a vector screen is notionally divided up into a plane of discrete points for addressing purposes. *(Diagram by the authors.)*

containing 1000 by 1000 dots, a quality just about acceptable for architectural drawings, will require a million bits (or 125,000 bytes) of memory. This *frame-buffer,* or *bit-map, memory* needed just to keep the picture displayed is therefore about the same as the total memory of many microcomputers. If the screen is in color, we need even more, since the choice is then between multiple colors instead of simply between a binary on or off. To be able to display any one of 16 (2^4) colors requires a nibble (4 bits) per pixel, about 500K at the same resolution as for black and white. The computer interprets the value of a pixel as saying "Display color x at this pixel," where x is the value of the pixel.

Most screens allow only a small number of colors to be displayed simultaneously but have a large palette from which to pick. In this case the number associated with each pixel refers not to a color directly, but to a *color table.* The color table contains the code for the actual color to be displayed. The computer interprets each pixel as saying "Display this pixel in the color shown by entry x of the color table," where x is the value of the pixel. If each pixel occupies a nibble, we are definitely limited to having 16 different colors on the screen at any one time. But if our color table consists of 16 entries of 1 byte each, one entry for each of the possible pixel values, then the color table can represent up to 256 (2^8) colors, from which we may select any 16. Further, changing the value of an entry in the color table means that all the pixels that refer to that entry will change instantly to the new color (Fig. A2.4).

In a *bit-mapped display* the pixels are mapped not only into the screen's own frame-buffer memory but also into the computer's main random-access memory, so that specific areas of the screen can be immediately addressed by the computer without affecting the rest of the image. Bit mapping allows instant update and the use of screen *windows* (Fig. A2.5). By mapping a window (rectangular area) of the screen into more than one set of corresponding computer memory locations, a part (or the whole) of the screen can be instantly changed from one image to another. One design feature that this allows is the use of command menus, which appear in temporary screen windows over the drawing area, as in the Apple Macintosh personal computer.

Raster displays have long been used for text, but until the early 1980s the resolution offered was too low for good graphics. For drawings, vector displays were the standard.

Vector display. In a vector display the internal surface of the screen is coated with a layer of phosphor (usually green) on which lines are "cut" by using a high-power positive electron beam to trace the image. Thus, although the vertices of the image must lie on a rectangular grid (typically 1000 by 1000 so-called addressable points, but it can be much higher), the lines joining these vertices are straight and sharp. Flooding the coating

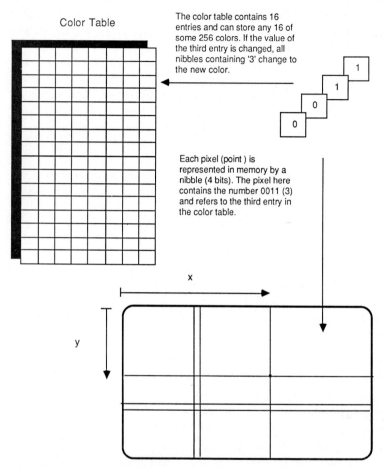

Color Table

The color table contains 16 entries and can store any 16 of some 256 colors. If the value of the third entry is changed, all nibbles containing '3' change to the new color.

1

1

0

0

Each pixel (point) is represented in memory by a nibble (4 bits). The pixel here contains the number 0011 (3) and refers to the third entry in the color table.

x

y

Figure A2.4   The lower diagram shows a graphics screen. Every point has an *x-y* coordinate, with the origin usually in the upper left-hand corner of the screen. Alphanumeric screens are typically divided into 25 lines and 80 columns, the latter a relic from the days of 80-column punch cards. The upper diagram shows that each dot or pixel on the screen is represented by half a byte (nibble) in the computer's memory. The value of each nibble refers to an entry in a color table. The value in this entry is then intrepeted by the computer as a color. A nibble can hold 2^4 (16) different values; hence, up to 16 colors can be displayed at any one time. Each entry in the color table is 8 bits, however, allowing a larger palette of 2^8 (256) colors from which to select. *(Diagram by the authors.)*

with a low-power positive electron beam causes it to fluoresce, displaying the image that has been cut.

These phosphor-coated tubes were first derived in the 1950s from the oscilloscope industry. The original vector graphics terminals were *refresh displays*, in which each individual line was stored in the display's own memory (the *screen buffer*) and redrawn on the screen at least 30 times a second. If they weren't redrawn this fast, the image started to flicker, so that the number and length of lines on the screen were effectively limited by the speed of redrawing. There were technical difficulties in keeping the number of lines that occur in architectural floor plans on a refresh screen without flicker, and any display that could remove most of the flicker was very expensive.

To bypass these problems, in the late 1960s Tektronix and others developed the *direct view storage tube (DVST)*, in which the phosphor itself retains an image for about an hour. Since this image is stored on the screen, it doesn't rely on memory and electronics to refurbish it continuously and it doesn't flicker. The corollary of these advantages, unfortunately, is that it is impossible to get rid of any part of a stored image without recharging the whole screen negatively and losing everything on it. Hence, to remove a table from a plan of a restaurant entails removing and redrawing the whole restaurant. This process is automatic, but it is inherently clumsy, and storage tubes are not as fast or flexible as refreshed screens.

Note the difference between the effect of resolution on vector and raster screens. On a vector screen, resolution influences only the number of addressable points (on which line ends must lie) and does not affect the apparent clarity of the image. On a raster screen, resolution controls the number of dots with which the picture is displayed and very much affects the clarity of the drawing.

A2.1.3   Printers

A VDU, of course, does not provide a permanent paper copy of output *(hard copy)*. Only a printer can do this (Fig. A2.6). The most commonly used printers in design offices are dot-matrix, daisy-wheel, laser, and ink-jet

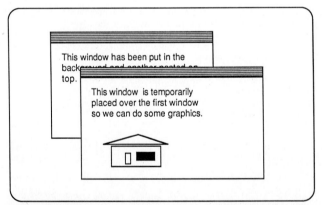

Figure A2.5   One of the most useful abilities of bit-mapped graphics screens is the display of multiple windows. Windows may be overlapped, as shown here, and moved around the screen. *(Diagram by the authors.)*

Figure A2.6   Impact printers (such as daisy-wheel printers, dot-matrix printers, and line printers) make an image by hammering a ribbon against paper. Shown here is a printer enclosed in an acoustic cabinet. Alternatively a smaller box, called an acoustic hood, is used. *(Courtesy of Knoll International.)*

printers. As the price increases, so does the quality of type and the speed of operation.

At the bottom of the price range are the *dot-matrix printers,* in which characters are formed by a print head containing a matrix of pins striking the ribbon. The quality of character formed depends on the density of the matrix. High-density print heads produce results of a quality called near-letter quality by the computer industry, fairly close to the quality of a cheap electric typewriter. Dot-matrix printers are cheap and fast. The very cheapest are quite slow, about 80 characters per second (cps), but the pricier ones are very fast indeed at around 500 cps, about a page every 10 seconds. Since the dot-matrix system is infinitely flexible, it can print any character that could be made out of dots, and most dot-matrix printers can also print graphic information straight from a screen.

The *ink-jet printers* are also cheap. They produce output similar to that of dot-matrix printers in that each character is formed from a matrix of dots, but instead of relying on an impact mechanism to form these dots, they squirt minuscule drops of ink onto the paper. Ink-jet printers are as quiet as dot-matrix printers are noisy, and they achieve speeds of 40 to 300 cps. Their major disadvantage is that the characters they form are not dark. The ink has to be fairly thin so that it can be sprayed quickly, so the impression tends to be light and spidery. They can also produce graphics, both in black and white and color.

Next in price range are the *daisy-wheel* and *thimble printers (letter-quality printers),* in which the characters are kept on a wheel shaped like a daisy flower or thimble that revolves to place the correct character in position over the paper, whereupon it is hit by a hammer to strike a ribbon, thereby printing the character onto the paper. Typically these are 4 times slower than dot-matrix printers (about 35 to 80 cps), taking about 2 minutes to print an A-size page (A4 metric). They are also noisy and are limited in the characters they can print by the range of daisy wheel or thimble offered by the manufacturers.

At the very top of the price range are the *laser printers*. These produce a bit image (a matrix of dots) onto an electrostatic drum, which then transfers the image to paper, rather like a photocopier. Laser printers are extremely fast, producing an A4 page in a few seconds or less at a quality close to that of typesetting. Their speed is one signal advantage, and another is their flexibility. A laser-printer can produce graphics almost as fast as it can produce text, and at a resolution usually much better than that offered by a VDU. Indeed, the quality is so good that a business letter produced by a laser printer looks a little strange, a bit too good. Although still expensive as printers go, laser printers will clearly supersede all other types in design offices.

A final sort of printer, the *line printer*, is rarely found in design offices. Still the standard with some minicomputers and all mainframes, it is intended for enormous throughput of low-quality text. It can produce an A4 page in a second or two, but its printing quality is simply awful. All those telephone bills and pieces of customized junk mail are produced by line printers.

Printers can do many interesting things, such as change pitch, switch to a new font or typeface, underline, and embolden. These features are activated by sending commands to the printer in the form of special sequences of characters called *escape sequences*.

The problem of having the printer distinguish between text that is to be printed and a command that is to be executed is solved by having the command sequences all start with the ASCII character called ESCAPE. As soon as the printer sees this character, it knows that the next few characters form a command, not text to be output. For example, on one printer the sequence ESCAPE followed by ")" (right parenthesis) may mean "switch to italic font." One of the irritating problems of the microcomputer world is that manufacturers cannot agree on common escape sequences. On another printer the ESCAPE then ")" may mean to backspace $\frac{1}{16}$ in (1.6 mm).

This leads to difficulties when matching a word processor with a printer. Naturally, a word processor has no idea what printer is being used with it, so an initial installation procedure must be carried out to tell the program which escape sequence does what. Most word processors come with a selection of printers for which this information has been encoded in the program so that initializing only involves choosing from a menu of possibilities, but to use a printer not in this selection means spending a good deal of time ferreting through manuals to determine the appropriate escape sequences.

A2.1.4 Plotters

Many dot-matrix, ink-jet, and laser printers can also print drawings as well as text, since in all cases the image is made up of a matrix of dots and these can as easily be combined to represent a drawing as a character. Computer-aided drafting and design systems usually have specific drawing plotters, capable of reproducing large drawings.

Until recently *pen plotters* (Fig. A2.7) reigned supreme, busily pushing a pen around under microprocessor control over any normal drafting paper or film with pen types from ballpoint to ink. Either the pen moves back and forth on an arm that in turn traverses over a flat sheet of paper (a flatbed plotter) or the paper is held on a drum that rotates to move the paper in one direction as the pen moves in the other axis (a drum plotter). There is a deep fascination in watching pen plotters at work, which is only marred when the pens dry up or make blotches or the paper tears. These events are only too common.

The present trend is toward *electrostatic plotters* (Fig. A2.8), by which the drawing is produced by an array of tiny nibs that make dots, using an electrostatic process akin to a photocopier. These nibs are closely spaced, typically producing between 125 and 400 dots per inch (5 to 16 dots per millimeter), the finer resolution being associated with more expensive equipment. A pen plotter takes about 45 minutes to draw a typical architectural layout drawing on a D-size sheet (A1 metric), the exact time depending on the complexity of the drawing since it can only draw one line at a time — but an electrostatic plotter takes less than a minute, and that time is independent of drawing complexity since the paper moves through the machine at the same speed whether or not any lines are being drawn. High-resolution electrostatic plotters are comparable with pen plotters. Above all, there is no ink in the nibs to clog up.

Figure A2.7   A trio of Hewlett-Packard pen plotters. Although much slower than electrostatic plotters, they produce very high quality output and can draw on tracing paper, polyester film, and vellum. Many offices have both types of plotter. *(Courtesy of Hewlett-Packard Inc.)*

Figure A2.8   A large electrostatic color plotter. Electrostatic plotters are very fast and reliable machines, although their drawing quality is not as good as pen plotters. *(Photograph courtesy of Versatec.)*

In the long run, laser plotters will probably replace them both. The major problem at present concerns producing laser plotters large enough to produce A1 or larger-size drawings.

A2.1.5   Pointing and graphic input devices

The obvious pointing device is a finger, and *touch-sensitive screens* record directly the position of a finger or other object poked at the screen. Some use a flexible screen that actually deforms when pressed; others use a grid of infrared beams that scan the face of the screen in two directions and respond to interruption. Sensitivity is low and only adequate for picking a series of options. The most common pointing devices, then, are not fingers but digitizers, light pens, and mice.

A *flatbed digitizer,* or *tablet,* consists of a grid of sensitive wiring in two directions that detects either a touch or electrical signal from a second cross wire in a movable top controller called a *puck, pen,* or *stylus* (Figs. A2.9 and A2.10). The signal is converted into x-y coordinates on the tablet and sent back to the computer. Movement of the pen over the tablet causes a marker or cursor (usually two fine lines at right angles to one another) to move around the screen in synchronization, so that end points of lines or other drawing elements can be indicated and items in a screen-displayed menu of command options can be picked. When the pen is touched firmly against the tablet, the computer registers its position and maps this loca-

Figure A2.9 A digitizing tablet being used with an IBM microcomputer and the Versacad Advanced drafting program. Until the early 1980s all CAD systems were mounted on minicomputers. The coming of relatively cheap systems such as displayed here has enabled even very small firms to experiment with computer-aided drafting. *(Courtesy of Versacad.)*

tion onto the image appearing on the screen. Tablet sizes vary from about a foot square (300 mm × 300 mm) up to the size of large drawing boards. A tablet is particularly effective for describing an existing drawing (overlaid on the tablet) to the computer.

Figure A2.10 A Hewlett-Packard stand-alone workstation for a computer-aided drafting system. The keyboard, puck, and tablet lie on the desktop in front of the screen, with the central processor and hard disk in the cabinet.

A *light pen* is similar to a tablet pen but is used to point directly to the desired position on the screen. This sounds simpler, but light pens, like touch screens, are tiring to use (requiring an arm to be held unsupported in the air) and cannot be positioned as accurately as a puck or digitizer. Other options are *thumb wheels* (rotating one wheel moves the cursor up and down, and rotating a second wheel moves it across), *direction* (or *arrow*) *keys* (the cursor moves in small steps as long as the key is depressed), or the *joysticks* found in computer games. None of these devices is common.

A *mouse* acts very much like a digitizing puck, but it is shaped to be pushed about like a toy car over a desk top or special plate. It registers movement either by using a photoelectric cell to count the number of grid lines it crosses on the special plate or by monitoring the rotation of a bearing on which it rolls. Movement of the mouse causes a pointer on the screen to move in synchronization, so that endpoints of lines or other drawing descriptions can be indicated and items can be picked from a screen-displayed menu of commands. A mouse will have at least one push button (and often several) to allow the user to communicate with the computer. A mouse cannot be used to digitize drawings, however, and sketching with a mouse has been likened to drawing with a lump of cheese.

The final sort of input mechanisms are the *automatic data-capture* devices (Fig. A2.11). These scan text or drawings with lasers or LCDs to produce graphics raster images, which are then converted to conventional

Figure A2.11   The Tektronix 4991 Autovectorizer, an automatic data-capture device for the direct conversion of drawings into computer format. The computer must first convert the image into raster lines and then into points, lines, and shapes. This is a very complex task, and these devices rely on substantial help from humans in structuring lines into represented objects. *(Copyright 1985 by Tektronix Inc.)*

text files or graphics files. This is a complex task, for the computer must translate a collection of black and white dots obtained from a raster image into letters, numbers, lines, and curves. Most use a combination of computer software to look for line ends and a human operator to structure the information. The time saved over wholly manual data entry is only about 50 percent. At present uncommon and expensive, they will no doubt become commonplace over the next decade.

A2.2   The Central Processor

The central processor, or CPU, is the heart of the computer, the thing that does all the actual computing. In microcomputers it is generally just a single chip, but in mainframes and minicomputers usually several. The overwhelming majority of microcomputers use one of perhaps three of four brands or makes of CPU. Each has its own characteristics, and these more than any other factor determine the true power of the system as a whole. CPUs differ in several ways, the most important being speed, native language, and word size.

1. Speed.   Speed is the easiest of these to understand. A chip that works faster than another is better (with the qualifications given below). The speed is often given in megahertz (MHz), or million cycles per second, and is typically 4 to 20 MHz. It is sometimes referred to as the *clock rate.* At every tick of the clock, some well-defined process inside the CPU takes place. It is difficult to use clock speeds for interchip comparison unless you know just what can happen in a clock cycle. For example, the Intel 8088 chip (used in the IBM PC) usually has a clock rate of 4.76 MHz, or 4,766,000 cycles per second. If we look up the right books, we find that the ADD instruction takes 3 ticks and the MULtiply instruction perhaps 50. On another chip, the ADD might take 1 tick or 10. So the actual speed at which things happen depends not only on the clock rate but on the timings of instructions.

Another measure of speed is *millions of operations per second (Mips),* although with this measure we run into the question of just what operations are being measured. For what it's worth, minicomputers run around the 1- to 5-Mips range, and mainframes run up to about 20 Mips. A similar problem exists with the measure of speed called *megaflops,* which stands for million floating-point operations per second.

2. Native language.   The *native language* of a CPU is the computer language that the CPU is designed to understand and utilize. This language is composed of instructions. Each instruction is directly understood by the circuitry of the chip and is executed very quickly. However, since each instruction only does one tiny simple task, many instructions must be used to carry out jobs that we would consider pretty easy, like adding two numbers together. One aim of CPU designers is to provide a chip with a native language, or set of instructions, that is powerful and comprehensive, thus enabling the circuitry to do complex calculations with as few operations as possible. One measure of the power of a CPU chip is therefore the richness of its machine code. The Intel 8088 has about 100 different sorts of instruction, and its successors in the Intel family, the iAPX 186, iAPX 286, and so on, added more.

Different CPUs have different machine languages. By and large, two different CPU chips will be utterly unable to understand each other, which is one reason for the difficulty in transporting programs between computers without some sort of translation effort. There are special programs called *cross compilers* that translate between CPU languages, but the results they produce are clumsy and inefficient. Unfortunately, many programs developed for the old 8-bit microcomputers were sold for the newer 16-bit computers after just such a translation, and they actually performed worse on the new machines.

Very few people actually write programs in machine language. A good machine-code programmer might write 10 debugged instructions per month. A whole program that does something reasonable may contain some 20,000 instructions, so you can see that this is not the way to meet deadlines. The advantage of writing in machine code lies in the ability to write extremely efficient, elegant programs. Like an illuminated manuscript produced by a monk, superb results are possible but take time. It is much faster to write in a high-level language (see Sec. 3.3.3).

3. Word size.   The final measure of a CPU's power is its word size. A *word* in computer parlance (see the Glossary) is not a fixed unit like a byte or a bit, but rather the basic unit of information the CPU is designed to handle. One common operation required of a CPU is to fetch some data from memory, and it does so usually in chunks a word big. Also, the instructions that make up the vocabulary of the CPU's native language are often designed to fit inside precisely one word. By and large, more powerful CPUs operate with longer words.

Until the late 1970s the standard word length for most microcomputers was 8 bits. At that time the standard word length for minicomputers was 16 bits and for mainframes was 32 to 60 bits. Nowadays the CPUs used in microcomputers are more powerful than the old 8-bit CPUs and operate on words 16 or 32 bits long; minicomputers have also progressed to using 32-bit words. This is the meaning behind the expressions "8-bit" or "16-bit" microcomputer. For a variety of reasons, none of them particularly convincing, word lengths have evolved in multiples of 8 bits. Traditionally, word lengths are referred to as 8-bit or 16-bit rather than 1-byte or 2-byte.

The word size, then, signifies the amount of information that can be stored in one memory location and transferred into the CPU at one time. Word length affects the accuracy of the results obtained by individual operations. The older 8-bit microcomputers used 8-bit words, each of which could hold a number from 0 to 2^8 (256). In order to manipulate the sorts of numbers found in the real world (the real numbers as well as large integers), four or more words had to be strung together. This entailed a lot of time-consuming word shuffling between the CPU and the internal memory. One of the more modern 16-bit microcomputers needs only worry about two words, and a 32-bit microcomputer only one word (Fig. A2.12).

Unfortunately, the situation about word sizes is a little more complex than this, and to continue the discussion we must venture into the internal memory.

A2.3   Internal Memory

Internal memory is used by the computer for the temporary holding of data and programs. The operating system lives inside the internal memory, as do many other things, all invisible to the user. This memory is often called *random-access memory (RAM)* since any particular location can be accessed at random, although "at will" would be a better way of putting it.

The internal memory of a microcomputer is *semiconductor memory.* This is an integrated circuit or microchip designed, obviously, to hold electric impulses. A single chip is about the size of a postage stamp and can hold hundreds or thousands of bytes. These chips are arranged in groups on a circuit board that is plugged into the computer's main circuit board. The memory is *volatile,* in that once the power goes, the memory forgets everything.

For the CPU to use the RAM, it must first be able to locate the particular location in RAM that it wants and then be able to read or write data to or

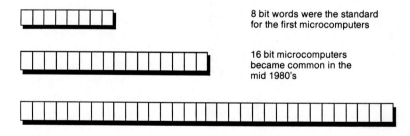

8 bit words were the standard for the first microcomputers

16 bit microcomputers became common in the mid 1980's

32 bit word lengths are now common for micro and minicomputers

Figure A2.12   Like words in a natural language, computer words are of variable length, although the variation is between machines. Every microprocessor is designed to manipulate memory amounts of some fixed length (the word). Each word has a certain number of bits. Microcomputer and minicomputer word sizes are multiples of 8 bits (a byte), but mainframes vary. *(Diagram by the authors.)*

8 bit Data Bus

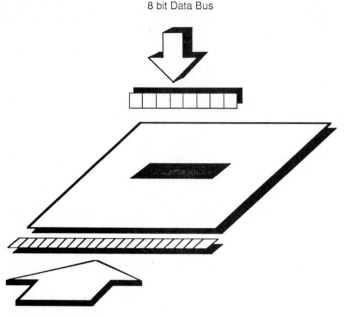

20 Bit Address Bus

Figure A2.13   A computer uses two buses to get information into and out of memory. The address bus is used to tell the memory *where* the data is to be stored (or retrieved from). The data bus transfers the data itself. The data bus is precisely as wide as the word length, so that exactly one word can be transferred at a time. When a microprocessor is said to be a "16-bit" chip, we are referring to the word size and the width of the data bus. The address bus is much wider and of a size independent of the data bus. The width of the address bus determines the maximum amount of memory that the microprocessor is capable of addressing. *(Diagram by the authors.)*

from that location. These jobs are accomplished through two important buses in the computer, the *data bus* and the *address bus* (Fig. A2.13). A *bus* is simply a set of tracks on a printed circuit board that carries electric impulses. Each bus has a width matching the CPU's design. Since the data bus transfers data, one would think that its width should precisely match the size of a word, so that an 8-bit CPU would have an 8-bit data bus, and so on, but some 16-bit chips still operate with 8-bit data buses and some 32-bit chips operate with 16-bit buses. This naturally obviates one major advantage of having a larger word size, namely, being able to transfer data in bigger chunks. However, the existence of a faster 16-bit chip utilizing an 8-bit data bus allows computer manufacturers to upgrade machines by simply replacing an old 8-bit chip with a new 16-bit processor. No changes need to be made to the circuitry in the rest of the computer.

The address bus is responsible for locating single portions of memory. Its width determines the largest amount of RAM that a microprocessor can use. For obscure reasons, 8-bit microcomputers typically have 20-bit address buses, which means that they can talk to 2^{20} bytes of memory, which happens to be 64K. This means that a computer with such an address bus could never use more than 64K of memory (which is not much, by the way). The Intel 8086 and 8088 have 24-bit buses, allowing them a more generous 1024K (1M). True 32-bit chips (such as the Motorola 68000) use 28-bit buses, allowing for a luxuriant 16M of internal memory.

The size of the RAM in a computer determines the largest program that can be run. A reasonable program for a microcomputer occupies between 40K and 300K of memory, in addition to which there has to be room for the data it uses. Modern microcomputers offer between 128K and 2048K (2M) of RAM. A program too big to fit into RAM all at once may be broken down into subsegments that are kept on mass storage until needed, at which time they are loaded into RAM (thereby overwriting the previous part of the program in RAM). The speed of data transfer between the mass storage and the RAM is about 10,000 times slower than between the RAM and the CPU, so this technique can slow down a program considerably.

A2.4 Mass Storage

Since the RAM is only a temporary memory storage, some form of permanent storage for programs and data must be provided. This role is filled by *mass storage,* also called *auxiliary memory, external memory, online storage,* or *secondary memory.* Mass storage uses interchangeable magnetic media, such as disks or tapes, to store information (although there are other methods, such as bubble memory and laser disks, magnetic storage is still the commonest form of mass storage). It thus has the secondary function of acting as a medium of data transfer between computers. The devices that read and write these media are called *disk drives* or *tape drives* and work rather like record players or tape decks. The CPU communicates to the disk drive not directly, but through special chips called *direct memory access (DMA) controllers.*

A2.4.1 Tapes

The simplest form of mass storage for microcomputers is the common cassette tape. A 1-hour audio tape holds about 250K, but information transfer is slow and unreliable; consequently, cassette mass storage is restricted to the home computer and hobbyist market.

For *archival storage* of data from minicomputers and mainframes, conventional reel-mounted tapes are used; because they are not immediately accessible by the computer, they are a form of *offline* storage. Used with large tape drives, these tapes cost more than most microcomputers and are never used as a form of mass storage with small machines. They do, however, possess one enormous advantage: The format in which data is laid down on a tape is standardized. A tape written by one mainframe or minicomputer can thus be transported to any other such machine. Tapes are used extensively as very cheap ways of transferring large amounts of data between mainframe and minicomputer sites and machines. Unhappily, this is not the situation with microcomputers.

A2.4.2 Floppy disks

The common form of mass storage on microcomputers is the use of floppy disks, which presently come in three sizes: 8, $5\frac{1}{4}$, and $3\frac{1}{2}$ in. Large (8-in) disks were the first to be developed and are now quite rare. Small ($5\frac{1}{4}$-in) floppies were the standard in the early 1980s but have given way to the tiny ($3\frac{1}{2}$-in) floppies. For the two larger sizes, the magnetic disk that stores the information is housed in a card jacket with a slot cut in it; these sizes are delicate and easily damaged. The $3\frac{1}{2}$-in floppies are housed in a rigid plastic case and can be treated with much less circumspection.

Information is recorded onto floppies on circular tracks divided into pie-shaped sectors. These tracks are not physically part of the disk but must be laid down by the computer before use. This initializing process is called *formatting* and must be done before the disk is used to store data. The great bane of the microcomputer industry is that manufacturers have chosen different ways of formatting disks, so that a floppy disk used in a Hewlett-Packard computer cannot be used in an Apple or an IBM. This is a staggering hindrance to the use of floppies as a means of transferring data. Software houses, unless they develop a program for one brand of computer alone, are obliged to release software on many disk formats. Some microcomputer makers purposely adopt the format of existing, popular machines (notably IBM and Apple) in order to avail themselves of the programs available for these. This is part of what it means to say that two computers are compatible.

A floppy disk is read by the disk drive, which contains a magnetic head that can move along the disk's radius while the disk is spinning rapidly. The time it takes for the head to move from one track in or out to the next is called its *seek time,* and the time it takes for a sector to spin round underneath the head is known as its *latency.*

A disk's *capacity* depends on its size and density and on whether it is single- or double-sided. Capacities range from about 80K to 1024K. Many machines offer disk drives in both single- and double-sided versions. However, while a single-sided disk can be read by a double-sided drive, the reverse is not the case. Programs are therefore distributed on single-sided disks regardless.

A2.4.3 Hard-disk drives

The standard mass storage device for minicomputers and mainframes is the *hard-disk drive.* Very fast and reliable, a hard-disk unit consists of a stack of rigid disks, each of which is accessed by its own magnetic head. This platter of disks is removable. Such disk drives can transfer data between 10 and 1000 times faster than a floppy-disk drive and can store much more data; typical sizes range from 80M to 1G (or about 80,000K to 1,000,000K).

Microcomputers use a much smaller version of these known as *Winchester drives,* in which the disk is sealed inside the drive case. This allows the engineering tolerances to be much finer than would be the case with a removable disk pack. A typical Winchester unit for a microcomputer holds anywhere from 5M (5000K) to 100M (100,000K). Many Winchester drives also come with a separate section that takes a removable disk pack.

Without a removable disk pack, users of Winchester drives would be faced with the problem of making a backup disk on some reserve medium. (Large computers don't have any problems; they just transfer the disk's data to a separate tape unit.) In recognition of this problem, most Winchester units are fitted with an auxiliary tape backup system. The system contains a tape in a large cassette that looks like a normal audio cassette with a glandular problem; you simply press the backup button and the unit transfers all the information from the Winchester to the tape. Such drives are called *streaming tapes.* In contrast to a normal tape drive, which is designed so that any part of the tape can be accessed fairly quickly and thus requires special buffering systems to prevent the tape from splitting, a streaming tape is designed simply to proceed from the start of the tape to the end without stopping and starting, so its engineering can be less delicate.

A2.5   Communications

A2.5.1   Local-area networks

A major trend over the last 10 years has been a progression away from single, large computers to distributed processing using many smaller computers. In its simplest form, the aim of the network is to provide all users with access to a single, large mass storage device. All the computers are connected as *nodes* in a star network to a master central computer called a *file server,* which alone handles mass storage memory operations. The computers can all function on their own, and if the file server fails, the only consequence is that they are denied access to the central disk (which may be serious enough).

This star system is one form of what are called *local-area networks (LANs),* or *internal networks* (Fig. A2.14). Such networks often arise when an organization expands from a single microcomputer to several, and instead of having its floppy disks in many places (and never the right floppy at the right machine), all its computers access one large hard-disk drive with its centralized store of data. Printers can also be shared among several machines, the file server handling requests to print documents.

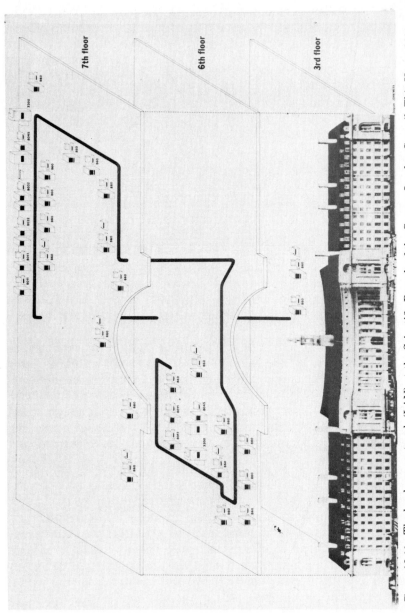

Figure A2.14   The local-area network (LAN) at the Scientific Branch of the Greater London Council. This Xerox 8000 network consists of 23 word processors and four more sophisticated graphics workstations, plus associated peripherals such as laser printers and mass storage devices. It is used by over 150 people primarily for word processing and electronic mail. Such netowrks are increasingly being favored over the older solution of a star network based on a central minicomputer. *(Hand-drawn and photo montage, used by permission of Architects Journal.)*

Star networks suffer from several problems. First, their functionality is limited to mass storage and printing. Second, the lines between the micro-computers and the file server must be complex high-speed links (since they now must handle the rapid transfer of data to mass storage), not the simple slow-speed lines that connect terminals to a central computer. High-speed cables are limited in length, however, whereas slow-speed cables can travel for hundreds of meters if necessary. Third, star networks do not allow the free connection of different sorts of computers to the one hard disk. Some do allow different machines on the network, but then files written by a type-X machine are only available to other type-X computers and not to any type-Z computers that may also be on the network.

An alternative to the star form of the local area network is provided by *ring networks* and *bus networks* (Fig. A2.15). In these systems the necessity to run cables back from each computer to the central device is eliminated. Instead, a single cable connects all the machines together through small auxiliary devices called *cable drops*. The motives behind installing this form of network are often different from those behind star networks, for in a ring or bus system each computer can talk to the others. Messages are not channeled through a single central machine, where data jams could occur. Moreover, different types of microcomputers can be connected together (in theory at least).

The major problems with these systems lie in handling the movement of data in such a way as to prevent confusion. In a star system a single computer handles all communications, but in a bus or ring network each computer must look out for itself. Each piece of data (called a *data packet*) must have an address associated with it, and only the addressee must accept it. The way in which data is organized in a packet so that both the sender and the receiver understand the message is known as the *protocol* of the system. The media that can be used for carrying the digital information through a network range from the familiar twisted pair of wires (the twist-ing reduces the effects of external interference) to shielded twin and coax-ial cable and to the newer fiber-optic wires (Byers, 1984). Fiber optics, since it uses light as the transmission medium, is immune to all forms of electrical interference. Other approaches do not use cables at all: with radio or infrared transmission, the signal is available anywhere within range of the transmitter and is picked up by any network node equipped with a detector.

In theory, local-area networks are the solution of choice in any system of more than one microcomputer. Problems occur in selecting the sort of LAN that best suits the application at hand. The first consideration is between a *broadband* and a *baseband* sort of network; these refer to the method by which data is electronically transmitted through the network. The *bandwidth* of a communications channel is a measure of the amount of information it can transfer without significant information loss. The

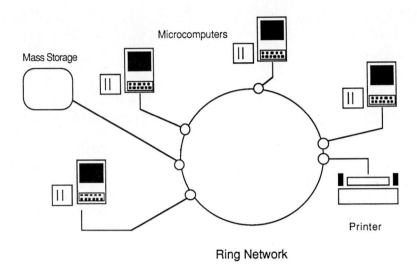

Ring Network

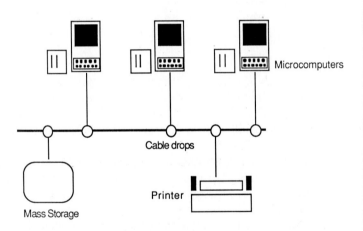

Bus Network

Figure A2.15 The two most common forms of local-area-network topology are the ring network and the bus network. *(Diagram by the authors.)*

greater the bandwidth, the better. Voice communication requires a narrow bandwidth, for example, while television requires a much wider one. A *baseband* system utilizes the entire bandwidth to transmit a single channel of information; a *broadband* system allows several different channels to be transmitted simultaneously. Baseband systems use cheaper cables and are easier to tap than broadband systems and are suitable for small networks on a single site; however, individual cable lengths are limited because of possible information degradation. Over large sites, the more complex and expensive broadband systems are the better solution. In both cases the total cable length is limited to about $2\frac{1}{2}$ miles (5 kilometers).

A second factor to consider is the speed of transmission. A low-speed network runs at about 1 Megabit per second (Mbit/s) (about 100,000 bytes or characters per second), a medium-speed system at 10 Mbits/s, and a high-speed one from 30 Mbits/s. These transmission rates sound fast but are not a proper indication of the effective utility of the network, for the limits of speed are usually set by the number of users and peripherals (or nodes) on the network and how often they access it. If several people try to access a hard disk simultaneously, they will have to wait their turn until the user who made the first access has finished. Naturally, the faster the network can send information to or from the first user, the less waiting time the other users will have. Networks require very fast data transmission times in order to maintain their response rates at a reasonable level.

A2.5.2   Long-haul networks

Long-haul networks allow computers to talk to each other over very long distances. The telephone system is the largest and oldest long-haul network, while the telex system has long provided a direct person-to-person means of international document distribution. Telex is a very old technology and transmits at very slow rates, typically 5 to 7 cps, usually referred to as 50 to 70 *baud;* the baud unit is roughly bytes or characters per second multiplied by 10. At this rate an A4 page takes about 5 minutes to be transmitted, woefully slow by modern standards. By comparison, a standard telephone line can be used to transmit information from a computer at 30 cps (300 baud or more), and a reasonable speed for direct machine-human communication (so that the human does not die of boredom waiting for the screen to fill) is considered to be at least 120 cps (1200 baud).

Most microcomputer users who wish to communicate with distant computers do so through the normal *public-switched telephone network (PSTN)* (Fig. A2.16). They buy a small box called a *modem,* which provides an interface between a computer and a telephone plug. A connection to another computer then involves the user literally dialing that computer's telephone number. (It is not quite this easy; there is a huge amount of work involved in the communications game, as discussed in Sec. A2.5.3.) Telephone lines readily support only 300- to 1200-baud transmission rates. The PSTN was not designed for digital data transmission, and the lines are often noisy as well as slow. However, they are quite adequate for low-speed uses and short connect times, such as occasional communication with public databases (see Chap. 4).

If you want to talk to some one specific computer, you can have a *dedicated line* installed between your computer and the other site. Some design professionals install CAD terminals in their offices, connected via dedicated lines to a computer owned by a bureau running a CAD package

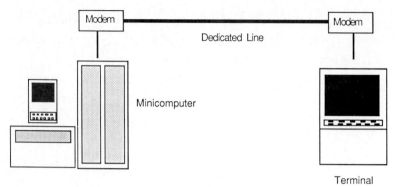

Dedicated Lines for High-Volume Transmission

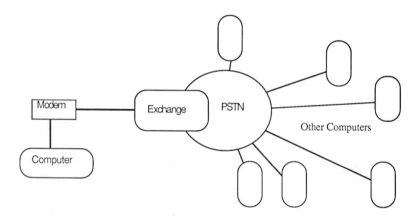

Using the PSTN to communicate

Figure A2.16   A dedicated line (above) is a permanent connection through the telephone system between two computers. Dedicated lines are used when transmission rates must be very high, as between a graphics terminal and its computer, or between two computers, and when large amounts of data must be transmitted at frequent intervals. Most microcomputer users are happy enough to use the everyday telephone system (below) to make casual connections to long-distance networks for database access or electronic mail. *(Diagram by the authors.)*

(see Chap. 8 for details). Dedicated lines miss out on the very noisy switching gear used in telephone exchanges and can support transmission speeds up to 96,000 baud, although 9600 baud is often as high as users want to push their machines. While 1200 baud is a reasonable speed for a simple alphanumeric terminal that can display only text, graphics terminals require faster transmission rates. The amount of graphics information in a typical working drawing is vastly greater than in a screenful of text, so correspondingly faster transmission speeds are required if the response time of the terminal is to be quick enough.

Local telecommunications authorities, of course, charge considerably for these fast transmission lines, usually based on an annual rental fee plus a charge for the quantity of data transmitted. However, dedicated lines are at present the only economical solution for those applications involving high data flow which must be done at high speed and which require long connect times, such as in computer-to-computer communications. The telephone system is just too slow, and dedicated lines too rigid, for a general-purpose system that would allow computers to talk to other computers with the same ease with which we can telephone anyone throughout the world. Moreover, the existing worldwide PSTN system is becoming overloaded with computer users monopolizing the lines for long hours of computer-computer transmission. At present there is in fact no universal large-scale computer network system, and all existing networks are implemented through dedicated lines or the PSTN.

However, telecommunications authorities throughout the world are developing new networks to replace the PSTN. Called *integrated services digital networks (ISDNs),* they will utilize broadband fiber-optic cables to transmit information at speeds of up to 300 Mbits/s (400 million baud) and will handle voice, visual, and computer data in digitally encoded form (Lamb, 1984). The importance of this development cannot be underestimated. The encoding of normally analog data (such as for telephone, television, and radio) into digital form is a significant advance toward more reliable and faster communications systems. The superiority of digital coding is evident in the audio quality of compact disks over conventional records, for example. The reason is that such encoding guarantees that information loss or corruption is minimized to almost zero.

ISDNs will make use of existing *packet-switched networks.* In such a system you can "dial" any other user also on the system, just as in the PSTN. Your information is divided up into discrete *packets* and supplied with a forwarding address, some information about the sender, and some data-protection information. It is then fed into the network and stored until an opportunity for forwarding the data presents itself. Unlike the PSTN, which maintains a single physical connection between sender and receiver for the length of the transmission, the packet-switched network constantly adjusts itself to maintain optimal performance. The network possesses several major switching nodes connected by high-speed transmission lines whose job it is to keep information flowing as fast as possible given the current traffic situation. Which node handles your particular packets varies depending on the current load of all the nodes in the system.

Packet-switched networks intelligently optimize their performance constantly, routing information to bypass overloaded or failed nodes. One important benefit is that they allow all sorts of computers to access them and operate independently of the transmission speeds and protocols of these different machines. Large users use items of equipment called *packet assemblers/disassemblers (PADs)*. A PAD translates data from the format given it by the individual computer into a format suitable for transmission through the network. Small users use a normal modem to transmit through the PSTN to a nearby public PAD, which does the job for them. So efficient is this sort of communication that packet-switching costs are independent of the distance traveled. Charges are made for the volume information transmitted, plus an annual fee.

A2.5.3 Getting a computer to communicate

A computer must be able to communicate with all sorts of external devices, such as printers, plotters, and modems. It does so through channels called *ports,* or *interfaces.* Microcomputer users are concerned mainly with two different types of ports, the Centronics and the RS-232C. Each port can be male or female and accept the appropriate type of connector. Each port has connections for 30-odd wires, not all of which are actually used.

The *Centronics port* was designed by a printer maker, and its main use is still in connecting up printers. It is known as a *parallel port* because each bit in a byte is sent down a separate wire so that the whole byte arrives simultaneously at the printer. Connecting equipment by means of Centronics ports is very easy, and far and away the method of choice for connecting printers.

The CPU talks to the various ports through special-purpose chips, and it does so in an elegant manner. The port appears to the CPU as 2 or 3 bytes in memory, a technique called *memory mapping.* To send a character, the CPU places it into what it thinks is a memory location. In another apparent memory location it places a value indicating that a character is ready to be sent. The input-output processor chip then does the rest and returns a value into one of the locations, indicating that the character has been sent. Quite an amount of the address space is taken up by such memory mapping, and this means that those addresses are not available for use as normal RAM. Hence, although a 16-bit CPU can address a whole megabyte of memory, only a portion of this can actually be RAM.

The *RS-232C port* is another matter. This uses *serial transmission,* which means that each bit is sent down the wire one at a time. The RS-232C port is used to connect computers to each other and to modems. Unfortunately, it is no simple task to do so. The two pieces of equipment must agree on the method of data transmission, and this involves several parameters. They must agree on what speed the data is to be transmitted, measured in baud. There are about 10 standard transmission speeds. Next, the *parity* of the data must be agreed upon. (Parity is a simple means of guarding against corrupt data and was explained in Sec. 2.4.2.) The parity may be even, odd, or ignored. Then the equipment must agree just how big a byte is; some pieces of equipment expect a 7-bit byte with a 1-bit parity bit, others 8 bits and then the parity bit, and so on. An added complication arises from the fact that the standard defining the RS-232C defines two types of equipment: data transmission equipment and data receiving equipment. These types are differentiated by what they expect to find on some of the wires that make up the interface.

Matters do not end there, though. The receiving machine must know where a bit starts and ends and where the boundaries between characters are. The two machines must also agree on the special characters to be used to start and stop a message so that the receiver can know when to start and stop listening. The data is probably sent to a small buffer in the receiver, so the receiver must have a way of telling the sender to pause in transmission if the buffer fills up. All these rules form a *protocol,* a collection of rules for forming and transmitting data. The major reason for using a protocol is to guard against data corruption in transmission. Protocols for transmission to and from microcomputers can be fairly simple because of the low transmission speeds and low volume of information flow. Mainframe protocols are much more elaborate. They can not only detect if an error has occurred but where it has occurred. If all this sounds terribly complicated, it is. Even getting a computer to talk to a printer is not an easy job.

A2.6 State of the Art: Future Developments in Hardware

A2.6.1 Advances in hardware and software

The development of hardware over the next 5 to 10 years is easy to summarize: bigger memories and faster CPUs. But this does not necessarily mean a corresponding increase in the performance of computers. A noted feature of the computer industry is that the state of software development generally lags behind the state of the art in hardware by 2 to 4 years. When a computer incorporating some technological advance is released on the market, the software available for that machine does not take full advantage of its sophistication. In the first year or so of the new machine's existence, most of the programs available for it are derived directly from earlier models. Software developers generally wait for the new computer to develop a reasonable market base before devoting resources to writing programs utilizing its greater abilities.

Once this market exists, software firms will probably turn their attention to developing programs designed from the start with the new computer in mind. These programs will often not be available for several months after the new computer's debut. If a new technologically advanced computer is released by a small firm, it has a correspondingly less certain market and developers will be reluctant to devote resources to a computer that may never get anywhere. The software lag will be even greater. While there will always be some enterprising developers who will take the plunge on the computer, the range of software will for many years be substantially smaller than that of an IBM or Apple computer.

These remarks are offered primiarily to disabuse designers of the notion that only the latest computer will do. Perhaps your machine can display a billion colors, but are there any programs that can utilize that ability? With that said, we can now turn to a look at hardware developments over the next few years.

A2.6.2 Developments in microprocessors and internal memory

Microprocessors will become faster, certainly a lot faster. They will do this through a variety of developments, such as increasing the speed at which the clock chip operates and increasing the word size that the CPU can handle. Many microcomputers today use 16/32-bit CPUs. This means that internally they work in 32-bit-size words but communicate with the other parts of the computer in 16-bit chunks. Naturally, it is best if the CPU can communicate in full 32-bit-size words, and this progression to full 32-bit chips will be completed in the next few years. Speed will also be improved by a technique called *caching.* In this sort of system the CPU in effect takes a guess at what the next instruction will be and prepares itself accordingly while actually executing the current instruction.

All these things can speed up a microprocessor so far and no farther, but the computer industry is now looking to two major developments for the next major speed increase. The first is *parallel processing;* the second is the use of *optical microprocessors.* In many computers today the workload is borne by a single CPU, which processes programs in a sequential fashion, carrying out one instruction before proceeding to the next. The sort of look-ahead abilities provided by caching are a minor but appreciable improvement on this. In those computers with several full microprocessors, each is dedicated to a single task, such as handling accesses to the disk drives and screen, and only one microprocessor acts as the CPU. Parallel processing arranges several CPUs together so that the central workload can be shared by all.

In theory, the advantages of parallel processing are substantial, promising enormous reductions in processing time. To take a prosaic example, consider a long specification in which a single word has to be changed to some other word. The conventional sequential processing computer must examine the entire document, starting at the very first word and proceeding to the very last. If the document could be broken down into 100 separate pieces, and each piece alloted to its own CPU, then the processing time would be reduced by (roughly) a factor of 100. This is a grand idea in theory, and well within the abilities of existing hardware. Such machines are available and in use. There are plans to utilize as many as 1000 or even a boggling 10,000 CPUs together. Since microprocessors are but a small part of the cost of a computer, such machines would not be correspondingly expensive.

In practice, one major problem is in deciding which parts of the program should be allocated to different CPUs. Programs today are written in sequential fashion simply because all the major languages are sequential. Only a very few languages, such as Ada and some artificial intelligence languages like PROLOG, have the idea of writing parallel pieces of code built in. As a consequence, it is difficult for the computer to know which portions of a program can be executed in parallel with other portions and which must be handled sequentially. Another major problem is in preventing the CPUs from tripping over each other or suffering from overlong waiting periods. These problems are not yet fully solved, although substantial progress can be expected before the end of the decade.

The second major improvement in processing speed will come from the use of optical chips, developed around lasers. At present, a major limitation on the speed of supercomputers is the amount of wiring inside them. The less distance electrons have to travel, the better, so supercomputers tend to be physically very compact. Light travels much faster than electrical signals, and optical switching elements can switch faster, and it is therefore natural to look to optical methods to develop faster computers. Although research has been progressing for many years, there are still many problems to be overcome and there is little prospect of an optical CPU reaching the market before the end of the decade.

Apart from speed increases, microprocessors will be able to address greater areas of RAM. As noted above, 8-bit chips were limited to 64K of RAM, and the early 16-bit chips to 1M (1024K). Modern microprocessors will be capable of addressing several gigabytes ($1G = 1024M = 1,048,576K$!). This would not be much use without the physical RAM actually available to be addressed. The advent of cheap, high-capacity RAM chips has ensured that this is possible.

A2.6.3 Other developments

We have seen magnetic storage media improve in storage capacity markedly over the past few years. The next great step will be the abandonment of such technology in favor of *electro-optical storage media*. Purely optical storage media are available but suffer from the disadvantage that they cannot erase information, for they depend on a laser burning and thus permanently alter the disk medium as they store the data. For the next few years at least, the future lies with hybrid electro-optical systems that can read, write, and erase; this technology promises vastly greater storage capacities than those provided by conventional magnetic media — by a factor of at least 1000. A single disk 4 in. in diameter could hold the name and address of every person in the United States. Sometime, one probably will.

These developments will have a significant impact on computer-aided drafting systems. Detailed working drawings represent large amounts of storage. Large projects consume megabytes or even gigabytes of memory. The only solutions at present are to store much of this on tapes, transferring to the computer as needed, or to invest in more, expensive hard-disk drives. The existence of small but very capacious mass storage devices will lead to smaller and hence to cheaper drafting systems. The fancy things that architects like to do with CAD systems, such as colored perspectives, are time-consuming for computers to carry out and will be rendered faster by the new microprocessors.

Architects should also be cheered by improvements to display screens. Color is enormously expensive in terms of memory, and the range of colors displayable at any one time is limited largely by the amount of memory available for the bit map. Larger RAM sizes will mean more colors, and screens of greater resolution. Resolution will also be improved in a new generation of display technologies that promises to replace the bulky screens now in use by screens a few centimeters thick.

3

Software

3.1 Introduction

In Chap. 2 we have described the computer industry and the components that go to make up computers and computer networks — the *hardware,* in the jargon of the industry. All this hardware does nothing without some instructions. The computer programs and their associated manuals that provide these instructions are called *software.* In this chapter we look at the building of computer software and some of the tools and techniques available for its construction.

Architects are users rather than makers of software, and we can certainly use programs without knowing how to create them. The aim here, then, is only to give enough information for an understanding of the processes and concepts involved. Most design offices that really exploit the technology contain at least one person who not only understands the concepts but gets involved in the practice of programming.

We begin with a discussion of the process of systems analysis and the design of software systems, then describe the nature and purpose of computer programming and computer programs. In the secondary text we look at two major concerns of computer programmers in constructing programs: (1) the structure and the languages with which they can describe processes and (2) the structure and methods with which they can store information in computer programs as databases. Knowing about such things helps us understand the tools a programmer employs and what is going on when a program is running.

3.2 Systems Analysis and Design

Computer software is associated with computer programming, but programming is merely a late and sometimes rather mundane stage in the process of developing computer solutions to problems. Much more important are the notions of *analyzing* systems and situations and *constructing models* of the procedures and domains within which computers might have some application. In the world of computing, *systems analysis and design* are the processes by which a new organization or computer system is developed to replace an existing state of affairs. Systems analysts use their professional skills to *investigate, analyze, design, develop, implement,* and finally *evaluate* a systems project (Fig. 3.1) (Capron and Williams, 1982). This does not sound too dissimilar to the work of an architect in collecting and analyzing the brief and then in designing and managing the construction of a building. Both require the ability to analyze a situation, synthesize some design proposal to improve the situation, and carry the project through to completion.

Typically, a systems analyst first attempts to understand how some organization or procedure works and then designs an appropriate computer-based solution which will at least increase efficiency and productivity and which may also allow a service or way of working that is quite impossible without computers. As in architectural design, the analysis includes some form of *initial feasibility study,* followed by the *gathering of data* and the *creation of a model* of both the system and the design proposal. More on models later. The design process begins by establishing what the new system is supposed to produce (the output requirements of a computer program, for example) in the same way as, but probably more precisely than, an architect might start by thinking of the kind of ambience or character that is sought in a new building before starting on the details. Given a specification of the desired results, the analyst can then consider

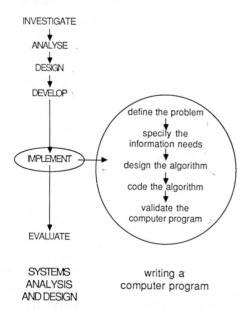

Figure 3.1 The process of writing a computer program is just a part of the process of systems analysis and design in which a new organization or computer program is developed. *(Diagram by the authors.)*

the form and nature of the information or data to be input to a computer system and design the procedures by which this input can be transformed into the desired output. Development then involves the translation of these procedures into computer code and, if necessary, the selection of suitable computer hardware. Finally, there are the obvious implementation, testing, adjustment, and training stages, all essential for the smooth running of a new system. Any major computer project, from an accounting system for a small business to the computerization of the Bank of America, has some kind of systems analysis and design behind it.

3.3   Computer Programming

3.3.1   Symbolic models

Systems analysis, then, is carried out to discover how some real system does or should work. Much of the work done by computer programmers concerns the building of special kinds of models of real systems, built in computer code that can be understood and operated by a computer. *Models* are constructs that enable us to represent ideas that would otherwise be difficult or impossible to comprehend. Architects are familiar with physical models: two-dimensional drawings of building elevations and plans or three-dimensional constructions of cardboard or balsa wood. The important point about models is that they never attempt to represent all the facets of reality, but only a few carefully selected characteristics of interest. Thus, a building plan models the spatial relationships between rooms of a building and, using a code that is well understood by architects, represents certain constructional characteristics. A plan is an entirely passive model: it does not tell us anything about a building's behavior in any dynamic sense. The real world, as we have seen, is a very active place. To get information on behavior, we can construct a suitable physical model and subject it to tests of some kind (for example, placing a model house on a heliodon and switching on a bright lamp to represent the sun), or we can construct a mathematical model and operate it either manually or by computer.

A *mathematical model* is an equation or set of equations that represents some facet of reality. Thus, $e = mc^2$ is a simple but powerful model of the relationship between energy and mass as a consequence of Einstein's theory of relativity. Other examples are equations representing heat flow, illumination, or other components of the physical environment. Typically, mathematical models consist of large numbers of operations where the output from one set of equations becomes the input to another set. Mathematical models imply *unambiguity*, the possibility of *strict deduction*, and *verifiability* by reference back to reality. They are based on the existence of some kind of algorithm. A mathematical model is one of the family of symbolic models, in which symbols are used to represent the elements of the system. We prefer the more general term *symbolic models* because many of the systems of interest in computing are not primarily mathematical.

3.3.2 Algorithms

An *algorithm* is a finite sequence of well-defined, executable actions or instructions, which together provide a blueprint for solving a problem. Each instruction in an algorithm must be meaningful, with its action being unambiguously performable in a finite amount of time. We are familiar with algorithms from recipes in cookbooks. A recipe is not just something *like* an algorithm; it *is* an algorithm: an unambiguous step-by-step process for solving a given problem. If our Black Forest torte doesn't turn out like the picture in the recipe book, either the algorithm is ambiguous or we have not followed it correctly. Recipes share the components of most problem-solving algorithms. They *input* material from the environment (ingredients in a recipe, data in a mathematical model), *check* that material to ensure its acceptability, *execute* some operations to transform that material into a new state, and *output* the transformed material back into the environment.

Most cookbooks show algorithms as a series of such steps. Turning from cookery back to architecture, or at least to building, we can devise an algorithm for calculating and working down the roof area and ridge length (top and hips) for three kinds of pitched roofs on rectangular buildings (Fig. 3.2). In our systems analysis here, we have decided that pitched roofs must lie between 10 and 60 degrees (otherwise, the chances are that the architect got the figures wrong) and have noticed the interesting fact that roof surface area is independent of roof type, whether monopitch, gable, or hipped:

1. Get roof length, width, pitch, and type.
2. If pitch <10 degrees or >60 degrees, then go back to 1.
3. Area is length × width/cos(pitch).
4. If type is monopitch, then ridge length is 0.
5. If type is gable, then ridge length is length.
6. If type is hipped, then ridge length is length − width + 2 × width × (1/cos(pitch)+1).
7. If type is neither monopitch, gable, nor hipped, then go back to 1.
8. Write area and ridge length.

Alternatively, we could use some special code. Perhaps the best known

ROOF TYPES

MONOPITCH   GABLE   HIPPED

FLOW CHART FOR CALCULATING ROOF AREAS AND RIDGE LENGTHS

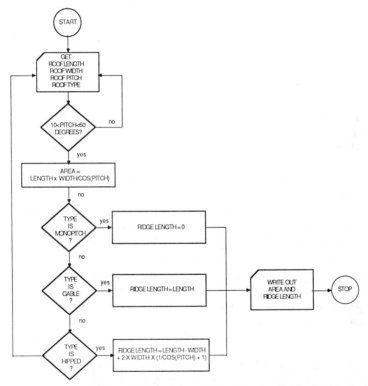

Figure 3.2   An algorithm for calculating the roof area and ridge length for three types of roof (above), expressed here as a flow chart (below) in which arrows show paths between "start" and "stop" points. *(Diagram by the authors.)*

special code is that used in knitting patterns, where an algorithm for transforming a ball of wool into a woolly jumper is coded in lines like:

Next row, K2, sl 1, K1, psso, K to last 4 sts, K2 tog, K2.

A roof area algorithm is difficult to represent as a knitting pattern, but in the next section we shall introduce another kind of code called a *computer language*. Fortunately computer languages are a lot easier to understand than knitting patterns, although unpicking a computer program is a lot more difficult than unpicking a woolly jumper (Fig. 3.3).

Complex problems tend to result in long and complex algorithms, which are difficult to develop, comprehend, or modify. The answer is to separate a complex model into a set of simpler, more or less self-contained, constituent parts. We then have one algorithm linking these parts, with independent simpler algorithms representing each separate component.

3.3.3   Computer code

If a symbolic model (or the algorithm describing its operation) is of any complexity, its execution by hand will be exceedingly tedious. If, however, the algorithm can be written in a *computer language,* the tedium can be

Figure 3.3   Once created, computer programs are notoriously difficult to unpick and adapt to new tasks, particularly if the computer code is not supported by adequate documentation on the algorithm and how it works. *(Cartoon hand-drawn by Ingram Pinn, used by permission.)*

subcontracted to a computer. Any fancy tricks you see computers performing have been instructed to it via algorithms written in computer languages. Thus, word processors, drafting systems, and computer games are
all based on complex algorithms that describe, step by step, the operations
the computer has to perform.

We shall translate our roof area algorithm into a very basic computer
language called, very appropriately, BASIC. This language is ubiquitous
among small microcomputers. Unfortunately, BASIC is ubiquitous but not
very standardized, so that it is slightly different for different machines
(like the dialects of human language). The algorithm translated into a
fairly representative example of BASIC looks like this:

A BASIC algorithm for calculating roof areas:

```
1 INPUT LENGTH, WIDTH, PITCH, TYPE$
2 IF PITCH < 10 OR PITCH > 60 THEN 1
3 AREA = LENGTH * WIDTH/COS (PITCH)
4 IF TYPE$ = "MONOPITCH" THEN RIDGE = 0
5 IF TYPE$ = "GABLE" THEN RIDGE = LENGTH
6 IF TYPE$ = "HIPPED" THEN RIDGE
    = LENGTH − WIDTH + 2 * WIDTH * (1/COS (PITCH) + 1)
7 IF TYPE$ <> "MONOPITCH" AND TYPE$ <> "GABLE"
    AND TYPE$ <> "HIPPED" THEN 1
8 PRINT AREA, RIDGE
```

We find, then, that the algorithm written in BASIC is easy to follow
without having learned any of the language at all. The only unusual symbols are the "$" after "TYPE," which tells the computer that the pattern of
bits contained in the memory location labeled "TYPE$" represents a
string of alphanumeric characters and not a number, and the "<>" in line
7, which is a BASIC symbol for "not equal to." An alphanumeric character
is a single alphabetic letter or numeric digit.

We could equally well represent our algorithm in some other computer
language. Here is the same algorithm written in FORTRAN, the first
so-called high-level language, which was first developed by IBM in 1954
and is still widely used:

A FORTRAN algorithm for calculating roof areas:

```
  PROGRAM ROOF
  REAL LENGTH, WIDTH, PITCH, AREA, RIDGE
  CHARACTER TYPE*10
1 READ*, LENGTH, WIDTH, PITCH
  IF (PITCH .LT. 10.0 .OR. PITCH .GT. 60.0) GOTO 1
  AREA = LENGTH * WIDTH/COSD (PITCH)
  IF (TYPE .EQ. 'MONOPITCH') THEN
      RIDGE = 0
  ELSEIF (TYPE .EQ. 'GABLE') THEN
      RIDGE = LENGTH
  ELSEIF (TYPE .EQ. 'HIPPED') THEN
```

```
        RIDGE = LENGTH − WIDTH + 2 * WIDTH * (1/COSD (PITCH) + 1)
    ELSE
        GOTO 1
    ENDIF
    PRINT*, AREA, RIDGE
    END
```

In fact it has taken 17 lines of FORTRAN to do much the same job as eight lines of BASIC, but it is still easy to recognize that this is the same algorithm and to follow it through. There are some superficial differences (the use of ".LT." and ".GT." instead of "<" and ">," and "READ" instead of "INPUT"), and also some more fundamental distinctions. In the first three lines, for example, we have given the whole algorithm a name ("PROGRAM ROOF") and declared in advance which of our variable names (LENGTH, WIDTH, TYPE, etc.) are going to represent "real" numbers (the word "real" means an ordinary decimal number, like 3.4 or 6.25), and which are going to represent strings of characters. Given its long history, it is not surprising that there are enormous numbers of computer programs written in FORTRAN (Fig. 3.4), and it is still the most commonly used language for scientific and technical work, including most computer-aided design systems. Fortunately, it is regulated fairly successfully by the International Standards Organization and is much more standardized than is BASIC, although the version used here (FORTRAN 77) has some significant differences from the previous standard, FORTRAN 66.

For completeness, here is the same algorithm a third time, now written in one form of Pascal. Again, it is fairly easy to follow it through.

A Pascal algorithm for calculating roof areas:

```
program roof(input, output);
    type
        RoofTypes = (GABLE, HIPPED, MONOPITCH);
    var
        Ridge:   real;
        Length:  real;
        Pitch:   real;
        Type:    RoofTypes;
        Width:   real;
    begin
        repeat
            writeln('What is the roof's length, width, pitch and type');
            readln(Length, Width, Pitch, Type)
        until (Pitch <= 60.0) and (Pitch >= 10.0);
        case Type of
            MONOPITCH: Ridge := 0;
            GABLE:     Ridge := Length;
            HIPPED:    Ridge := Length − Width + 2 * Width * (1/cos(Pitch) + 1)
        end;
        write('Area =', (Length * Width / cos(Pitch)):3:2);
        writeln('; Ridge length =', Ridge:3:2)
    end.
```

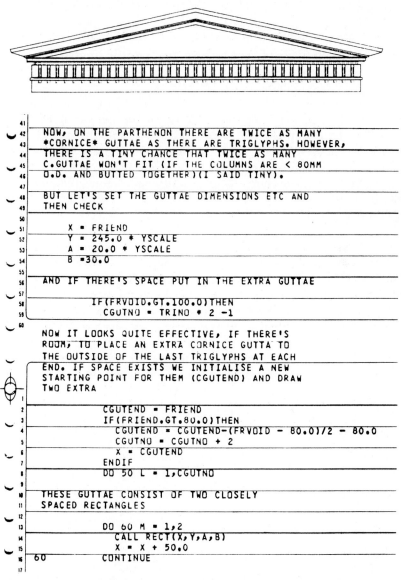

```
41
42   NOW, ON THE PARTHENON THERE ARE TWICE AS MANY
43   *CORNICE* GUTTAE AS THERE ARE TRIGLYPHS. HOWEVER,
44   THERE IS A TINY CHANCE THAT TWICE AS MANY
45   C.GUTTAE WON'T FIT (IF THE COLUMNS ARE < 80MM
46   O.D. AND BUTTED TOGETHER)(I SAID TINY).
47
48   BUT LET'S SET THE GUTTAE DIMENSIONS ETC AND
49   THEN CHECK
50
51       X = FRIEND
52       Y = 245.0 * YSCALE
53       A = 20.0 * YSCALE
54       B =30.0
55
56   AND IF THERE'S SPACE PUT IN THE EXTRA GUTTAE
57
58       IF(FRVOID.GT.100.0)THEN
59           CGUTNO = TRINO * 2 -1
60
     NOW IT LOOKS QUITE EFFECTIVE, IF THERE'S
     ROOM, TO PLACE AN EXTRA CORNICE GUTTA TO
     THE OUTSIDE OF THE LAST TRIGLYPHS AT EACH
     END. IF SPACE EXISTS WE INITIALISE A NEW
     STARTING POINT FOR THEM (CGUTEND) AND DRAW
     TWO EXTRA
 1
 2       CGUTEND = FRIEND
 3       IF(FRIEND.GT.80.0)THEN
 4           CGUTEND = CGUTEND-(FRVOID - 80.0)/2 - 80.0
 5           CGUTNO = CGUTNO + 2
 6           X = CGUTEND
 7       ENDIF
 8       DO 50 L = 1,CGUTNO
 9
10   THESE GUTTAE CONSIST OF TWO CLOSELY
11   SPACED RECTANGLES
12
13       DO 60 M = 1,2
14           CALL RECT(X,Y,A,B)
15           X = X + 50.0
16   60      CONTINUE
17
```

Figure 3.4 A classical pediment and a short extract, printed on a line printer, from the FORTRAN 77 program that draws it. The code controls the lines to be drawn very directly: *CALL RECT (X, Y, A, B)* causes a rectangle to be drawn of length *A,* width *B,* and origin *X-Y* in a two-dimensional coordinate system. About half the lines here are not computer code, but comments written by the programmer to explain the code and assist anyone who later tries to modify the program. *(Written by Jonathon Rowbotham, Department of Architectural Science, University of Sydney.)*

The algorithm has been improved over the BASIC and FORTRAN versions by adding an action to write out some instructions to the program user. If executed, it will keep demanding to know the roof's length, width, pitch, and type until the pitch is between the specified limits, when it will write messages for the area and ridge lengths. The ":3:2" in the code just specifies how the numbers are to be written.

There are many other languages, and computer programmers tend to think that their favorite language is fantastic and all others are bunk. Among the most common are COBOL, almost as antique as FORTRAN and used extensively in commercial applications, and C, a more modern language similar to Pascal but with a richer vocabulary. Most computer programmers, and most computers, are multilingual, able to communicate in several languages. Not all are as easily followed by the uninitiated as the ones we have cited.

This computer program for calculating roof areas and ridge lengths is really very short and simple. It also concentrates on the process of calculation rather than on the storage and management of data, which is the second important aspect of designing programs. In the secondary text we look at programming languages (Sec. A3.1) and the structuring of information in programs or program components called databases (Sec. A3.2).

To sum up very briefly the last few sections, in which we have traveled rather quickly from systems analysis to computer programming, remember that in order to write any computer program successfully the system analyst and/or programmer must carry out at least the following five operations:

1. *Define* the problem in precise terms, which is often the most difficult task of all.

2. *Specify* the information requirements, both input and output.

3. *Design* the algorithm, which requires a complete understanding of the system being modeled and the information or data that needs to be stored.

4. *Code* the algorithm in a computer language.

5. Finally, *validate* the resulting computer program, to ensure that it is correct.

All this is a considerable creative effort and we should never underestimate the achievement of producing a good, bug-free program, however seemingly simple. There are a number of well-known aphorisms in computer programming, among them that no major project is ever completed on time, within budgets and with the same staff that started it, or does exactly what it was intended to do. No less a design effort goes into a good program than into a good building. Fortunately, most of us spend more time using computer programs than writing them, and to use a program we only need to know how to get the computer running and how to drive the program, providing we can find one that matches our needs.

3.4 Programs

3.4.1 Applications software

We have seen, then, how an algorithm can be written in a special code that makes it comprehensible to a computer as well as to a human. Programs of instructions like this, together with the data on which they operate (the actual values for lengths, widths, types, and pitches in our roof example) and the documentation that describes their operation, constitute what is known as *computer software.* In fact, our program for calculating the area and ridge length for a roof is a piece of *applications software,* which is simply the name given to programs intended for some specific business or technical application (Fig. 3.5). A word processing program, a program to calculate a PERT network or optimize a steel frame, a computer drafting program, and a program that acts as an expert system for building regulations are all examples of applications software, and such programs are the topic of Chaps. 4 to 7. Because architects have been perceived as a small market in terms of the global use of computers, the range of applications software directed specifically at architectural problems has been slow to develop. In the last few years more have appeared, often developed by architectural and engineering organizations who have wanted them for their own use and then thought they might as well try to recover their costs by selling the product to others. Their designers were often engineers or architects first and programmers second, self-taught or home-grown and quite unlike the computer professionals in the mainstream of the commercial computer industry.

The easiest way to buy programs is to purchase a complete package straight off the shelf, and this is indeed the way in which most software is acquired. It should be the most trouble-free approach, but here are other options.

First, we could start with one of the *software tools,* a database management system (DBMS) or spreadsheet (see Chap. 4). It is possible to simulate many dedicated programs with these tools, and adopting this method allows the creation of systems precisely tuned to our way of doing things without having to start from scratch by writing a new program. However, some skill is required to exploit such tools, and while it is certainly possible to use them with no knowledge of programming, a little helps. A system so created will also be slower and clunkier than a well-designed tailor-made package.

Second, we could write an entirely new program, but programming is not

Figure 3.5 Computer software includes not only the computer code but also the instruction manuals and other documentation explaining its operation. *(Copyright Design Council, used by permission.)*

something to be entered into lightly. There are already so many very bad programs in the world that we should feel distressed at encouraging others to add more. Building a programming vocabulary is not easy and is done much as one builds an architectural vocabulary, by looking and reading. A bad program that just works is not too hard to get going, but one that will last for years is another matter. Another aphorism from the world of computing: Programs are written quickly until they are 90 percent complete, but they remain 90 percent complete forever.

Third, we could enlist a consultant or software house to modify an existing package or write one *de novo*. A *software house* is something like the computer equivalent of the architectural practice in the world of building. Modifications might be simple, such as getting a word processor to operate correctly with a printer, or might require major revisions. The latter are always expensive and may cost more than the unmodified program. Even more expensive is having a whole program written from scratch, since this is still a labor-intensive activity for both the programmer and the one who commissions it.

3.4.2 Operating systems

Applications programs written are not the end of the story; they make up only a part of the world of software. The other major part for our purposes consists of the less public *operating systems* that lie inside computers to manage their resources, maintain communications, and translate from BASIC, FORTRAN, Pascal, or whatever into the kind of binary signals really meaningful to an electronic machine (Fig. 3.6). They are visible to the computer user as a series of *commands* that allows him or her to do such fundamental tasks as running a program, storing some results, or changing the language in which programs are written. Some, at least, of these commands have to be learned. Much of the system's work, though, is done implicitly, without being told to act by any mere human.

For example, an operating system must include a *translator,* a program that translates from a high-level language into machine language. BASIC was developed as an interpreted language; its instructions are stored in the

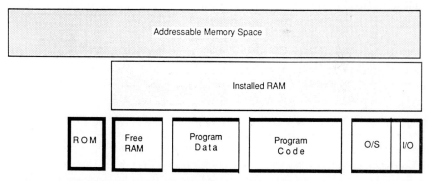

Figure 3.6   Inside the computer's internal memory. The addressable memory space is the theoretical maximum size that the microprocessor can use. This is a design constraint of the chip. Some part of this is occupied by read-only memory (ROM), which contains programming and data in exactly the same way that random-access memory (RAM) can, except that it is nonvolatile. Typically, in addition to other utility functions, the ROM contains a boot program that directs the computer to load the operating system from disk into RAM at start-up. The installed RAM is the amount of internal memory (RAM) that the manufacturer decided to include in the computer; most install less than the maximum and sell memory expansion kits. Part of this RAM is taken up by input-output (I/O) buffers and memory mapping. The operating system (O/S) also consumes part. When a program is run, it occupies some of the RAM, too, and reserves part of the RAM to hold its data. The RAM left, if any, is free. *(Diagram by the authors.)*

computer memory and translated line by line by the *interpreter* during execution, in the same way that a human language interpreter might translate from French to English one line at a time at an international architects' conference. This allows a very high degree of interaction. In BASIC, for example, we can type "PRINT 6+7" and see the result "13" right back on the computer screen with no delay. Pascal, FORTRAN, and most other high-level languages are *compiled.* This means that the translator puts together the complete machine-code version of the program in one go, before anything is executed. If it finds any mistakes in the language, it causes *diagnostic error messages* to be printed and scraps the compilation process. The diagnostic messages are intended to be helpful. Once complete, a compiled program will always run faster than an interpreted one, often 10 to 100 times faster. On the other hand, it is often more difficult to eliminate errors (known as *debugging*) in a compiled program than in an interpreted program since the syntax of the language (but not the logic; getting the logic right is another and often harder problem) has to be just right before it will deign to work. There are now several compilers available for previously interpreted languages like BASIC, and interpreters for compiled languages like Pascal, allowing us the best of both worlds. A program can be tested and debugged with the interpreted version, then compiled into efficient machine code when complete.

Organizing the reading and writing of information to and from disks or other forms of computer memory is also a task of the operating system. This complex process can be handled in many different ways. A disk written with one *disk operating system (DOS)* tends to be frustratingly useless when confronted with a computer operating under a different one, a major incompatibility problem in the computing industry. Further, most programs that are sold are developed to run with some particular operating system and take advantage of the special features offered by that product but not by others. Sofware houses tend to write programs for the most popular systems only, so that a computer using a little-known or eccentric operating system will inevitably have a relatively small selection of programs available to it. For professional computing, then, the selection of an appropriate operating system is a matter of much importance. Usually it is linked to the choice of computer. CP/M and MSDOS (for microcomputers) and Unix (for microcomputers and minicomputers) are examples of operating systems that have made the jump from acceptance on single models to many different makes of computers.

3.4.3 Human-computer communications

The way in which computer programs and operating systems expect humans to communicate with them has changed over the years from methods that are suited entirely for the convenience of computers to methods that are at least partly designed for the convenience of the human.

The jargon expression is *user friendly*; every program that doesn't actually require the users to stand on their heads and work with three hands is described as user friendly.

Early *batch programs* expected the data on which they operated to be prepared in advance in a fixed format and a predetermined order. Data and instructions were typed on a machine that punched holes in a thin cardboard computer card, one item per card. One stack of these cards constituted the program, another stack the data. There was no interaction between system and user during the running of the program; since everything was predetermined, there was no reason for interaction. The first *interactive programs* that did interact with human users in the course of their operation used questions and answers (Fig. 3.7). The program caused a prompt to be written on the computer screen and the user replied; note that our Pascal program for calculating roof areas uses just this approach. Here it is the system controlling things and asking the questions, not the user saying what he or she wants. It works reasonably well with small programs that afford few options in the way they are used, but not with programs affording any variety in their use.

Instead of the system deciding what questions to ask, the next stage was to allow users to decide what commands to issue. Systems using *command languages* employ a fixed vocabulary of commands and sometimes a restricted language of commands, modifiers, and data, with a syntax controlling the way they are used. The commands can be typed on a keyboard, sometimes spoken into a microphone, or more often chosen from a list of commands shown as a menu on a tablet or the computer screen; the latter are called *menu-driven systems*. A list of commands can be expressed as words or as pictures illustrating actions, or as a mixture of the two. Most drafting systems are menu-driven. They are a big advance on the question-and-answer technique but require users to learn the language, and the issuing of a series of discrete commands is hardly a natural way for a human to draw, write, or control any process. It is rather like trying to drive a car by typing commands to turn left, increase speed, or brake. As a technology of communications, it parallels the steamship captain shouting down a voice tube to the engine room.

The intense and prolonged effort to make the use of computers more natural for their users led the Xerox corporation to the *iconic interface* used in its astonishing Star word processing system and popularized by Apple in its Lisa and Macintosh computers. Typically, the screen of such a system shows a row or column of small symbols called icons, representing common functions of the program. The user manipulates a cursor (sometimes an arrow or one of those cute little pointing hands beloved of nineteenth-century compositors) to the desired symbol in order to execute a function. The screen cursor may be moved by labeled arrow keys on the keyboard or by a small mouse resting on the desk beside the keyboard. Each icon graphically represents its function. To retrieve a document for processing in the Apple

(a) Question and answer interface

Draw a line?
   no
Draw a rectangle?
   no
Draw a circle?
   yes
Input centre of circle (x,y coordinates)
   10,10
Input radius of circle (x,y coordinates)
   5
Input line thickness (1,2, or 3)
   2
Draw a circle?
   no

(b) Command language interface

**LINE THICKNESS 2
DRAW CIRCLE CENTRE 10 10 RADIUS 5**

(c) Menu driven interface

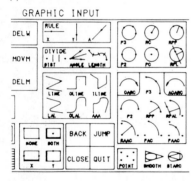

(d) Iconic interface

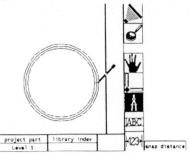

(e) Natural language interface

**I'ld rather like to draw a circle
with a middling line thickness
and a radius of 5 inches and
a centre twice the radius up and
across from the bottom left
corner of the sheet, please.**

Figure 3.7 Communicating with a computer: *(a)* With a question-and-answer interface, the program has control and prompts each response from the user — not the easiest way to get a circle drawn, but sometimes appropriate. *(b)* With a command language, the user can issue any valid command in a fixed vocabulary and syntax. *(c)* In a menu, the commands are set out to be picked rather than remembered. *(d)* An iconic interface uses tools to carry out appropriate actions; here a circle is drawn by selecting pen and compass icons and using them in combination; the center position and radius can either be judged by eye or entered as numbers. *(e)* A natural-language interface allows the computer to understand and implement required actions stated in a human, natural language. *(Diagram by the authors.)*

Macintosh operating system, for example, the user moves the cursor to an icon that looks like a filing cabinet. This icon is replaced by a set of icons like suspended files and then by a set of manila folders. To delete a file, it is dumped in the wastepaper basket icon, and so on. Drawings are made by using a pencil or the paintbrush icon, and the conjunction of different icons has its own meaning, so that a pen combined with a grid might ensure that all lines are rectilinear. Often the user may define windows on the screen in which different tasks may be displayed, a facility requiring multitasking computers. The windows may be stretched or squeezed to accommodate the user, and they may be overlain.

These advanced interfaces use high-quality screens, fast microprocessors, and large amounts of central memory and mass storage to be effective (see Chap. 2 for an explanation of these terms). Iconic interfaces require microcomputer hardware that only became readily available in the early 1980s. They typically require a good graphics resolution on the screen, perhaps 1000 by 1000, and the use of bit mapping. The processor must be fast enough to control the graphics and the other things happening. Because the 16-bit processors are barely fast enough, 32-bit microprocessors are really required. More than with command languages, the essence of iconic interfaces is that things happen quickly and intuitively.

3.5 Summary

A computer program is an algorithm that can model some selected aspect of reality (or fantasy, as in computer games, and apparently as in some of the programs supposed to calculate energy use in buildings) in the same way as a physical model can represent some selected aspect of reality. The correctness of the results from a computer program depends on the correctness of the information used by the program ("garbage in, garbage out" is a pithy computer saying) and on the correctness of the models employed. In this last respect consensus is not always a guarantee, since it is quite possible internationally to agree on a wrong algorithm. Consensus is marvelous for producing consistency among programs but may not bear much relation to the real world. A computer program cannot be better than the algorithm on which it is based, and that (so far) always comes out of somebody's brain and not out of another, brighter, computer. Architects (and others) have tended to regard computers either as of no use whatever or as capable of independent, almost mystical, power. This displays a binary way of thinking that maybe suits the topic, but the truth, of course, is somewhere in between. Since what computers can do depends entirely on human imagination and humans have a regrettable tendency for occasional error, so do computer programs.

Models are descriptions of existing or desired reality. They represent selected aspects of reality that are of interest, rather than attempt a complete description. We introduced symbolic models as a particular form of model which makes use of mathematical and other symbols (instead of the drawn lines or pieces of balsa wood we find in familiar physical models) and which is based on the existence of some sort of algorithm. A computer program is merely an algorithm expressed in a particular code. Once it exists, the program can be used to tell us something about reality and, in turn, itself becomes a part of reality: the world of banking today, for example, is so fundamentally dependent on its computer software that a systems analysis of the banking process would spend much of its time looking at existing computer processes.

The act of computer programming, then, is just a part of this cycle. There is no magic involved, although there are some in the computer industry who would like the rest of us to think that there is. The ability to translate instructions into this special form is really rather a mundane skill, necessary but not particularly exciting and not nearly as intellectually demanding as the process of systems analysis and design. In architecture, we use another kind of code called drawings to represent our ideas about building form and construction, but the ability to draw does not make an architect. When we look at Jorn Utzon's famous competition drawings for the Sydney Opera House, we rate the quality of the ideas and the architecture — the imaginative leap that suggested the solution — as much more significant than the line quality of the sketches.

When you see a really good computer drafting system, don't think "What clever programming" but rather "What brilliant systems design." And don't make the mistake of believing that creativity exists only among architects and has no place in the computer industry.

SECONDARY TEXT
Languages and Databases

A3.1 Programming Languages

A computer language provides the means by which a person may communicate with a machine. Languages come in many forms, designed for all sorts of functions, but all represent a compromise between what is natural for a human to write and what is easy for a computer to understand. A language consists of a *vocabulary* and a *syntax*; the vocabulary specifies the meaningful commands in the language, and the syntax specifies how they are put together. Programming languages are not the only ones of interest; the commands understood by a word processor constitute a language, for example, as do the commands available in an operating system. Many programs have their own language. A drafting system may have its own language in which "Draw elevation" uses two words in its defined vocabulary specified in the correct syntactic way (verb, then noun) to draw an elevation on the screen. Such languages are sometimes called applications languages because of their specific task-oriented nature.

Programming languages are divided between *low-level* and *high-level languages*. Low-level languages are very tightly bound to the particular language understood by the computer's central processing unit; they are discussed in Sec. A3.1.2. High-level languages are independent of the particular computer they are running on; they are discussed in Sec. A3.1.3.

The many languages from which to choose were created for varying reasons and have evolved in different environments. One of the major initiatives behind the creation of COBOL was the desire for a straightforward business data processing language. One of the things people want to do with business data is sort it: sort checks by number, by payee, by date, by expenditure category. So COBOL was designed with a sorting ability built into it, and sorting is easy to do in a few lines of COBOL. FORTRAN was intended for scientists and engineers, and they hardly ever sort things, so this ability was not included in the language. Carrying out a standard COBOL sort therefore requires a couple of pages of FORTRAN code.

A3.1.1   Structured programming

High-level languages were developed to make life more pleasant for programmers and to allow programs to be ported (short for "transported") to different machines. Programs written in any human-readable language must ultimately be translated into machine code. Programs called assemblers do this for assembly languages, programs called compilers do this for compiled languages, and interpreters do this for interpreted languages. Interpreted languages are by far the easiest to work with, program in, and debug and provide a quite different working environment to compiled languages. To program in an interpreted language, such as BASIC, you first run the interpreter. The interpreter provides editing facilities for writing and altering a program, and facilities to run the program. A programmer does not interact with the operating system, but with the interpreter. BASIC is such a popular language because of the friendly environment it provides.

Programming is so hard an activity and the possibility of error is so great that much thought has been devoted to improving the productivity of programmers. The methodology called *structured programming* is a result of this activity. It applies a tight discipline on the sort of code that a programmer can write, and it encourages defensive programming, which means planting lots of checks and tests in a program to ensure that everything is proceeding smoothly. Using structured programming is a bit like systems building techniques that use prefabricated building components instead of bricks, mortar, and timber. Bricks are so small and flexible a building element that it is quite easy to construct wavy walls or to misread a plan and put a wall where it shouldn't be. A lot of small mistakes can happen that might not be detected until too late. But prefabricated elements come ready-made and therefore (hopefully) mistake-free. Most mistakes are the result of improper placement, or because the junctions with other elements are badly designed. With structured programming, the aim is to assemble several medium-size pretested parts of code into a complete program. Most mistakes occur because of incorrect assembly of the units.

Structured programming techniques can only be followed if the language of choice has the required building blocks. Such a language is called a *structured language*. In this respect, BASIC is atrocious: in no other language is it so easy to write a really horrible program. Unfortunately, these horrors are concealed. As in building, most of the activity in programming is maintenance and conversion. Programmers spend more time converting other people's programs than in writing wholly new ones, and BASIC is unpopular among professional computerists because the lack of structure makes it very difficult to understand what is going on or to change a part without upsetting the whole. It is a good language for writing short programs, programs that are going to be thrown away, or programs that will never ever be modified (about as common as buildings that will never ever be modified). For anything else, a modern structured language is a must.

A3.1.2 Low-level languages

The very first method of programming involved setting switches and making plug connections. This was superseded by the writing of programs in *machine code*, the language directly comprehended by the computer's central processing unit (CPU). It is important to realize that every type of CPU understands only its own machine code and that everything else has to be translated into this language in order to run. Moreover, different CPUs understand different machine languages. The machine code used by the Macintosh's Motorola 68000 processor is completely unintelligible to an IBM PC's Intel 8086 processor. Machine code is as close as we can get to the processor, and this is really too close for comfort. The 8086 processor has about 100 instructions, and the instruction that halts it looks like this: 11110100.

No one likes writing a lot of 1s and 0s for a living, and programming at this level is tedious, error-prone, and unwieldy. An *assembly language* is the next step up, a sort of machine code made easy. It provides handy mnemonics and takes care of some of the things a programmer prefers not to worry about, so that in assembly language the halt instruction is simply written as HLT. It also allows a programmer to write reusable program chunks, called *macros*. If we have already written some code to do a task, there is no point in writing it out again. We do it once, make sure it works, and then use it with confidence later in a different context.

The reasons to write code in an assembly language are either to do something that cannot be done in the high-level language of choice or to write code that will run much more quickly than the same process written in a high-level language. The ability to delete a file, for example, is rarely found in high-level languages and is a good candidate for assembly language if a program is required to do it. Deleting files is a task handled by the operating system, so assembly language is often used to make the abilities of the operating system directly available to programs.

In theory, anything that can be done by the computer can be programmed in assembly language, but the problem lies in finding out just how to do it. We might know a great deal about the assembly language, but we also need to know a great deal about the computer: how it stores information in memory, what bits of memory it reserves for special functions, how input-output operations are conducted, how to access disks, and so on. Discovering such information is often extremely difficult, particularly if it is an obscure computer and the manuals are in a foreign language, the dealers ignorant, and the manufacturer unhelpful.

A3.1.3   Major high-level languages

BASIC.   Developed as a beginner's language, BASIC is the language that most people learn first. It started out life as a subset of the venerable FORTRAN language without FORTRAN's nitpicking syntactic features. Because BASIC programs were intended to be written and used by real people, as opposed to programmers, its designers included some elegant features to handle dialogue between human and machine. They also included the ability to manipulate character data easily, a surprisingly uncommon property of computer languages. When BASIC was invented, microcomputers were still a long way into the future. Its straightforward features made it a natural for these new people-oriented machines, and as microcomputer manufacturers proliferated, so did versions of BASIC; consequently, learning the language means learning the particular version implemented on the computer we wish to use.

C.   So-called because it was the third language developed by its inventors, C is modeled on Pascal and ALGOL. Its history is intimately connected to the Unix operating system, which was developed concurrently. The key idea was that a very small part of Unix was to be written in assembly code, which of course varies enormously from machine to machine, and that the rest would be written in C. Much of C is actually written in C itself. It is similar to Pascal but has a much richer vocabulary. Conceptually, it operates at a level closer to the computer than do other high-level languages.

COBOL.   A year or two younger than FORTRAN, COBOL is the great commercial language. The impetus behind its design was for COBOL to understand speakers of English. This aim was quickly downgraded to having speakers of English understand COBOL. The result is a language with a very wordy syntax, but the vast quantity of software written in COBOL gives it a momentum of its own.

FORTRAN.   FORTRAN was the very first high-level language to be widely implemented on different computers, way back in the 1950s. It is fairly tightly regulated by international standard, and so there is little variation between implementations. The language carries many curious fossils from its long heritage and is quite primitive compared to more modern structured languages. It is at its best handling arithmetic problems and complex formulas, but it suffers from poor input-output facilities. Nonetheless, most minicomputer-based CAD systems are written in FORTRAN and it remains a major language for technical work.

Pascal.   Pascal was developed by an academic computerist as a vehicle to teach good programming; it then emerged in the late 1970s as a proper commercial language. Modeled on ALGOL, it provides excellent structured programming facilities but is much harder than BASIC to learn. Pascal has a sparse vocabulary and allows very elegant programs to be written. It is widely used on minicomputers and microcomputers but may be replaced by C.

PL/1.   Programming Language 1 was intended by IBM to replace FORTRAN and COBOL. It combines the concise statement structure of the former with the data-handling abilities of the latter; however, its overrich vocabulary has limited its role.

A3.1.4   Some other high-level languages

Ada.   Like COBOL, Ada was created by the U.S. Department of Defense as its universal language. Although a source of much controversy, and critized as being even more of a kitchen-sink language than COBOL, Ada contains many advanced concepts (such as allowing for parallel processing) and is the structured language par excellence.

ALGOL.   ALGOL was intended more as a method of writing mathematical algorithms than as a computer language, and in this regard it has enjoyed great success. ALGOL was the very first of the modern structured languages and has served as model to many others. Pascal and C have almost entirely superseded it in common use.

APL.   Like ALGOL, APL started out as a notation for expressing algorithms. Subsequently implemented as a programming language, APL is unique in its symbology, which uses a host of special characters, many borrowed from Greek and Cyrillic. This has been a major factor retarding wider use, for special keyboards are needed and the computer must be capable of displaying all the symbols. Another unique aspect is its treatment of the array as the fundamental storage unit, not as the simple scalar variable. APL is an extremely rich language, and it has many operators that carry out functions requiring dozens of lines in other languages.

Unfortunately, programmers tend to go out of their way to make unconscionably terse programs, full of tricks.

FORTH.   FORTH enjoys a small but strong cult following. It is a most unusual language; developed for microcomputers, it produces extremely small programs that run quite fast.

LISP.   Developed particularly for artificial intelligence work, LISP was designed for handling complex lists. It is a very sparse language, sometimes seeming to consist mainly of brackets. There are now computers designed specifically for the LISP language.

LOGO.   This is a simple but powerful language, originally developed for teaching graphics to children. It serves to clarify many fundamental concepts from computer science that other languages tend to mask. LOGO will probably acquire greater prominence as its use spreads in schools in competition with BASIC.

PROLOG.   Rather than being based on the sequential execution of a linear algorithm, PROLOG is based on the declaration of facts about and relationships between objects from which inferences can be drawn about other facts and relationships. Like LISP, it is used in artificial intelligence work, and like APL, it has its own determined enthusiasts for whom no other language will suffice.

A3.2   Structuring Information: Databases

One of the most pervasive notions in modern computing is that of the database. A *database* is a structured set of information. A dictionary is a database, a telephone directory is a database, and so is a card file of names, addresses, and telephone numbers. All applications programs manipulate data, and most maintain their own separate data files, structured for the particular needs of the program. This means that programs working on similar data must use some translation process to transfer data between them, or rely on a human to do the job for them.

   As an example, consider (1) a microcomputer-based CAD system that maintains geometric data about the external walls of a building and (2) a thermal analysis program that uses the geometric and thermal properties of a building envelope to calculate thermal gains and losses. As things stand in the microcomputer software business (but not necessarily in the minicomputer market), these programs could probably not communicate with each other. Having sketched a building, a designer would have to close down the drafting system, start up the thermal analysis program, and retype the lengths and heights of the walls into the program. A better solution, of course, would be for the thermal analysis program to read the data stored by the drafting system directly, leaving only the thermal data to be entered by the designer. Even better would be a situation in which all the properties of a wall (height, length, construction, finishes, resistances, U-value, sound transmission class, opacity, connections to other walls, identities of adjoining rooms) could be stored in the one structured collection so that many different programs could access it.

That is what database methodologies are all about: the construction of unified, comprehensive, single collections of data that can be accessed by many different applications. Ideally, every piece of information is stored precisely once (no redundancy) and any program or person wanting to know something about the data can interrogate it easily. The basic unit of the database is the *record*, which is subdivided into *fields* (or *attributes*). A record represents a single entity, such as a single wall, and each field is a small piece of information about the entity. Height, length, and U-value would each constitute a field, for example. A group of related records constitutes a *file*. A single file would contain all the wall data.

Both of the two programs above can be looked upon as database processors, albeit for their own special uses. Each relies on the database being structured in one particular way, resulting in *data dependency*. Programs must know the physical layout of fields within a record; otherwise, they would not know, for example, whether a record that commenced with the numbers "7.5 10.3" meant a wall 7.5 m high with a U-value of 10.3 or one with a length of 7.5 m and a height of 10.3 m. The programs must agree as to what they expect to find in the database. If the database is physically restructured, the programs must be altered.

A3.2.1 Database models

Clearly, it would be better if this dependency could somehow be removed so that programs and program writers did not have to know the physical structuring of a database, only its *logical structure*. A program that can say in effect "Provide the height of the wall" instead of "Provide the number that starts 25 characters from the beginning of the record" is more flexible and robust. A database nowadays is designed to be looked upon from three viewpoints, or as three models:

1. *External model (a user's view).*   This is the viewpoint taken by a particular applications program. A drafting system sees only the geometry and topology of the walls; a thermal analysis program sees these as well as the thermal properties, but not the acoustic ones. Such models are examined and manipulated by using a high-level software language called a *data manipulation language (DML).*

2. *Logical model (the programmer's view).*   The logical model is created by

using a high-level language called a *data definition language (DDL),* or *data description language.* This language implements the logical model as a physical model.

3. *Physical model (the computer's view).*   This refers to the way the data is physically organized into fields, records, and files and to the software mechanics used to interconnect the whole. The physical organization is completely independent of the logical model of the database and can be altered without affecting it. Ultimately, the physical model is implemented as a machine-code program, as are all compiled or assembled programs.

The data manipulation language and the data description language, plus a few ancillary tools, constitute a *database management system (DBMS).* Such a system is a software package that allows programmers and users to construct, alter, and interrogate databases (in the same general sense that a word processor is a program for creating and editing documents). The data description and manipulation languages may be interpreted, translated by the database management system itself into machine-code instructions in the same way that a BASIC interpreter translates BASIC statements into machine code. They appear to the programmer as yet other languages to learn. An interpreted data manipulation language (often referred to as a *query language*) is ideal for human use, but not so for use by applications programs. Programs need more direct communication. For this purpose, a database management language may be present as a set of program instructions that can be caused to execute a program written in Pascal, C, COBOL, FORTRAN, or any other high-level language.

A database management system must fulfill several requirements. First, records must be accessed quickly. Most processing by a DBMS consists simply of searching for the right record ("Find the U-value of the northern wall") or of sorting ("List all the walls in order of finish"). Since the data is kept on mass storage, the relatively slow access times of disks (as compared to accessing the main memory), even of hard disks, can mean that the sheer volume of data to be examined causes lengthy delays, particularly on microcomputers.

Second, the DBMS must be designed to achieve space efficiency, ensuring that a large database doesn't consume more mass storage than it has to. The DBMS must also allow for ready updating of information — for adding, deleting, and changing records efficiently. For these reasons of efficiency, DBMSs are particularly hard for professional programmers to design.

A final and most important issue is that of security and protection. Access to key data must be limited to the right people, and the data must be safeguarded against program malfunction, hardware failure, and accidental or willful destruction.

A3.2.2 Types of databases

There are three fundamental logical models for databases: the *hierarchical* (or *tree*), the *network* (or *plex*), and the *relational.* Each has advantages and disadvantages (Fig. A3.1). The hierarchical and network models are the oldest and the most widely used on mainframes. Relational database systems are very popular on microcomputers, and their use is spreading to minicomputers and mainframes.

Relational model.   The most recent model, this is also conceptually the easiest to grasp (Fig. A3.2). Data is organized into tables, each row being a single record. Each column represents a single field or attribute within a record. Such tables, called *tuples* in the jargon, are no more difficult than all the sorts of tables we come across all the time. They have five constraints:

1. Each row must be unique; that is, no two rows can be absolutely identical.
2. Each column represents the same field or attribute throughout all the rows.
3. Every column has a distinct name.
4. The rows must be in no particular order.
5. Each row must have a means for uniquely identifying it.

This fifth constraint is accomplished by providing a single column or combination of columns with a unique name. This name is used to locate the row and is called a *primary key.* For example, a table of walls would have to have a column named something like "Wall Number" that contained a unique number for each wall. Locating a particular row in the table, is, in theory a brute-force process, requiring a search of all the rows until the row with the right primary key is located.

Quite often one is not looking aor a particular row but for a number of rows that have common properties, such as all walls with a plaster internal finish. This would involve a search of the field containing that wall finish.

Door No.	Height	Width	Core	Frame	Lockset	Handle
T7	1820	410	Hollow	Timber	Whitco D/L	Astra CK.14
T8	1820	410	Hollow	Timber	Whitco D/L	Astra CK.14
P35	1820	410	Hollow	Steel	Whitco S/L	Astra CK.14
E3	1820	820	Solid	Steel	Whitco S/L	Merroni Premiaviri

Figure A3.1   An abbreviated door schedule. This is used in Figs. A3.2, A3.3, and A3.4 to illustrate different sorts of database structure. It contains four doors, each of which has a door number, a size, a core type, a frame type, a lockset type, and a handle type. *(Diagram by the authors.)*

Doors Relation

Door No.	Height	Width	Core	Frame	Lockset	Handle
T7	1820	410	Hollow	Timber	W1	A1
T8	1820	410	Hollow	Timber	W1	A1
P35	1820	410	Hollow	Steel	W2	A1
E3	1820	820	Solid	Steel	W2	M1

Locksets Relation

Code	Manufacturer	Catalogue No
W1	Whitco	D/L
W2	Whitco	S/L

Handles Relation

Code	Manufacturer	Catalogue No.
A1	Astra	CK.14
M1	Merroni	Premiaveri

Figure A3.2 Relational database structure. The data is taken from Fig. A3.1. The relational type of database is conceptually the easiest but the most recently developed. The data is broken down into tables (relations) that must obey a few rules of construction. The Doors Relation (top) contains the information on each door. Each line is called a tuple and each column a domain. The primary key is the domain Door No. The Locksets and the Handles relations contain information applying to each sort of lock and handle. If Whitco were to drop its lock D/L, the code W1 would have to be allocated to some other lock and doors T7 and T8 would be identified as possessing this sort of lock. This change is easier to do (it requires changing only one tuple in the Locksets Relation) than altering all the lock references in the original table. *(Diagram by the authors.)*

A field used in such a way is called *secondary key*. It does not constitute a primary key for the very reason that many walls may have the same finish.

The attractiveness of relational databases lies in the wonderful flexibility with which they may be interrogated. It is easy to ask difficult or unusual questions of a relational database, such as "List all walls more than 6 m long with a plaster finish and a sound transmission class of at least 25." Several tables can be joined to form larger tables, and columns can be excerpted to produce new ones. Since the rows are in no particular order, additions to the database can always go at the end of the table, instead of being squeezed between other items. The database can be put to many uses not envisaged by the original database designer. When coupled with a good query language, a relational database is quite easy to work with, even for unskilled users. It excels in producing odd and ad hoc reports.

The price paid for this is in performance. A pure relational database requires a lot of brute searching. This speed penalty has been the major factor in retarding the spread of relational systems, and although invented in 1970, it is only since the early 1980s that fast, efficient relational DBMSs have been available. Quite often they achieve this by maintaining the logical purity of a relational system while speeding things up with some physical programming techniques. The most common of these is *indexing* on the primary and secondary keys. Searching an index is much faster than searching the bulk of the database, thus considerably shortening the access time.

Hierarchical (tree) model.   The hierarchical type of database is best used to model data that is also hierarchical in form (Fig. A3.3). Consider, for example, spatial organization in buildings. At the top of the hierarchy is the "Building." Next beneath it is the "Floor"; each building can have many floors. A "Building" is said to *own* a "Floor," and the "Building" is also said to be a *parent* of the *child* "Floor." This sort of relationship is called a *one-to-many* relationship. A "Building" can own many "Floors," but every "Floor" belongs to one and only one "Building." Next below the "Floor" is the "Room," another one-to-many relationship. A cardinal rule of hierarchical systems is that while a parent can own many children, each child has a single parent. This is a significant restriction, given that few relationships in reality are that simple.

Network (plex) model.   Many relationships between data entities are actually of the *many-to-many* type. Buildings in which rooms may extend through two or more floors provide an example. A single "Floor" would still own many "Rooms," but a "Room" might belong to more than one "Floor." Such relationships can be modeled in network databases (Fig. A3.4). These databases are more complex to design and program, but much less restrictive than hierarchical systems.

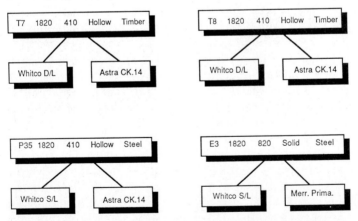

Figure A3.3   The hierarchical (or tree) database structure. Each of the four doors is a record containing most of the information about each door. The locksets and handles have been separated out into their own records. Each door can own at most one lockset and one handle record, and each lockset and handle can be owned by one door. This last limitation requires duplication of the lockset and handle information. *(Diagram by the authors.)*

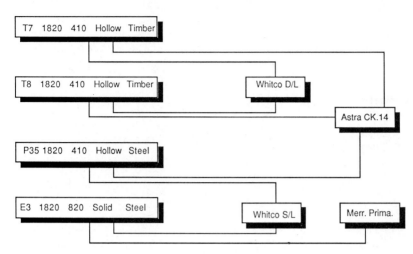

Figure A3.4   The network (or plex) form of database structure. This consists of three types of record: doors, locksets, and handles. Each door still owns precisely one lockset and one handle, but each lockset and handle can be owned by several doors. The information about each different type of lockset or handle need be recorded only once. *(Diagram by the authors.)*

Both hierarchical and network database systems are superior in search and access times to a relational system but labor under several disadvantages. In these systems the links between data are built into the design of the database, but in a relational system the links are created by the user at will. To reach a particular "Room," a nonrelational system starts with the "Building" and proceeds down through the "Floors." This is vastly more efficient than a blind search through a mass of data but imposes a rigidity on the system: The database designer must foresee all possible uses of the database so that he or she can build in all the desired access paths.

Current trends are strongly towards relational database systems, particularly when they are intended for direct access by a user. However, the database systems underlying most drafting systems are still hierarchical or network models, since at present these best provide the very rapid access required.

Applications

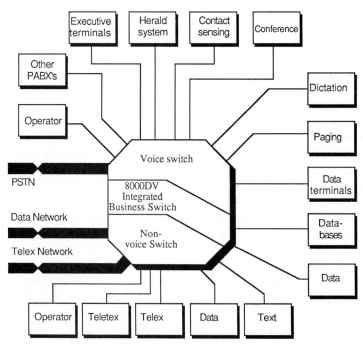

Figure 4.1   The Philips Business Systems EBX 8000DV office automation system exchange integrates data processing and voice communications. With the advent of integrated services digital networks (ISDNs), these exchanges will become commonplace. *(Used by permission of Building Services.)*

the rising executive puts his conference presentation together with the help of "my Lisa," which does everything except deliver the coffee. There is, unfortunately, a catch: The document has to be typed, and typing has until now been an ability required only of flunkies. Great efforts have been made to remove this managerial embarrassment, mainly in the direction of voice recognition, but so far such methods are still cumbersome and unreliable. For the foreseeable future, typing is the only method of getting substantial amounts of information into a computer, and with office automation typing is assumed to be a universal skill.

4.3   General-Purpose Packages

Five software packages have become so widely accepted in the business world that they have become standards across many businesses and professions. These are programs for word processing, electronic spreadsheets, business graphics, database management, and finally (but probably most important of all) for electronic communications. In the following sections we shall examine each in turn.

4.3.1 Word processors

In 1970 the sign of a very small business was its use of a mechanical rather than an electric typewriter. In the 1980s the sign is its use of a typewriter rather than a word processor. Once a word processor enters our life, it is universally agreed, we can never do without one again. This does not mean that the typewriter is useless; we do not give up walking just because we buy a car, and for many purposes walking is better.

All word processors allow us to *create and edit text* by searching for and changing words, inserting new material, and moving pieces of text around. We can locate individual words or phrases or change all occurrences of one phrase into another. A process called *boilerplating* allows us to create a standard letter and insert names and addresses, for example, kept on another file, or to insert other documents into the current document. All this is standard stuff, and programs differ largely in terms of how easy they make these tasks and of how versatile they are. We may only want a single paragraph from a file extracted, but older programs require the whole file to be inserted and then edited to delete the unwanted sections. More recent word processors allow us to work with several documents simultaneously, pulling bits from there and placing them here at will.

In the mid-1970s most word processors were dedicated machines: word processing was all they did. They were generally sold by people in the minicomputer or business machine field, such as Lanier, Wang, Digital Equipment Corporation, or Remington-NBI. At bottom, a *dedicated word processor* conceals a quite normal microprocessor, but surrounding this is a sophisticated user interface designed from the start with the word processing function in mind. The people writing the word processing software would work closely with those designing the hardware to provide an integral package. The keyboard has lots of extra keys on it, suitably labeled SAVE DOCUMENT or MOVE PARAGRAPH to make life as easy as possible for the operator. The ergonomics of the system is carefully thought out, and the whole system is optimized for its single function.

Since the early 1980s, dedicated word processors have been stiffly challenged by *word processing programs* on general-purpose microcomputers. Using such programs has been rather more clumsy than using a dedicated machine. Most microcomputers have about 10 special-function keys to which the complex command sequences of word processing programs could be assigned, but this is rather less than the typical number of commands used by a word processor. The most common way of overcoming the shortfall is to implement commands as arcane key combinations, often using the control key (usually symbolized $\wedge$) or the escape key. The greater the ability of the word processor, the more commands must be provided and the trickier it becomes to key sequences, with a consequent burdening of the user's memory. The more recent alternative has been to use an iconic interface or menu-driven system (see Sec. 3.4.3), and current programs offer features comparable to dedicated machines at a fraction of the cost.

Linked to these developments has been a change in emphasis from content to form in what might be considered second-generation systems. Word processors are lineal descendants of programs called *text editors*, which were designed for programmers writing computer programs. Programmers, of course, are concerned with the textual content of a program, not with typography. Early word processors inherited this concern, but modern ones have been strongly influenced by *typesetting systems* in which the form of the text is important. So now people want different typefaces (or *fonts*), emboldening, subscripting and superscripting, and all the sorts of things of interest to typographers (Fig. 4.2). Further, people now want their word processors to show them these things on the screen, a feature called *reproductive fidelity*. To display characters on a screen as they really will be printed out requires good graphics ability (through bit mapping, see Chap. 2) and the right operating system and underlying hardware.

The really difficult problem with modern word processors attempting reproductive fidelity is in transferring the screen image to paper. A daisy-wheel printer is as versatile as its range of daisy wheels allows. Printing a document with several fonts on a daisy-wheel printer involves printing a page first with one wheel, then feeding backward, loading another wheel, and printing again. This is tedious and liable to inaccuracies. An alternative is to use a dot-matrix printer capable of transferring a graphics image on the screen to the page. The printed page is then as good as the resolution

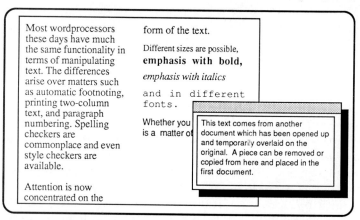

Figure 4.2 Document production is a universal function of business. Except in the very smallest firms, most documents are prepared with word processors rather than typewriters. This does not mean that typewriters are redundant; they are still useful and faster for short documents. Architects often seek automatic paragraph numbering for specification writing, but this is still an uncommon feature of word processors. *(Diagram by the authors.)*

of the dot-matrix printer, which, in spite of high-quality printers, is still only so-so. The best way to do things is without doubt to use a laser printer. Cheap laser printers (in the low thousands of dollars) are now available, with resolutions of 300 dots per inch, more than adequate for text. In the next few years we can expect laser printers to replace daisy wheels, and to a lesser extent dot-matrix printers, as the standard choice for word processing.

4.3.2 Electronic spreadsheets

Spreadsheets should perhaps be called number processors, since they do for numbers what a word processor does for words. The name comes from their appearance, because presented on the screen is a sheet of rows and columns, forming boxes, into which are entered numbers or formulas to manipulate numbers. This is a very simple conceptual model, easy to understand and manipulate. To sum the numbers in a column, for example, we might simply put a formula like "sum (C)" into the box at the bottom of the column. The total is then instantly calculated and placed into the cell containing the formula (the formula itself is normally invisible). If a number in the column is changed, then the total is instantly recomputed. A typical sheet might allow 100 columns by 500 rows, only part of which is visible at any one time.

The power of these programs lies in the ways that the boxes can be accessed and in the nature of the inbuilt functions provided. Setting up a spreadsheet can be a tricky exercise, and usually involves establishing various auxiliary calculations on out-of-the-way parts of the sheet. The program proceeds in a generally linear fashion, calculating those formulas which use only raw data first, then those which use the first obtained results, and so on. The more calculations it has to do, the slower it becomes. Often subsidiary sheets are needed to pass data to controlling sheets.

Model and data are intimately connected in a spreadsheet. It is easy to change data, but not to expand or contract the amount of it. A simple example concerns adding columns of numbers: Once a column of 50 numbers has been set up, it is impossible to add only 10 of the numbers or an additional 20 in the same column without deleting or inserting rows. Moreover, a spreadsheet leaves all its workings in full view, and this is dangerous if naive or unskilled people are called on to operate it because they could damage the elaborate structure that has been created. It can also be very difficult to verify the correctness of the structure. All in all, spreadsheets are powerful but subtle tools, much easier to get working than a purpose-written computer program but needing much thought and skill to exploit. Fortunately, there are many books to guide a novice through the setting-up process, and they are well worth acquiring.

Spreadsheets have many potential uses in the architectural office (Fig. 4.3): for financial feasibility studies, cost estimates, and general project

```
ELEMENTAL COST ESTIMATE for a small  Church Extension
Area of  Building    43.75 m2    (Extension only)
VISICALC PRINTOUT         April 1983      ARCHILAB
Costing @    450 /m2   = 19687.50 (not inc overheads etc)   (-rough estimate
!!!!!!!!!!!!!!!!!!!!!!!!!!!!!!!!!!!!!!!!!!!!!!!!!!!!!!!!!!!!!
  Item                     COST    Cost/m2 %of COST
  OVERHEADS etc
Prelims & Insurances      1600.00   36.57    7.95       8% of the building cost
Contingencies             1000.00   22.86    4.97       5% of the building cost
     Sub TOTAL    2600.00
  SUBSTRUCTURE            ...............        units  £/unit    No.  £amount     Descriptn
Demolitions, Alterations  1300.00   29.71    6.46
Foundations                980.00   22.40    4.87       m    17.50   56.00   980.00 Strip Foundation
Floor Construction         600.00   13.71    2.98       m2   40.00   15.00   600.00 Domestic-type Concrete Floor
     Sub TOTAL    2880.00
  STRUCTURAL ELEMENTS     ...............
External Walls            2700.00   61.71   13.42       m2   69.00   39.00  2691.00 allows for forming openings, Insuln
Roof    Main area         2000.00   45.71    9.94       m2   44.00   45.50  2002.00 Inc beams in roof
Roof    Verges etc         550.00   12.57    2.73       m    34.00   10.00   340.00 Add allowance for gutter £200
Windows Main Elevations   1800.00   41.14    8.95       m2   12.00  150.00  1800.00 Hardwood framing, coloured glass
Windows Rooflights        1820.00   41.60    9.05       m2   13.00  140.00  1820.00 Inc clerestory & Veluxes
Windows to Stage rear      450.00   10.29    2.24       m2    3.00  150.00   450.00 allows for forming openings
External Doors             110.00    2.51    0.55       no    1.00  110.00   110.00
Partitions                1200.00   27.43    5.96       no    1.00 1200.00  1200.00 Folding Partition to stage
Internal Doors              60.00    1.37    0.30       no    1.00   60.00    60.00 Hatch to Kitchen
Ironmongery                225.00    5.14    1.12               Mainly Window catches & panic bolt
     Sub TOTAL   10915.00
  FINISHES AND FITTINGS   ...............
Wall    Finishes           380.00    8.69    1.89       m2   69.00    5.50   379.50 Plastering
Floor   Finishes           600.00   13.71    2.98       m2   40.00   15.00   600.00 Carpet Tiles & Skirtings painted
Ceiling Finishes           286.00    6.54    1.42       m2   44.00    6.50   286.00 Plasterboard & skim
Decoration                 250.00    5.71    1.24       m2   84.00    3.00   252.00 Ceiling and wall painting
Fittings                   350.00    8.00    1.74       m2    7.00   35.00   245.00 Platforms and    Kitchen
     Sub TOTAL    1866.00
  SERVICES
Waste, Soil & O'flow pipes 240.00    5.49    1.19               gutters etc
Heating                    900.00   20.57    4.47               mods & new Boiler
Electrical                 320.00    7.31    1.59       no    8.00   40.00   320.00
Drainage                   400.00    9.14    1.99               Mods to RW Drainage
     Sub TOTAL    1860.00
-----------------------------------------------------
Total Excluding Ext Works 20121.00  459.91  100.00
External Works             329.00                       Concrete path & Gate
TOTAL    Building Cost   £ 20450.00 (----
-----------------------------------------------------
Allowance for Inflation   1500.00              During Money raising period
Professional Fees         2250.00              10% of Building Cost + exp
Local Authority Fees       200.00              Planning & Building regs
Insurance, Expenses        180.00              Employers Insurance
-----------------------------------------------------
TOTAL                    £ 24580.00 (----
```

Figure 4.3 Spreadsheets are very useful tools for a whole range of tasks, especially in the small firm. This figure shows an initial cost estimate for a small church extension. Most of the numbers are raw data, entered directly by the user. The cells labeled "Sub TOTAL" and "TOTAL," although displaying monetary sums, actually contain formulas directing the sheet to add the figures above. Likewise, the column headed "% of COST" consists of 25 cells, each containing a formula that divides the cost to the cell's left by the total building cost. Much of the power of a spreadsheet comes from the ease (or lack thereof) with which such formulas can be constructed. *(By D. Nicholson-Cole, used by permission of Architects Journal.)*

cost control as well as office accounting (Nicholson-Cole, 1983). They are particularly useful for exploring options and asking "What if?" questions, such as investigating the effect of variations in interest rates in a feasibility study. It is possible to set up just a framework on the spreadsheet (made up of the form layout and formulas, but no data) for use in similarly structured but separate problems.

4.3.3 Business graphics

Architects, of course, generate drawn as well as written information, but the generation of drawings is such a large topic that we shall leave it to the next chapter. So-called business graphics systems (Fig. 4.4) specialize in transforming numerical information into pie charts and graphs, using

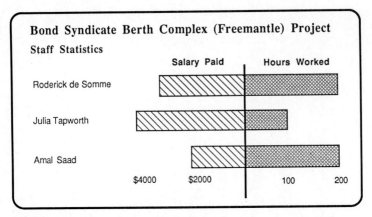

Figure 4.4 Business graphics packages basically present numerical information in graphic format. All provide various sorts of bar and pie charts. A major factor in selecting such a package is whether it can extract and use data from other programs, such as a spreadsheet or database management system. *(Diagram by the authors.)*

low-level graphics but sophisticated algorithms for their semiautomatic creation. Ideally, information should not have to be retyped into a business graphics program. Direct input from a spreadsheet or database management system is the preferred means.

4.3.4 Database management systems

A great deal of time is taken up in the architecture business in looking for and collecting *information*. Most practices have dozens of books, folders, manufacturers' catalogs, and plan chests containing huge quantities of information in more or less disorder. All that information must be transformed into quite a different form: a set of drawings and specifications to be transformed by a builder into real, solid objects for people to live and work in.

The term *database* is applied to any structured set of information, generally stored in a computer and amenable to computer processing. Database processing is a large field within computer science and has evolved many sophisticated techniques and an advanced mathematical theory. The most common types of databases (relational, hierarchical, and network) were described in Sec. A3.2.2.

A database management system (DBMS) (see Sec. A3.2.1) is a self-contained program that manipulates databases to extract information. Some DBMSs use their own language to do things, at which point they merge into the so-called fourth-generation languages (see App. 2). Typically, a DBMS allows us to set up forms on the screen for the input of data in a nice way and contains a report generator that allows for the rapid design of standardized reports (Fig. 4.5). A good example of DBMS use is given in

MacDougall (1983). He created a database of plants and trees for land-scaping. Instead of sifting through a book to locate a suitable tree, he could interrogate the database with questions like "Find all the trees that grow to less than 3 m, like shade, and have a wide canopy." The essence of such systems is the ability to search them by combinations of different keys (here the words "trees," "less than 3 m," "like shade," and "wide canopy") to find all instances of records in the database that contain all the nominated descriptions.

Of course, a DBMS is of little use without data to manage. A DBMS is useful for large amounts of information or for handling difficult queries. There is little point in transferring a small card file to a DBMS; it is much easier and faster just to look up a card. We are only justified in using a DBMS instead of just looking up a book if our information is voluminous and scattered through several works. In an architect's office it might be used in marketing (maintaining data on past, present, and prospective clients and projects), in personnel management (employee records), and in keeping track of equipment, records of past work, and technical information.

As with spreadsheets, anything that can be done with a DBMS can be done by writing a program in a high-level language, but the effort is much less. The price paid is in computational efficiency. A well-written special-purpose program in a high-level language will probably be faster and more

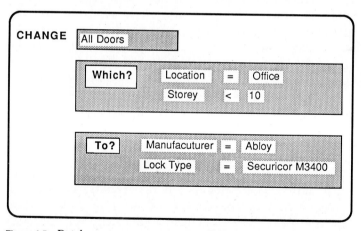

Figure 4.5 Database management systems allow firms to store large quantities of data in a manageable format. Perhaps the major features to be looked for are the ways in which this data can be examined and changed. In this diagram, a DBMS has been used to store door schedules for an office complex. One of the clients, who occupies all the offices above the 10th story, has decided on a different type of lock for those rooms. The old locks are replaced with Abloy Securicor M3400 locks with a simple command (CHANGE, in this case). Not shown here is all the other information that the DBMS has stored about the doors; door identification number, handedness, and so on. *(Diagram by the authors.)*

secure than one written with a DBMS, but the DBMS approach has the enormous advantage of flexibility and most of the difficult work in structuring the data has already been done. As with spreadsheets, too, the first difficulty in using them is in formulating what we want to do in the kind of format that such a general-purpose tool can handle.

4.3.5 Electronic mail and online databases

A *communications program* enables a computer to turn data into signals for transmission and to convert incoming signals into a form that can be processed and stored. Communications can either be via the public telephone system (simply dialing up a computer elsewhere with a local or long-distance call) or through a public network designed specifically for computer communications (Fig. 4.6). Such a network is known as a packet-switched data network because the data is divided up into small, discrete, labeled packets (see Sec. A2.5.2). In addition, many privately run networks, such as Telenet and Tymnet in the United States, CSIRONet in Australia, or Transpac in France, link up all sorts of media to large computers that have something to sell to other computer users. These are called *value-added networks* to distinguish them from networks that simply act as communications media. Catalogs of the services available on these networks are available from local telecommunications authorities. We investigate which service or services we need, select the appropriate service on the appropriate network, and are given account numbers and passwords for the system as a whole and the services in particular.

The services provided by value-added networks are mainly of two types: electronic mail and database access. *Electronic mail* is just what it says. A message is composed on the computer and mailed to someone or sent to a public bulletin board. When the recipients next connect up to the network, they are notified of pending mail. They can also scan the bulletin board for interesting messages, indexed by keyword. *Database access* entails extracting information from a database established by someone else. This promises to be of great importance in the future.

Electronic mail. Electronic mail is not new; the telegraph service, after all, dates back to the 1800s, and telex has existed for over 50 years. The difference in the new view of electronic mail is that there is no physical form of the message at either end of the link. Typically, the system uses an "electronic mailbox," which is used as an address by a message sender and is periodically checked for mail by message receivers. It is not, then, an instantaneous system and does not depend on the receiver being present (or even on the receiver's computer being hooked up) at any critical moment. Like much in computing, there are no international standards in electronic mail; different systems work side by side in commercial competition.

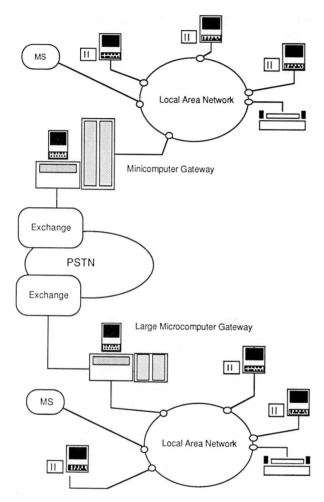

Figure 4.6   Electronic mail promises to assume great importance over the next decade or two. This diagram shows two firms, each with its own local-area network, who use an electronic mail system to communicate with each other. One computer in each network, called a gateway, handles the interface between the telephone system and the local-area network. Messages are transmitted through the public-switched telephone network to the other gateway computer, which stores the mail until the addressee logs onto the network. Another way to do this is to subscribe to a single computer on a large-scale network that offers electronic mail. Individuals often use these systems. *(Diagram by the authors.)*

The process goes something like this. Our microcomputer, word processor, or computer terminal is linked to public telephone or data networks. As registered users, we can access a private workspace in a host computer by using a password and can send an addressed message; there are online directories linking names to mailbox addresses, and we can set up the system so that if we just send a message to "Fred," it will append Fred's mailbox number. Part of the address number identifies the computer, and part identifies the box number within that computer. There are also word processing facilities and spelling checkers in the system, or we can prepare messages in advance with our computer's own word processor and enter them quickly to the host, once connected. The message is transmitted to the address (or simultaneously transmitted to many destinations, if required) and stored in computer memory in the receiver's country or area; a message sent on the ITT Dialcom system from the United States to an address in Australia will be stored in the Minerva system computer in Sydney. When the receiver calls to check for mail, he or she can scan any messages to see the sender's name, time of dispatch, and subject, with express messages topping the list. Any messages can then be read, forwarded on to another address, filed away for later reference, or replied to. If the sender requests, an acknowledgement can be sent back to the originator automatically when a message is read. Costs depend on connect time, storage, and the facilities used. It is all very simple, but very useful.

Online databases.   Online databases (information systems) have been available since the early 1960s, so these, too, are hardly a recent development. *Database vendors* make a number of databases available to the general public. *Database producers* are organizations that collate and make available the information in databases, often the same organizations that produced the earlier print versions. Indeed, many of the electronic databases began as a spin-off from the production process of these printed documents. The information they contain is typically bibliographic (listing only the sources of information on a topic), sometimes numeric (such as statistics), and increasingly the full text of documents.

Most database management systems behind online systems work in the same kind of way. They use a dictionary of the contents that "knows" for each word in a document its document number, its field number (where the field might be the title, author, source, and abstract of a document), its sentence number within the field, and the word number within the sentence. They then use boolean operators that define *and, or,* and *not* combinations of nominated terms, so that we might ask for documents that mention architecture *and* design *or* manufacture but *not* landscape. The search is narrowed by combining the boolean operators with proximity operators, which specify whether the nominated terms have to be used together (in the specified order), in the same sentence, or in the same field. We need to use such systems fairly regularly to keep familiar with their contents and methods of inquiry; otherwise, it is more efficient to go through an *information broker*, who specializes in the task.

Gretes (1984) has noted six benefits of using large-scale networks to access large databases:

1. *Keeping current.* The ease with which electronic databases can be updated means that they are always more current than corresponding information in print.

2. *Comprehensiveness.* Databases can store huge amounts of information.

3. *Precision.* Databases can be searched with finer precision than one can search manually. Searching is done by posing questions about the topics of concern, the replies being lists of references or perhaps their number.

4. *Speed.* An online search is extremely rapid.

5. *Cost-effectiveness.* Less personnel time is required to conduct a search.

6. *Ease of access.* We don't have to leave our office.

The American Institute of Architects has established a facility called ArchNet, available free of charge to members ("AIA Computer Network," 1983), that provides information of interest to architects. This is provided as part of The Source, one of the services available on Telenet. The Source provides an electronic mail service in which we can send letters to anyone else who is also a member of The Source, or post them to a public bulletin board accessible to all members. Mailgrams can be sent, airline seats booked, selected databases scanned, the news read. ArchNet is mainly in the electronic mail category. Gretes (1984) has noted several databases of interest to architects: Compendex (13 years of the Engineering Index); Standards and Specifications, produced by the U.S. National Standards Association; the Avery Library's index of international periodicals; and Health Planning and Administration.

In Britain the construction industry is establishing several databases (Atkinson, 1984b). The Royal Institute of British Architects, the Greater London Council, and other groups have set up library databases, mainly for internal use. The Building Research Establishment maintains a database of over 100,000 references to building science and technology; the Timber Research and Development Association operates a database called TINKER; the Building Services Research and Information Association maintains a database called IBSEDEX of building services references; and the British Architectural Library is transferring its catalogs to an online database. In 1985 the information contained in the library of the Property Services Agency, responsible for all construction activities, supplies, and transport for British government departments, became the source for the PICA database with initially around 45,000 records dating back to 1974 and the promise of about 5000 new items to be added each year. Among the topics covered are rules and legislation on construction, contracts, various building types, and (of course) computer-aided architectural design.

Architects in practice are probably most interested in a full text products database, a facility that will be of enormous utility. The old product services (which were always incomplete, out of date, and unwieldy) will be replaced by one central system updated daily, covering every product supplier in the country. But this will require an effort of coordination unusual in the building industry, and it is unlikely to be fully implemented before the end of the decade.

4.3.6 Integrated systems

In the late 1970s and early 1980s we could buy a word processor, a spreadsheet, and a business graphics program. Data transfer between the three was difficult if not impossible. Our financial estimates were generated by the spreadsheet but had to be typed afresh for the business graphics program and for the report we were preparing with the word processor.

The earliest attempts to get the disparate parts working together began when software houses released the details of how their programs stored data. Clever programmers could write programs that transformed the data made by the spreadsheet into a form the business grapher could understand. We still had to leave the spreadsheet, invoke the translation program, and enter the business grapher to get things done. The next wave came when software developers created *family lines* of programs, which used a common data format so that the files the programs created could be interchanged. This is certainly a better solution, provided that we stick with the one software line of products. In the early 1980s the trend proceeded to its logical conclusion as firms released single programs that incorporated several previously disparate functions, usually word processing, spreadsheet, and graphics.

The goal of such *integrated programs* is to make the seams between the various functions invisible. The major obstacle is that each function uses conceptually quite different data structures. A word processor operates on characters, lines, paragraphs, pages, and documents; a spreadsheet works with cells of numeric data and formulas; a business graphics program works on arrays of numbers. Combining these so that they can access a common database is very difficult. To date, the attempts adopt one form of data structure and force the other functions into a more or less happy fit.

4.4 Management Software

4.4.1 Practice management

Practice management (or business management, such as of an architectural firm) requires information for financial, personnel, and project management; marketing; accounting; and the management of technical information, job records, and part jobs. The spreadsheet and database management programs outlined in the previous section have a role in this process, and we have described some of their uses. In this section we look at software specifically for the management of architectural practices.

Financial management systems (Fig. 4.7) have been available for many years on many different systems. As Laurie (1983) has noted, the early ones suffered the lamentable disadvantage that they were designed by accountants, who made the computerized systems look just like the old manual ones, even to the extent of entering the same information several times over. We might call these disintegrated systems, as opposed to modern integrated systems that unify the various separate accounting records into the one package. No one should have to enter identical data twice. A further difficulty for architects is that most accounting systems are designed for the small retail business, with an emphasis on stock control.

Systems for professionals are a little more difficult to come by, but since 1982 several packages specifically for architects have been developed, often by architectural firms themselves. Thanks to the wide differences in how principals choose to run their firms, it is difficult to select one or two of these programs as the best. Further, like most microcomputer software, customization is difficult or is available only at a price. Fanning (1983) and

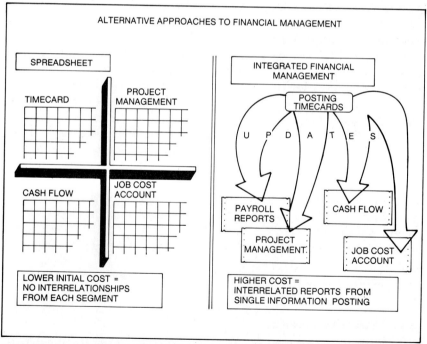

Figure 4.7 A spreadsheet can be used to conduct an office's finances, but it requires some work to set up and maintain; keeping track of relationships is complex, and errors can occur. A better (even if more expensive) way is to buy an integrated finance package, in which all the accounting functions are preprogrammed. *(Diagram by W. D. Hooper and D. R. Levy, used by permission of Architectural Technology.)*

Witte (1985a) have suggested some guidelines. They recommend that a program suite include the five major functions: general ledger, accounts payable, accounts receivable, payroll, and project costing. Security provisions are a necessity for medium to large firms, so access to critical data files is restricted.

A typical session with a financial management system might involve adding some new projects, entering time sheets, and printing some project or accounting reports. The system will keep track of the various kinds of expenses and their attribution to projects or to the office generally. What is important is the ability to abstract information at varying levels of detail, from summaries to individual detailed items, and to organize that information in reports suited to different purposes. Thus, a *project report* might list the various stages of the design process (from briefing to construction documentation and so on), the actual and budgeted hours and costs allocated to each stage for the current time period and for the total to date, the balance left, and the percentage of the budget expended. It might also list direct and reimbursable expenses and a summary of fees billed and received. A *personnel report* might list the staff with hours worked, projects worked on, and vacation and other time totals, with summaries for each department and for the whole firm. A *billing report* will detail labor charges and other expenses, such as printing, photocopying, travel, and special computer use, with the total to be charged, the estimated total charge, and the amount billed to date. A *project profit-and-loss report* will list the actual fees received and receivable, other recoverables, and the various expenses and compare these with the budgeted amounts.

All these reports are generated from the same integrated database; the key advantages are the ease with which that data can be entered and the flexibility with which it can be extracted to provide meaningful information. For example, some programs summarize transaction data after a month, and others keep it accessible indefinitely. A few programs provide graphic output directly, providing management with easily understood summaries at a glance. In lieu of this, an interface to a spreadsheet or database management system with graphics ability is often offered. This is a handy feature, for it allows a firm to manipulate the data for its own special purposes.

Good support for accounting programs is critical, as a program failure can throw a firm's finances into chaos (Witte, 1985a). For financial management, reliable ongoing support (or at the very least a thorough manual and tutorial) is probably more important than advanced features.

4.4.2 Project management

Project management involves project scheduling, project costing, and resource scheduling. It applies during both the design and the construction phases of a project, the tools for the former overlapping with those needed in practice management.

Project scheduling is the sequencing of the operations or subtasks necessary to complete a project and has to be done implicitly or explicitly on all jobs (Fig. 4.8). Large building contractors have been using the techniques of critical-path project scheduling for many years, and computers provide architectural firms with the ability to develop project schedules without the hours of tedious arithmetic otherwise necessary (Krawczyck, 1984).

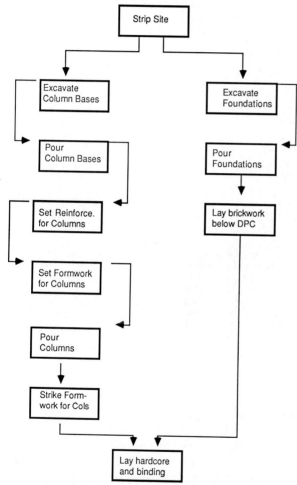

Figure 4.8   This precedence network shows the initial steps in a small building project. After the site is stripped, excavations can begin. The relationships between the first three events are called finish-to-start relationships, since the two excavation processes can only start when the site is stripped. Pouring foundations does not have to wait until all the foundations are excavated, but can proceed in parallel and slightly behind the excavation. The relationship joining "Excavate Foundations" and "Pour Foundations" is a start-to-start one, showing that the second can commence after some specified delay from the start of the first. *(Diagram by the authors.)*

The fundamental theoretical basis is the critical-path method or its allied technique, PERT, both of which describe the activities in a project as a network. The most used variant is the *precedence scheduling network,* in which each node constitutes an activity and is connected to other nodes that cannot start until each preceding node's activity is completed. Each node possesses a duration. The total duration of the project is given by the longest path, called the *critical path.* Some activities, but not all, will be on this path. Any alteration in the timing of activities on the critical path will affect the overall time of the project. Noncritical activities can be late (within limits) without affecting the outcome. Applying a calendar to the network will provide a set of earliest start and latest finish dates for each activity.

This is the bare bones of project scheduling. Entering a whole network is a time-consuming job, so a program should allow for the storage of small subnetworks containing often-used subtasks that can then be assembled into a larger network. The very simplest programs will determine the critical path, but the quality of project-scheduling software lies in the additional abilities provided. One of the most important is in allowing sophisticated relationships between activities. An activity that cannot start until another finishes is easy to model, but some activities can overlap others. For instance, a builder does not excavate footings and then commence pouring; the pouring starts a few days after excavation commences and proceeds in parallel and slightly behind. Flexibility in the specification of a calendar is also important. Some activities may proceed by days, others by weeks, months, quarters, or years. From the number of working days in a week, holidays must be allowed for, and these may differ for different trades. Provision for altering the network as activities finish early or late must also be included.

The type and nature of reports vary from program to program. We need to be able to report which activities are being done on time and which are ahead of or behind schedule. A few programs allow us to designate a few critical activities or dates as milestones, which can then be reported as achieved or not. Good programs also provide various levels of summary. For instance, given that the network for a medium-size building project contains hundreds of nodes, all of which we may not want to see at once, good programs provide a simple working summary in a bar chart, or Gantt chart. They are also capable of producing progress summaries in terms of late activities and of the amount of activity completed. Finally, computer programs differ in their abilities to produce hard-copy reports of a whole network. All programs can display it all on screen, but few microcomputer-based programs can produce a hard copy of it; most only produce the output of Gantt charts (Fig. 4.9). Minicomputer packages, however, are commonly able to produce the entire network. To print a large network, a plotter is necessary.

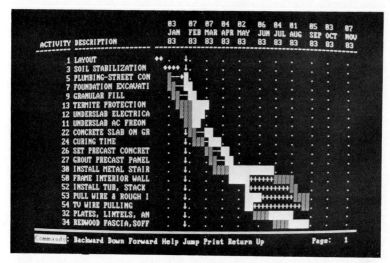

Figure 4.9 A bar chart from a project management program, Primavera Project Planner, showing a calendar of activities in implementing a project. *(Courtesy of Primavera Systems.)*

Most activities consume *resources* as well as time, and we need to know just what resources are needed when (Fig. 4.10). A good program allows resources to be specified in terms of money, people, and man-hours, broken down into jobs and specializations (trades or subcontractors in the building process, consultants in the design process). It should provide reports and charts showing cash flow and resource consumption. We can then

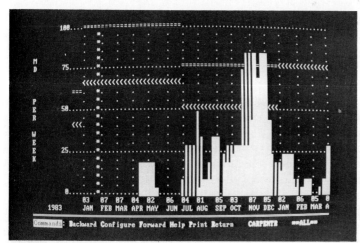

Figure 4.10 A manpower allocation chart for the carpentering trade. The ability to present information in meaningful forms is as important as the ability to calculate results. *(Generated by Primavera Project Planner, courtesy of Primavera Systems.)*

delay or accelerate activities to fit limited resources; some programs can partially automate this by doing their own resource leveling. Project *costing* can be tackled using a combination of database management system and spreadsheet, or through a program written specially for the purpose using an office's costing techniques.

Project management is an area that could be exploited by architects much more than it has been; perhaps no other development exemplifies the failure of architects aggressively to expand (or even maintain) their services than the rise of a separate profession of project managers, instead of the development of a specialization within the profession. When introduced to computerized project scheduling, the response of a few architects is "It's just what we've been looking for to help us." The majority think, "What do we need this for?"

4.4.3 Facilities management

Given a large building, a complex of buildings (such as a hospital or university), or a portfolio of buildings in a dozen different cities (such as a government department or a commercial organization might own or lease), how do we keep track of the efficient use of space and the real costs of building use? How do we plan for change? Since for most buildings the long-term operating costs are more significant than the initial capital costs, these questions are important. Traditionally, they have been dealt with on an ad hoc basis with inadequate information. *Facilities management programs* attempt to provide an integrated basis for the task by providing a comprehensive database about buildings and about the activities, people, and equipment within them, coupled with problem-solving software that links into the database (Mitchell, 1985b). They have as their goal the structuring of the complex interaction of facilities (or physical objects) on the one hand and of people on the other in order to improve the relationship.

The first group of issues addressed by such programs concerns *continuing operation*, the regular problems of running a building. Examples are the ongoing scheduling of activities to appropriate spaces at required times (a major problem in universities), the scheduling of routine maintenance programs and the recording of maintenance histories, the monitoring of building costs (such as energy use, maintenance, and government charges), and the allocation of costs to the correct cost center in a multiuser or multisection organization. At the very least, they should keep track of the relationship between people, equipment, and buildings (what person is in what room and with what furniture) and maintain purchase and stock lists of equipment and spare parts. The second group of issues concerns *future planning*, the anticipation of the implications for building and equipment stock of an organization's policy decisions (Fig. 4.11). At its simplest, this

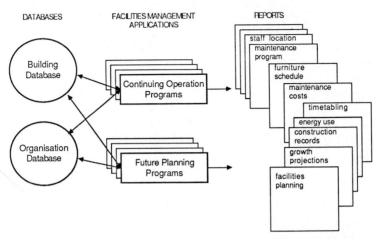

DATABASES   FACILITIES MANAGEMENT   REPORTS
                        APPLICATIONS

Building
Database

Continuing Operation
Programs

staff location
maintenance program
furniture schedule
maintenance costs
timetabling
energy use
construction records
growth projections

Organisation
Database

Future Planning
Programs

facilities planning

Figure 4.11 A facilities management system uses a database of the building or set of buildings and its physical contents (spaces, furniture, equipment, etc.) and a database of the organization or organizations that occupy the building (people, organizational structure, departments, etc.). Applications programs use this database to produce reports to use in the day-to-day operation and future planning of the facilities. One aspect, facilities (or layout) planning, is discussed further in Sec. A6.4. *(Diagram by the authors.)*

involves the application of growth or contraction factors to figures in the database, but knowing that more or less space is required is only the first stage in developing a strategy for managing change. Other basic decisions include whether to build or sell, lease or rent, or simply to reorganize and replace units within existing boundaries. These are followed if necessary by the management of design processes, by project implementation, and by the purchase of furniture and equipment.

A facilities management program needs to be able to represent the different parts of the facility and the relationships between them. For the building, the design description created in the course of its documentation in a computer drafting system (see Chap. 5) might be carried over into the facilities management process to provide an ongoing resource; drawings can be used directly in providing a spatial key to equipment location and maintenance needs ("the desk needs to be moved from here to there"). For the organization, the description needs to represent not only the numbers of people but the organizational tree and the need for proximity between different sections. For the equipment, it needs to keep a catalog of items and the locations of each type of item. All of this can add up to large quantities of information to be handled, and the system is required to provide printed reports, diagrammatic reports, and building drawings. The result is a very sophisticated piece of software.

A key characteristic of facilities management programming, then, is that the process is dynamic, not static. Databases are generated and continually updated as an organization develops and changes over time. The majority of facilities management systems have probably been sold to end-users, not architects, and it is easy to see that a large organization could quickly become dependent on its facilities database. It fits with the perception of buildings being no longer static and unchanging, but responsive machines to be tuned and managed. It is taken further in the notion of "intelligent" buildings (described in this chapter's secondary text). Whether architects can, or wish to, capture this management function remains to be seen.

4.5 Summary

Although management is not the most exciting function of architectural practice, it is an essential function. All architects should be using at least a microcomputer to manage their own firms; considering that microcomputers are used extensively by small businesses throughout the world for management, not to do so seems almost perverse.

We have described the aims of office automation and the five basic software packages: word processing, electronic spreadsheets, business graphics, database management, and electronic communications. Beyond this, practice management programs are of use in accounting and job control, and project planning and facilities management open up opportunities for architects to extend their activities. The secondary text to this chapter looks at building management systems. Most of this chapter has been concerned with the processing of written and numerical information; in Chap. 5 we turn to the processing of drawn information.

SECONDARY TEXT
Building Management Systems

Most of this book is concerned with building design and with the role of computers in the design and documentation of buildings and the management of that process. In this section we digress into the role of computers in the management of building services systems. In what have become known as *intelligent buildings*, a network of sensors gathers information about the internal and external environments and the building's use and feeds it to a computer that controls the response of heating and cooling plants, lights, elevators, fire and security alarms, and other building services. The building acts as a dynamic system working on feedback, not as a static object. The computer system may also pinpoint locations of equipment failure and, through expert systems (see Chap. 7), help in diagnosing faults.

A4.1   The Control of Building Services

Microprocessors have made possible extraordinary advances in the monitoring and control of mechanical and electrical systems. Before modern technology was introduced into buildings, all these were independent entities. Such monitoring information as existed was presented to operators on a series of gages and lights on machine panels. The operators would then travel from panel to panel to press buttons, open valves, and close switches according to readings jotted down on their clipboards. In the early 1960s the various indicators and monitoring devices were equipped with wires or pressure systems to transmit their information back to a central control board. Operators at this board could monitor the sundry building functions and adjust the heating and electrical systems to cope with changing conditions. After the introduction of transistorized electronic components, monitoring systems became more sophisticated in the information they could send to the control board, providing operators with more information presented in better forms (Abramson, 1981).

Modern forms of control systems are often called building management systems (BMSs), building control systems, or building automation systems. Older versions used pneumatic control lines to actuate valves and motors in response to commands from a central computer. Information from sensors was crude and limited, and the devices could only be controlled to certain set points (Carolin, 1983). Pneumatic signals had to be converted to digital ones and vice versa by bulky transducers. They were expensive, difficult to operate, and relied on the uninterrupted functioning of the central computer. Over the past decade microprocessors have increased the quantity and quality of information and allowed direct links between monitoring and control systems. Sensors have been miniaturized and automated, and pneumatic signals replaced by direct digital control. The ability of computers to handle large quantities of disparate information allows varied sensors to feed into one integrated system, allowing the monitoring of intruder sensors and of fire and plant-failure alarms by the one processor. Analysis of incoming signals is possible, allowing sophisticated and flexible responses and the filtering out of false alarms. (Perks, 1984; Sennewald, 1986).

There are two kinds of BMS: *Rigid systems* operate under fixed programs and are left unattended except for maintenance and regular checks; *interactive systems* provide for monitoring of systems, active computer control, and operator intervention (Atkinson, 1984). A major trend is toward distributing many control functions to microprocessors located near or in the plant and monitored by an overwatching central computer (Fig. A4.1). This allows a system to be constructed in modules, incorporating additional functions in stages, and provides for easier fault detection. The extensive cabling required is often of the two- or four-wire type,

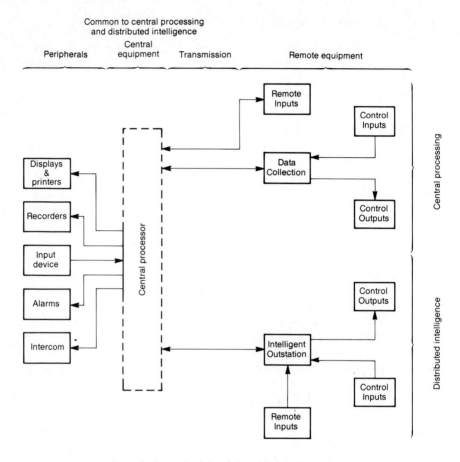

Composition diagram of central processing and distribution intelligence systems.

Figure A4.1   Older building management systems relied on central processing (that is, large central computers) to run the building's functions. Distributed systems rely on intelligent outstations to process much of the data before sending key information back to a central computer. *(Diagram by D. Oughton, used by permission of Building Services.)*

compatible with normal telephone systems to transmit signals, which allows a substantial savings in cabling (Oughton et al., 1983).

A4.2   Energy Management

The overwhelming majority of building management systems are concerned only with energy management and have five functions: *scheduling*, which turns a plant on or off according to a predetermined schedule; *optimum start/stop*, which involves calculating the best time to start and stop the plant based on outside temperatures; *duty cycling*, which activates the plant for a short time each hour to reduce energy consumption; *load shedding*, which involves shifting the electrical load toward cheaper off-peak periods; and *data logging*, which is the recording of the system's performance.

Such systems are usually justified on the basis of energy savings, typical figures being a 12- to 36-month payback period. For a fully integrated BMS, current experience indicates a minimum economic building size of 538,000 ft^2 (50,000 m^2). However, such justification relies on a comprehensive energy and systems audit having been carried out. Documented energy savings have been as much as 20 percent, but BMSs have been subject to criticism. A survey by the U.S. National Bureau of Standards revealed that half of the owners of BMSs were dissatisfied, mainly because of exaggerated energy-savings claims, improper installation, and poor integration with the rest of the building's equipment. Some users have argued that computerized scheduling is no more effective than simple time clocks, that duty cycling increases plant wear, and that load shedding reduces occupant comfort and violates building codes (Fisher, 1984).

An insight into the kinds of problems that can arise is provided by the experience of the Property Services Agency in London (Oughton et al., 1983). The agency wanted to install a building management system involving a number of inner-London buildings, all connected by telephone lines to a central site. Several objectives were set down: to save energy; to improve maintenance management; to provide a central control facility for all the buildings that would be simpler, more efficient, and more accurate than the existing system; to enable rapid response to plant failure; to reduce ad hoc alteration of control set points; and to provide a more effective means of maintenance planning. They decided on a standard microcomputer as the central control facility and on a set of intelligent local stations that could operate independently. Each local station was set to work one by one, and when proven was brought into the network and connected to the central computer. Although all the software and hardware had been laboratory-tested, problems arose that required considerable skill to diagnose. Remedial work was often lengthy, particularly when the problem lay with the software. Persistent problems were encountered, too, with the data transmission equipment, with the telephone lines failing to disconnect at the end of routine transmissions (giving rise to very high bills), and with data corruption caused by the normal noisiness of telephone equipment and by interference from the start-up of plants near the locations of sensors. All sorts of other troubles arose: The optimum start control only started when the building was occupied, instead of before; the system responded to marginal temperature changes in the zoned heating system by cycling to full on or full off; data from the central computer failed to arrive at the local sites and failed to tell the central site of this; and various components failed in the hostile environments of the boiler rooms.

All these troubles were eventually surmounted, and they probably indicate more about the state of the art at the time than anything else. After the troubles, the good news: Energy savings ran at the 15 percent level, giving a payback period of less than 3 years.

A4.3   Integrated Systems

The most sophisticated building management systems attempt to integrate as many functions as possible (Fig. A4.2). A British example is Cutlens Gardens, one of the largest office developments in Europe, largely in refurbished warehouses of the Port of London (Heard, 1982). A minicomputer controls the heating, security, and fire systems. By monitoring its many sensors, the computer reports to the main desk and operates switching devices according to its programmed instructions. The main boilers and air-conditioning are timed to start based on calculations the computer makes concerning the previous day's temperature and the current external temperature. The external perimeter of the building and all internal courtyards are monitored. External lighting is programmed to come on at dusk and to fall to security levels after working hours. Entry to the car park is by card access, also monitored by the computer. The eleva-

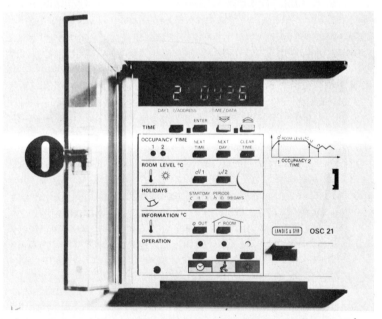

Figure A4.2   Small units such as the Sygmagyar OSC 21 controller are used in building management systems to monitor and control temperatures in building zones. They can be programmed to account for occupancy times and holidays. *(Copyright by Design Council, used by permission.)*

tor alarm is linked to the system and a series of checkpoints is placed along the night watchman's route, so that should he fail to reach one in the allotted time, the control desk is notified. All external doors are wired into the system. As well as these security functions, the computer also provides an emergency management package.

An American example is City Place in Hartford, Connecticut (Carolin, 1983). The elevator systems, heating/ventilating/air-conditioning (HVAC) plant, security monitoring, lighting control, emergency telephones, garage carbon monoxide monitoring, and telephone are integrated into the one computer system. Tenants can also use it for word processing and other office automation needs. Fiber optics is used for the data cabling. All information is transmitted digitally, including voice data. The outstanding feature of the building is the extraordinary degree of integration of the whole; computer vendors often talk about unifying communications, computing, and control, but it is still rarely accomplished. Interestingly, it was designed by a subsidiary of United Technologies, Building Systems Company, whose president commented that "Buildings are the most disjointed systems that exist. . . . Decisions are made on the basis of price alone — technological advances (which may be unique), system integration, operating costs, and serving factors are disregarded" (Carolin, 1983, p. 117).

Systems, though, must be flexible enough to accommodate human idiosyncracies and unusual demands. It seems very reasonable to have the lights work through sensors so that they switch on when there are people about and the ambient level of daylight is low, and switch off when the last late worker leaves for home. It is reasonable, but not always appropriate. A speaker at a seminar in the United Kingdom wanted to show some slides and drew the curtains. Reacting to the lowered light level, the building control system promptly turned on the lights. There was no manual override; the only way to get darkness in working hours was to disconnect the fluorescent tubes individually. There is a wider moral to the anecdote. At the start of this brief description of building management systems, we wrote that the buildings they manage are often called intelligent buildings. This kind of control displays a rather limited intelligence, certainly compared with what we mean when we ascribe the same adjective to humans. Intelligent buildings still have a long way to go, even with the best examples.

5

Computer-Aided Drafting

5.1 Introduction

In architecture, the act of drawing is intimately linked with the act of *design*. Traditionally, architects are supposed to make their creative leaps while sketching with 6B pencils on the backs of used envelopes. If there are not enough envelopes around, then butter or drafting paper are just about acceptable. They don't design first and draw later; rather, the process of designing takes place in parallel with the processes of drawing, erasing, modifying, and redrawing (Akin, 1978; Lawson, 1982). Right through the design and documentation sequence, details are refined as the drawings are reworked. Further, architects develop their own personal style of drawing that expresses something about their personality, taking pleasure in choosing and mixing line styles, line intensities, and techniques for expressing texture and materials. Indeed, in architecture, this pride in drawing leads to some confusion about the end product of the process. People talk of a "fine drawing" as an end in itself, quite independent of the building being described, and the job satisfaction of many a draftsperson and junior architect comes as much from producing pretty drawings as from participating in the intended purpose of building.

Given this close relationship between drawing and design, it is hardly surprising that there is some concern over rejecting the habit of 500 years and abruptly replacing pen and pencil with keyboard, digitizer, and mouse (we explained these in Chap. 2). The concern is entirely justified; Marshal McLuhan (1964), among others, has argued that the medium by which the creative process is expressed affects the resulting product. Using computers instead of pens and pencils certainly modifies drawing styles and may change the architecture (Radford and Stevens, 1983). Playing safe, or just because it is the most likely application to be cost-effective, computer drafting in most architectural offices is firmly restricted to the documentation stages after the design decisions are supposed to have been made. The only exception is the occasional computer-generated perspective or axonometric drawing of design proposals to communicate ideas or to confirm expectations.

A drawing is a *model* of the artifact or scene it depicts. In manual drafting, the model physically consists of particles of ink or graphite on paper; we interpret the particles as parts of lines, polygons, and surfaces, but there is no internal structure that establishes such entities. In computer graphics there has to be some internal *structure,* if only to relate a pattern of bits stored in the computer memory to an image on a computer screen. This structure is the reason why graphics systems are so useful. The computer model will have properties quite independent of the object it is describing. Generally, the less structure in the model, the easier it will be to use but the less powerful it will be in use. In this chapter we describe the modeling of shape in two and three dimensions in computers and the operation of computer drafting and modeling systems. In the secondary text we look in more detail at the process of using a drafting system to construct some drawings and views of a small building.

5.2 Modeling in Two Dimensions

5.2.1 Points, lines, and objects

The simplest way to model an image in a computer is to represent it as a *set of points,* or *pixels,* on a two-dimensional grid mapped on a raster screen (see Sec. A2.1.2). The drawing is represented by the points on this grid that are turned "on" and show black rather than white (or vice versa) on the screen. A color drawing is stored by associating a color with each point. There is no structure to the computer's knowledge of the drawing other than the set of points. This limits what can be done with the drawing. We can't work with lines or objects because the computer knows nothing about them. We can only work with individual pixels (turning them on or off; the "fat bits" feature of the celebrated Apple Macintosh MacPaint system facilitated this at a very direct level) or with subareas of the grid containing pixels. For example, to move an object on a MacPaint drawing (perhaps a door or window on an elevation), we typically have to identify the appropriate points by "lassoing" them and dragging the pattern across the matrix, together with the surrounding pixels of drawing caught within the lasso (Fig. 5.1).

The next level of modeling is to represent the drawing as a *set of lines.* Now we are interested in the endpoints of lines (say, x and y coordinates in a two-dimensional coordinate system) and the attributes (thickness, color, and perhaps type — continuous, dashed, dotted, etc. — which we can think of as a texture) of the line between them. Again, the representation limits

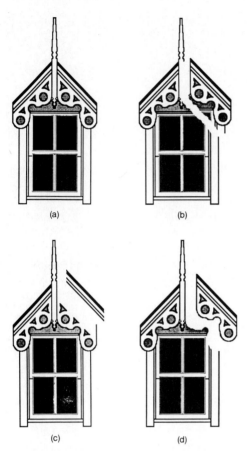

(a) (b)

(c) (d)

Figure 5.1 *(a)* The image of a dormer window can be modeled as a set of points (pixels), lines, or objects. *(b)* As a set of points, there is no structure to the drawing; moving an element (here the right-hand bargeboard) involves moving all the points in that area of the drawing. *(c)* As a set of lines, individual lines are recognized as entities and can be moved without disturbing the surrounding image. *(d)* As a set of objects, elements can be recognized as entities and moved without disturbing surrounding elements. If the two bargeboards and the central upright are set up as objects, they can be moved as wholes. *(Window drawn by Patrick Trinh; modified by Zol Nemes-Nemeth, University of Sydney.)*

what can be done with the drawing. We can move or delete lines as entities, rather than as contiguous pixels, and the computer can calculate intermediate or intersection points on lines from the endpoint information. It might be able to recognize polygons by tracing intersecting lines and to associate colors or textures with those polygons. There is, however, no recognition of higher-level structures. To move an object on the drawing, we would identify the appropriate lines by lassoing them or by identifying each constituent line in turn (there is still no recognition of the lines together combining to form a higher-level entity) and reposition the pattern of lines somewhere else on the drawing.

The third level of modeling, then, is to represent the drawing as a *set of objects* (also sometimes called elements, components, macros, or blocks) (Fig. 5.2). We are then interested in the discrete objects depicted in the drawing and the position of those objects in space. In a drawing of a building elevation we might have objects like a window, a door, a step, a balustrade panel, and so on. Some of these objects will be repeated several

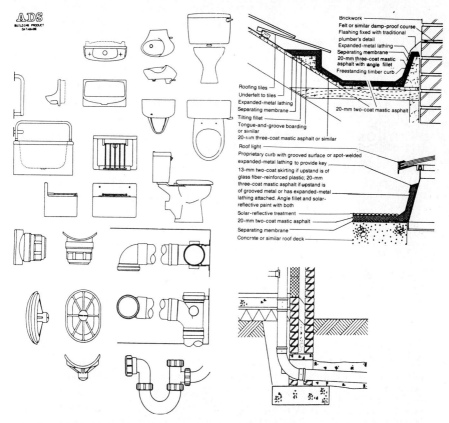

Figure 5.2   Some components from the building products database prepared by Architectural Data Systems Ltd. (United Kingdom) on behalf of product manufacturers and made available in digital form with the help of CAD system vendors. The database contains plan, elevation, and sectional views of individual elements that can be treated as objects in the drafting system, such as these basins and toilets from Armitage Shanks (top left) and piping components from Key Terrain (bottom). It also contains some complete annotated drawings showing how products should be used, as in the details prepared by the Mastic Asphalt Council and Employers Federation Ltd. (top right). *(Used by permission of Architectural Data Systems Ltd., Curry Mallet, Taunton, England.)*

times; technically, each time it appears is called an *instance* of the object. To move an object, we have only to identify it (by pointing; there is no need to lasso it since the lines that depict it are linked as a single entity) and move the whole object across the drawing.

These three levels of modeling are hierarchical, and a description at a higher level can be transformed into a description at a lower level. In practice that is what happens; the objects have associated with them a list of the lines by which they are depicted, the lines have endpoints, and from the endpoints the pixels on a two-dimensional grid that are occupied by drawing elements can be calculated. The map of these pixels (called a bit map) is used to control the turning on or off of the pixels, of a raster-based computer screen, or of an electrostatic or laser plotter. With a vector screen or pen plotter, we stop with the line model and use that to control the movement of the beam on the screen or of the pen in a plotter.

With a drawing described as a set of objects, though, we are not limited to describing the objects only in terms of lines. We can describe them as combinations of any other defined entities, whether objects or lines, and we can associate nongeometric as well as geometric *attributes* with objects. Lines have few attributes of interest (we have mentioned thickness, color, and type), but objects may have many. They almost always have a semantic interpretation as a "real" thing, and we can associate the attributes of the "real" thing with its drawn image. Thus, an image representing an object called "chair" might have associated with it the attributes of cost, manufacturer, and code number. The number of instances of such objects appearing on a drawing (or set of drawings) can also be counted, allowing the production of reports on the numbers and types of doors, windows, chairs, and so on, that are shown to exist (Fig. 5.3).

5.2.2 System operation

This object-oriented model is adopted by all useful drafting systems for technical drawing. Since drawing accounts for about 60 percent of the work hours in most offices, it is only to be expected that with computers this is the activity in which the largest investments are required and from which the most significant changes in office organization often result and the greatest benefits are sought. The essential equipment consists of a *computer,* a *screen* to preview drawings, a *plotter* to print drawings, and a *memory* to store drawing descriptions. Optional equipment (necessary in some systems) includes a second display screen to show a detail or text while the main screen is showing the overall drawing, some means of describing an image to the computer by pointing to its vertices, and a long-term memory to store semipermanent records. On larger systems several *workstations* (the screen and any attached devices) can share the same computer, memory, and plotter. Indeed, only the workstation needs

```
GDS DATA REPORT

FILE #>X02143 >JTDEMO

DRAWINGS:  PLLR
           PLMR

OBJECTS:   ##
```

FLOOR NAME	ROOM NAME	ITEM	MANUFACTURER	DESCRIPTION	COST	QTY	CST&QTY
LEVEL 12	-	-	-	-	800.00	18	
LEVEL 12	ASS. MAN. DIR	Coffee Table 3	B & B Italia	Piediferno black marble top on lacquered cast iron base	800.00	1	800.00
LEVEL 12	ASS. MAN. DIR	Lounge 1.1	Artifort	Single seat fully upholstered in leather on furniture guides	1500.00	1	1500.00
LEVEL 12	ASS. MAN. DIR	Lounge 1.3	Artifort	3 seater fully upholstered in leather on furniture guides	4000.00	1	4000.00
LEVEL 12	ASS. MAN. DIR.	Visitors Chair	Steelcase	451 MB	480.00	3	1440.00
LEVEL 12	ASS. MAN. DIR.	Managers Desk	Rosenthal Studio	STC with arms, charcoal thermal plastic base, wool upholstery Prisma desk, silk matt black polyester varnish finish with integral clock and lamp	4000.00	1	4000.00
LEVEL 12	DINING	Dining Room Chair	Rosenthal Studio	Folio fully upholstered in leather, on slides, stainless steel legs	800.00	12	9600.00
LEVEL 12	DINING	Dining Table	Rosenthal Studio	Prisma, Silk matt black polyester varnish finish to table top on marble slab supports	7000.00	1	7000.00
LEVEL 12	GENERAL OFF. 1	General Chair	Steelcase	451MB	400.00	6	2400.00
LEVEL 12	GENERAL OFF. 1	Typist desk	Tecno	STC with arms, charcoal thermal plastic base, leather upholstery Systems Graphics Scrivania white laminate slab desk and mobile pedestal	2500.00	5	12500.00
LEVEL 12	GENERAL OFF. 1	Right Return Unit	Tecno	Systems Graphics Contenitori white laminate storage unit	600.00	3	1800.00
LEVEL 12	GENERAL OFF. 1	Left Return Unit	Tecno	Systems Graphics Contenitori white laminate storage unit	600.00	3	1800.00
LEVEL 12	GENERAL OFF. 2	General Chair	Steelcase	451MB	400.00	6	2400.00
LEVEL 12	GENERAL OFF. 2	Typist desk	Tecno	STC with arms, charcoal thermal plastic base, leather upholstery Systems Graphics Scrivania white laminate slab desk and mobile pedestal	2500.00	6	15000.00
LEVEL 12	GENERAL OFF. 2	Right Return Unit	Tecno	Systems Graphics Contenitori white laminate storage unit	600.00	2	1200.00
LEVEL 12	GENERAL OFF. 2	Left Return Unit	Tecno	Systems Graphics Contenitori white laminate storage unit	600.00	4	2400.00
LEVEL 12	GENEREAL OFF. 1	Typist desk	Tecno	Systems Graphics Scrivania white laminate slab desk and mobile pedestal	2500.00	1	2500.00

Figure 5.3 A schedule of furniture objects can be generated from attributes associated with their graphic descriptions in a drafting system. The attributes here include each item's name, manufacturer, description, and cost. A report generator looks for the number and location of instances of each object in the drafting system's database, adds up their numbers, and calculates a total cost. (*Reproduced courtesy of Jackson Teece Chesterman Willis and Partners Pty. Ltd.; generated using GDS by Applied Research of Cambridge, a McDonnell Douglas company.*)

to reside in the architect's office: the computer, memory, and plotter may be located and maintained at a central bureau and be shared by several offices. All this equipment is described in Chap. 2.

At a very basic level all drafting systems work in essentially the same way. A drawing is built up from *entities,* which are basic elements (such as lines and curves) or defined components (such as a plan of a column, a standard window, or a piece of furniture). A component can be a simple box or a complex group that is itself made up of other components. Once it has been defined, it can be reused endlessly on the same or other drawings of the same or other buildings simply by locating the point at which it is to occur (Fig. 5.4). Conceptually, a computer drafting system can be regarded as a graphic equivalent of a word processor: it edits, repeats, transforms, and translates graphic elements instead of words. There is no necessary connotation of a computer generating or creating a drawing any more than of a word processor writing a report (Figs. 5.5 and 5.6).

Using manual drafting as an analogy, what we have is something like an infinitely large drawing sheet on which can be located elements from an infinitely flexible sheet of transfer images. But not only can we define our own images with this tool, we can also use those images on a drawing as often as we like and at any size we like. And if we are so inclined, we can reflect the images, stretch them, or use a different line style from the

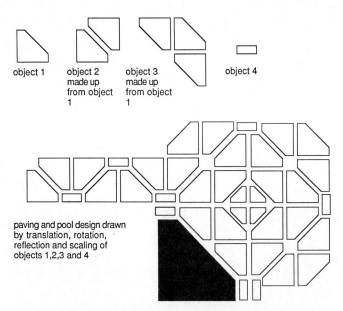

object 1

object 2
made up
from object
1

object 3
made up
from object
1

object 4

paving and pool design drawn
by translation, rotation,
reflection and scaling of
objects 1,2,3 and 4

Figure 5.4   A design for a small pool and paving layout is built up from two basic objects, numbers 1 and 4. Objects 2 and 3 are constructed by rotation, reflection, and repetition of object 1, and the paving also uses scaling. *(Diagram by the authors.)*

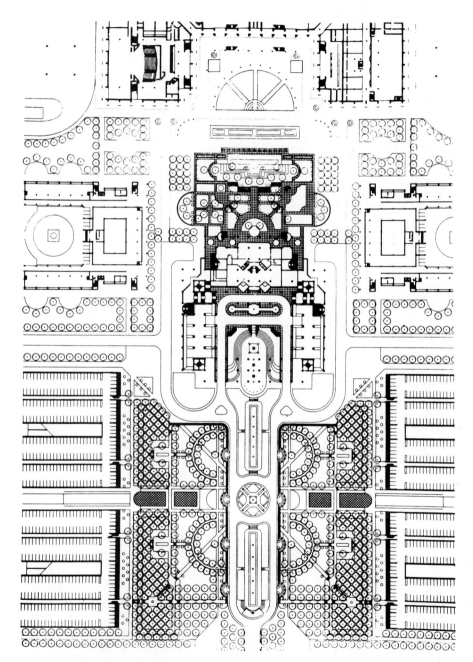

Figure 5.5 Drawing by Ian Whitefield of Scott Brownrigg and Turner, Architects, the first computer drawing to be accepted by the Royal Academy, London, for the prestigious Summer Exhibition of 1982. Note the structure of the drawing—and how it was created by the reflection, rotation, and repetition of objects. *(Drawn using GDS by Applied Research of Cambridge, a McDonnell Douglas company.)*

Figure 5.6 The Queen Victoria Markets, Sydney, designed by George McRae in 1893. Symmetry and the repetition of bays ease the definition of a complex building facade. *(Drawn on Calcomp System 25 by Peter Calf at Datamatic, Sydney, using data provided by Ipoh Garden Berhard.)*

originals. We might even have a set of two or more alternative images that are automatically substituted when the drawing is reproduced at different scales: an outline of the object for small-scale drawings, and a more detailed version for large scales. We can also place parts of drawings on different *layers,* which are analogous to different layers of drafting film and can be combined or separated at will, so that if the electrical fixtures are placed on one layer and the plumbing on another, we can produce drawings with one, both, or neither of these services shown.

The most obvious advantages of drawing by computer are *quality* (the drawing quality can be superb), *consistency* (all drawings are produced in the same way from the same set of building component descriptions), *speed* (once defined, an A1 drawing can be produced in about 45 minutes on a pen plotter and in less than a minute by an electrostatic printer), and the *ease of modification* by which drawings can be updated and revised. For a particular component, it is generally possible to modify a single instance or all instances on the drawing or on all drawings of a project. Dimensioning may be automatic, requiring only the specification of the endpoints of the dimension required. Sheet outlines and title boxes are stored in the machine's memory, and drawing sheets are built up by locating individual drawings within this outline on the screen. Users of drafting systems also have to be aware of the very different management processes required when working with electronic rather than physical drawings: the lack of any concept of an "original" drawing, the proliferation of different versions that can easily arise, the need to keep track of and index large quantities of retrievable graphic information, and the need to make backup copies regularly on tape or disk to avoid disaster if serious problems arise.

All this graphic information is stored in the drafting system database and recorded as a file in the computer's internal memory or on disk or tape. The precise way in which it is stored varies from system to system, but architects and others want to exchange drawings in electronic form. The

Initial Graphics Exchange Specification (IGES) describes a neutral format for file structures, language, and the representation of geometric, topological, and attribute data. Different drafting system vendors then provide preprocessors and postprocessors for converting files between the IGES standard format and their own chosen format.

The big difference is between those drafting systems in which the drawings produced are essentially unrelated two-dimensional images (even if using the same component definitions) and those in which the drawings are all based on a single internal description (model) of the building. The drawings produced by both types may look the same, but only if an internal model exists will the system "know" that if the designer moves (for example) a window on the plan drawing, it is also to be moved on the elevation drawing.

5.3   Modeling in Three Dimensions

5.3.1   Cells, edges, surfaces, solids, and objects

When we turn from two to three dimensions, things get more complex, but the principles essentially remain the same. The advantages of modeling in three dimensions are not only the ability to generate three-dimensional (3-D) views but also the consistency and integrity that can be obtained when all the 2-D views (plans, elevations, and sections) are generated from the same computer model. A change in one view can then be propagated to all other views.

The simplest approach is to model space as cells (called voxels) in a 3-D matrix and a scene as the *set of cells* occupied by matter (sometimes called a spatial occupancy representation), but the computer memory required to store this representation makes it useless for space of any reasonable size or detail. A more practical option is to represent solids by the *set of edges* between their enclosing planes. We then need to know the endpoints of the edges, now coordinates in a 3-D coordinate system. But if all we know is the edges, we cannot distinguish between polygons representing enclosing surfaces and polygons representing open space; the 12 edges of a cube could represent a solid mass, a hollow rectangular section with four closed and two opposite open faces, a box with one open side, or a wire frame with no surfaces at all. The representation is ambiguous. This means that we can only generate *wire-frame* views, showing all the edges whether they would in fact be obscured or not, giving a futuristic impression of see-through architecture.

The minimum useful level, then, is to model a 3-D form as a *set of surfaces,* where each polygonal surface is recognized as an entity and has associated with it a set of bounding edges and attributes, such as color and

Figure 5.7   The Breuer chair, with and without arms, is drawn as a wire-frame perspective by the CAPITOL modeling system on a small Apple II microcomputer. Objects are built up by digitizing, by extrusion of 2-D shapes, and by combinations of a library of standard objects. *(Webster, 1984; reprinted by permission from the Proceedings of the CAD 84 Conference, published by Butterworths Scientific Ltd. and sponsored by the journal Computer-Aided Design.)*

texture (Figs. 5.7 to 5.9). If the model knows about surfaces, it is possible to calculate which surfaces and edge lines are hidden when the scene is viewed from a particular angle. The next level again is to model form as a *set of solids,* with the recognition of closed polyhedra bounded by polygonal faces. A solid model allows the calculation of the results of intersecting, of adding and subtracting solids, and perhaps of spatial clash checking (whether two or more objects occupy the same location in space: for example, whether a duct passes through a beam), an often-talked-about but little-implemented attraction of computer drafting and modeling.

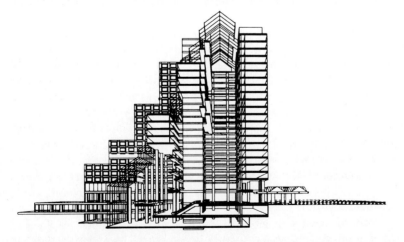

Figure 5.8   Sectional perspective through a building, with hidden lines not shown. *(Drawn on HOK Draw, courtesy of HOK Computer Service Corporation.)*

Figure 5.9   A surface model generated by a landform modeler is used to visualize a proposed reservoir. *(Ground modeling using SITE, visualization using SVS, both products of Applied Research of Cambridge, a McDonnell Douglas company.)*

Above all of these lies the description of a 3-D scene as a *set of objects,* each object being made up of some linked combination of other objects, solids, and/or surfaces. As with 2-D objects, we can associate the attributes of a "real" element with its modeled form. In addition to those suggested earlier (manufacturer, cost, and code number), an object called "window" might have associated with it physical characteristics like density, U-value, light, and sound transmission. These can be used via applications programs to calculate the environmental conditions associated with another object called "room." Indeed, the model can become as important for nongraphical as for graphical reasons (the use of models for design feedback is discussed in Chap. 6). With such *integrated building description systems,* as they are sometimes rather long-windedly called, we come to a computer replacement for manual drafting that can be linked to other design tools in a way for which there is no equivalent in manual drafting.

When we ask for a line drawing of a scene from a 3-D modeling system, the implementation sends us back down the track of these levels of models. The description of an object points to descriptions of its constituent solids, these point to the surfaces, and the surfaces point to their edges. Since we can only view a scene as a 2-D view, the edges are transformed into lines on a picture plane and the lines are decomposed into a string of points stored in a bit map and displayed on a raster screen. (With a vector screen we stop, as before, at the line endpoints.) Interestingly, when we view the screen we reverse the process: we interpret contiguous points as lines, closed polygons of lines as faces of solids, and assemblies of solids as representing real objects.

In three dimensions we can treat color and texture just as in two dimensions, simply as attributes of surfaces that remain the same no matter how a scene is viewed. But that is not how we see real buildings, and the resulting images appear flat and cartoonlike. Buildings exist in ever-changing natural environments causing light and shade, highlights, and spectral reflections. Technically all this can be simulated by computer to generate realistic photographlike images. As a first step, it is reasonably easy to model the diffuse shading of surfaces according to their angle to and distance from one or more light sources, and this shading helps define shapes (Figs. 5.10 and 5.11). It does not, however, give us cast shadows.

Calculating the shadows cast by one object on a variety of other objects is a complex task. The comprehensive approach is to trace the path of each ray of light that reaches the picture plane of the viewer's image back to the surface seen, and then through any reflection or refraction back to other surfaces (Fig. 5.12). At each intersection with a surface there is a test for shadows to determine whether that point is directly illuminated by a light source; this is done by checking whether the light source can be "seen" from the point or whether it is obscured by other objects. The final intensity and color of the pixel on the picture plane through which the ray is propagated is determined by calculating the contributions of each intersection point, using a model that simulates how light will be absorbed, transmitted, or reflected at that surface. All this takes a lot of computation, and ray tracing requires considerable computing power to do in reasonable time.

5.3.2 System operation

The operation of a 3-D modeling system uses the same equipment and is conceptually similar to that of a 2-D system, except that we are now building up an assembly of solids and surfaces instead of lines and planes. The problem is how to describe these solids and surfaces. The general approach is to use a combination of swept volumes, the assembly of primitives, and the explicit definition of vertices as coordinates.

A *swept volume* is a 3-D volume created by the rotation or translation of a 2-D surface. If we have a coordinate system in which x and y coordinates define a point in horizontal space and a z coordinate defines it in vertical space, a rectangle in horizontal space will be described in the system's database by the four pairs (x, y) of coordinates of its vertices. For a 2-D drawing (a plan), that is all we need. If we then specify a vertical elevation for the plane on which the rectangle lies, the pairs (x, y) become triples (x, y, z), where the z coordinate identifies the elevation. Translating this plane to a new elevation defines a parallelopiped (a rectangular prism with parallel sides) with its base at the original level and its top at the new level, fixing a volume in space. Using translation, we can generate any solid of constant cross section (the same as if we extruded a material through a cutting mold). We could, for example, extrude a wall described in plan between a floor plane and a ceiling plane to describe it in three dimensions. Rotation gives us a means of generating solids of constant distance from one axis

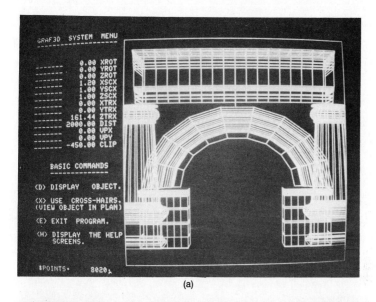

(a)

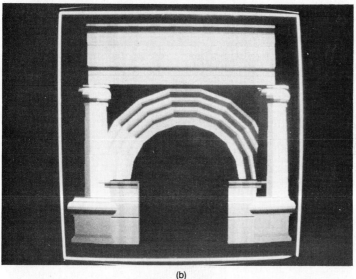

(b)

Figure 5.10 *(a)* An edge "wire frame" drawing and *(b)* a surface "hidden surface" drawing of a group of building elements are displayed on a computer screen. The surface drawing is generated by ordering the surfaces from farthest to closest to the observer. Each surface is then "painted" in order on the screen, so that front surfaces are painted last and overpaint those behind, with diffuse shading on the surfaces according to their angle and distance from the light source. *(Drawn by Jerome Chen using Graf3D at the Graduate School of Architecture and Urban Planning, University of California, Los Angeles.)*

Figure 5.11   Textures are attached as attributes and mapped onto the surfaces of rectangular blocks; these could also be colored. Any two textures can be combined to derive a third, giving a rich palette with which to work. The textures are generated procedurally, not as stored images taken from photographs. The wood grain, for example, is first generated as concentric ellipses, which are then "disturbed" by moving points on the ellipse by random negative or positive increments within a small specified range. These patterns are simply superimposed images; to get realistic results, both the geometry of the texture (its bumps and hollows) and its spectral properties (the differential absorption of different wavelengths of light) must also be modeled. *(Drawn by TEKTON at Ohio State University; Yessios, 1982; reprinted by permission from the Proceedings of the CAD 82 Conference, published by Butterworth and Co. Ltd. and sponsored by the journal Computer-Aided Design.)*

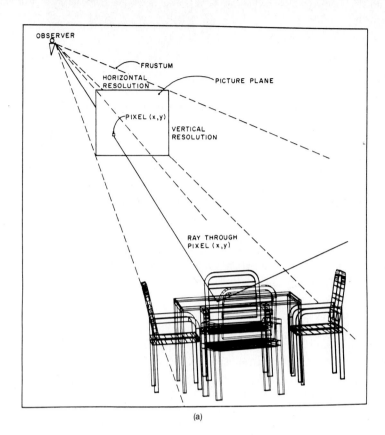

(a)

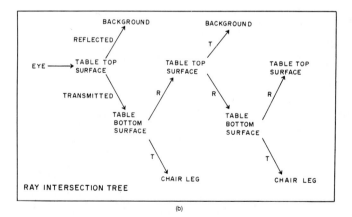

(b)

Figure 5.12 "Ray tracing" in the realistic rendering of a scene involves tracing *(a)* the ray of light reaching the observer through each pixel of the picture plane back through *(b)* a ray intersection tree. Properties associated with each surface describe its reflectance, transmittance, and color. The final color and brightness of the pixel depend on the contribution of each path through this tree. *(Greenberg, 1984; reprinted from Architectural Record, Sept. 1984, copyright 1984 by McGraw-Hill, with all rights reserved.)*

(the same as a material worked on a lathe). For example, a line perpendicular to an axis can be rotated to become a disk, a circle becomes a sphere, and a rectangle becomes a cylinder. In practice, many of these and other basic volumes (sometimes called *primitives*) may be preprogrammed in the system as parametric objects, which we can then use by providing values for the parameters (origin, height, width, etc.) for the situation.

What can be done with the solids so created depends on the degree of modeling supported by the system (Fig. 5.13). Many systems can rotate and reposition solids in space. A true solid-modeling system affords a full range of what are known as boolean operations: the intersection, subtraction, and addition of volumes to make more complex wholes. To describe the form of a simple house, we could describe the gable end, extrude it to make a solid lump of house, intersect this lump with a vertical rectangular prism to provide a chimney, and then subtract volumes equivalent to the internal rooms and to the door and window openings. It is not a way that architects are used to working, but it opens interesting possibilities in the perception of architecture as the designing of solid and void spaces.

If we cannot describe all of a 3-D object by the conjunction of volumes generated by swept volumes or preprogrammed primitives, we are left with its direct definition by the coordinates of its vertices in space. To create the sloping plane of one side of a hipped roof, for example, we should define the vertices (as numerical coordinates, by pointing to their position in both plan and sectional drawings or by using a 3-D equivalent of a digitizing pen that measures position in vertical as well as horizontal space), draw edges between the vertices, and then define the closed polygon as a surface.

5.3.3 Modeling approximations

The information required to describe an object fully in three dimensions is vastly more than the information required for two dimensions: it is comparable to the difference in effort between drawing a plan and constructing a complete physical model of a house. Because of this, most computer modeling systems use representations which are geometrically incomplete and which approximate the 3-D description only to a degree adequate for their intended function. Many modeling systems are oriented toward mechanical engineering, in which the typical design problem is to create a single component to be machined from a solid piece of metal. The boolean operations of a solid modeler enable them to cope with such features as drilled holes and the complex intersection of different volumes. However, the intended purpose for building is rather different from that for most other applications. The typical architectural design problem is concerned with the assembly, rather than the creation, of a very large number of different

elements. The one simplifying characteristic of buildings is that they tend
to consist of planar surfaces which are either vertical or horizontal and
which are organized in layers corresponding to building floors.

Being designed by clever people, commercial modeling systems intended
specifically for architects make use of these characteristics to simplify the
modeling problem. Some of them model the physical building as a set of
paralellopipeds whose faces are each perpendicular to at least one axis.
Some handle only a limited number of components, restricting their ability
to model complex buildings. A few support only one particular method or
style of construction. So most building modeling systems are not capable of
true, full, 3-D modeling but something less, often figuratively called 2.5-D

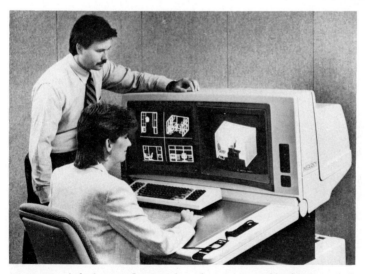

Figure 5.13   A dual-screen Intergraph workstation is used by Steelcase in the
construction of a surface model of an office workstation using elements from a
database of its own furniture products. The draftsperson-designer can work
concurrently in plan, section, and perspective, all shown in different windows of
the quartered left-hand screen. Locating an element in plan and section fixes it
in three dimensions. Steelcase, which is the world's largest designer and manufacturer of office furniture and systems, has developed a range of computer
drafting and design tools to complement its products. *(Courtesy of Steelcase.)*

modeling to indicate some intermediate step between two and three dimensions. This is not necessarily a disadvantage, since by not using a true 3-D representation we bypass much of the tedium and difficulty of describing objects in three dimensions. Typically, linear elements such as walls are defined in plan with either a specified constant height (a swept volume) or a "gap filling" property where they are assumed to extend from soffit to ceiling, whether flat or sloping. Smaller components are described in plan and four other orthogonal elevations or sections as required. This is sometimes called *box geometry* since a component such as a washbasin is described by the images it projects on an enclosing box (Fig. 5.14). This is fine if we draw all our building views and sections on the perpendicular axes, but if we try to draw a diagonal section we get a wrong image (usually a foreshortened version of the orthogonal projection), and we may also have problems with components that have a variable cross section along their lengths. The system designer has to compromise between simplicity and universality.

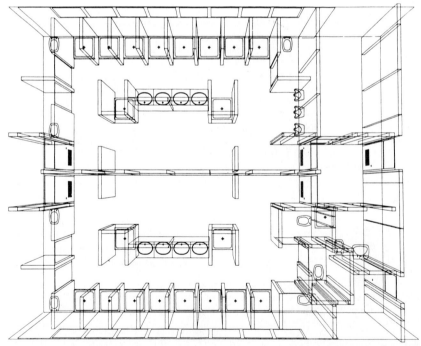

Figure 5.14   Box geometry is an approximation of 3-D representations by placing 2-D plans and elevations on the faces of 3-D boxes that envelope the object being depicted. In this view, the shower and washbasins are shown in plan but are depicted at the right level as images on an enveloping box. The definition of the walls as a series of boxes is also apparent. *(Drawn on the BDS system of Applied Research of Cambridge, a McDonnell Douglas company.)*

5.4   Human-Computer Communication

As a human designer or draftsperson, we have a mental picture of what we want to draw or model; we may already have hand-drawn sketches. As a drafting system, the computer program has a data structure ready to accept and store that picture and to make it available in graphic form as plans, sections, and perspectives. What is left is the problem of human-computer communication: how to get the description of the building or other object from brain to computer memory.

To use any tool efficiently, we need a clear conceptual model of how it works. We have such a conceptual model of what to expect from a pen and T square. Faced with a computer drafting system, we have to construct such a model anew. Since this drafting system is more powerful than a pen and T square, it requires a more sophisticated conceptual model, but it should retain many of the same characteristics: *consistency* (the same actions always produce the same results), *universality* (any action can be taken at any time), and *simplicity* (the minimum and most obvious action will produce the desired effect).

Almost all systems are driven by a *command language,* whereby the command elements are entered at a keyboard or selected from a *tablet or screen menu.* For keyboard control, we remember and type; to use the system, we have to know the language and its syntax. For menu control, we look and point; to use the system, we have to be able to find the command on the menu and have to know the syntax of how parts of a command go together. The menu command may be displayed as a word or as a picture representing the action (Figs. 5.15 and 5.16). There may also be a hierarchy of submenus; it is rarely possible to fit all the commands onto a screen at one time, so the screen menus are generally hierarchical, with commands on a main menu causing submenus to appear for drawing, editing, dimensioning, and other tasks. These either replace the main menu or, with a bit-mapped display, temporarily "pop up" or "pull down" over areas of the screen. Where a system offers a choice of menu and typed commands, we find that beginners use the menu (the visual clues act as a prompt in remembering what to do), while experts use the keyboard (the hands stay in one place and the process is faster). Many actions require a combination of menu, keyboard, and pointer. Simply to draw a line of a fixed length and angle, we might have to point to the LINE command on the menu (or type "line" on the keyboard), point to a starting position with a cursor on the screen, and type in a numeric length and angle.

A drawing, then, is typically constructed by a sequence of individual commands, plus the positional and numeric data with which they operate. Returning to the notions of algorithms and computer languages introduced in Chap. 3, a series of these commands can be regarded as instructions in a high-level computer language. Starting from a blank sheet of paper, the series that positions and draws a stairway is an algorithm for drawing that

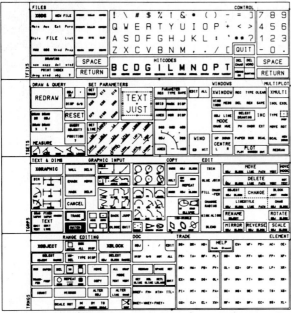

Figure 5.15 A tablet menu to be overlaid on a digitizing tablet. Pointing with the digitizing pen to an item on the menu causes the command to be carried out. As well as the letters and numbers that we would find on a keyboard (top right), the menu contains commands for manipulating files and driving the drafting system. Some of the commands are shown pictorially rather than by words. Note the extent of the menu concerned with copying and editing, actions for which there are no easy manual equivalents. This is menu number 5; the same architects use other menus for choosing from different selections of objects or for other specific purposes that need different commands. *(Mitchell Walker Wright, Architects; used by permission.)*

stairway. Many systems allow such sequences to be grouped and stored in what is known as a *macro language* so that the whole sequence will be executed by just one command to start the macro (Fig. 5.17). Moreover, the macro language typically allows variables and expressions, as well as numbers, to be used in the data with which commands operate, so that the result is tailored to a specific situation. A DRAW STAIRWAY command might ask for the width and number of steps in the stairway and then use the values that one keys in as the values for the variables in the individual DRAW commands in order to generate the stairway image. A good macro language is important. It allows a drafting system to be tailored for a particular task or office and is the beginning of the incorporation of knowledge (in this example, the knowledge about how to draw a stairway) into the system itself instead of coming each time from the system user.

As we issue these commands, the drawing is displayed on the computer screen. To continue, we need feedback on the results of our actions; imagine trying to draw blindfolded. We need not only good human-computer communications but also good computer-human communications.

Much depends on the characteristics of the equipment we are using. A high-resolution screen gives a clearer picture than does one of lower resolution. And color, quite apart from its use in the colored rendering of the images themselves, allows us to differentiate between drawing elements and to separate, say, construction lines from element lines. Interestingly, when microcomputer drafting systems offer users a choice between a black-and-white display and a lower-resolution color display, most users

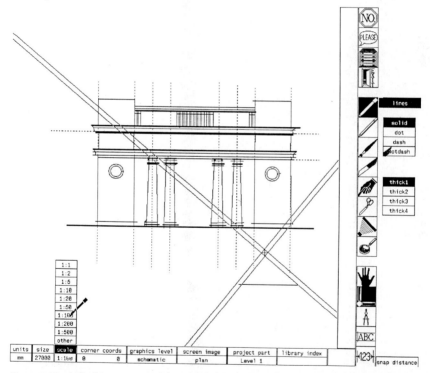

Figure 5.16   A drafting system with an icon-driven interface. The tools in the menu at the right-hand side are used to carry out tasks analogous to, but more powerful than, their manual drafting equivalents. Thus, for example, the pen will draw not only lines (in varying styles and thicknesses) but whole objects. Among other icons, the paintbrush is used for filling areas with texture, the scissors for cut and paste, the copier for copying (multiplying) objects, and the magnifying glass for zooming and panning. Combinations of icons have meaning; here, the pen (in reverse image) and the T square are used together so that the pen is constrained by a clamped T-square template to draw at a particular angle. Pointing the pen (or another tool) at boxes in the bottom menu causes further pop-up submenus to appear. *(ICADS prototype drafting system, University of Sydney; Cornell, Sambura, and Gero, 1984).*

```
#### STD/WALL1.CMD
#### WALL CREATION COMMAND FILE
ECHO OFF
SWITCH OFF
RUBOUT ON
IFERROR
!Wall creation
!
SUP M
ASK 'Wall width (default,',V81,')':V81
DO STD/WALL3S
IF V90>0:GOTO 2
TELL S35
GOTO 0
        LABEL 2
ASK 'Wall height (default ',V82,')':V82
DO STD/WALL4S
IF V90>0:GOTO 4
TELL S35
GOTO 2
        LABEL 4
ASK 'Hatch type (default ',V83,')':V83
IF V83<1 : !Must be greater than 0!;BELL;GOTO 4
DO STD/WALL1S
DO STD/WALL2S
LET S35=<V83>
LET S28= W ^26 ^27 ^35
SUP
IFERROR
LET S29=STD/^28
GET ^29
IFOK GOTO 16
IFERROR
LET S29=S28
GET ^28
IFOK GOTO 16
DO STD/WALL5S
UNS
GOTO 1
        LABEL 16
UNS
KIL
        LABEL 1
LET S2=P11
POINT 11
!Vector to start of wall
?(Hit RETURN for current control,
  E if you have finished) :S2
IF S2='QJ' : S2='Q'
IF S2=Q:GOTO 20
```

Figure 5.17 A command file consists of a sequence of drafting system commands that can be stored away, recalled later, and processed. In this file for wall creation, variables are used for the wall width, height, and desired hatching pattern. A command file will set up parameterized components, whereby an image will be generated to suit the particular situation after questions have been answered about parameters such as size and location. Command files can also be written to carry out engineering, evaluation, and costing calculations. *(ACROPOLIS, BDP Computing Services, United Kingdom; used by permission.)*

choose color because of the additional level of information it allows. The ideal, of course, is a combination of both high resolution and color.

As a drafting medium, the computer is much richer and more versatile than our traditional media. The problem has been in making this richness and versatility available without letting the difficulty of using the medium intrude too much on attention that should be focused on what is being drawn. In Secs. A5.1 and A5.2 we describe in more detail the process of creating a set of drawings with a computer drafting and modeling system.

5.5 Summary

In this chapter we have described drawings as models of the objects they depict, described approaches to building these models in computers, and explained the limitations that the form of the model imposes on what can be done with it.

In two dimensions we can work with points, lines, or objects. In three dimensions we can work with cells, edges, surfaces, volumes, or objects. A useful technical drawing system recognizes objects and allows their manipulation as entities. At the risk of gross oversimplification, the technique of computer drafting is something like overlay drafting with an infinite selection of transfer symbols, all done electronically instead of by playing around with scissors and physical sheets of drawing film and transfers. The big difference is between systems in which the drawings produced are essentially unrelated and those in which the drawings are all drawn from a single coherent model of the building. The invention of the typewriter did not make handwriting obsolete, but handwriting is no longer used for technical reports and documentation. The invention of computer drafting systems will not make hand drawing obsolete, but hand drawing will cease to be used for technical work and documentation.

SECONDARY TEXT
A Drafting/Modeling Example

A5.1 Drawing with a Computer

Let's take a closer look at a "typical" (if there is such a thing) computer drafting system in an architect's office and look at the kinds of operations that go into creating a drawing by computer. Our aim here is not to describe any real drafting system but to give an impression of the use of computer drafting and to describe some of the features that can be expected. A word of warning, though: Because this is a simplified description, it all seems easier than it does in practice, and a single operation mentioned here might in reality take a sequence of actions to achieve. Remember that a plotted drawing produced via a cheap drafting system on a cheap microcomputer can be indistinguishable from the same image produced via a million dollars worth of hardware and software. The differences lie in the systems' power, flexibility, and ease of use.

If this is a single-screen workstation, then the screen area will probably be divided by the system software into a drawing area, a smaller menu area used for displaying verbal or graphic menus, and room at the foot of the screen for a few lines of alphanumeric text that show the system's dialogue with its user.

If it is a two-screen system, all the alphanumerics may be on the subsidiary screen, leaving the graphics display with a larger drawing area. If it has a bit-mapped display, a mouse, and an icon-driven interface, then part of the screen will house the icons and main menu, and subsidiary menus will appear in windows when they are triggered. Otherwise, the system will probably employ either a screen menu, a tablet menu (a printed overlay to the tablet, with the overlay registered in position so that pointing to a box on the menu indicates a certain instruction), a language of commands to be entered at the keyboard, or a combination of these.

A5.1.1 Starting a drawing

Typically, we sit down in front of the workstation and, using the keyboard, get access to the drafting system by entering some cryptic commands. Let us assume that we want to create a new drawing of a floor plan for a pavilion café. The drafting system will ask us to identify the job and will ask whether this is a new drawing or an old one that we wish to modify. We type in a job number and specify that this is a new drawing.

We will probably also need to specify either a scale at which we will draw (which determines the size of a building or detail that will fit on the screen) or the size that the drawing area of the screen is to represent (which determines the scale). Most drafting systems store a drawing in memory at actual full-size dimensions and then scale these to fit any screen or plotted image, so the scale at which we choose to draw is not of great import. We can change it later.

Finally, before we start drawing, we should think about which *layer* of the drawing we want to be working with; we will set our layer to "BUILD-ING" or some such name. Most drafting systems have explicit *layering mechanisms,* whereby different parts of drawings are overlayed as if we were drafting on film and using the overlay system of manual drafting. The layer on which we are working is called the *active layer;* the others, which we can see but not alter (equivalent to all but the top layer of film in overlay drafting), are called the *echoed layers.* Anything drawn goes onto the active layer; other layers cannot be amended unless they are first made active. In our drawing we shall use different layers for the building, the furniture, and the landscaping.

We also have a choice of drawing in free space or on a rectilinear grid. With a grid, all lines and linear elements are assumed to lie on the grid (Fig. A5.1), easing the definition process.

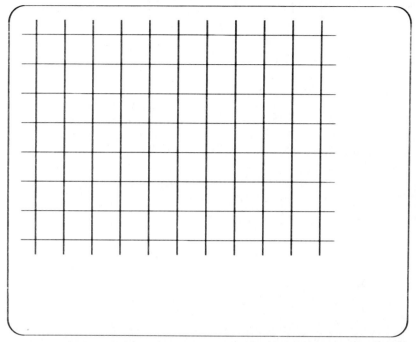

Figure A5.1   A grid is displayed on the computer screen of a single-screen graphics workstation after a user enters the drafting system, issues commands for setting up a new drawing, and specifies a grid interval. The grid interval and all drawing dimensions are specified as real full-scale dimensions; the system will scale the image to fit on the screen. Here, the area to the right of the grid is reserved for the display of screen menus and the area below for displaying a few lines of the dialogue (questions and commands) between the draftsperson and the drafting system. *[This and the following "screen images" (Figs. A5.2 to A5.19) were drawn by Roy Hill of CADCOM, Sydney, using its Eagle drafting/modeling system running on a Sun supermicrocomputer.]*

A5.1.2   Locating objects and lines

Our pavilion is modular, with the external wall set beside grid lines; thus, drawing it is fairly easy if we use a grid. We specify a horizontal and vertical grid interval and cause it to be drawn on the screen. We also instruct the system to interpret any point we indicate in space as a point referring to the nearest grid intersection, a function known as grid snap or grid lock. Now we are ready to draw a wall.

If the drafting system lets us use predefined *linear elements,* we can draw walls and floors as entities (for example, two leaves of brickwork and a cavity complete with cross-hatching) in one operation rather than building them up from lines. We shall assume that our system allows for such elements and that we have a library (produced earlier by the office or purchased with the system) of different wall types. We might have to work with code names or numbers (usually compressed into small numbers of characters, so that we are faced with a choice between names like "brkcav270," "brklf110," "block280," and "blockvav"), or we might have a system that displays images of the wall types in the menu area (Fig. A5.2), permitting us to select the appropriate construction by sight. To choose one, we issue some kind of DRAW WALL command and indicate our selection by typing its name in response to a system prompt or by pointing to a screen or digitizer menu.

Now we can actually place the wall in space. To place it on plan, we move the screen pointer (by light pen, keys, stylus, or mouse) until it is close to a grid intersection where we want a wall to start, then issue a START POINT command (by key, button, or pressing down a light pen or stylus). The grid lock we turned on means that we do not need to be too accurate in hitting this intersection, since the system assumes that we want this point. We do the same where we want the wall to end, and, with a bit of luck, there it is on the screen extending between the two points and lying on the grid line (Fig. A5.3). To draw another wall, we repeat the operation (Fig.

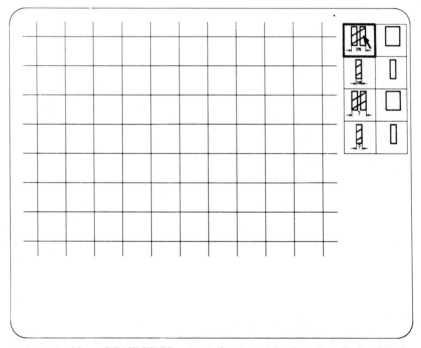

Figure A5.2 After a DRAW WALL command, a menu of wall types is displayed in the menu area. Here it is a pictorial menu, showing images of the plan view of the wall rather than verbal descriptions. A wall type is selected by pointing to it with a mouse or other pointing device, whereupon it becomes highlighted or (in this case) surrounded by a heavier box to provide the draftsperson with feedback that the element has been chosen. The "?" in the dimensions of the lower two walls of the menu shows that these are parametric objects; they will be assigned a thickness in response to a question of the system user and will be drawn with that thickness.

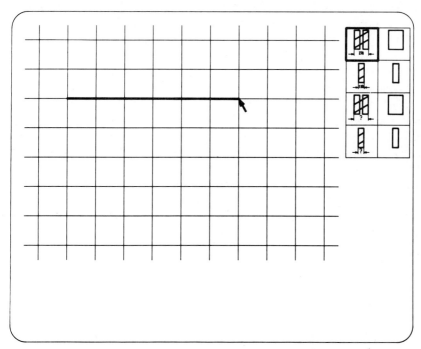

Figure A5.3   A wall is drawn by indicating its beginning point and endpoint, here by pointing to the grid intersections at which the wall is to start and finish. If the drawing is "locked" to the grid, these points will snap to the nearest intersection. Often, as here, the wall is indicated first by a single line, either its centerline or (because it is more useful when working with brick-size increments) its inner or outer edge.

A5.4). At an angle in the wall, a good drafting system will automatically sort out the junction of linear elements; thus, for example, internal and external leaves of brickwork will meet but not overlap. To simplify this process, many systems will show the wall first as an edge or centerline and not draw the full section until we issue a WALL END instruction (Fig. A5.5).

Generally, two other ways of drawing are available to us. If we turn off the grid lock, the system will not connect our line ends to the nearest grid intersection and we can draw anywhere we like on the screen. If we don't use a pointer to define line ends, but use the keyboard instead, we can make the lines we draw of fixed length and angle by using a standard syntax of commands. At its simplest, these will simply state that the line is to be drawn to a point in space defined by x and y coordinates, either relative to a global "0,0" point on the drawing or relative to the last point drawn. But most drawing systems accept that new lines on a drawing are usually positioned in relation to existing lines and make it as easy as possible to do so. Some systems use a set of *modifiers* to describe these relationships;

thus, to draw a line parallel to a specified line and n units away, we would use an instruction something like

INS LIN PRL n: $D1$ $D2$ $D3$ $D4$

where INS, LIN, and PRL are commands that are either typed or identified on a menu, n is a number in the units of the drawing, and $D1$, $D2$, $D3$, and $D4$ are points on the drawing identified by the digitizer pen. The first ($D1$) marks the line to which the new line is parallel, the second ($D2$) marks the side on which the new line will be drawn, and the third and fourth ($D3$ and $D4$) mark the extent of the new line. Other syntaxes allow new lines to be drawn exactly perpendicular to or at a specified angle to existing lines or at a tangent to an arc or circle. Other systems employ *hit codes* to affix a digitized point to some existing graphic element; thus, the indicated point may be affixed to the nearest grid intersection or line, the midpoint of the nearest line, the intersection of two lines, etc. With a mouse and icon-driven interface, we might use different buttons on the mouse to specify

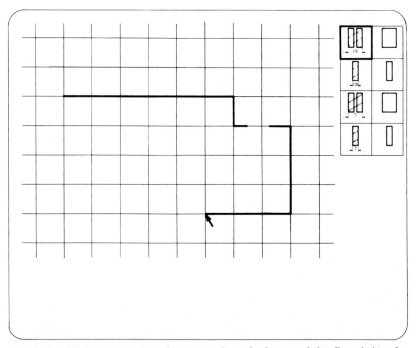

Figure A5.4 Each line is assumed to start where the last one left off, so it is only necessary to provide a series of endpoints unless the wall is specifically stopped and started again to leave a space for a door or window. Drawing on the grid ensures that all lines are orthogonal. A door opening has been left by specifying a length for two wall segments rather than by snapping to grid intersections.

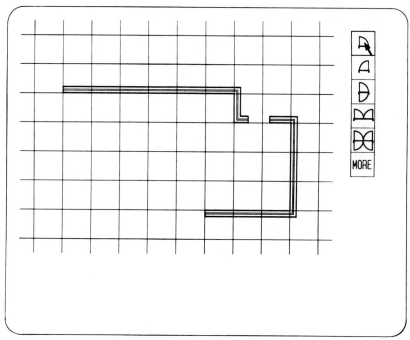

Figure A5.5   After an END WALL command, the single-line model is replaced by the full-wall image, scaled to fit with the grid. The line thicknesses have been set up as attributes in the wall description. To place a door in the wall opening, the user issues commands that cause a menu of available doors to be displayed. A door type is picked in the same way as a wall type.

some of these relationships. Most systems also have special means for constructing circles, arcs, rectangles, and triangles from the minimum number of specified parameters.

Our plan is progressing nicely, but we could do with a door to fill the gap in the wall. Images of such things may well be available as elements or macros already defined in the system database, and we find them either by consulting a printed catalog of drawings and code numbers or by interactively exploring a library of available images on the screen. Once a macro is chosen, we still have to position it on the drawing. The usual method of doing this is by *anchor points,* by which we "anchor" the image in the right location (Fig. A5.6). We pick a point on the drawing in the same way as we pick a point to start a line or linear element. One point on the component image (usually the geometric center or the lower-left-hand corner) is defined as the point that will actually be mapped onto this indicated position on the drawing. All other lines and points will be located relative to this anchor point; to fix their position, we also have to specify an angle to the horizontal at which the image is to be set. Some systems also ask for a scaling factor, allowing the component to be used not only at its originally specified size but also at larger or smaller sizes. This scaling factor has nothing to do with the drawing scale, since both the building walls (to quote our example) and the component will be stored with full-size dimensions in the computer database. What it does is specify that this particular instance of the object is going to be at a different size from the original.

All this can also be done implicitly by using three anchor points instead of one. On the component image, then, are three small crosses labeled 1, 2, and 3. Using a pointer, we identify three corresponding points on our drawing. The component image appears on our drawing so that anchor point 1 is located at the first of these points, 2 at the second, and 3 at the third. Using three points enables us to specify transformations (stretch, rotation, location) implicitly by the position of the anchors we define — a very simple procedure, but in practice difficult to execute precisely. Instead, most systems opt for numeric values for size and angle.

If we keep on specifying new anchor points, we can keep repeating the same element with the same or different dimensions and orientation. On our drawing of the pavilion café, we use the same procedure for windows,

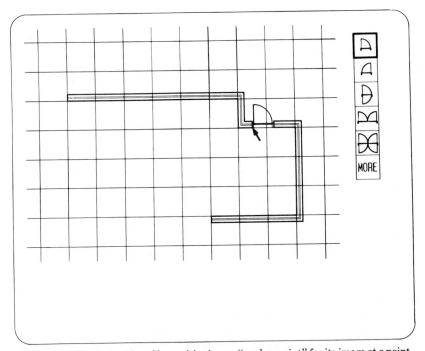

Figure A5.6   The door is placed by positioning an "anchor point" for its image at a point on the drawing and, if necessary, rotating or reflecting the image to suit the situation. Drafting systems recognize that objects are placed in relation to other objects already on the drawing and make it possible to snap to line intersections, ends, midpoints, and other key locations as well as grid intersections. The ease with which this positioning can be done is very important in the overall ease of using a system.

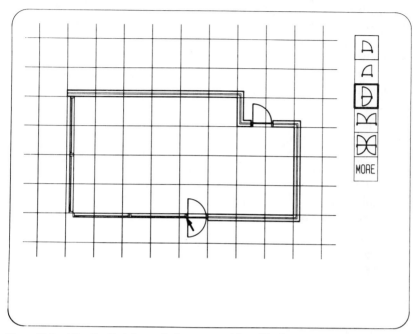

Figure A5.7 After the first door, windows are positioned in the same way (some of these have been rotated), and the door menu is redisplayed to locate a second type of door. Each use of an object is known as an instance of its use; here, there are four instances of a window type and one instance each of two types of doors.

for another door, and for any other components we wish to go on the "Building" layer of the drawing (Fig. A5.7). If they are all predefined in the system's library of elements, this process of location is very fast indeed. Otherwise, we need to create new elements either from scratch or by the combination of previously defined elements; we give these a name and type and store them away for future use. Most systems come with a set of predefined elements supposedly suitable for architectural drawings, although the supplier's conception of a suitable set of elements may differ from our own.

Since the process of creating drawn elements can be time-consuming, we might best repeat certain elements. To draw a particular chair really nicely (with accurate curves and a variety of line styles) could take an hour or more, particularly if we want to draw a set of elevations as well as a plan. If this chair represents a real, purchasable piece of furniture, it is clearly easier to keep using the same one than to repeat the drawing process. Maybe this repetition will follow through to the contract, and offices will standardize on a small range of carefully chosen chairs.

Now we shall add some furniture, but in this case we want to be able to draw our building sometimes with and sometimes without furniture, so we need to keep it separate; we therefore change layers. Using a library of

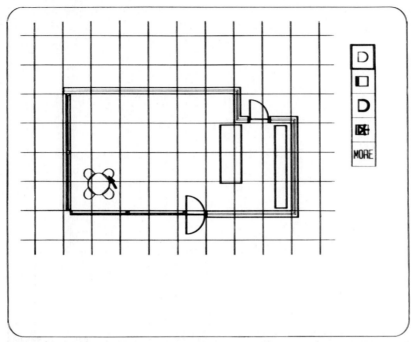

Figure A5.8 A counter and shelf are added by using parametric rectangles as objects and providing values for lengths and widths; then a table and four chairs are positioned by using another menu. This furniture might represent particular real items, and the images and associated descriptions might be provided by the product manufacturer. Some systems set up a spatial or angular matrix for the repetition of an object; thus, here it would be possible to set up a 90-degree angular grid, position one chair, repeat it 3 times, and then rotate the whole by 45 degrees.

predefined furniture elements, we lay out items of furniture in much the same way as we have already laid out doors and windows. We place a table on the plan, then put a chair 4 times around it (Fig. A5.8). We want to repeat this group of table with chairs, but rather than placing another table individually, we can define the first group as an assembly and simply repeat the whole entity. We could have picked each member of the group individually, but most systems allow us to delineate a box (often called a *fence*) around the table-and-chair group by pointing to its two opposite corners; using anchor points, we then repeat the whole group. Perhaps we like the result so much that we decide to repeat the pattern of tables and chairs again; using the same procedure, we put a fence around both tables and their chairs and copy them elsewhere on the drawing (Fig. A5.9).

A5.1.3 Editing a drawing

This is fine, but suppose one of the chairs is now obstructing the door and we wish to delete it. As with moving the table and chairs, our first task is to identify just what entities on the drawing we wish to act on. Again, we can point to each entity in turn (since the chair is a single object, we only need to point once) (Fig. A5.10) or delineate an area to be deleted by a fence (all lines or objects lying entirely within the fence will be removed). Most systems will give us visual confirmation of the items we have picked by highlighting them or redrawing them on the screen in a different line style or color. If we have failed to identify the right entities, we can cancel the operation and start again. Many systems also include some kind of UNDO command that reverses the last operation, so that if we delete more than we expected, we can always get the lost items back.

What happens if we want to change one of these now numerous chairs? Generally, drafting systems let us modify a single instance of a chair or other element simply by erasing or changing the lines by which it is drawn, but this does rather confuse the system. If we add arms to a chair on the plan, are they part of the chair or not? What happens to those arms if we later change all the chairs to a different type? It is disconcerting to find the disembodied arms left hanging in space after the chair has been deleted. To be safe and consistent, the better way of modifying the chair is to create a new element, an armchair, and use that on the drawing (Fig. A5.11). Some drafting systems are cleverer, but this is an example of the kinds of prob-

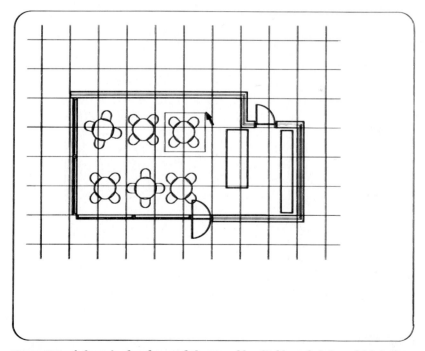

Figure A5.9   A fence is placed around the assembly of table and chairs, which is then copied 5 times, sometimes rotating the image again to vary the chair positions. There are now 6 instances of a table and 24 of a chair, although only one of each was defined in the database of objects.

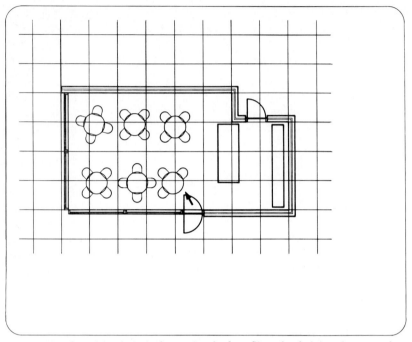

Figure A5.10   One of the chairs is obstructing the door. Since the chair is an instance of an object and therefore an entity in itself, it can be removed by issuing a DELETE command and simply pointing to it. Most systems give visual feedback on the items that have been picked by highlighting them or redrawing them in a different color, then asking for confirmation of the command.

lems that drafting system designers have to sort out. We can probably classify it "on the fly" as a new element, give it a code name, and then change all the desired instances of the old type to the new type.

Deleting, changing, and moving objects around a drawing are common actions with drawing systems; the ability to modify a drawing easily is one of the major reasons for using them. The object is identified by pointing in its vicinity with the cursor. We can tell which one is meant just by looking at the screen, but the drafting system cannot do this; instead, it must conduct a *search* of its database to find which element is nearest the digitized location. If the database contained 1000 objects (a respectably large number for a drawing system) then all 1000 would need to be examined. Now, searching happens to be a very time-consuming process, even for a computer, and one of the tasks facing programmers is to make such searches as efficient as possible (the secondary text to Chap. 3 discussed the database concerns of programmers). After all, if we want to change a chair, we expect a quick response. A wait of more than 2 seconds for such an action would be annoying, and half a second would be more agreeable.

There are several methods to reduce this search time, varying in complexity. All involve adding a bit more information to the database, but not much more. The obvious way to accomplish our aim of making the search as quick as possible is to use some devious and extremely quick method of conducting the search itself. A more subtle approach is to reduce the number of elements searched. This can be done by maintaining within the computer a list of the macros currently displayed. An operator cannot point to a macro that isn't on the screen, so as long as the system keeps track of visible macros, it can reduce the number of those searched from a thousand to perhaps a couple of dozen. But there is still the task of identifying which of these macros is the chosen one. Since a macro is only a collection of points and lines (and maybe some other appendages), each line of each macro must be examined in turn to determine which is closest to the digitized location. A macro may contain a few dozen lines, so once again we have a searching problem. One technique for speeding this search up is by storing information on each macro's bounding rectangle. A *bounding rectangle* is the smallest imaginary rectangle that completely encloses a figure or macro, and it serves as a simplified approximation of the shape. The system can then make the assumption that the digitized location will

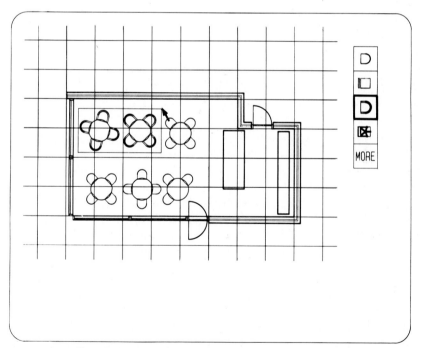

Figure A5.11 Changing some of these chairs to armchairs involves range editing: it is necessary to define the range (one instance, all instances, or a subset between the two) over which the change is to be made. Here it is done by drawing a fence around a part of the drawing, getting back the chair-type menu, and issuing a CHANGE command to change the chairs within the fence to the new model.

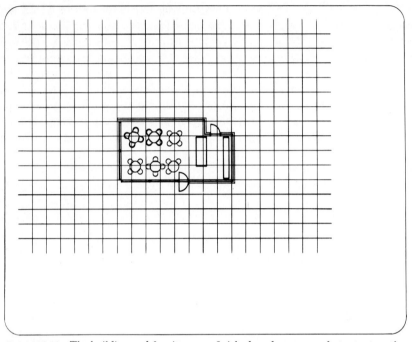

Figure A5.12   The building and furniture are finished, and we are ready to start on the landscape around the building. To show more of the surrounding area, the drawing is *zoomed* out so that it is shown on the screen at half the previous scale. Since all the dimensions are stored full-size in the system's database, the scale on the screen is only relevant to our convenience in drawing. We will probably place the furniture, building, and landscape on different layers so that they can be separated or combined as different images.

be within one of these bounding rectangles. A search then involves testing the location against each macro's bounding rectangle, a rapid process with little calculation. In many cases the location turns out to be within the bounding rectangle of only one macro, and the problem is solved. If not, we get back to searching all the lines within the macros concerned in order to determine which is the closest. A little bit of sophisticated database design has reduced the problem from a search of maybe 20,000 lines to, at best, no lines at all, and at worst perhaps 100 or so. Once again, good design pays, whether the object of the design is a building or a drafting database.

A5.1.4   Adding detail

Now we want to add some landscaping around the building, which means that we need to see a bigger area on the screen. This is easy; all reasonable systems have zooming and panning commands of some kind. *Zooming* changes the scale of the image on the screen (both up and down), while *panning* moves the image across the screen to reveal surrounding space. In Fig. A5.12 we zoom with a scale factor of 0.5, so that the area seen is doubled in width and height.

Next we define a new layer of the drawing; we don't want the landscape contractor to get the furniture layout mixed up with her landscape plan, so we keep them on separate layers. Then we add to the drawing some lines representing path edges and planting beds. We could choose from a set of available line styles (thin or thick, continuous or dashed) or accept the default style. *Default* is a computer jargon term meaning what you get if you don't specify anything else, and all drafting systems make extensive use of default options. It would be good to crosshatch the plant boxes; usually there is a *polygon-filling* capability whereby we can choose an infill pattern from a set of options ranging from solid black to hatching and to some more varied textures, then point with the cursor or digitizer to a polygon on the drawing that we want filled with the hatching or other pattern (Fig. A5.13). The pattern spreads out until it meets a boundary of a line on the same layer of the drawing or until it meets an explicitly delineated boundary that has been selected. We might also want to add some elements representing trees and bushes, in the same way as we have already placed elements of furniture and building components.

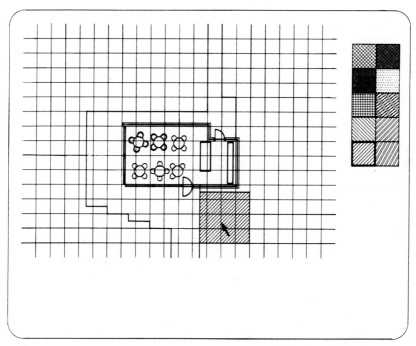

Figure A5.13   After drawing some lines to indicate the edges of paths and planting areas, we add some texture to the drawing. (These lines are in fact the first that we have actually drawn; everything else has been done by using predefined objects). The texture is selected from a menu and is placed either by indicating a single point, from which the texture will spread out to the nearest completely bounding set of lines (if it finds a gap, it "leaks" through to the next boundary), or by explicitly defining a boundary fence within which it is to apply.

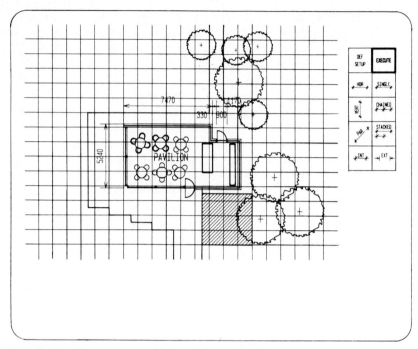

Figure A5.14 Some trees are added, and then some dimensions. There is only one tree image here; it is just used with differing scaling factors. The dimensions are calculated by the drafting system from the drawing database; all the draftsperson provides are the endpoints of dimension lines, the positions of those lines, and the type of dimensioning selected from a menu. Because the dimensions all come from the same database, they will be consistent. Usually they are placed on their own separate layer so that the drawing can be displayed with or without the dimensions. After the dimensioning, the plan drawing is complete.

A5.1.5 Dimensions and text

That completes the drawing, apart from *dimensions* and some text. Guided by the user, drafting systems will often calculate distances (which is easy, since the system stores the drawing's description at its full-size dimensions), provide projection lines where necessary, and print the dimension between those projection lines with arrows (Fig. A5.14). There will probably be some options on how dimensions are displayed (such as above, on, or below dimension lines) and on the size of text and numbers. For text, generally, we can choose a font or type style, a character height, width, and slant, and whether the type is to be centered or justified left or right. Usually it is sufficient to indicate where we want the annotation to appear and to type the actual text on the keyboard. Once the text and dimensions are on the drawing, it is possible to move or modify them or, of course, to remove them altogether.

A5.1.6 Assembling images on a drawing sheet

Now, or in a different session, we might also produce sections and elevations of our building, using the drafting system's capabilities in much the same way as for the plan. In a two-dimensional drafting system there is no automatic correlation between what is on the plan and what is on the elevations; the system doesn't know, or care, if we put the windows in a different place in plan and elevation. A three-dimensional modeling system can keep track of such things. Further, a modeling system may generate automatically much of an elevation or section from information given to it in the process of drawing the plan. These initial images may need further work to make them complete, but they save time and ensure consistency. The next step is to put the separate images of plans, sections, and elevations together on a drawing.

Typically, we define a sheet size and a sheet type (Fig. A5.15) (one of the office's standard borders and title panels, resembling the preprinted sheets of tracing paper we used to use in the old days of manual drafting) and, using our pointer, position our scaled images within the outline of the drawing sheet. There is some confusion in computer drafting terminology about whether *drawing* means an individual image or an assembly of

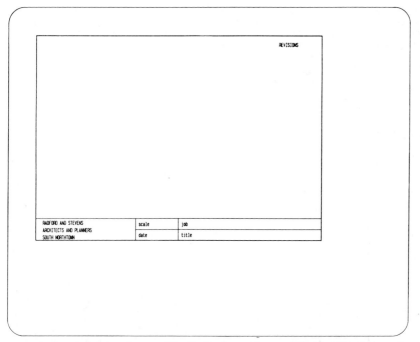

Figure A5.15 A drawing-sheet outline is simply another predefined object that can be selected from a library and displayed on the screen at an appropriate scale.

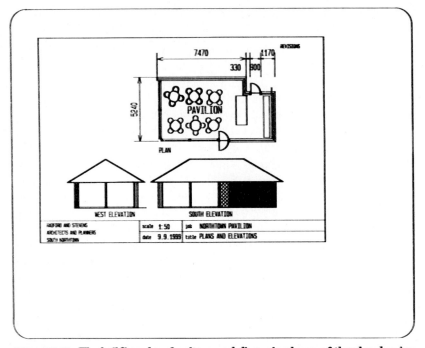

Figure A5.16 The building-plan, furniture, and dimension layers of the plan drawing, together with two elevations created at a separate session, are positioned on the drawing sheet. This positioning is interactive, and there is no need to sort out how a drawing sheet containing several images will be laid out until the images are complete. Some additional text is added, and the drawing is sent to the plotter.

images on a sheet, but the context usually makes its meaning clear. If we are not happy with our initial efforts, any of these images can be moved and rotated until we are content; a raster or refresh screen might allow us to drag them dynamically into position. We then fill in the title box on the drawing and label the separate images, using the text operations as on the plan image (Fig. A5.16).

Finally, two more operations: (1) We should *store* the drawing, which means that this particular drawing sheet and set of images will be stored on the computer disk for future retrieval. In fact, what may be stored is data that associates with the drawing's name a sheet outline, text, and constituent images rather than another version of the whole set of points and lines. This means that if we later change the plan or any other image, the changed version would appear if we reprinted the drawing. (2) At last, we issue a PLOT DRAWING command and rush off to the plotter to see the results of our work on paper. With an online plotter, the computer is linked to and sends information to the plotter throughout the plotting process, whereas with an offline system (more expensive and less common) the computer produces a tape that is read separately by the plotter.

And that is all. Here we have only described a part of the drafting system's capabilities and simplified most of the operations. A better (or at least more realistic) impression is gained, of course, from *using* a system than by reading a generalized description.

A5.2   Modeling with a Computer

So far we have concerned ourselves simply with drawing in two dimensions, although we have noted some of the implications of working with a 3-D system. Before parting with this example, we should look briefly at what could be achieved by adopting different degrees of modeling.

Since we have been working with elements (the doors, windows, and furniture), our computer should be able to print a report on the numbers of each type of element. If we had associated other attributes with these components, we could generate schedules complete with the appropriate code numbers and manufacturers. That's about as far as we can go in two dimensions. With a 3-D model, the information we can extract from the model depends on its purpose and how it has been set up: Is it just for visualization, or is it the basis for a design information system that will use the building description for nonvisual performance prediction?

A5.2.1   A model for visualization

Let's look at how we might construct a 3-D model of our pavilion café. Instead of providing 2-D information for the walls, windows, furniture, and so on, we would need to provide 3-D information. We shall assume that our system will generate 3-D form using swept volumes, that is, translating and/or rotating a 2-D set of data to create a 3-D set. The simplest transformation is by translation between end planes. To describe our walls, then, we might first set a base level (the bottom end) in relation to some constant datum level, then set an upper level (the top end), and then describe the horizontal cross section as with the 2-D drafting system. With one system, for example, we use an ELEVATION command to set or change these base and top levels, and all entities drawn on plan are then assumed to be extended through a vertical slice of space between these heights. A point becomes a vertical line, a line becomes a vertical plane, a rectangle becomes a parallelopiped (box shape), and a circle becomes a cylinder. These base and top levels stay the same until another ELEVATION command is used to change them. Other systems allow the vertical extent to be indicated directly on a section drawing shown concurrently with the plan. Any elements (such as doors, windows, and furniture) have anchor points expressed in three dimensions rather than two and are located in vertical space according to the current base level or by an explicit indication (by number or graphics pointer) of the desired height.

With our 3-D system, we have been placing not just plan views of doors and windows next to a plan view of the walls, but 3-D objects that can equally be seen from their sides or in axonometric or perspective view. This means that we have to think in three dimensions — in terms of the complete building rather than just of its plan. If the door does not extend to the top of the wall, what fills in the gap above? Perhaps a special panel goes there; if so, we need to place it as a separate element, with a base height equal to the height of the top of the door frame. What goes under the door? Perhaps we should also place a floor slab under the building, if we did not do so at the beginning. If we are working in three dimensions, we can periodically view the building in perspective to check that the model is being created in whole, and not just in plan. The concept of layering (to separate furniture from structure and so on) still applies in three dimensions, except that the layers are not horizontal surfaces with a direct correspondence with manual overlay drafting — but separate 3-D spaces which not only have different components described within them but which can also be combined as desired.

If we are only interested in appearance, we need only construct enough of a 3-D model to look right into the views we are going to need. Assume that we want to generate some external perspectives of our pavilion café (Figs. A5.17 and A5.18). The only elements we need to describe in three dimen-

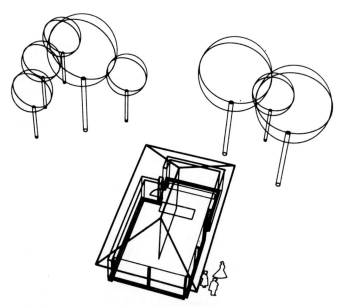

Figure A5.17   If a 3-D model of the building is constructed instead of just a 2-D plan, it can be viewed from many angles. Here the walls and window frames are generated by translation of end planes to make solids, the trees by the assembly of cylindrical and spherical primitives, and the roof by joining vertices defined in both plan and elevation to fix them in 3-D space. The people are only defined in two dimensions, like cardboard cutouts in a physical model. In this wire-frame drawing, all the edges of surfaces are shown, whether or not they are obscured by other surfaces.

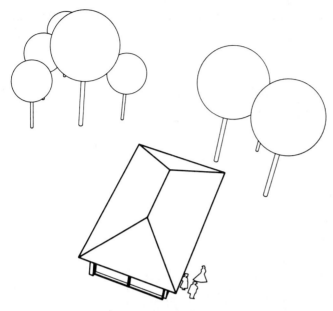

Figure A5.18 A "hidden line" drawing is produced by calculating which parts of edges are obscured by other surfaces nearer the viewer and not displaying or plotting those parts. In fact, the two elevations of the pavilion shown with the plan in Fig. A5.16 are simply hidden-line views of this same 3-D model as seen from directly in front of and beside the building.

sions are external: the walls, windows, and doors. The furniture and doors we can leave in two dimensions; when we draw the perspective view we shall probably omit that layer, anyway, to save computer time in calculating which lines are hidden. The roof we can construct as surface planes, and we can ignore eave soffits. What we have bothered to describe becomes apparent if we produce a wire-frame drawing of the pavilion, so that the edges of all surfaces appear. If the building has only been described for external appearance, we may find that the counter and shelves are lying on the floor, the wall cavities don't extend through the height of the walls, and right in the middle of the building is a vertical plane that never appeared on plan but has been added to make it easier to locate the ridge of the roof. Nonetheless, the description is appropriate for our purposes; we can use it to generate as many external views as we wish, either as line drawings (Fig. A5.19) or, if the system is capable of the task, as the basis for a colored surface view.

A5.2.2   A model for performance analysis

If, however, our windows have been given attributes of light transmittance and maintenance factors, our internal walls have been given an attribute of light reflectance, and we have also described floor and ceiling elements

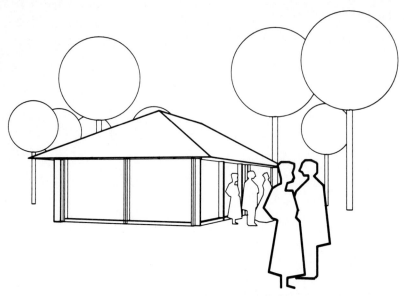

Figure A5.19   The main purpose of this 3-D model, of course, is to help us visualize the completed building from many different viewpoints. Here, the pavilion and some of its customers are seen from across the lawns of its surrounding parkland.

with their light reflectance, then this same model could potentially be used in the prediction of daylight factors within our pavilion. Clearly, the spurious central vertical plane would then have to go. Given other attributes and a more complete model, we could also predict heating and cooling loads, or perhaps calculate the total cost of all the elements or predict the number of bricks we need for the walls and the quantity of timber for the roof structure. The model then becomes much more than a simulation of future appearance. It becomes a central repository for all the information about the design, and the process of designing the building becomes almost synonymous with the process of constructing, elaborating, and testing the model.

6

Computer-Aided Design

6.1 Introduction

Why do people choose to become architects? Is it because they enjoy writing letters, filling in forms, and administering contracts? Is it the attraction of working with U-values, decibels, bending moments, and plot ratios? Or is it the heady egotistic lure of the chance to be creative, to design, to leave a mark on the physical world with a product of their imagination?

Design in dictionaries is defined with words like "indicate," "contrive," and "destine," but these do not help us much in understanding the undeniable fascination of design as an activity. J. Christopher Jones in his influential book *Design Methods* (1970, p. 4) cites the more useful descriptions that design is "a creative activity — it involves bringing into being something new and useful that had not existed previously" and is, more simply, "the imaginative jump from present facts to future possibilities." Design is exciting because it is creation, birth, "imagination in action," as Neil Hanson (1983) puts it. The particular province of design in architecture is the articulation of space, both as spatial massing and spatial enclosure. Sculptors, too, are concerned with space, but only a few architects get as excited by sculpting as by designing buildings. What puts the spice into architecture is that this creative act, the synthesis of form that becomes a building, is shot through with human, functional, financial, and physical imperatives — so that the architect has to create spaces not as abstract forms in an empty gallery, but wrought as functional entities in a world of demanding and conflicting constraints.

If the fun in being an architect, then, comes from being *creative,* how do computers affect that creative process? In this chapter we want to look at how a computer performs as a design medium and to see whether we can go further and assert that the computer itself can in any sense design and be creative. The secondary text examines a way of classifying computer design models (as being concerned with simulation, generation, or optimization) and describes some examples of each kind of model. Let us begin by looking briefly at the nature of the design process in architecture.

6.2   The Computer as Design Medium

6.2.1   A process that cannot be processed

Design is an intensely personal activity. At one extreme there are those who believe that it is centered on skilled intuition and that looking too closely at the process is dangerous: if we try to understand what is going on, perhaps the creative muse will fly away. This "designer as magician" theory, sometimes known as the *black-box school,* implies that design cannot be taught or externalized. Students have to acquire the skill through a mixture of God-given talent and osmosis from recognized masters. Since we cannot define the process, we certainly cannot put it into a computer. In contrast, the *glass-box school* looks at design as a teachable discipline with recognized methods and procedures that can improve performance.

Among the many models of design that have been put forward by researchers, most agree that it involves three identifiable processes of *analyzing* the problem, *synthesizing* a solution, and *evaluating* the result against preconceived aims. Most also agree that this sequence is not linear, but cyclical, so that the result of the evaluation leads to a reassessment of the problem (analysis) and a return to the synthesis of a new solution, gradually working from the general scheme to the detailed specification. Indeed, design in architecture can be a horribly complicated procedure. Architects are *solution-oriented* designers. They will jump to a solution as soon as possible, even before analysis has properly begun, as a way of clarifying the problem. They attempt synthesis at a very early stage and are prepared to resynthesize at a very late stage; many an architect has had the embarrassment of explaining to his client why his scheme proposals have drastically changed since their last meeting, when all was apparently fixed. Nor do architects follow an ordered pattern from design concept to detail, often finding themselves thinking of window details before deciding where those windows should be. Nigel Cross (1977b, pp. 19–20) quotes studies which suggest that while town planners and engineers tend to work in a neatly ordered sequence ("a distinct hierarchy of decision areas; once the designers had made a decision at one level, it led to a clear set of options at a lower level, and so on"), architects reveal something closer to chaos ("almost every decision was affected both by those that had gone before and those that were yet to come").

The design process in architecture, then, does not look like something that can be processed easily and automatically by computers. We cannot put a brief in at one end and get a building out at the other end. That sounds like good news for architects; no one likes to be automated out of existence. On the other hand, there is not much future in perceiving design to be a solely internal process that cannot be communicated. With complex projects requiring multiple designers, some externalization of the design process is essential, and checklists such as the U.K. Royal Institute of British Architects' Plan of Work already attempt to put some order into the process. If computers are to play any role in design, and CAD stands for computer-aided design instead of just computer-aided drafting, we need to externalize (but not necessarily too rigidly) at least some of the design process.

6.2.2 Characteristics of design media

If design is an activity that goes on within the brain, pencil and paper have traditionally served as the extension of the brain. We can record ideas on paper, express our explorations of space and form, and make calculations for nonvisual characteristics. Paper is not only a medium of communication to others (codesigners, client, builder) but also a kind of information overload device to which we resort when we cannot hold the necessary complexity of ideas within our brain. This is a very intimate relationship between user and medium, and one which we understand and feel confident about because we have grown up with it since our earliest years. Moreover, paper is a passive design medium: we get back exactly what we put down, with no processing or other response. The computer is both a new and an active medium. It responds to our actions, and as an extension of the brain it begins to impinge on areas traditionally reserved to the brain itself. Using computers, it is possible to mirror most of the design activities of using paper, but it is also possible to do much more.

Back in Chap. 3 we wrote about models and representations and the difference between the symbolic models used in computers and the physical models used in drawing. In design, as in any other complex task, the representation adopted influences the result obtained. With computer *symbolic representations* it becomes possible to use the same model as the source for many different design operations. We have seen in Chap. 5 how different spatial images (plans, perspectives, and axonometrics) could all be derived from the same building description. By adding information about the nonvisual attributes of building elements to the description (costs, thermal properties, structural characteristics, and so on), we can use the same model for performance and functional relations as well as for spatial modeling. This gives us the prospect of a design medium that will tell us the cost of our design proposals, floor areas, energy usage, and other performance indicators that inform us of the quantitative as well as the qualitative characteristics of our design ideas. Such integrated media are sometimes called *design information systems,* based on integrated building descriptions, and several exist or are under development. They are concerned more with the storage and management of information about designs than with producing drawings. The future probably belongs to this integrated view of a single computer system that will support the designer in all areas of design activity. Much of the pioneering work in exploring this direction took place in England, with systems such BDS (Building Design System, developed by Applied Research of Cambridge, which was founded by researchers at Cambridge University) and Gable (originally developed by Graham Lawson and others at Sheffield University). These are able to provide not only two- or three-dimensional images of a building design but also various environmental, financial, and scheduling items of information.

The difficulty with increased integration is the amount of effort involved in getting a comprehensive enough symbolic model set up within a computer. The use of the tool can come to dominate the design process, so that more time is expended in understanding the tool and making it work than in thinking about the design problem. We believe this to be a temporary state of affairs, our justification for optimism being the very early stage of development that these existing offerings represent. In design, the interface (a jargon word, but there is no suitable alternative) between the computer system and the designer is critically important. The great thing about pencil and paper is that we don't need to think about that interface at all; we pick up a pencil and draw. Until designers can feel as comfortable with a computer screen and mouse as with a pencil and paper, much design will continue to be carried out using the traditional media.

Right now the majority of computer design tools do not draw from an integrated design information system but use their own individual description, needing to be separately constructed for each application and gaining nothing from the potential for consistency that a multipurpose model promises. In the following sections we shall describe some of these design tools in isolation, without drawing the distinction between discrete and integrated systems.

6.2.3 Design studies in form and color

Perhaps the fundamental skill of an architect is the ability to visualize in three dimensions, to see a building, space, or detail in the mind and to construct from nothing a mental image of complex interrelated planes and volumes. The great English architect Sir Edwin Lutyens used to tell the story of a blind architect who described to him the memorized detailed design of a cathedral. Yet most of the time architects express these volumes on paper in two dimensions, in the abstractions of plan, section, and elevation. We would argue that this abstraction is a result of the design and documentation medium we use rather than a desirable choice. Moreover, a two-dimensional model encourages two-dimensional thought. We all know of buildings in which the real construction difficulties have been in three-dimensional junctions of walls, roofs, structures, and services, which not only did the drawings fail to describe but the designer failed to foresee. Architects do not, cannot, know what it is like to work consistently in three dimensions because they have never had the tools to do so. But we also know that many of what are widely recognized as the "best" architects in history have made extensive use of perspective sketches and physical models as part of the creative as well as of the presentation process.

Durinski (1982, p. 41) describes the creative stimulus of using a computer for something as apparently simple as typography design, traditionally "viewed only as ink on a printed page," but now: "What if the type font had depth? What might that particular face look like from the side, or the top, or if seen in perspective? Should the font's cross section be a square, a diamond, a hexagon, or an irregular shape?" Durinski urges more awareness among creative people, observing that "computer scientists appear to be learning design faster than designers are learning computer technology."

Very few architects have used computers to explore design ideas for buildings in any comparable way to the work of graphic designers and artists. Of his work with three-dimensional shape modelers, Harold Borkin (1983) of the University of Michigan reported that "only once or twice" had he been able, through the addition and subtraction of component volumes, to create a space that could not be predicted by mental visualization, "but that's exciting when it happens." Given a free hand on a three-dimensional-surface modeling system to explore form and color in architecture, the potential richness of the computer as a design medium becomes very clear.

Design studies using the computer as a medium have a different pace and style from a conventional design process and are likely to discover different things. Particularly, computers facilitate the generation and consideration of *variants.* There are essentially two ways of describing an image: by its form (for example, the coordinates in space of the vertices of its edges) or by a procedure that will generate the image. The list of objects, lines, and endpoints created in a drafting system's database describes (given a correct semantic interpretation) the form of an image. The sequence of instructions in a drafting system's macro language can describe the procedure to generate that image. The advantage of procedural descriptions is that the same procedure can be used to generate many different instances simply by making some dimensions and quantities functions of variable parameters that control the result. The variation of these parameters then provides a means to transform a design into new states (Figs. 6.1 and 6.2). The basic geometric transformations are rotation, translation, reflection, and scal-

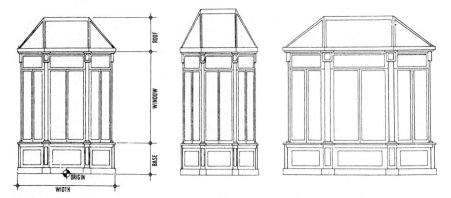

Figure 6.1 Parameterized objects allow the object to be used on a drawing with different sizes and proportions. This bay window is drawn by a procedure that asks for values for the four variables of width, base height, window height, and roof height. It is positioned on the drawing by locating the anchor point at the origin, the center of the window base. Different values for the variables give the opportunity to explore very different appearances to instances of the bay window. *(Drawn and generated by Michael Stuart at the University of Sydney.)*

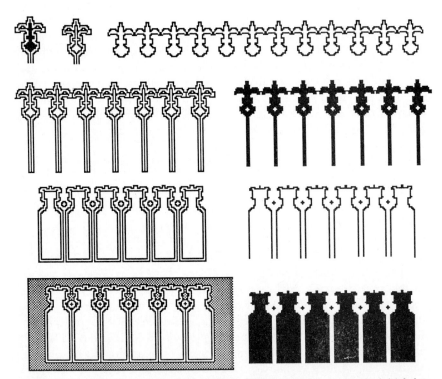

Figure 6.2 Variations on a theme of fleur-de-lis. Using a painting system, an initial shape (half a fleur-de-lis) is reflected, repeated, and then transformed by replacing single lines with double lines, painting enclosed polygons, and adding and subtracting elements. *(Rivka Oxman and Patrick Trinh using Macpaint, University of Sydney.)*

ing, and all computer drafting systems contain some procedures for applying such operations. In a production environment they are used for the modification of predefined elements to fit a specific situation, as described in Chap. 5, but they can also be used to explore a family of designs and design issues, such as proportion, symmetry, repetition, rhythm, pattern, color, and composition. These are basic design issues, and their exploration should lead to a deeper understanding and a consequent confidence in their articulation and manipulation. This is particularly important for design students. William Mitchell (1985a) at the University of California, Los Angeles, pioneered the use of computer models in the *parametric variation* of two-dimensional geometry and three-dimensional compositions of lines and color polygons (Fig. 6.3).

Color variation is particularly significant. Since in a computer database the color of an object, like its geometry, is described numerically, it is possible to extend the concept of parametric variation from geometry to color. Exploring hue, saturation, and brightness with a pot of paint demands a degree of skill and patience that most students and practitioners simply do not have. Working with a computer system, changing color relationships (complementaries, contrasts, gradations, and so on) becomes a task of the same type and difficulty as changing geometric relationships. If we want to, we can design from the start in color.

6.2.4 Design studies in environmental performance

Much of the early work with computers in architecture was not with the modeling of space and form but with the exploration of quantitative aspects of design — the investigation of the *structural, economic,* and *environmental performance* of buildings. For architects, the most exciting area is in exploring the physical environmental (light, shade, temperature, sound) and the creation of buildings and cities that appeal to all our senses. Only in the past few years have designers explored the pattern and availability of sunlight, shading, and daylighting in and around buildings in any depth, for computer programs have made such studies relatively easy, whereas prediction by physical models or manual calculation had been tedious. By a geometric projection of rays from the sun's direction onto the walls and floors of the room, computer programs can trace the *patterns of insolation* cast by sunlight through a window (Fig. 6.4). By a similar geometric projection, they can plot the *shadows* cast by buildings on the ground or other buildings. They can establish *sunlight access* to an urban scene or group of buildings simply by plotting a perspective with the sun as the viewpoint (Fig. 6.5); anything the sun can "see" is in sunshine. They can calculate the *distribution of daylight* in a room by using standard daylight-factor calculation algorithms and plotting the results as numbers on a grid or as contours of equal daylight factor. Similarly, they can calculate the luminance distribution from an *artificial lighting* scheme and present the results as numbers or as shades of color or greyness on a drawing of the room (Fig. 6.6).

They can predict *sound transmission* and *acoustic conditions* by model-

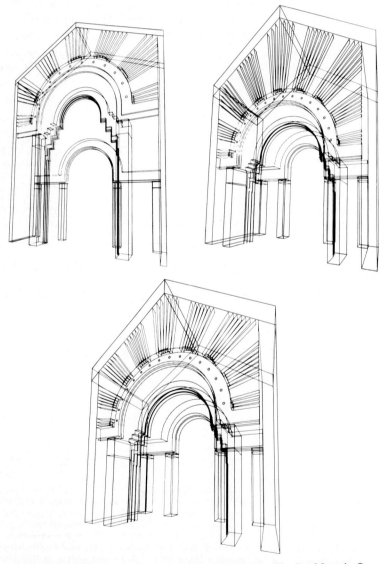

Figure 6.3   Studies of the design of the entrance for Charles Moore's San Antonio Art Center in San Antonio, Texas, generated at the Graduate School of Architecture and Urban Planning, University of California, Los Angeles.

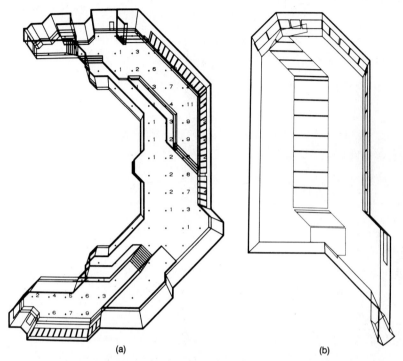

(a)   (b)

Figure 6.4 The same geometric model of a building can be used with many different applications programs to explore building performance. Here *(a)* daylight factors on the working plane and *(b)* sun patches on the floor and walls have been calculated and shown on an overhead view of a room. *(Anonymous, used by permission of the Architects Journal.)*

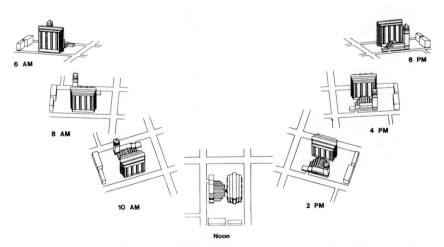

Figure 6.5 Sun study of an urban space by viewing the building on the site from the angle of the sun over a chosen day. Anything visible will be in sun, and anything hidden will be in shade at the corresponding time. *(Courtesy of HOK Computer Service Corporation.)*

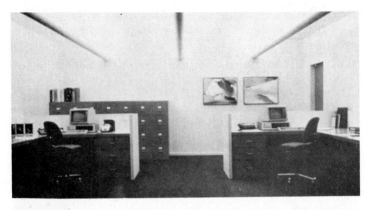

Figure 6.6   A full-scale mock-up of an office (top) is compared with its computer simulation (middle), which provides a designer with feedback on the luminous environment in the room. The program is intended for the comparison of luminous and luminaire arrangements, so that the appearance with open fluorescent uplights (middle) can be compared with that of direct and indirect prismatic luminaires (bottom) and others. This kind of simulation of appearance is sometimes called an *experiential* simulation; it stimulates the experience of being in the proposed room rather than presenting results as graphs, contours, or tables of numbers. *(Miller, Ngai, and Miller, 1984; used by permission of International Lighting Review.)*

ing sound waves and calculating reverberation times, although models for acoustic behavior tend to fall into two groups: extremely simple (almost simplistic for real-life situations) or extremely complex (beyond the scope of generalist architects). In this field, however, the majority of available computer programs concern *thermal performance,* motivated by the evident superiority of computers in handling the complex calculations involved and by the perceived importance of energy conservation as a factor in design. Many different energy analysis programs are available, the best-known including DOE-2 (Hunn, 1979), BLAST (Hittle, 1979), ESP (Clark, 1978), and NBSLD (Kusuda, 1974).

Energy-conservative design is a two-part problem; (1) designing the building to minimize the heating or cooling load on mechanical plant and (2) designing installed plant to meet these loads while minimizing the consumed energy. Services engineers have traditionally concerned themselves with this second part of the problem. The first part is clearly as much an architect's as an engineer's province. Indeed, many building codes in Europe and the United States now require that building designs meet specified thermal standards, either by demonstration through computer calculations or by restricting the form of acceptable building solutions through compliance with "deemed to satisfy" provisions. Such programs will identify heat flow through different elements of the building (Figs. 6.7 and 6.8) and annual or seasonal heating or cooling loads in the whole or in individual zones of the building, and some will interpret the loads in terms of consumed energy, given a description of heating and cooling plant. BLAST, for example, consists of three major subprograms:

1. *Space-load prediction.* This part calculates hourly space loads from solar gain, heat conduction, and internal sources based on a user description of the building and on weather data.

2. *Air distribution system.* This part calculates chilled water, hot water, steam, gas, and electrical demands based on the space loads calculated in the first part and on an additional user description of the building's air-handling system.

3. *Central-plant simulation.* This part calculates monthly and annual fuel and electric power consumption, using the results of the air-distribution-system simulation and an additional user description of the central plant to simulate chillers, boilers, and on-site power-generating and solar energy systems. It will also perform a life-cycle cost analysis based on initial costs, full costs, and maintenance costs (Ding et al., 1984).

In a computer thermal analysis program like BLAST, the computer is used to model the dynamic (time-varying) flow of heat through the building fabric. Dynamic models can also model flows of liquid (typically, storm or surface water flowing down a drainpipe system), people (one useful

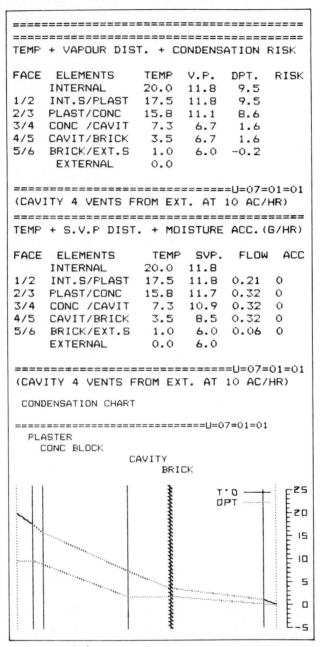

```
=============================================
=============================================
TEMP + VAPOUR DIST. + CONDENSATION RISK

FACE   ELEMENTS     TEMP   V.P.   DPT.   RISK
       INTERNAL     20.0   11.8   9.5
1/2    INT.S/PLAST  17.5   11.8   9.5
2/3    PLAST/CONC   15.8   11.1   8.6
3/4    CONC /CAVIT   7.3    6.7   1.6
4/5    CAVIT/BRICK   3.5    6.7   1.6
5/6    BRICK/EXT.S   1.0    6.0  -0.2
       EXTERNAL      0.0


============================U=07=01=01
(CAVITY 4 VENTS FROM EXT. AT 10 AC/HR)
=============================================
TEMP + S.V.P DIST. + MOISTURE ACC.(G/HR)

FACE   ELEMENTS     TEMP   SVP.   FLOW   ACC
       INTERNAL     20.0   11.8
1/2    INT.S/PLAST  17.5   11.8   0.21   0
2/3    PLAST/CONC   15.8   11.7   0.32   0
3/4    CONC /CAVIT   7.3   10.9   0.32   0
4/5    CAVIT/BRICK   3.5    8.5   0.32   0
5/6    BRICK/EXT.S   1.0    6.0   0.06   0
       EXTERNAL      0.0    6.0


============================U=07=01=01
(CAVITY 4 VENTS FROM EXT. AT 10 AC/HR)

CONDENSATION CHART

============================U=07=01=01
  PLASTER
    CONC BLOCK
              CAVITY
                BRICK
```

Figure 6.7   Part of the output from a microcomputer heat-flow analysis program, highlighting where there is a condensation risk because the temperature is lower than the dew-point temperature. These are also plotted in the section through the wall construction. The assumed internal temperature is 68°F (20°C), the external temperature 32°F (0°C). *(Burberry, 1982; used by permission of Architects Journal.)*

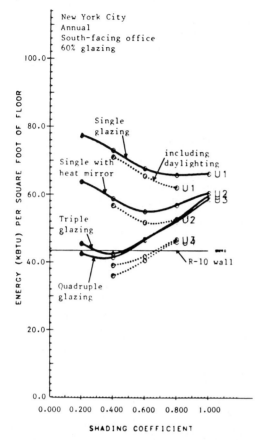

Figure 6.8 Energy analysis: A daylight illuminance simulation program, SUPERLITE, is combined with a thermal load and energy simulation program, DOE2, to investigate the energy implications of different window strategies for a multistory building in New York City. The rest of the design is kept constant while first the glazing type and then the degree of shading is varied. The solid lines assume no use of daylight (artificial lights are kept working all the time during occupied hours); the broken lines show the lower energy used if the artificial lighting responds to available daylight. (*Selkowitz, 1984.*)

application is a simulation of the emergency exit of a building's population through its fire-escape routes), goods (into and out of a warehouse), traffic (most urban traffic authorities use computer simulation models of the flow of traffic to test proposals for road or traffic-light alterations), or money (simulating income and expenditure over a long-term period for a redevelopment project as part of a feasibility study).

This kind of computer program, which takes a design proposal, models its behavior, and predicts its performance, is called a *simulation* program; it simulates real-life behavior. Because the models are often complex, preparing the necessary data and interpreting the results are not always easy. The models often require very detailed descriptions of the building form and fabric, which are only available very late in the design process. Most programs include default values (preset values that are used if the program operator does not specify any particular value for that parameter in the design), but if the program is run with many default values, it has to be recognized that the building being modeled is not the one that may finally be built. Examples of programs intended for early and late stages of design are described in Sec. A6.2.

The results from a simulation program are usually presented in multi-valued form (internal temperatures at different times or heat flows through different parts of the building fabric for a thermal program) with no direct indication of the goodness or badness of the results. To improve and develop solutions, we need to understand how to improve performance by modifying one or more of the design variables. In the process of *appraisal* (Maver, 1977; Markus et al., 1972), a first approximation is nominated by the designer and its performance predicted. The architect then decides whether modification of the solution is necessary, and if so, what form that modification should take. The success of this process depends on the designer's ability to formulate a useful hypothesis by which to modify the solution, and that demands either a theoretical knowledge of the field or some clear trend emerging from a series of simulations, or both. If a modified solution is very similar to the original (perhaps changing only one variable at a time in a parametric study), it is easy to understand the reasons for changes in performance, but the range of design options explored is small. If the modified solution is radically different from the original, it becomes impossible to attribute variations in performance to individual design changes.

6.3   The Computer as Designer

Using computers for design feedback keeps them at arm's length from that act of creation, or "imagination in action," which the synthesis of a design idea represents. Although they might lead to the modification of a design, they are not advising on just how the design should be modified to improve performance. So can computers design?

Interestingly, much of the early research about using computers in architecture sought the automatic synthesis of a plan for a building from some basis of desired functions or facilities and the relationships between facilities. The process is known as *layout planning*, or *facilities planning*. Typically, the designer specifies the areas required by each item and the importance of the relationship on an ordinal scale between each pair of items. The computer program produces a cluster, or "bubble," diagram that can be modified by the designer, allowing her to compare any derived solution to the originally specified relationships. The bubbles can be replaced by scaled rectangles to be manipulated in much the same way as an architect might manually work with scaled pieces of card, but with the benefit of feedback information measuring the "success" of his solutions in meeting the prescribed relationships. Alternatively, the facility areas may be fitted directly into available areas or zones within a given outline or building perimeter (Fig. 6.9). The resulting diagrammatic layout can be linked directly to a drafting system or to a wider appraisal package that measures cost and environmental performance as well as circulation (see Sec. A6.4).

Clearly, such planning aids are only useful where the spatial problems to be solved are nontrivial, such as hospitals, some industrial buildings, and large bureaucratic organizations. Indeed, although they have been available to architects in practice for many years now, they have not had a major impact, perhaps because only a small proportion of design involves planning problems of such complexity. But in recent times there has been a revival of interest in automated facilities planning and in the association of integrated packages for this work with facilities management (see Chap. 4) and with drafting and modeling systems.

These layout-planning programs work by *optimizing* a numerical measure of performance; they usually minimize circulation distances subject to any necessary constraints on particular spatial locations. Optimization seeks to answer the designer's fundamental question of what is the "best" solution. Moreover, if we can put the optimization algorithm into a computer program, we can argue that the computer is designing the optimal solution to the given problem. There are a number of examples where this has been tried, primarily in layout planning but extending to environmental design, site development, building services, structures, and other aspects of building (Radford and Gero, 1980). Clearly, however, this is a pretty weak model of design. For a start, optimization only works where the index of performance is measurable, which is fine if we limit the purpose of building to minimizing circulation, energy use, or cost, but which is not too good if we think that aesthetics has some role in architecture. Secondly, most applications of optimization have taken just one criterion in isolation, so that we get a building that minimizes circulation or perhaps energy or cost, but not all three. Architectural design is much more concerned with the trade-offs between different design aims and with finding an acceptable compromise than it is with optimizing for any single objective.

This does not mean that optimization is useless; far from it. For a designer, it is useful to know about the building forms that might, say, minimize energy use. We don't have to go on and build that form. Instead, we can use it as an item of useful information in the same way that we use

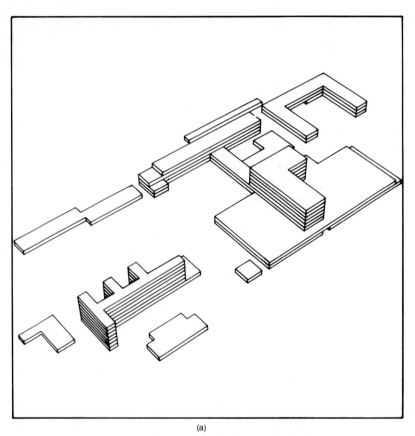

(a)

Figure 6.9 The TOPAZ (Technique for Optimal Placing of Activities into Zones) program was used in the investigation of different redevelopment strategies for the 581,000 ft² (54,000 m²) Royal Canberra Hospital in Canberra, Australia. Facilities were allocated to available zones of space in a way that minimized the total costs less benefits of allocation over a series of time periods to allow for phased development. The costs reflected both the interaction between facilities and the establishment costs (construction or alteration) for each facility. Here, *(a)* the massing of the existing hospital is compared with *(b)* a layout generated by **TOPAZ**, *(Crawford, Mitchell and Booth, 1980; courtesy of CSIRO Division of Building Research, Australia.)*

information from books and design guides — but perhaps it is more pertinent, for the computer optimization can take into account the *particular* conditions and constraints of our site and of our design problem instead of providing us with generalized advice. Further, we can use multicriteria optimization to give us trade-off information on the conflicts between designing for different objectives (Radford and Gero, 1980).

This is still restricted to the measurable aspects of architecture, or at least to the orderable aspects (in the sense that we can assert that one performance is better than another). Does this mean that computers are out of the design game as soon as we bring in qualitative, nonmeasurable

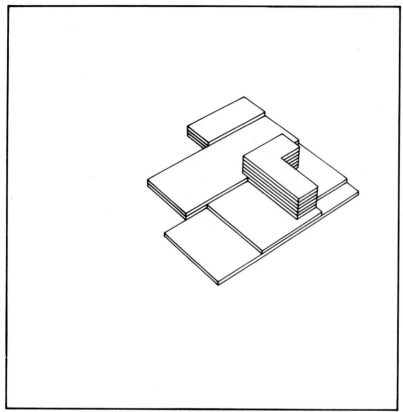

(b)

goals such as beauty and style? Perhaps not; George Stiny, James Gips, William Mitchell, and others have led a fascinating excursion into the role of shape grammars in architectural design. *Shape grammars* are concerned with the generation of form through the application of defined rules which constitute a grammar (analogous to a grammar in human languages) and which can be used to express the way that the elements of a design are composed in a style. In architecture, it has proved possible to identify grammars that appear to underly the design of certain Palladian villas (Stiny and Mitchell, 1978), Frank Lloyd Wright's Prairie Houses (Koning and Eizenberg, 1981; see Sec. A6.3.2), Mughul gardens (Stiny and Mitchell, 1980), and numerous other examples. So far, this work has concentrated on historical descriptive studies, but there seems to be no reason why shape grammars should not form part of a design system for new projects. It should be possible, for example, to "plug in" the shape grammar for a Georgian terrace house in order to design authentic infill buildings in a Georgian conservation area, if that is what we want to do.

6.4   Summary

In this chapter we have looked at design and the design process and the role of computers in that process, comparing traditional pencil and paper as a design medium with computers. We have argued that computers offer a design medium that is much richer, and therefore perhaps more difficult to use, than pencil and paper. We have also argued that computer design is possible, in the sense that computer programs are able to generate design solutions through the operation of algorithms.

A pencil is accepted as merely a tool, a medium, a means toward the goal of good design. A computer will be no more (and no less) important in the future. But as a tool it should not dominate, and as a professional the architect must accept the design responsibility, whatever tools are chosen. If the architect does not find a computer terminal a conducive medium for the development of aesthetically pleasing sketch designs, then much of the design activity should remain centered on the drawing board. Architectural design will remain a largely intuitive activity learned through experience and through study of the work of others, and neither computers nor structured design methodologies can replace the need for experience and good judgment. Neither should the tools be used for their own sake. Over 10 years ago an architect with Skidmore, Owings, and Merrill wrote of computer programs that designed and laid out spaces: "I thought that is what we did best, or at least what we enjoyed most. In other disciplines people are not so misguided as to let a machine do all the fun work while they do all the drudge work" (Davis, 1973, p. 389).

Computers today are much less concerned with numerical calculations than with making decisions according to rules. As such, they are not restricted to the numerical, measurable aspects of architecture. In fact, the most exciting developments in the use of computers in design lie in the fields of artificial intelligence and knowledge engineering. That is the subject of Chap. 7.

SECONDARY TEXT
Design System Examples

A6.1   A Classification of CAD Tools

With very few exceptions, all computer-aided design tools fall into one of three categories:

- *Simulation.* The computer is used to predict the consequences of a design proposal in some performance area. The design decision-making process is outside the computer model.
- *Generation.* The computer is used to explore the consequences of applying an ordered set of design rules. There is no separate performance

measure; all designs that conform to these rules are equally acceptable.

- *Optimization.* The generation mechanism is accompanied by the ability to simulate performance in a specified criterion in order to identify solutions that offer the best performance in that criterion.

Unlike simulation, then, in generation and optimization the computer model can be regarded as making design decisions of some kind. Rather than catalog areas in which computer methods can impinge on design, in the following sections we shall illustrate each of these three fundamental approaches in turn and discuss their attendant advantages and disadvantages.

Because they are based on known algorithms that are open and available, all three kinds of computer design tools necessarily belong to a glass-box view of design activity. J. Christopher Jones (1970, p. 50) characterized glass-box methods of design as follows:

1. *Objectives, variables,* and *criteria* are fixed in advance.

2. *Analysis* is completed, or at least attempted, before solutions are sought.

3. *Evaluation* is largely linguistic and logical (as opposed to experimental).

4. *Strategies* are fixed in advance; these are usually sequential but may include parallel operations, conditional operations, and recycling.

Christopher Jones argued that for some kinds of design problems, glass-box methods work better than the black-box approach, whereas in other cases they end in confusion, from which designers revert to their accustomed black-box behavior.

Our rationale for using computer tools in quite simple. We believe that design is almost always better when the designer thoroughly *understands* the design problem. Most of the design aids we describe here are concerned, in some way, with increasing that understanding. The standard by which they should be judged is whether they are increasing understanding about the really important, central aspects of architectural design or whether they are diverting the architect's attention away from these central problems toward the periphery, where computer models happen to be available. We are still quite short of computer design aids that address the really important problems in architecture.

A6.2 Simulation Models

Most computer design aids are based on *simulation models;* given a description of the relevant characteristics of a design proposal, they will simulate the behavior of the design in order to predict its performance in some area of interest to the designer. Simple manual simulation models have long been used for predicting structural performance and such environmental measures as daylighting and heat gains and losses. Consequently, computer simulation methods can occupy an established and well-defined position in design activity.

A6.2.1   Static and dynamic simulations

Simulation methods can model either *static* or *dynamic* behavior, the former ignoring and the latter taking into account the effect of time: a photograph is a static view of the world, a movie a dynamic view. Most manual simulation models deal with static behavior, and there are many examples of accepted manual algorithms simply having been translated into computer code. U-value calculations for walls and roofs, daylight factor calculations, bending moment calculations, and cost analyses all fit into this category. The advantages are speed, accuracy (if the algorithm is coded correctly, there is much less room for error than with manual methods), and a consistent presentation of results in a standard form adopted by the output of the computer program. It is with dynamic behavior, however, that we get into an area where reality can be simulated by computer in a way that would be far too time-consuming to do manually.

An analysis of the thermal behavior of buildings is a case in point. Heat flow into and out of a building is constantly changing with external weather conditions, with the effects of internal heating or cooling, and with time delays caused by the thermal inertia of the building. Traditionally, this dynamic behavior has been modeled by a static approximation which uses external and internal design temperatures and which assumes a steady state in heat flow between the two. With computers it becomes possible to model complex, dynamic time-varying behavior. This raises an issue of the matching of models to the stages of the design process.

To run a sophisticated dynamic model, we often need quite detailed knowledge of the building; in fact, if we are to use the model fully, the building must sometimes be almost completely designed. We also need design tools that are appropriate for use at the very beginning of a project, when many of the decisions affecting a building's ultimate performance are being made but when the design only exists as outline sketches of mass and form. This is when fundamental decisions are made about orientation, verandas, clerestories, and other building characteristics that affect or follow from strategies for low-energy design, costing, lighting, and so on. To be effective, programs intended for this stage need to match the pace and nature of the design process during sketch or scheme design: easy and fun to use, with easily assimilated results, and fast both in execution and in the preparation of data for its execution.

A6.2.2   Simulating thermal behavior

A model for such programs is provided by SOLAR5 (Milne, 1982 and 1984), which addresses passive energy design. From a minimum of information (the city, building type, floor area, and number of stories of the proposed project) the program itself creates a schematic "base-case energy-conserving building" using its own "design knowledge" or rules of thumb drawn from many sources (see Sec. A6.3 and Chap. 7 for a discussion of design knowledge as rules). The *base case* blocks out the building's depth, length-to-width ratio, percentage glazing on each facade, sun-shade cutoff angles, U-values, internal loads, and so on. It is intended only as basis for modification by the architect, a first rough guess to provide a starting point for improvement. The architect can revise, refine, and at any time request a 3-D graph of the total annual thermal loads for the buildings or for any building components (particular walls, windows, or roof) as these loads vary over the hours of the day and the months of the year (Fig. A6.1).

These graphs provide both qualitative and quantitative information. Qualitatively, the shape of the pictures and the position and relative magnitudes of peaks and troughs give an immediate impression of the thermal behavior of the building over time. Quantitatively, the vertical scale gives a numerical value to these loads within the accuracy allowed by the schematic models used. Architects find this kind of graphic display intriguing and very easy to understand (Milne, 1982), much more so than tables of figures to portray the same results. Because of the speed of the operation, one can explore refinements and variations and the resulting changes in behavior.

As a design develops, more data about it become available and more sophisticated models can be used. As an example, the Environmental Systems Performance (ESP) program (Clark, 1978) uses three sets of data:

1. A geometric description of the building, including the overall shape of the building and the position of windows, internal walls, and so on.

2. A thermal properties description of the materials used in the building, including their density, conductivity, and reflectance.

3. A description of the external climate and any incidental heat gains within the building.

The program is run interactively, and the design description can be changed to explore different building forms or to react to unsatisfactory predictions (Figs. A6.2 to A6.4).

As program users, we have several options. If we assume a constant internal air temperature, the program will calculate the required heating- or cooling-plant capacity and the annual energy consumption. If we assume a given plant capacity, the program will calculate the varying internal temperatures that will result when the plant capacity is insufficent to maintain constant conditions. Alternatively, we can let the internal temperature vary within an acceptable range, allowing for different temperatures at different times of day, and look at the necessary plant capacity and energy consumption. The results are presented as diagrams as well as numbers, where diagrams help to clarify the behavior of the building. Most

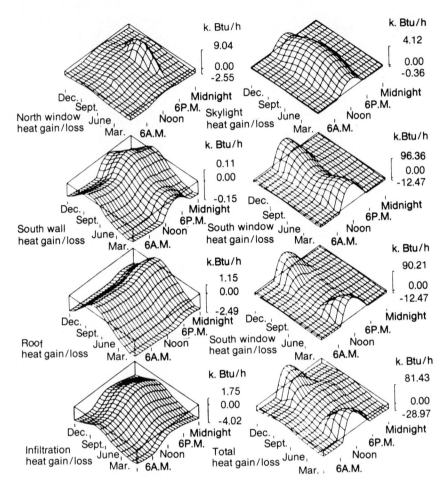

Figure A6.1 Qualitative and quantitative information on heat gain and loss through elements of a northern hemisphere building at the early stages of design is provided by these three-dimensional graphs from the SOLAR5 simulation program. The left-hand column shows heat transfer through a north window, a south wall (notice the 4-hour time lag), the roof (notice the damping effect of high mass construction), and infiltration. The right-hand column shows the results for a skylight (its "heat mountain" shape shows its poor passive solar performance), a south window (its "saddle" shape demonstrates good passive solar performance because it gains more in winter than in summer), a south window with overhang (eliminating much of the summer overheating at the cost of only a little winter gain), and finally the total heat gain and loss (internal thermal storage will prevent winter passive gain from temporarily overheating occupied spaces). *(Milne, 1982; reprinted by permission from the Proceedings of the CAD 82 Conference, published by Butterworth and Co. Ltd. and sponsored by the journal Computer-Aided Design.)*

importantly, it is possible to analyze the *paths* by which excessive heat gain or loss arises and establish where any apparent deficiencies exist. By systematically varying one design parameter (such as glass type, wall insulation, or orientation), it is possible to quantify the effect of design decisions. It is then up to the designer to take measures to improve thermal performance: simulation programs are predictive rather than prescriptive, and the user must interpret the results and decide what to do about them.

A6.3   Generative Models

In a *generative model* the model itself generates a design solution according to prescribed rules. Compare the most common methods for daylighting and artificial lighting design: For daylighting, the designer chooses a window size and checks by computer program or daylight protractor the resulting daylight factor in the room (simulation); for artificial lighting, the designer decides on a required design illuminance on the working plane, and generates a design solution by the lumen method in terms of a number and layout of luminaires. The type of luminaires can be either a part of the performance specification or a part of the solution. In SOLAR5 a genera-

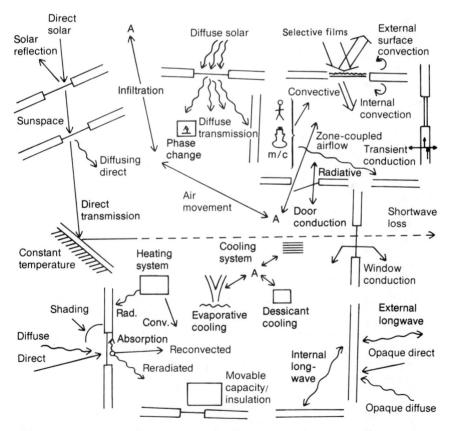

Figure A6.2   Energy exchanges in a multisided enclosure are represented in the computer thermal simulation model ESP as equivalent nodes, the dots on the diagram. All these paths are considered in simulating the thermal performance of a building. *(Lansdown and Maver, 1984; reprinted by permission from Computer-Aided Design, vol. 16, no. 6, May 1984.)*

tive model creates the base case for the first simulation of thermal behavior.

A6.3.1 Generating sun-shade designs

A computer program for the design of fixed external sun shades developed by Edna Shaviv (1978) provides a classic example of a generative model. The traditional approach to sun-shade design has been simulation: The shape of the shade was assumed, and checks were carried out to see if it worked. Shaviv inverts the problem: For each point on an imaginary grid over the window to be shaded, the program finds the necessary projection of a pole sufficient to cast a shadow to the edge of the window between given days and hours. The result is a matrix of pole lengths, presented graphically as a perspective of the window, the grid, and the poles, with lines drawn between their outer tips. Any shade which envelopes the top and sides of the lattice, or which envelopes the top and sides of the lattices projected from subareas of the window, will shade the window or part of the window for the desired period (Fig. A6.5). Thus, we get not just one solution but the whole field of feasible solutions.

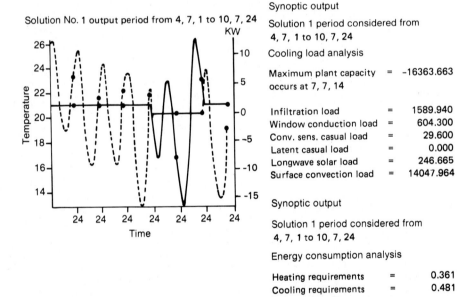

Synoptic output

Solution 1 period considered from
4, 7, 1 to 10, 7, 24

Cooling load analysis

Maximum plant capacity   =   -16363.663
occurs at 7, 7, 14

Infiltration load	=	1589.940
Window conduction load	=	604.300
Conv. sens. casual load	=	29.600
Latent casual load	=	0.000
Longwave solar load	=	246.665
Surface convection load	=	14047.964

Synoptic output

Solution 1 period considered from
4, 7, 1 to 10, 7, 24

Energy consumption analysis

Heating requirements	=	0.361
Cooling requirements	=	0.481

Figure A6.3 An analysis of thermal loads and energy requirements over a 7-day period in July for a building using ESP. The internal temperature is held constant at a user-specified value by allowing both heating and cooling to be applied as necessary. The synoptic output lists the different loads encountered (through infiltration, window conduction, a convective sensory casual load and a latent casual load, and longwave solar radiation and surface conduction loads), the maximum plant capacity and when it occurs, and the energy consumption required for both heating and cooling. *(Clark, 1978; reprinted by permission from the Proceedings of the CAD 78 Conference, published by IPC Science and Technology Press and organized by the journal Computer-Aided Design.)*

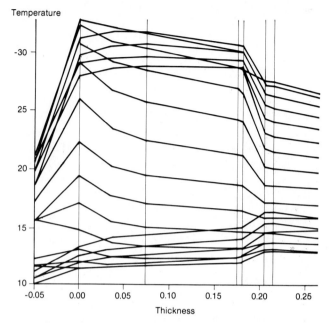

Figure A6.4 Output from a thermal simulation model, ESP, used to explore the variation of the temperature gradient in a south-facing wall (northern hemisphere) over a 20-hour period. The left-hand side shows outside air temperature in degrees centigrade. Each line follows the temperature gradient at a particular hour. The higher temperature at the wall surface (the 0.00 thickness) demonstrates the effect of incident solar radiation; then temperature levels fall through the multilayered construction. The right-hand side corresponds to internal conditions, in this case assuming no artificial heating or cooling. *(Clark, 1978; reprinted by permission from the Proceedings of the CAD 78 Conference, published by IPC Science and Technology Press and organized by the journal Computer-Aided Design.)*

Using this information, designers can consider all the possibilities that meet the shading requirements and still retain aesthetic control. Shades can have straight or sloping sides and straight or angled edges, have a vertical front, and have the form of small-scale egg crates or a large single shade. Instead of tending to standardization, this design information makes possible the design of many variations of efficient nonstandard shades, with a consequent enrichment of building design (Fig. A6.6).

A6.3.2   Shape grammars: Frank Lloyd Wright's unbuilt houses

The rules for generating the form of these sun shades are derived by analyzing the geometry by which the shape of a shade causes it to obstruct the sun's rays and deducing a set of rules for the shape of shades that ensures a certain performance result. A *shape grammar* formulation allows

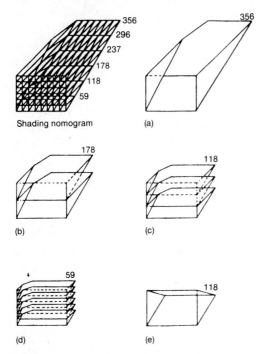

356
296
237
178
118
59

Shading nomogram   (a)   356

178   118

(b)   (c)

59   118

(d)   (e)

Figure A6.5   A shading nomogram and several possibilities of sun shades based on the nomogram are generated to shade a southeast window (northern hemisphere) from 8:00 A.M. daily from March to October.
The possibilities are established by following the outline of the projected rods at the top and sides of the
proportion of the window to be shaded by each shade.
For the whole window *(a)* we follow the top and outer
edges, for a third of a window *(c)* we follow the projection from the second highest of the six grid lines, and so
on. The shade at *(e)* has a sloping top, so that the outer
edge follows the fifth grid line. *(Shaviv, 1978; reprinted
by permission from the Proceedings of the CAD 78 Conference, published by IPC Science and Technology Press
and organized by the journal Computer-Aided Design.)*

for algorithms to be defined directly in terms of shapes and is one of the
most fascinating areas of recent research in architecture. There are four
components to a shape grammar (Stiny, 1980):

1. A finite set of *shapes*

2. A finite set of *symbols*, which are used to label the shapes

3. A finite set of *shape rules* of the form "shape *A* becomes shape *B*"

4. An *initial labeled shape*

The shape rules apply sequentially; a shape *A* is said to be generated by the shape grammar if there is a finite series of labeled shapes beginning with the initial shape and ending with *A* such that each shape but the first is produced by applying a shape rule to its immediate predecessor. Shapes can be two- or three-dimensional. But rather than present a theoretical discourse on shape grammars, we shall describe some work on the spatial composition of Frank Lloyd Wright's prairie houses carried out by Hank Koning and Julie Eizenberg (1981) at the University of California in Los Angeles. In this case a shape grammar is used to describe a language or style within which a designer works. Wright, of course, wrote a number of books on his work, but he did not set out any explicit rules for design. Instead, Koning and Eizenberg used clues in Wright's books to infer the shape rules from a study of 11 of his houses, chosen to cover a variety of plan types within the prairie style. They were looking at spatial composition rather than at decorative detail, and their rules concern the interpretation of building volumes, the position of different functional zones, and important features such as roof lines, balconies, chimneys, and porches (Fig. A6.7).

A shape grammar needs an *initial labeled shape.* For Wright's prairie houses, the key is the fireplace, both the symbolic and actual hearth of the home. Around it, rooms radiate outward toward the prairie. In this shape grammar, the initial shape is neutral, a symbolic asterisk at the origin $(0, 0, 0)$ of the building, but the first two shape rules replace this asterisk by a fireplace at some location *(x, y,z)* on the site. One of these two rules must be applied. Rule 1 generates a single-hearth fireplace; rule 2 generates a double-hearth fireplace. The symbols *A, K,* and *D* are used later. A *living zone* is then added by applying one of the rules 3, 4, 5, or 6 to replace one hearth and symbol *A* with a rectangular space with one of four specific relationships to the hearth. No other relationship is allowed within the grammar. Again, the symbols *L, D,* and *M* and the dots and arrows are used later. A service zone is added to the living zone by applying rule 7, which creates a double space, symmetrical about the arrowed line along one edge of the living zone. This is the core unit of the house, and it is distinguished by associating the symbol ". " with each of its corners. The symbol *A* on the long sides of the core means that the plan must grow in these directions (meaning that extensions are required), while growth is optional on the other two sides labeled *a.* Thus, the labels in a shape grammar determine how and where future rules can be applied to the developing shape.

Rules 8 to 11 provide for *extensions;* one of these rules must be applied exactly once to each side of the core unit labeled *A.* How these rules work is closely controlled. If rule 8 or 10 is applied, for example, the axis of the fireplace must fall within the middle third of the block being added. Added blocks must be smaller than the core unit, but no less than a quarter of its size. The rules determine not only the position of the addition but also how it relates to the space. Rules 8 and 9 generate separate wings, while rules 10

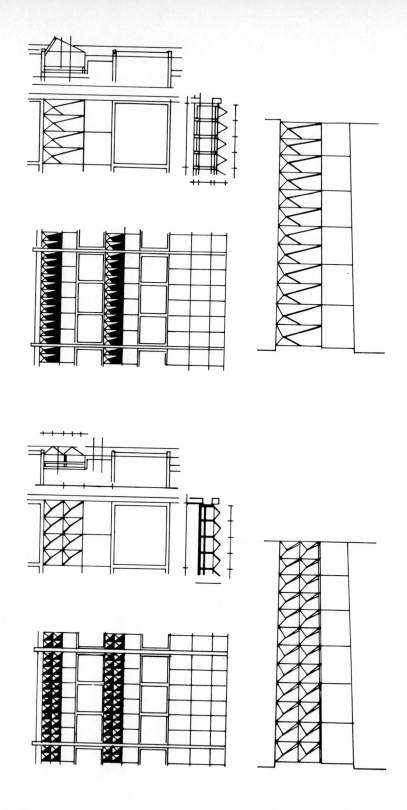

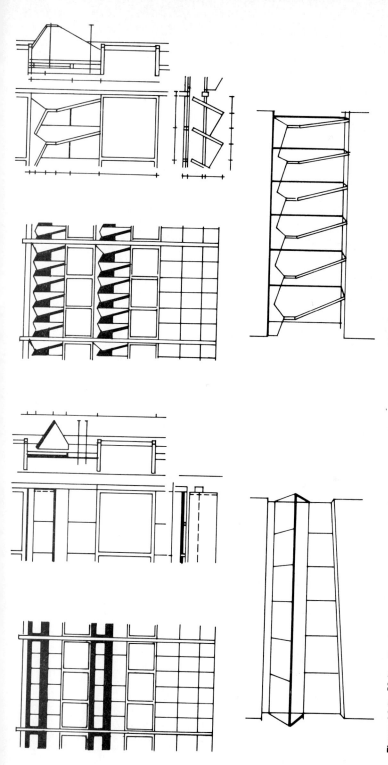

Figure A6.6 Using the computer-generated nomograms, a rich variety of shades can be designed to satisfy the performance requirements. Here, computer-drawn perspectives, building elevations, and details are shown for four alternative designs for the same window. (*Shaviv, 1978; reprinted by permission from the Proceedings of the CAD 78 Conference, published by IPC Science and Technology Press and organized by the journal Computer-Aided Design.*)

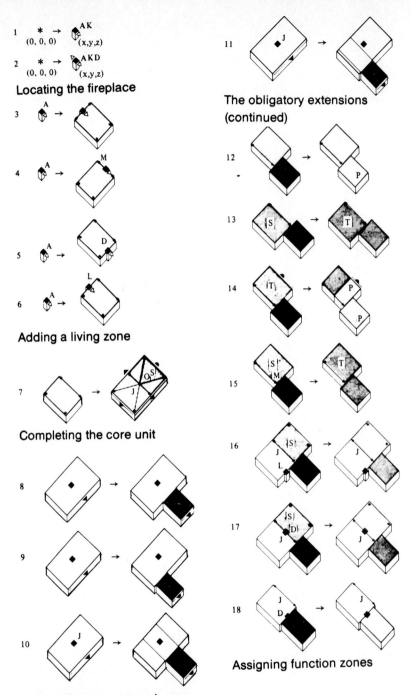

Locating the fireplace

Adding a living zone

Completing the core unit

The obligatory extensions

The obligatory extensions (continued)

Assigning function zones

Figure A6.7 An extract from the transformation rules developed by Koning and Eizenberg for the composition of designs in the style of Frank Lloyd Wright's prairie houses. The rules state that if the pattern on the left of the arrow exists in the design, then it can be replaced by the pattern on the right. Some rules are mandatory, some optional. For example, rules 1 and 2 state that if there is a point on the site that can be considered the origin of the building, then

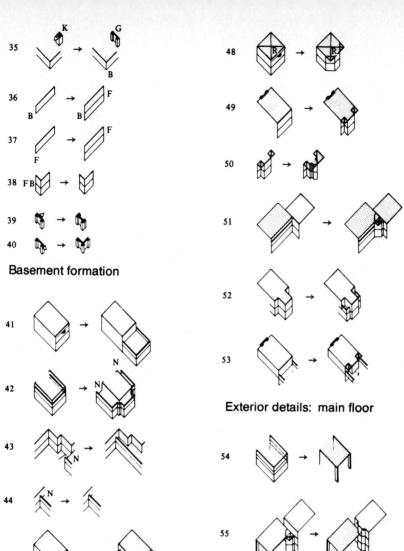

Basement formation

Adding terraces

Exterior details: main floor

Creating portes cocheres

57 → ⟨s_φ, {(0, 0, 0):J}⟩ → ⟨s_φ, ∅⟩
58 → ⟨s_φ, {(0, 0, 0):S}⟩ → ⟨s_φ, ∅⟩
59 → ⟨s_φ, {(0, 0, 0):T}⟩ → ⟨s_φ, ∅⟩
60 → ⟨s_φ, {(0, 0, 0):P}⟩ → ⟨s_φ, ∅⟩

Erasing main-floor nonterminal label

that point can be transformed into a one- or two-way fireplace. One of these two rules must be applied. Rules 3 to 6 show four ways in which the state of the design can be transformed into a fireplace with a living zone. Moving on, rule 47 states that if the design contains an internal corner, then a terrace can be placed in that corner. Rules 19 to 34 and 61 to 99 are not shown. *(Koning and Eizenberg, 1981; used by permission of Environment and Planning B.)*

and 11 generate extensions that interpenetrate the existing core unit. Note that the rules place the *a* symbol on the end wall of the wing, so that the design cannot be extended farther in that direction. The diagonals and *O* symbol are again used in controlling the application of future rules.

The next set of rules assigns *functions* (service or living zone extensions) to these added wings in ways that reflect Wright's tendency to group services together so that they do not interrupt living zones. The result is one of 89 basic compositions for Wright's prairie-style houses. The remaining rules in the grammar (99 of them altogether) *elaborate* these basic compositions to produce a variety of complete designs. Some of them (including those which add roofs or basements) must be applied; others (including those which add porches, terraces, portes cocheres, and further extension wings) are optional. Rules 41 to 47, for example, deal with the possible addition of terraces on the end of a wing (rule 41), in an internal corner (rule 47), or in other ways. These rules can be applied once, several times (as long as the necessary conditions and labels exist in the design to be modified), or not at all. The result, then, is a rapidly expanding set of possible designs legal within the grammar. If the grammar is right and the rules are right, any of these possible designs should fit into the style of Wright's prairie houses. We can judge for ourselves whether this is true: Koning and Eizenberg used the shape grammar to develop the Stiny house (Figs. A6.8 and A6.9), one which Wright himself never got around to designing.

Both the drawings and the grammar in this example have been executed by hand, but it is quite feasible to implement a shape grammar as a computer program. As Mitchell (1979) points out, if we want to generate computer designs that can be taken seriously as architecture, then we must define languages of architectural form that are both interesting and elegant. For these prairie houses, the language has been drawn from an existing and highly regarded body of work. The result is a tool of architectural criticism, helping us to understand something about the history of architecture. If we want to use shape grammars as tools in the creation of a new architecture, we need new grammars. But if we are generating designs automatically, where is the creativity? It lies in the creation of the rules themselves, and perhaps it also lies in the choice of which of the optional rules to apply. If we take an English linguistic grammar as a parallel, correct application of grammatical rules ensures legal English prose but is no guarantee of great literature. Perhaps shape grammars will be a means of achieving legal (meaning competent and consistent) rather than great architecture. Perhaps not, though; if the greatest designers design the grammars, we should get the best architecture.

The major problem with generative models is establishing the rules in the first place. Very rarely it is possible to identify an algorithm quite as elegant as Shaviv's for generating functionally satisfactory building elements, or a set of rules quite as effective as Koning and Eizenberg's for

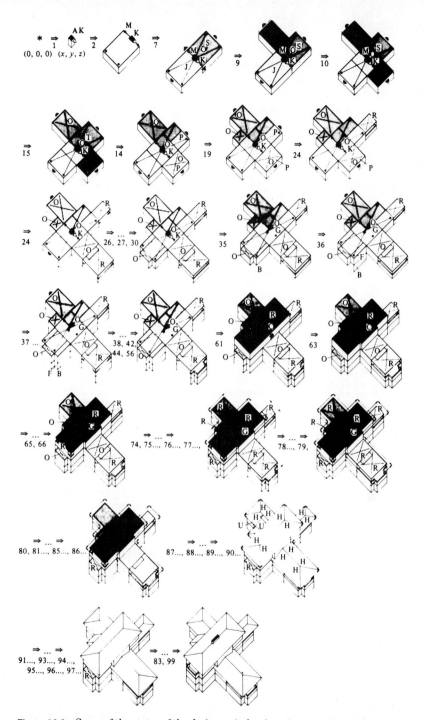

Figure A6.8 Some of the states of the design as it develops from a point on the site to the overall massing of a house. The labels help control which rules are eligible to be applied; they are later removed by other rules. The shading denotes functions assigned to parts of the house. *(March and Stiny, 1985; used by permission of Environment and Planning B.)*

Figure A6.9 A hand-drawn sketch of the house resulting from the sequence of rules shown in Fig. A6.8 and named the "Stiny House" after George Stiny, one of the pioneers in work on shape grammars in architecture. The windows, piers, and base courses are not results of the grammar but have been added in the spirit of Wright's work. *(Koning and Eizenberg, 1981; used by permission of Environment and Planning B.)*

generating building form. But even if we have the rules, we still need to provide direction or control in their application. In the prairie-house shape grammar, for example, the choice of early rules limits the choice of later rules and there is no direct mechanism for ensuring a particular kind of house within the grammar. The shape rules of a shape grammar are a particular instance of what is known as a production system, and both production systems and this problem of control also arise in the computer field of knowledge engineering. We shall return to them in Chap. 7.

A6.4 Optimization Models in Facilities Planning

Optimization, in a rigorous mathematical sense, means achieving the very best solution to a problem. The simplest optimization method is to generate every possible solution within the problem constraints, apply some rule for measuring their relative performance in a desired objective, and pick the best. This exhaustive enumerative approach is simple but not very practical: there are over $3\frac{1}{2}$ million ways of arranging just 10 blocks in a row, and architectural design problems have many more variables than 10 blocks.

In mathematics there are some well-established algorithms for finding an optimal solution to problems that can be expressed in a suitable mathematical form. Classical calculus might be familiar from school algebra lessons, linear programming is a favorite technique from operations research and management, and various heuristic methods have been developed for particular problems. A heuristic method does not guarantee an optimum but appears to approach it, or at least to do better than the unaided human. Mitchell (1977) describes examples of all of these techniques applied to architectural design.

Most attempts to use optimization in architecture have been in research studies rather than in practice (Radford and Gero, 1980), a reflection of the state of development in this area and the difficulty of formulating relevant architectural design problems in the necessary mathematical form to bring these optimization techniques to bear. The major exception is in facilities planning, where algorithms not only exist but really do get used in practice.

Facilities (or layout) planning is the process of laying out rooms, spaces, or facilities within an existing building or as a part of new building design. The facilities might be the departments of an organization, the plant in a factory, sections of a supermarket, or any other appropriate entities. Here we shall look at two approaches to this task: one which adopts and extends the familiar "association matrix and cluster diagram" approach beloved by many an architect as a manual method of articulating the problem, and the other which uses a location/allocation optimization algorithm to assign facilities to spaces according to a best-fit measure of association.

A6.4.1 Association matrix and cluster diagram

The simplest programs will generate cluster diagrams based on association (or proximity) values and allow those clusters to be translated into a rectilinear layout. This layout can then be tested according to criteria for adjacency, orientation, and access.

To use them [we shall use SPACES2 (Th'ng and Davies, 1972) as a model], we first need to assemble a list of the required spaces, including their areas and any desired orientation (north, south, east, west, or none) and access requirements ("access" meaning full or partial views from the space to a specific boundary). An adjacency constraint can also be applied, specifying whether any pair of spaces should or should not share a common boundary. This is all information that would be needed in any brief to design a building.

Next we construct an *association matrix* (Fig. A6.10), which represents the relative importance of circulation or interaction between the spaces in the building. This association matrix is expressed on a constant scale (1 to 10 is common) and is multiplicative, so that 4 implies half the strength of

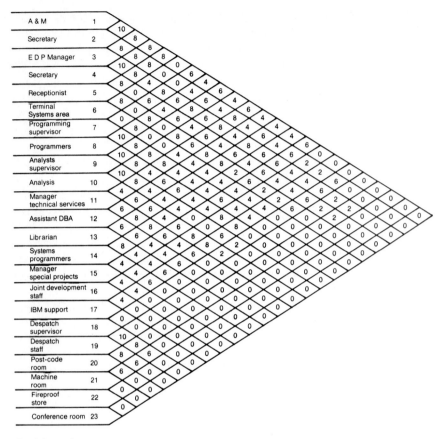

Proximity matrix

Figure A6.10 In an association (or proximity) matrix, the degree of interaction between pairs of functions is indicated on an ordinal scale, here the numbers 1 to 10. *(Courtesy Mitchell Walker Wright, Sydney, using SPACES2 software, University of Strathclyde.)*

8 in representing the importance of a close association. A 0 means that it does not matter if the spaces are close or near, while a 1 means a weak connection, which, in relation to the other values, implies that the spaces should be far apart. The numbers reflect not only the number of trips likely to occur between the spaces but also any relative weighting of the people making the trips, so that a managing director can get preferential treatment over the mail clerk. Usually, of course, the managing director gets the corner office with the best view, whatever any computer program might suggest.

Where do these numbers come from? Any brief will contain some indication of the spaces that need to be close to each other, but it is not normal to specify these relationships in quite this comprehensive and mathematical a fashion. The values might come simply from talking to representatives of the client organization and agreeing upon a matrix of association after much discussion, or from a survey in which members of the organization keep records of their movements or are counted and checked as in a traffic census. This is often a trial-and-error process; once the program suggests a layout, there is much reference back to the association matrix to understand why a particular pattern has been produced, and if the client does not agree with the result, the matrix is modified to reflect any new information and the process is repeated. This way the computer's layout-placing program becomes a vehicle for developing the brief as much as a means of designing the building, and the architect avoids the problem of justifying his or her numbers.

Typically, cluster diagrams (Fig. A6.11) are layed out on the computer screen so that the distances between the centroids of the bubbles are inversely proportional to the numbers in the association matrix. The ideal solution is one in which the result of multiplying the association by the distance between every pair of spaces in the layout is a constant, achieved when all the distances are inversely proportional to the degree of association. For clarity, the area of each bubble is proportional to the area of the space it represents. It is, of course, possible to produce many different sets

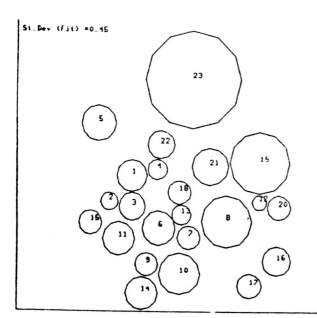

FUNCTION RELATIONSHIP MODEL
(BUBBLE DIAGRAM)

Figure A6.11 A cluster (or bubble) diagram is generated from the association matrix such that the sizes of the bubbles indicate the relative sizes of the spaces needed by different functions, and their distances apart indicate their relative degrees of interaction.

of bubbles that reflect the association matrix equally well, particularly if many of the spaces have no defined interaction. Note, too, that a weak association forces bubbles representing the relevant spaces to be far apart in the diagram, even if there are no other spaces between them.

With some programs the bubbles can be converted into rectangles (Fig. A6.12), which can then be interactively manipulated into position to form something more akin to a sketch plan (Fig. A6.13), like shifting cutout cards around on a drawing board. As this is done, the program calculates the performance, using indexes for the original criteria of adjacency, orientation, and access.

Such models fit into this section on optimization because they optimize (by a heuristic search method) a layout of bubbles to minimize a mathematical objective function. The optimization ends with a cluster diagram, not with a plan; deriving the plan from the diagram (whether or not the architect chooses to stay with the computer to convert bubbles into rectangles) depends entirely on the architect's skill. There are, however, other computer programs that lay out spaces directly.

A6.4.2 Stacking and blocking

The earliest, and still the most common, mechanism for laying out spaces directly is an algorithm that allocates a list of required facilities to a set of available locations in a way that minimizes the total "circulation cost,"

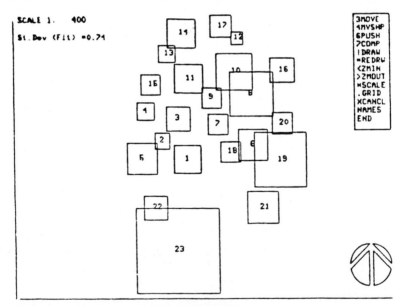

IDEAL FUNCTIONAL RELATIONSHIP

Figure A6.12   The bubbles of the cluster diagram are replaced by rectangles, which are more indicative of a plan form for a building layout.

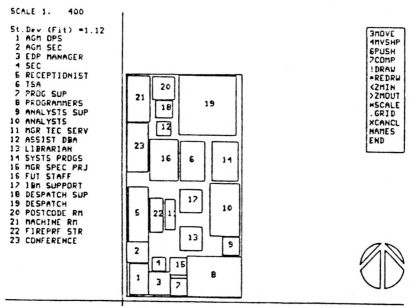

SCALE 1.   400

St.Dev (Fit) =1.12
1 AGM OPS
2 AGM SEC
3 EDP MANAGER
4 SEC
5 RECEPTIONIST
6 TSA
7 PROG SUP
8 PROGRAMMERS
9 ANALYSTS SUP
10 ANALYSTS
11 MGR TEC SERV
12 ASSIST DBA
13 LIBRARIAN
14 SYSTS PROGS
15 MGR SPEC PRJ
16 FUT STAFF
17 IBM SUPPORT
18 DESPATCH SUP
19 DESPATCH
20 POSTCODE RM
21 MACHINE RM
22 FIREPRF STR
23 CONFERENCE

3MOVE
4MVSHP
6PUSH
?COMP
!DRAW
=REDRW
<ZMIN
>ZMOUT
*SCALE
.GRID
XCANCL
NAMES
END

MANIPULATED FUNCTION RELATIONSHIP

Figure A6.13   The rectangles representing the areas needed by different functions are interactively manipulated into a plan form by the program user.

using what is known as a quadratic-assignment formulation of the problem (Mitchell, 1977). Because this is one application in which the computer is clearly functioning as a design tool, it is worth describing the process in some detail.

We shall assume that our particular task is to fit a new organization into an existing multistory office building, so we already have floor plans showing the available spaces (Fig. A6.14). We begin by creating a database containing the *project description,* the *spaces* and their areas and the *activities* to be housed and the areas they require. The system itself (we shall use Calcomp's software as a model) may be able to generate a diagram of the organization showing the hierarchy of departments and subdepartments so that functions at any level, high or low, can be selected.

A facilities-planning program typically operates in either section or plan, assigning facilities to floors of a building, known as *stacking* (Figs. A6.15 and A6.16), or assigning them to zones or areas on a floor, known as *blocking* (Figs. A6.17 to A6.19). In an office building we might first want to sort out the floors to be occupied by different departments, then the positions on each floor to be occupied by sections within departments. For both tasks, we use adjacency matrices to specify the degree of interaction between facilities. We might also wish to preassign some areas (we might want the staff canteen on the top floor despite the fact that its interaction

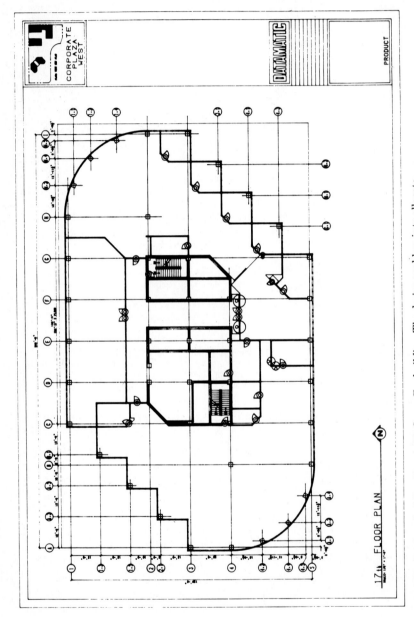

17th FLOOR PLAN

N

Figure A6.14 A typical floor from a 20-floor office building. The design problem is to allocate a list of activities (office departments) to floors in this building and to lay out the departments within any one floor. (*This and Figs. A6.15 to A6.19 were generated at Datamatic, Sydney, using Calcomp System 25 and facilities-planning software.*)

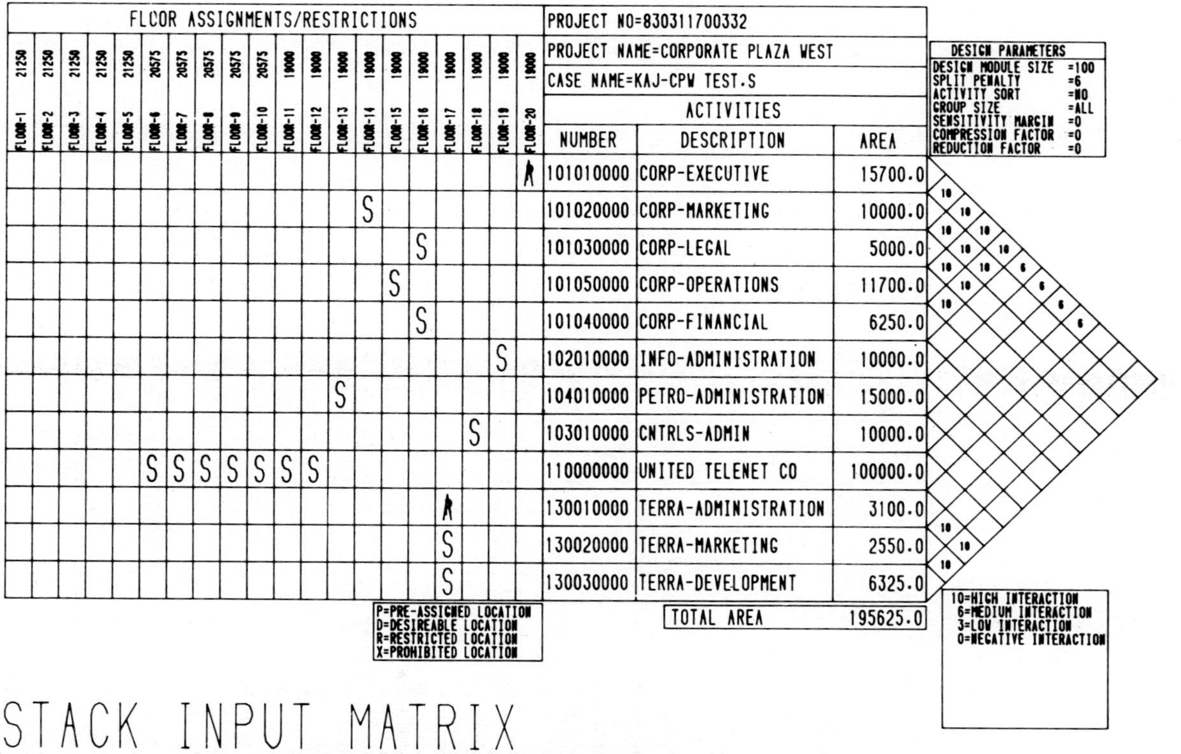
FLOOR ASSIGNMENTS/RESTRICTIONS
FLOOR-1 21250
FLOOR-2 21250
FLOOR-3 21250
FLOOR-4 21250
FLOOR-5 21250
FLOOR-6 20575
FLOOR-7 20575
FLOOR-8 20575
FLOOR-9 20575
FLOOR-10 20575
FLOOR-11 19000
FLOOR-12 19000
FLOOR-13 19000
FLOOR-14 19000
FLOOR-15 19000
FLOOR-16 19000
FLOOR-17 19000
FLOOR-18 19000
FLOOR-19 19000
FLOOR-20 19000
PROJECT NO=830311700332
PROJECT NAME=CORPORATE PLAZA WEST
CASE NAME=KAJ-CPW TEST.S
ACTIVITIES
NUMBER
DESCRIPTION
AREA
101010000 CORP-EXECUTIVE 15700.0
101020000 CORP-MARKETING 10000.0
101030000 CORP-LEGAL 5000.0
101050000 CORP-OPERATIONS 11700.0
101040000 CORP-FINANCIAL 6250.0
102010000 INFO-ADMINISTRATION 10000.0
104010000 PETRO-ADMINISTRATION 15000.0
103010000 CNTRLS-ADMIN 10000.0
110000000 UNITED TELENET CO 100000.0
130010000 TERRA-ADMINISTRATION 3100.0
130020000 TERRA-MARKETING 2550.0
130030000 TERRA-DEVELOPMENT 6325.0
TOTAL AREA 195625.0
P=PRE-ASSIGNED LOCATION
D=DESIREABLE LOCATION
R=RESTRICTED LOCATION
X=PROHIBITED LOCATION
DESIGN PARAMETERS
DESIGN MODULE SIZE =100
SPLIT PENALTY =6
ACTIVITY SORT =NO
GROUP SIZE =ALL
SENSITIVITY MARGIN =0
COMPRESSION FACTOR =0
REDUCTION FACTOR =0
10=HIGH INTERACTION
6=MEDIUM INTERACTION
3=LOW INTERACTION
0=NEGATIVE INTERACTION
STACK INPUT MATRIX

Figure A6.15 The activities are input and listed with their areas and code numbers in a *stack input matrix.* In the triangular section on the right, the degree of interaction between different activities is indicated on a scale of 1 to 10, with a 0 denoting negative interaction (to be kept apart) and a blank denoting no interaction. The rectangular section on the left allows activities to be preassigned to or prohibited from the particular floors listed along the top.

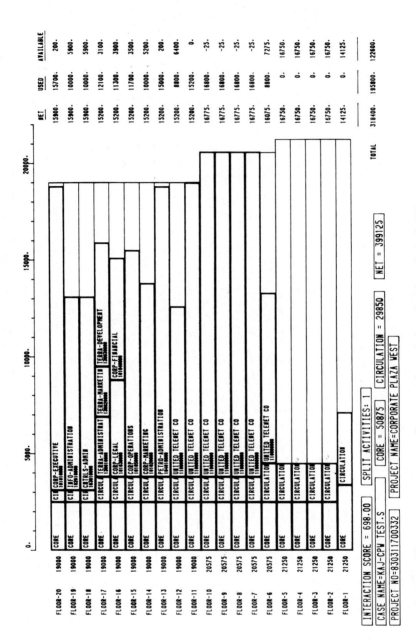

Figure A6.16 The program generates a diagrammatic vertical section through the building showing the activities that the layout algorithm has allocated to each floor. On the right are the net area, the area already allocated, and the remaining available area on each floor, with their totals for the building. At the bottom is an *interaction score*, which signifies the relative success of the allocation in meeting the specification of the interaction matrix in the stack

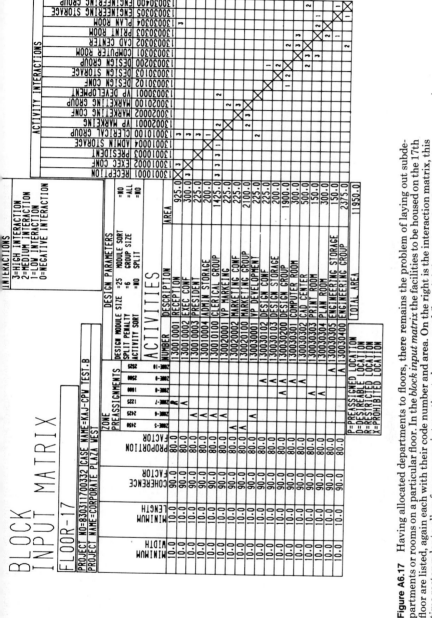

Figure A6.17 Having allocated departments to floors, there remains the problem of laying out subdepartments or rooms on a particular floor. In the *block input matrix* the facilities to be housed on the 17th floor are listed, again each with their code number and area. On the right is the interaction matrix, this time rectangular to allow for one-way interaction to be expressed (here it is important for the reception area to be close to the plan room, but not vice versa) and with the interactions expressed on a scale of 1:3. On the left is a record of the preassignment of facilities to particular zones (parts) of the floor, any constraints on minimum width and length, and the coherence and proportion factors. A high coherence factor indicates a need for the activity to interact with itself and therefore to be pulled together rather than spread out. A high proportion factor indicates that the facility should occupy a square space rather than an elongated one.

217

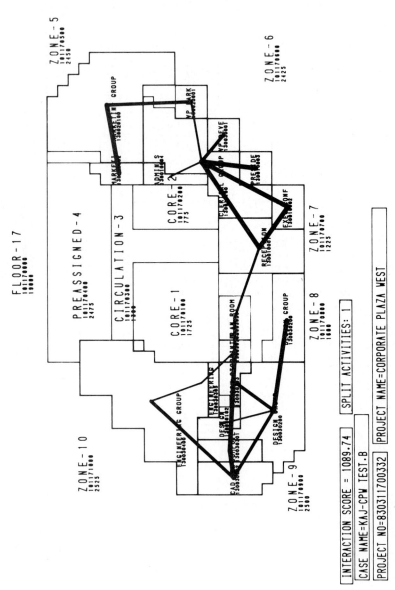

Figure A6.18 From the block input matrix and a description of the building geometry and zones, the program generates a diagrammatic floor plan with its spatial allocation of the different facilities. The superimposed lines link the centroids of facility areas where an interaction has been specified, the lines' widths illustrating the degree of interaction on the same scale of 1:3. As with the floor allocation, there is an interaction score to provide a basis for comparing different solutions.

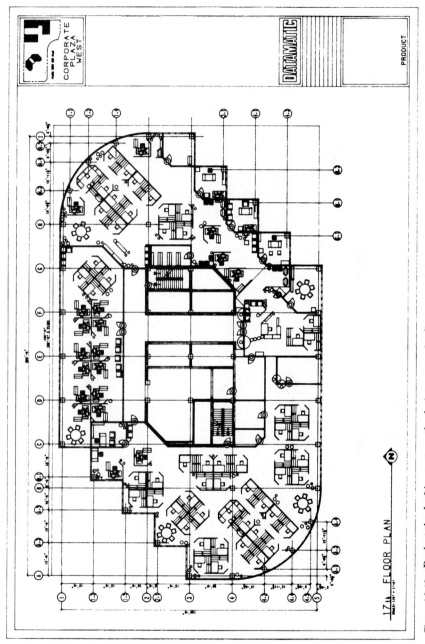

CORPORATE
PLAZA
WEST

DATAMATIC

PRODUCT

17ᵗʰ FLOOR PLAN

Figure A6.19 Back at the drafting system, the designer uses the diagrammatic layout plan as a basis for placing furniture and partitions to fit the different facilities in their appropriate positions.

with the office's departments suggests it go in the middle), to set some parameters that penalize or encourage the splitting of facilities over different floors or zones, and to impose constraints on the lengths, widths, and proportions of individual areas in a floor plan.

This association matrix is the basis for the automatic solution of the planning problem. As with the cluster-diagram programs described above, the result is described as both a diagram and an "interaction score" that provides a numerical index to compare with other possible solutions. This is useful if we wish to move individual activities interactively in either the stacking or blocking diagrams (perhaps in recognition of other design requirements not expressed in the matrix) and want to see the effect on circulation. Indeed, a facilities-planning program can be a useful tool in representing and expressing the planning problem without any automatic layout optimization at all.

With facilities-planning programs we always have the problem of finding the numbers that represent associations and determining their credibility as the generators of plans. First, are these numbers, however carefully chosen, really reflective of the need for different spaces to be close to one another over the lifetime of the building? Second, is a criterion that takes only the circulation cost into account really an adequate representation of the many goals and implications of layout planning?

Sometimes maybe yes, but usually these tools are better used as a part of the articulation and clarification of design problems than as a generator of immutably perfect solutions. They allow clients to be involved in interactive sessions in which multiple solutions are generated and feedback is used to modify the associations and constraints before trying again, a process that combines ideas from optimization and appraisal. Used in this way, the programs help in identifying those groups and organizations of space which remain stable even when some of the numbers change. The optimization is used to provide design information, not a design.

7

Computer-Aided Knowledge

7.1 Introduction

There is a change in the perception of computers from being sources of computational power to being sources of knowledge. The field is called *knowledge engineering,* a beguiling title that combines the connotations of knowledge (brainpower, erudition, and experience) with those of engineering (control, strength, and the construction of large structures from small parts). In fact, knowledge engineering simply attempts to transform knowledge, instead of just facts and procedures, into a form that can be represented in computer systems. It is closely related to two other fascinating topics in computer research, artificial intelligence (Winston, 1984) and expert systems (Hayes-Roth, Waterman, and Lenat, 1983). *Artificial intelligence* is, as it sounds, concerned with endowing machines with some of the characteristics of intelligence normally associated with humans, including the ability to understand and communicate in natural language. *Expert systems,* more modestly, are computer programs that model the performance of human experts within their domain of expertise.

In this chapter we shall look at the characteristics of expert systems and knowledge-based design systems, the problems of knowledge acquisition in architecture, and the implications of this new view of the role of computers in the design office. In the secondary text we shall describe two prototypical examples of expert systems: a diagnostic system for building regulations and a generative system for construction details.

7.2 Expert Knowledge and Expert Systems

Expert knowledge, of course, has been the traditional basis for the professions, and the notion that computers might intrude into this area can be rather alarming and will certainly have far-reaching implications. Doctors know about bodies, engineers know about stresses and strains, and architects know about buildings. Experts in any field possess a rich and diverse store of knowledge, drawn from their education, from reference libraries, and above all from their working experience. As new knowledge is acquired, it is related to what is already available, and this occurs in a psychologically complex way that is not fully understood.

7.2.1 Facts and relationships

At the risk of oversimplification, we can list three classes of knowledge:

1. *Facts.*   The simplest kind of knowledge is simply about facts: houses have roofs; Frank Lloyd Wright was born in 1869. This is the kind of knowledge that can be encoded in traditional databases. One of the keys to the future is access to the encyclopedic knowledge of large databases with millions of entries.

2. *Relationships.*   A skill like designing involves knowledge beyond mere facts. We need knowledge about procedures, or *how to do things:* how to calculate the U-value of a wall or how to decide what kind of floor construction to use in a house. We need knowledge about relationships between facts and procedures — and about the *inferences* that can be made from an available set of facts and relationships. If procedures can be expressed in a reasonably simple algorithm (as for a U-value calculation), they can be fairly well represented by a traditional procedural computer program. If they cannot, and most knowledge about relationships and inferences cannot, then procedural computer programs are likely to prove clumsy.

3. *Metaknowledge.*   Experts also use knowledge about what they know and how to apply it, called metaknowledge. Experts know their personal strengths and weaknesses and their level of expertise in different domains; they know where they can act authoritatively and where to do so will court a lawsuit for professional negligence. More importantly, they are able to relate new knowledge to their existing store of knowledge.

The key to *human knowledge* is that we do not simply look up a memorized database of facts and techniques to find an exact match for the situation at hand; if we did, we would be very restricted in our abilities and would never learn from experience. Human knowledge includes the ability to infer new facts from existing facts and new techniques from existing techniques. For familiar objects, the process is immediate: Given a wet day and water dripping from the ceiling, we can infer that the roof needs repairing. For unfamiliar objects, the process is difficult or impossible. We go to an expert or specialist when the situation is outside our own domain and we cannot make the necessary inferences ourselves. The skill of an expert lies not in knowing all the answers, but in knowing the right questions (what is needed to be able to deduce an answer) and in being able to explain any decisions made or inferences drawn the process of obtaining an answer.

7.2.2 Automating inferences

An *expert system,* then, is a computer program that incorporates and makes explicit the kind of knowledge that an expert applies to a problem (Fig. 7.1). Typically, the system asks users questions and provides one or more of the recommendations that follow from their responses. The questions are likely to be asked in the jargon of the specialist field, and users will probably be given the opportunity to ask the system how it arrived at its conclusions. The advice might be a *diagnosis* of a fault (why the roof is leaking), a *recommendation* or requirement for action (what to do for passive solar energy), a *classification* (what type of development the proposed building is under the planning regulations), or an *interpretation* (whether the proposed design meets the minimum requirements for floor area and height of rooms).

Existing examples of expert systems are clustered around individual disciplines in which expertise is an expensive commodity, such as medical diagnosis, chemical analysis, geological prospecting, and electronic circuit design. The best known are probably MYCIN in the medical field, which is used to diagnose certain infectious diseases and recommend appropriate drug treatments; PROSPECTOR in mineral exploration, used to deduce from geological information the likely sites for mineral deposits; DENDRAL in chemistry, used to interpret mass spectograms; and R1-XCON in computing, used to design installations of DEC's VAX computer systems in a fraction of the time needed by skilled technicians.

If an expert system is to act like a human consultant, then that system has to process its underlying knowledge in a way analogous to that of its

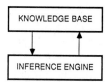

Figure 7.1   All computer programs contain knowledge of some kind. The key characteristic of an expert system is that the knowledge is kept separate (in a knowledge base) from the mechanism (often called an inference engine) that is able to draw on that knowledge and infer new knowledge to provide expert advice or solutions. *(Diagram by the authors.)*

human counterpart. This means that it has to display the following characteristics (Lane and Loucopoulos, 1985):

1. It must be able to *acquire* knowledge from one or more specialists.
2. It must be able to *represent* this knowledge within a computer in a form that allows the making of inferences.
3. Its underlying knowledge must be *accessible* for update and refinement as a result of experience.
4. Its *communication* with the user should be easy and reasonably natural, in the same way that human experts can communicate with their clients.
5. It must be able to *explain* its line of reasoning so that the system is not a mysterious black box, unable to justify its conclusions.

Acquiring knowledge, either for the initial system or for its later updating, is not easy. Experts do not carry their knowledge around in a form devised for convenient incorporation into computer systems, nor are they always very keen to part with their accumulated expertise. The process of extracting this knowledge and mapping it onto a system as a domain-specific knowledge base has become the role of the specialist *knowledge engineer.* The simplest approach is to try to break the knowledge down into discrete self-contained rules (e.g., "If A is true and B is true, then C is true") and literally spell out these rules in the knowledge base. The more desirable objective is that expert systems should be able to gain their knowledge by induction, reasoning from the observation of particular instances. Work toward this goal is proceeding; for example, Davis (1982) describes a program called TEIRESIAS that is intended to acquire new knowledge for the medical expert system MYCIN. TEIRESIAS employs a "tutorial session" in which human user (tutor) sets the system (student) working on challenging problems and fills in evident gaps in the system's knowledge. Indeed, one of the best ways to prize knowledge out of experts is to get them to disagree with the reasoning of a computer expert system and to analyze their explanations.

For *representing* knowledge, there are several possible approaches, and none has yet been proved superior to all others in a general sense. In Sec. 7.3.2 we shall describe a particular method using facts and rules, which is probably the most popular approach so far. The important characteristic is that the knowledge is represented explicitly in an expert-system knowledge base, not implicitly buried in the computer code that controls the program processes.

For the *user interface,* it would be nice to think that communication could be based on natural language — that we could chat with our expert system in the same way that we can chat with a human expert and could get to the point only after discussing the weather and the football results. So far, though, natural-language interpreters have proved rather fragile when used in realistic situations. In the foreseeable future a restricted vocabulary and syntax seems more likely, and it need not be difficult to learn. A restricted language can avoid the pitfalls of ambiguity and grammatical error that plague the developers of true natural-language systems.

The *explanation* facility, last in our list of five characteristics, is in fact much more important than might at first sight be apparent. Human experts are credible because they can justify their recommendations, and a professional report from a firm of consultants usually contains many more pages of justification than of recommendation. Similarly, a good expert system is able not only to answer any inferences that it makes but also to justify any requests for information from the user. It answers questions of "How?" and "Why?" from the user, examines suggestions, and gives reasons for not accepting a user's alternative hypothesis (Fig. 7.2).

7.2.3   Doubts and plausibility

So far in our discussion of expert behavior, we have assumed certainty: If it is raining and there is water dripping from the ceiling, then there must be a leak in the roof. This follows our implicit assumption that the deduction is subject to the strict rules of logic, as in the *modus ponens* axiom:

If   A is true
and   A implies B
then B is also true.

In practice, however, experts most often have to deal with situations in which there is no certainty (no absolutes). In the general case, various propositions might only constitute items of evidence contributing to the plausibility of a particular hypothesis. If we could quantify the plausibility, we could make statements like these:

If A is true, we can be 40% sure that B is true.
If C is also true, we can be 80% sure that B is true.

Although human experts use words like "possible" and "likely" rather than figures like "40%" and "80%" to describe their strength of belief in a hypothesis, in a computer it is much easier to use numerical values. They allow probabilitylike mathematical manipulations and are adopted in the plausible-inference mechanisms employed by such systems as MYCIN and PROSPECTOR. In theory, a well-understood technique called Bayesian probability analysis is ideal for such systems because it links probable causes with probable effects and, given new knowledge, allows the updating of the probabilities associated with possible effects (Lansdown, 1983),

```
             BUILD
A GENERAL EXPERT SYSTEM BUILDER

COMPUTER APPLICATIONS RESEARCH UNIT
DEPARTMENT OF ARCHITECTURAL SCIENCE
        UNIVERSITY OF SYDNEY

AUTHOR : M A ROSENMAN              DATE : JUNE 1985
```

```
do you want the list of command options ? - (y(es)/n(o))
? n.
```

```
                         RETWALL
* A KNOWLEDGE BASE FOR SELECTION OF EARTH RETAINING STRUCTURES *
* Language:  Quintus Prolog    Equipment:  SUN Workstation *
* Author:  Peter Hutchinson    Date:       October 1985 *
```

```
This program selects the most appropriate form of earth retaining
structure for your given application. Earth retaining structures
are used when soil banks have to be retained at slopes steeper than
those they would naturally assume; when for some practical reason
abrupt changes in ground levels have to be introduced; or when it
is necessary to protect soil banks against destructive agencies.

Because retaining walls are expensive, unless space or other
considerations are paramount, an embankment or battered cut, if
feasible, is always preferable to a retaining wall.

enter command

? find 'design of earth retaining structure'.
```

```
The type of application for earth retaining structure is_ ? - enter value (no
w/why/explain)

options for values are :
temporary or marine or emergency or domestic or commercial or industrial or r
oad or railway or heavy vertical load/abutment

? road.

type of application for wall is_ road

The site case most applicable (as shown in the diagram) is_ ? - enter value (
how/why/explain)
?
```

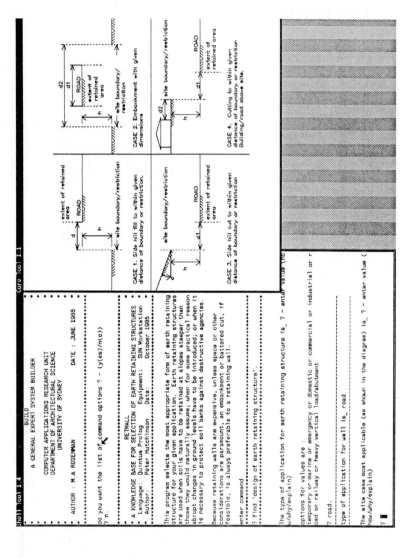

CASE 1. Side hill fill to within given distance of boundary or restriction.

CASE 2. Embankment with given dimensions

CASE 3. Side hill cut to within given distance of boundary or restriction

CASE 4. Cutting to within given distance of boundary or restriction. Building/road above site.

(a)

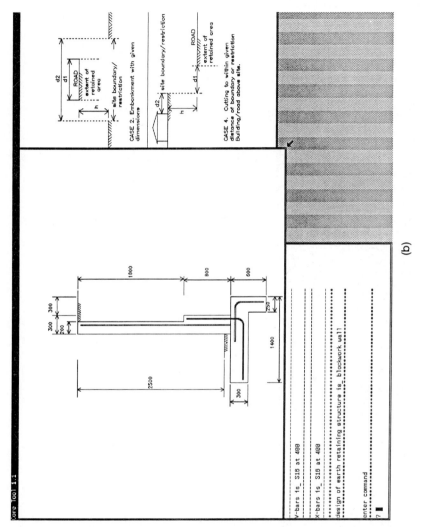

Figure 7.2 An expert system for selecting the most appropriate form of earth-retaining structure for a given application. The inference engine is provided by BUILD, a general expert system builder which infers new facts, given the necessary existing facts and rules, and which also provides the mechanisms needed to answer questions of "how," "why," and "explain" from the system user. The knowledge is provided by RETWALL, a knowledge base established from the technical literature of the field, and by interviews with experienced engineers. (a) The "case" diagrams are used to describe the possible types of application and the parameters for which the system will require values. (b) After a series of questions, depending on the situation, the recommendations of the expert system are presented in both words and a dimensioned cross section of the wall construction. *(Expert system builder written by Michael Rosenman, knowledge base and graphics implemented by Peter Hutchinson, University of Sydney; Hutchinson, 1985.)*

but in practice it is not so easy; thus, existing systems use a variety of modifications to strict Bayesian probability (some modifications seemingly rational in a logical sense, and others justified purely by the fact that they appear to give reasonable results). PROSPECTOR, for example, uses two numerical measurements in calculating the probability evidence (they are, in fact, measures of *sufficiency* and *necessity* in the hargon of PROSPECTOR); their values are fixed in the expert system to allow the evaluation of Y in a statement like:

If we are X% sure that A is true, we can be Y% sure that B is true
where only X is known.

But where do all these numbers come from? As Lansdown (1983) argues, it must be difficult enough to get experts to agree on suitable figures in scientific subjects like geology and medicine that have histories of numerical analysis, let alone in a subject like building that has largely ignored mathematical techniques. This is clearly an area in which further research is needed.

7.2.4   Example: An expert system for subfloor structures

Everything is clearer with examples, so the following describes a very small expert system for choosing between suspended and slab-on-ground subfloor constructions in a domestic-scale building. The example is drawn from the work of Richard Coyne (1986) and is based on *experiential knowledge,* meaning the knowledge that might be derived from the working experience of an architect specialist rather than from established theory. The system uses a plausible-inference engine with numerical measurements, as described in Sec. 7.2.3.

The system can be represented as two inference trees. The first shows the evidential propositions (possible pieces of evidence in a particular situation) that contribute to the plausibility of the hypothesis that "slab on ground" is the best method of subfloor construction, and the second shows propositions that contribute to the alternative hypothesis that "strip footings and piers" is the best approach (Fig. 7.3). Percentage figures are used to represent directly the strength of each proposition's contribution to the appropriate hypothesis. The knowledge is stored as eight rules that link a proposition to a hypothesis and associate a numerical strength with the contribution that this evidence would make to the hypothesis.

The system asks questions of the user, but instead of giving "yes" or "no" answers, the user responds with a percentage weighting to indicate the degree of certainty attached to the proposition: there is a 20 percent chance, for example, that an impervious floor finish will be required (Fig. 7.4). A tally is kept for the two competing hypothesis of "slab on ground"

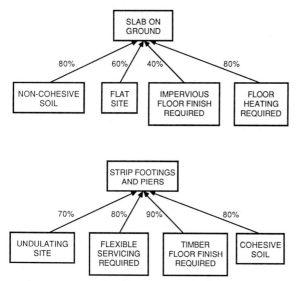

Figure 7.3   A plausible inference net, showing those proportions (and their respective strengths) which have a bearing on two competing hypotheses for a suitable floor construction, namely, "slab on ground" and "strip footings and piers." *(Coyne, 1986.)*

and "strip footings and piers"; initially, the tally for each hypothesis is zero, but as evidence is added, the tally is updated. This updating process is a simplified version of the approach taken by MYCIN and other expert systems; it uses a formula for calculating the probability of an event being true, given two other events that are conditionally independent of each other. Eventually the tally for "slab on ground" reaches 98 percent and that for "strip footings and piers" reaches 62 percent. Given this tally, the system regards the "slab on ground" hypothesis as "true," meaning that this is the most appropriate subfloor structure.

7.2.5   Applications in architecture

This brief example has been very much simplified, but it does give something of the flavor of expert systems and indicates where they can be usefully employed, given the present state of the art. Principally, they are suited to domains of expertise in which the rules are known (or knowable) and in which experts are able to articulate their knowledge. Within this area, they work best where the rules required to make the system work are of manageable quantity (although MYCIN extends to many rules, so manageability is relative) or where the knowledge can be subdivided into manageable groups of rules that are semi-independent.

In architecture, expert systems at the *briefing stage* might assist in de-

Evidential Reasoning System

(enter ?begin.)

: ?begin
Enter percentage weighting for the following ...

impervious floor finish required ? ... 20.
(tally for - slab on ground - 8%)
(tally for - strip footings & piers - 0%)

flexible servicing required ? ... 50.
(tally for - slab on ground - 8%)
(tally for - strip footings & piers - 40%)

flat site ? ... 90.
(tally for - slab on ground - 58%)
(tally for - strip footings & piers - 40%)

undulating site ? ... 30.
(tally for - slab on ground - 58%)
(tally for - strip footings & piers - 53%)

timber floor finish required ? ... 20.
(tally for - slab on ground - 58%)
(tally for - strip footings & piers - 62%)

heaving soil ? ... 95.
(tally for - slab on ground - 90%)
(tally for - strip footings & piers - 62%)

cohesive soil ? ... 0.
(tally for - slab on ground - 90%)
(tally for - strip footings & piers - 62%)

floor heating required ? ... 80.
(tally for - slab on ground - 98%)
(tally for - strip footings & piers - 62%)

** true

Figure 7.4 A dialogue between expert system and user for an illustrative evidential reasoning system for ground-floor construction. The user is prompted to supply a measure of his or her conviction about each proposition. As each question is answered, the system presents the progressive tally for each competing hypothesis and finally advises that slab on ground is the most appropriate subfloor structure. *(Written by Richard Coyne, University of Sydney; Coyne, 1986.)*

termining the feasibility of a project, in ascertaining the spatial and functional needs of clients and users, and in establishing project priorities. At the *design stage,* expert systems might help in site analysis, in design decision making (as in the subfloor decision system described above), and in the checking of design proposals against fire authority or other building code requirements (Fig. 7.5). At the *documentation stage,* expert systems might help determine what working drawings and specifications are required in order to describe the building adequately and might check that the necessary contract documentation has been produced. In *construction,* they could assist a site agent in the ordering and management of a complex building site and assist an architect in the quality control of a building at various stages of construction. With *completed buildings,* expert systems can help in controlling building services systems and in diagnosing building faults and problems (dealing with "ill" buildings in the same way that MYCIN deals with ill people); Lansdown (1983) has developed some prototypical systems dealing with the identification of molds and fungal growths in structural timber and joinery. These are all fairly obvious potential areas of use: expert systems have application wherever knowledge extends beyond the trivial and universal and into areas where particular skill and experience is required.

7.3   Knowledge-Based Design

7.3.1   Knowledge in CAD systems

So far we have described expert systems as self-contained entities that exist quite separately from other computer-aided design systems. Equally, if not more, important is the notion of imbedding explicit knowledge (of

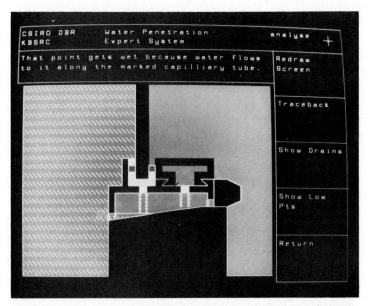

Figure 7.5   Screen image from an expert system for drained joint design for aluminum windows, running on an IBM AT with professional graphics. The system establishes where and how water penetration occurs so that existing designs can be analyzed and modifications evaluated. Extensions will cover other kinds of joints in building facades designed to resist water penetration. *(Developed by John Thomson at the CSIRO Division of Building Research, Melbourne, Australia; used by permission.)*

the kind encoded in an expert system) within more general computer design tools. Thus, a drafting system for building working drawings might "know" something about the way buildings fit together and make use of that knowledge for the semiautomatic detailing of common constructional problems.

This is not as exotic as it sounds. Any computer program for design purposes contains implicit knowledge imbedded within it, so that a program for calculating U-values "knows" the procedure for calculating U-values. A computer building modeling system may similarly make use of knowledge about some fundamental characteristics of buildings (floors tend to be horizontal, walls vertical, and buildings are made up of a series of horizontal layers) in its organization of the building description database and in its ability to update elevations or sections to match a change in the plan drawing. Going further, a few drawing systems automate such procedures as the laying out of timber studs and noggins in a stud partition wall according to preset rules about stud spacing and the handling of junctions and openings. Systems are also available for the semiautomatic layout of concrete reinforcement and similar tasks. An example is a stair-generation module developed by Jung/Brannen in Boston (Kemper, 1985); it generates macro-language commands for a computer drafting/modeling system to produce both graphic and nongraphic information for stair cores. Given answers to questions such as floor-to-floor height, door locations, quality and cost parameters, materials, and the federal, state, or local building codes to be applied, the system generates small- and large-scale plans, typical sections, specifications, and details for critical joints drawn from libraries of standard details and templates. The aim is to generate information that is 90 to 95 percent rather than 100 percent complete. These forms of automated layout use expert knowledge just as surely as self-contained expert systems do, and they are available now.

The knowledge imbedded within most of these existing computer systems is embodied in the computer code itself, so that changing the knowledge means reprogramming the computer. The disadvantage is that even if the programmer's view of the user's world is not out of date before problem development is completed, it is very likely to become so soon after. Moreover, knowledge once encapsulated in computer code is notoriously difficult to unpick and recreate (Bijl, 1982). The fundamental feature in the handling of knowledge as we think of it here, whether in an expert system or within a drafting system or other CAD tool, is that the *knowledge is kept separate,* thus represented explicitly rather than implicitly and able to be modified without recoding the computer program.

A CAD tool that is *knowledge-rich* (meaning that it contains a considerable amount of knowledge about the practices and conventions of the intended user's world) can be much more effective than one containing little knowledge. Aart Bijl (1982) makes this point when he distinguishes between dumb and intelligent drawing systems. A *dumb* drawing system produces drawings by following instructions from a user about where to place lines on paper. An *intelligent* system is, in addition, able to interpret the arrangement of lines as descriptions of the real-world objects depicted in the drawings. The advantage of a dumb system is that it is general; by avoiding any association between lines and real objects the same system can serve users in very different fields. The advantage of an intelligent system lies in its ability to make use of its inbuilt knowledge about the attributes and relationships of what is drawn. Bijl cites the example of obtaining construction quantities from a drafting system in the building industry. A dumb system can count the instances of groups of lines that the user has explicitly labeled as building components, thus providing a schedule of quantities for distinct components. An intelligent system can identify not only these distinct components but also different junction details and ways of putting components together in order to produce something closer to a production bill of quantities. Further, if the system can recognize different ways of putting components together on a drawing, it can, in theory at least, begin to know how components ought to be put together and can externalize that knowledge as computer-generated lines on paper.

The obvious *motivation* for using knowledge-rich systems is the potential for increasing productivity by automating low-level design decisions and procedures, encoding within a computer program the knowledge on which they are based. Other motives may be just as significant. The great majority of failures in building construction result from the nonapplication of existing recorded knowledge, so there is much to be gained from making this knowledge available at the point where it is most valuable, that is, in the production of building construction information. Westlake and Waight (1984) suggest other arguments for knowledge systems, including the avoidance of the dilution of an organization's expertise through its dissemination to numerous individual draftspersons and (conversely) the ability to apply that knowledge to an expanding workload without a delay in training staff. In some situations there might also be a desire to protect trade secrets, although this is rarely a factor in architecture.

7.3.2 Design critics and design generators

There are essentially two places where the knowledge that resides in computers can be injected into the design process: after the synthesis of the design, as a *design critic,* and before the synthesis of the design, as a *design generator.*

Design critic.   The design critic approach parallels the performance prediction of simulation and quantitative analysis in computer-aided design by using judgmental knowledge acquired from human experts to test the

Shell [00] I.I
archsc![14]: r1vka% /usr/local/rp_src/screen)/tmp/r1vka5

K

A TYPICAL DESIGN SESSION

CHECKING THE DESIGN

GRAPHICAL DISPLAY

core [00] I.I

corridor plan

SUGGEST
EXPERT
CLEAR
QUIT

Shell [00] I.I
USE LEFT HAND BUTTON TO TERMINATE
locate the center of counter on wall
[3,391.864,784.81]
locate the center of counter on wall
[3,403.546,435.506]
locate the center of counter on wall
[2,481.44,588.86]

----

classification of kitchen size is medium

----

the approval of kitchen counter is true

[3,391.864,191.244]
locate the centre of the sink
[3,429.164,884.026]
[3,815.424,715.186]
locate one corner of the window
[3,307.84,725.577]
locate other corner of the window
[3,582.445,721.427]

----

area of window in sqm is 4.11986

----

light is sufficient is true

----

the approval of kitchen window is true

[3,638.6,164.235]
locate center of fridge
[3,621.907,488.571]

(a)

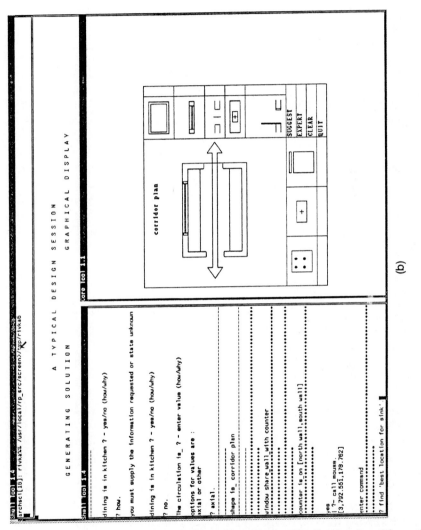

Figure 7.6 A design session with a prototypical expert system for the planning of domestic kitchens. *(a)* As a design critic, the system checks the designer's actions in placing components; here, it approves the size and position of the kitchen counter and, after calculating its area and daylighting capabilities, the kitchen window. *(b)* As a dedisn generator, the system asks the user questions about the use of the space (whether people will be dining in the kitchen), circulation patterns, and other parameters and generates a design solution. *(Written by RIvka Oxman, University of Sydney.)*

adequacy of design proposals. Consider the design of a domestic kitchen (Fig. 7.6). Design critics would check the proposed length and width for sufficient space and acceptable proportions and would check that the stove, sink, and worktop form an acceptable working group, that the window provides enough daylight, that the cupboards are big enough, and so on. This evaluative approach is analogous to that of a diagnostic expert system, in which the design critic tries to *diagnose* a fault in the design, given a description of the design.

The major implementation difficulty is matching a geometric model of the kitchen to a semantic model (what the parts are and mean) within which the knowledge can operate. If the design is initially described only within the geometric model, then the semantic model must be constructed by the recognition of particular elements in the description, which is part of the general problem of pattern recognition in artificial intelligence. More likely, the design will be described by a combination of geometric and semantic descriptions (so that a kitchen counter will be described as such and will have associated with it a material, surface finish, size, etc.), but it will still be necessary to calculate from the geometric database the tolerances, clearances, circulation patterns, and other factors not explicitly described but necessary as input to the knowledge rules. For example, given a rule in the knowledge base,

Counter is acceptable
if   there is one window
and   room shape is corridor
and   window is on long wall
and   counter shares wall with window

the system needs to interpret the meaning of "corridor shape" and to establish its validity from the database descriptions of the room plan and door positions.

The design critic approach allows flexibility in the design process and in the design solutions that can be developed, although there can always be debate about the applicability of the knowledge base to all kinds of designs that might be proposed by the designer.

Design generator.   This alternative approach questions whether it is really necessary to interpret the design: Why not simply get the design right in the first place by implementing generative rather than evaluative rules? A generative production rule for "counter is acceptable" would be

if   there is one window
and   room shape is corridor
and   window is on long wall
then counter shares wall with window.

For a domain in which the design is assembled from a fairly restricted library of components with relationships between them, some of this knowledge can be represented in a relational database or as procedures that can be associated with a general-purpose drafting system (Westlake and Waight, 1984). The relationships enable the occurrence of one component to be the necessary and sufficient condition for other components to exist, even if not specifically placed by the designer. The specification of a kitchen, then, will imply the occurrence of stove, sink, counter, and so on, both on the drawings and in schedules of components:

If   standard kitchen
then   add stove
and   sink
and   kitchen counter.

The *rules* that control such associations are themselves defined within the database and are executed by relations to other rules. The knowledge used is tailored and domain-specific to the user of the system. Within such domains, the way in which components fit together in assemblies is standardized and of limited variety; for instance, the word "add" in the rule quoted just above implies an understood and established set of dimensions, fixings, positions, and tolerances. The design generation leads to a single form of solution that follows from the initial specification of the design problem, although because the specification will vary in many subtle ways, no two solutions may be identical. Knowledge-based generative systems become more difficult to implement as the domain becomes more general. The number of possible final design states then quickly approaches infinity, and the problem of control and of achieving desired designs becomes considerable.

The aim of a generative expert system as a synthesis tool is to allow designers to *work at a high level* of design descriptions, subsuming lower-level synthesis in the generation of such designs. The higher level could be the complete or partial building or detail. Since designers currently do much of their work at high-level states, there is nothing fundamentally new in this notion. An architect designing a building typically produces first a sketch design, then an outline design, then a detailed design. The first two assume that the details implicit in the outline specification of the final design are capable of being generated later, meaning that either the architect or others have the knowledge to design those details. The significant notion here is that this assumed knowledge will lie within the computer design system. The specification of a given design state will imply reference to the lower-level design states and to the knowledge necessary to reach those states.

7.4   Implications

Much of what we have described in this chapter concerns the future rather than the present: the search for ways of making computers more responsive to real human needs and to the way that humans work. It will be some time yet before we turn to a consultant computer rather than a consultant human as the first source for most building problems.

Nonetheless, expert systems are beginning to appear (Lansdown, 1984a and 1984b), and the new drafting systems aim to incorporate more knowledge about buildings than did earlier systems. The result will be computer tools that address the central area of a professional's skill and thus, at first sight, pose the kind of threat to professional employment and status that robots and word processors appear to pose to factory and clerical staff. Certainly we can expect future computer-aided architectural design systems using knowledge engineering concepts to be very different from the ones with which we have become familiar. On the credit side, this means that designers should be able to work at a higher level than is now possible, using computer-resident knowledge to supplement their own expertise. It should also give small practices something of the range of expertise in different areas that is presently the preserve of the large office. Moreover, because this knowledge can be represented explicitly and the tools that use it need not be black boxes, expert systems (or expert system components of wider systems) can explain their reasoning and make it possible for a human user to learn from the use of a computer consultant. All this should produce more completely designed buildings.

On the debit side (perhaps), the use of computer systems of this potential power will almost certainly cause some structural change in the profession, especially in the relationships between architects and other consultants in the building industry.

Their use also raises profound issues of *professional liability* and of the *ownership* of and *responsibility* for the knowledge contained within computer systems. The journal *New Civil Engineer* ("CAD Methods," 1983) reported a case of a multistory car park where "reinforcement has been fixed to a pattern 90 degrees out of orientation, it is alleged, with misuse of software the root cause of the mistake." The journal's source is reported as saying that "engineers are blaming the computer software used to design the slabs. Faulty programming resulted in the reinforcing steel being put in incorrectly. It looked alright superficially but the slabs were light of steel in the direction of span where they should have been heavy." Whether or not the report is true, it is eminently believable; all who have used computer programs know the difficulty a user faces in trying to judge the accuracy of the results of the program. As practices base more of their work on computer systems, and as these systems incorporate more knowledge about their field of application, such problems are bound to occur. It is going to make quite a lot of lawyers wealthy. The only safeguard is a theoretical understanding that would enable the user to recognize when something is badly amiss. Where the expertise is represented in the computer code explicitly (as in our definition of expert systems) rather than implicitly, this problem of checking the knowledge is very much easier, but a sound theoretical understanding is still necessary.

We could present all this as an ethical question concerning whether it is desirable to transfer human knowledge into inanimate computer memories and write off the job satisfaction lost by the "drains experts" and human "building regs encyclopedias" who presently inhabit every large office and derive their status from knowing more about a select topic than anyone else in the organization does. Instead, we shall suggest the blossoming of creativity that might emerge from designers who are able to work with increased confidence in their ideas and decisions because of the computer-resident knowledge that they have been able to tax.

7.5 Summary

Artificial intelligence might suggest a future of synthetic superbrains taking over from humans, but the present reality is that the artificial version of intelligence is no match for the richness and versatility of the human brain. Expert systems, the chief products of artificial intelligence research for design, operate within limited domains of knowledge with limited possible results; they run out of knowledge abruptly at the edge of their domain and, unlike humans, cannot make an intelligent guess beyond that edge. On the other hand, expert systems will apply their store of knowledge tirelessly, consistently, and often more quickly than humans. They can take care of the repetitive solution of well-defined classes of problems, freeing the human to work at higher levels of intelligence. Indeed, the combination of human and knowledge-based computer system can make a powerful team. Whereas computer graphics was probably the most exciting and fruitful area of computer development in the 1970s and early 1980s for architects and the design professions, knowledge engineering and artificial intelligence constitute the most exciting area in the late 1980s and the 1990s.

SECONDARY TEXT
Expert-System Examples

A7.1   A Diagnostic Expert System for Building Regulations

Building regulations combine a large amount of causal and experiential knowledge, but there are two major difficulties in using them: They are large and complex, and they require substantial understanding on the part of the user. Finding and interpreting the necessary information is often difficult and time-consuming, not only for designers but also for the government authorities whose task it is to administer the codes. Continual use makes the process easier, and people can become experts on certain codes. An expert system dealing with building regulations should carry out the same functions as a human expert, providing a coherent and consistent structure to the knowledge and providing a solution to a particular problem by applying the available knowledge in as efficient a manner as possible (Rosenman and Gero, 1985).

Part 49 of the Australian Model Uniform Building Code deals with minimum requirements for the floor area and height of rooms in certain situations, a limited but representative domain of knowledge. An expert system covering part 49 needs to establish the minimum floor area, the minimum room width [for toilets (water closets) only], and the minimum height of a room in any of the building types covered by these regulations. It will have to ask users the questions necessary to enable it to infer the answer to any of these goals. The dialogue between system and user ranges over the building type, its class according to the regulations, the type of room, and further details depending on the type of room. For example, if the room is a bathroom, the system will need to know about intended showers or baths, water closets, and any combination with clothes washing facilities (Fig. A7.1).

The advice provided is the required area or dimension, as appropriate, but providing this answer is only a part of the capabilities of such a system. Among their other characteristics, expert systems can typically answer "how" and "why" replies to their questions and explain their line of reasoning in answering the query. Questions are generally asked in a "top down" order. The user may have information at a higher level than the most primitive information level in the system and should be given the opportunity to provide that information directly. Users who cannot answer a query can ask "how" (how do I answer this?). The system will then search for any knowledge it already has that may help it in inferring an answer and will ask any necessary lower-level questions. For example, if the user of this building regulation expert system asks "how" to the high-level question "The increase in floor area required for clothes washing is?" the system will turn to the lower-level question "The bathroom or shower room contains a washing machine or copper (yes/no)." Given information in its knowledge base, answers to these allow the system itself to infer an answer to the original question. Of course, there is a bottom level at which the system's response to "how" is simply "You must provide the information."

The reply "why" (why do you want to know?) causes the system to look at the reasons for asking the question (what it is trying to infer) and to transmit that information to the user. In the same expert system, if the

```
!!!!!!!!!!!!!!!!!!!!!!!!!!!!!!!!!!!!!!!!!!!!!!!!!!!!!!!!!!!!!!!!!!!!!!!!!!!!
? list goals.
!!!!!!!!!!!!!!!!!!!!!!!!!!!!!!!!!!!!!!!!!!!!!!!!!!!!!!!!!!!!!!!!!!!!!!!!!!!!


g1 : required minimum floor area of room in sq m
g2 : required minimum width of room in mm
g3 : required minimum height of room determined


enter command
!!!!!!!!!!!!!!!!!!!!!!!!!!!!!!!!!!!!!!!!!!!!!!!!!!!!!!!!!!!!!!!!!!!!!!!!!!!!
? find g1.
!!!!!!!!!!!!!!!!!!!!!!!!!!!!!!!!!!!!!!!!!!!!!!!!!!!!!!!!!!!!!!!!!!!!!!!!!!!!


The building is_a ? - enter value (how/why)

options for values are :
dwelling-house or flat or other

? flat.

The room type is_ ? - enter value (how/why)

options for values are :
habitable room or non-habitable room

? 'non-habitable room'.

The building classification is_ ? - enter value (how/why)

options for values are :
Class I or Class II or Class III or Class IV or Class V or Class VI or Class VII or Class VIII or Class IX or Class X

? why.

building classification is_ Class I or Class II or Class III or Class IV
room is_a bathroom
not_true(the bathroom is provided with a bath and shower that is not above the bath or increase in bathroom/shower room floor area r
equirement)
      needed to prove
required minimum floor area of room in sq m is_  0.2200000000E+001

The building classification is_ ? - enter value (how/why)

? 'Class II'.

The room is_a ? - enter value (how/why)

options for values are :
bedroom or living room or lounge room or music room or television room or kitchen or dining room or sewing room or study or playroom
  or sunroom or bathroom or shower room or water closet or laundry or other

? bathroom.

the bathroom is provided with a bath and shower that is not above the bath ? - yes/no (how/why)
? yes.

increase in bathroom/shower room floor area requirement ? - yes/no (how/why)
? how.

the bathroom or shower room contains a water closet pan ? - yes/no (how/why)
? yes.
--------------------------------------------------------------------------------
increase in bathroom/shower room floor area requirement is true
--------------------------------------------------------------------------------
```

Figure A7.1 Part of the dialogue between the system user and a prototypical expert system for building regulations. The knowledge base deals with required floor areas and heights of rooms in certain situations under Australian building code proposals. One of three "goals" is selected and the system attempts to "find" an answer to the goal, asking the user to provide values for facts it needs to know. Note the "why" and "how" responses to the system's questions; a "why" response causes the system to point out why it needs the value in order to prove some intermediate goal, and a "how" response causes it to ask lower-level questions in order to infer the value of a fact that the user does not know *(Rosenman and Gero, 1985; written by Michael Rosenman, University of Sydney.)*

user replies "why" to the question "The building classification is?" the system responds that it is trying to establish that the required minimum floor area is some specific value and to do this needs to know the building classification, that the room is a bathroom, and that the room is not provided with both a bath and a separate shower. Finally, the explanation facility (Fig. A7.2) will explain how a conclusion was derived, why all other conclusions failed, or why a particular conclusion did not succeed.

```
##########################################################################
? explain proof.
##########################################################################
required minimum floor area of room in sq m is_ 0.4700000000E+001
   proved true by rule No. r16 because
building classification is_ Class II
room is_a bathroom
the bathroom is provided with a bath and shower that is not above the bath is true
increase in bathroom/shower room floor area requirement is true
increase in floor area required is_ 0.1900000000E+001
  0.4700000000E+001 is_equal_to 0.2800000000E+001+ 0.1900000000E+001

increase in floor area required is_ 0.1900000000E+001
   proved true by rule No. r20 because
increase in floor area required for W.C. in sq m is_ 0.7000000000E+000
increase in floor area required for clothes washing in sq m is_ 0.7000000000E+000
increase in floor area required for clothes drying in sq m is_ 0.5000000000E+000
  0.1900000000E+001 is_equal_to 0.7000000000E+000+ 0.7000000000E+000+ 0.5000000000E+000

increase in floor area required for clothes drying in sq m is_ 0.5000000000E+000
   proved true by rule No. r27 because
the bathroom or shower room contains a clothes drying cabinet is true

increase in floor area required for clothes washing in sq m is_ 0.7000000000E+000
   proved true by rule No. r24 because
the bathroom or shower room contains a washing machine or copper is true
the bathroom or shower room contains a washtub is false
not_true(the bathroom or shower room contains a washtub) is true

increase in floor area required for W.C. in sq m is_ 0.7000000000E+000
   proved true by rule No. r22 because
the bathroom or shower room contains a water closet pan is true

increase in bathroom/shower room floor area requirement
   proved true by rule No. r19 because
the bathroom or shower room contains a water closet pan is true
```

Figure A7.2 Having found an answer to the goal, the system is asked to "explain proof." This causes it to trace back through the series inferences it has drawn in order to find the answer; it lists the rules it used and the intermediate facts it inferred in the process (Rosenman and Gero, 1985). Here, rules 19, 22, 24, 27, 20, and 16 in the knowledge base were used in deriving an answer.

In most expert systems of this type, the "knowledge" about the domain is stored separately from the program that asks the questions and makes the recommendations. It is stored as a series of facts and "if . . . then" conditions that record in a different form the clauses of the building code. An expert system without any knowledge is known as a *shell* and can be used with a number of different files of knowledge. Thus, the knowledge base contains the specific knowledge about the specialism or domain, while the shell contains the mechanisms for inference and the "why," "how," and "explain" operations, and the means for communicating between system and user. Both shells and full expert systems vary in the degree of sophistication of their interface with users and in the ease with which knowledge can be inserted into the knowledge base. A sophisticated interface contains elements of natural-language understanding and makes the system easy to exploit by an unfamiliar user. An unsophisticated interface works very close to the programming language of the implementation and requires both the knowledge and the answers to be formulated in particular and unusual ways.

A7.2   A Generative Expert System for Building Details

The *working detail* in architecture is the means by which an architect describes to a builder how the parts of a building are to be fashioned and assembled. Its purpose is to ensure both functional sufficiency and aesthetic consistency. Architects design a building using a personal vocabulary of responses to design problems, and this vocabulary extends to the details.

Many architectural practices maintain sets of standard details to cover recurring situations, and it is possible to buy books of "good practice" standard details, published by some authoritative organization or individual. Existing computer-aided drafting systems facilitate the organization, transfer, and management of such sets of standard details. They are correct for the single, specific design situation for which they were originally created. The junction of a wall and window, for example, may be based on an exemplary detail showing the way in which a "typical" wall should meet a "typical" window, with the associated flashings, fixings, and sealants. Since architecture is characterized by variety, however, the standard case rarely applies.

As descriptive drawings, *working details depict facts:* the sizes of members, the topological and geometrical relationships between components, and (via notes) the materials and finishes to be used. The *knowledge* employed in establishing these facts comes from the designer and is rarely explicated in the drawing. Because standard details deal only with facts and with final designs, they contain no intrinsic basis for their modification; consequently, a decision on what may or may not be varied rests entirely with the user of the detail. The knowledge is embodied in the drawing and is not retrievable. It is, indeed, implicitly assumed that an architect or draftsperson altering the detail has access to the same body of knowledge that was available to the original designer, but this may not be true; in fact, a reason for using standard details is not only to increase productivity but also to overcome a lack of such knowledge.

An expert system for detailing should be founded on providing the knowledge for synthesizing particular solutions. Ideally, the knowledge should be contained as one description of the solution and should be retrievable. As an example, we shall consider an illustrative *generative expert system* for eave details. In fact, the expert system will only generate eave details to match Australian domestic construction around the years 1910– 1912; by developing a set of design rules (a grammar) within a coherent and established style of architecture, the aesthetic consistency of the language of designs within the grammar is ensured by the rules themselves. Any resulting detail will be aesthetically acceptable.

The generative knowledge is represented as a sequence of "condition and consequence" production rules (Fig. A7.3) of the same generic form as those in shape grammars (see Sec. A6.3.2). Thus, rule 1 of the grammar proposes that

> *If*   there is a single-leaf brick external wall and a pitched roof
> *then*   a wall plate shall terminate the wall
> *and*   the wall plate shall be fixed to the wall by straps.

As rules are applied, the design passes through a series of intermediate states (first wall, then wall with wall plate, then wall with wall plate and rafter, and so on) until the complete design is generated. In a traditional detail only the shape is described (by a drawing), with appropriate annotations. Computers allow the maintenance of many different descriptions of the same design. A detail can be described symbolically (for the internal convenience of the computer), by two- and/or three-dimensional shape, by written specification, by cost, by a record of the course of its creation, by the knowledge implicit in the decisions taken during its creation, and by any other appropriate form. Moreover, with computers it becomes very easy to switch between these different descriptions. Thus, the state of the eaves detail after applying rule 1 might be specified by:

1. The shape.
2. The specification: i.e., "Fix 4-in × 2-in (100-mm × 50-mm) sw wall plate to single-leaf brick external wall using 1-in × $\frac{1}{16}$-in (25-mm × 1.5-mm) galvanized ms straps at 10-ft (3000-mm) centers tucked under minimum 6 courses of brickwork."

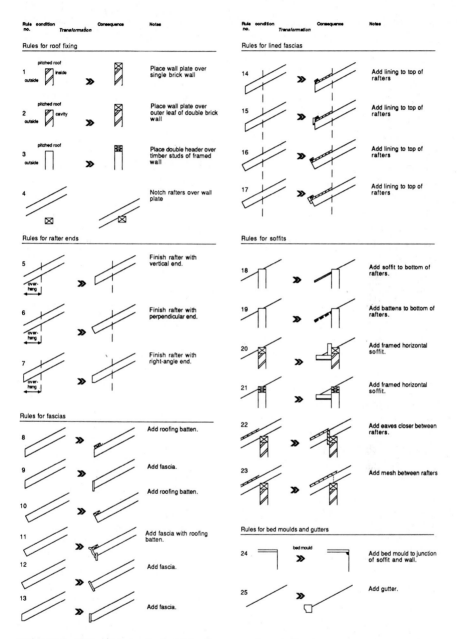

Rule no.	condition	Transformation	Consequence	Notes

Rules for roof fixing

1 — pitched roof / outside / inside ≫ — Place wall plate over single brick wall

2 — pitched roof / outside / cavity ≫ — Place wall plate over outer leaf of double brick wall

3 — pitched roof / outside ≫ — Place double header over timber studs of framed wall

4 — ≫ — Notch rafters over wall plate

Rules for rafter ends

5 — overhang ≫ — Finish rafter with vertical end.

6 — overhang ≫ — Finish rafter with perpendicular end.

7 — overhang ≫ — Finish rafter with right-angle end.

Rules for fascias

8 — ≫ — Add roofing batten.

9 — ≫ — Add fascia.

10 — ≫ — Add roofing batten.

11 — ≫ — Add fascia with roofing batten.

12 — ≫ — Add fascia.

13 — ≫ — Add fascia.

Rules for lined fascias

14 — ≫ — Add lining to top of rafters

15 — ≫ — Add lining to top of rafters

16 — ≫ — Add lining to top of rafters

17 — ≫ — Add lining to top of rafters

Rules for soffits

18 — ≫ — Add soffit to bottom of rafters.

19 — ≫ — Add battens to bottom of rafters.

20 — ≫ — Add framed horizontal soffit.

21 — ≫ — Add framed horizontal soffit.

22 — ≫ — Add eaves closer between rafters.

23 — ≫ — Add mesh between rafters

Rules for bed moulds and gutters

24 — bed mould ≫ — Add bed mould to junction of soffit and wall.

25 — ≫ — Add gutter.

Figure A7.3 The complete set of rules for the generation of a class of eave details in section, in the form "if the condition on the left exists, then the condition on the right can replace it." Some rules are mandatory (there must, for example, be a wall plate of some kind), while others are optional. Applying the rules leads to a variety of possible design solutions, but all are inherently defined by the rules themselves. *(Diagram by Zol Nemes-Nemeth, University of Sydney.)*

3. The quantities: i.e., "X m of 4-in × 3-in (100-mm × 75-mm) sw, Y No. 20 × 1-in × $\frac{1}{16}$-in (500-mm × 25-mm × 1.5-mm) galvanized ms straps," where X and Y are calculated from the length of external wall over which the detail applies.

4. The cost: i.e., "Timber $A, straps $B, fixing $C, total $D," where A, B, C, and D are calculated from facts about the costs of materials and labor in assembling materials.

5. And finally, the knowledge: i.e., "Wall plate needed for nail fixing of rafters. 4 in × 3 in (100 mm × 75 mm) is traditional size. 4 in × 2 in would work but would not look right. Straps needed to hold down roof against wind uplift."

This description of the state of a design in terms of the knowledge imbedded within it is different from the "why" mechanism described in Sec. A7.1 that enables expert systems to explain their conclusions. The response to a "why" question in such systems is to interrogate the train of inferences that leads to a particular conclusion. This is also useful in a generative expert system to explain the present rule in terms of future design states, but we need more. We need, too, to understand the knowledge of why a consequent state in a transformation rule takes that particular form, and that is what is provided by maintaining a separate parallel description of the knowledge imbedded in the system. Given such a description, the expert system becomes an educational tool as well as a production tool.

The implementation issues, as with an generative expert system based on production rules, concern the encoding of the rules within a computer system, the representation and recognition of design states, and mechanisms for control and for tracing back from a complete design to the lower-level states that it subsumes (Coyne, 1986; Coyne and Gero, 1986). The simplest control mechanism is to ask the system user to accept or reject the consequences of each rule in turn, trimming the number of possibilities by a process of interactive selection. What we usually want to do, though, is to specify some salient points about the desired result and let the expert system sort out which valid rules will generate a design with those characteristics. Whereas most shape grammars begin from an initial state (a point on the site for the Frank Lloyd Wright grammar described in Sec. A6.3.2) and work toward a catalog of feasible designs within the grammar (known as forward chaining), for a detailing expert system we need to work backward from characteristics of final designs (Fig. A7.4) to the rules and conditions that allow those characteristics to exist (backward chaining).

Generative systems allow designers to concentrate their work on the new and different aspects of a design, rather than diverting attention to the re-solving of detailed design problems where there are already acceptable and well-established solutions available. They provide a base level on

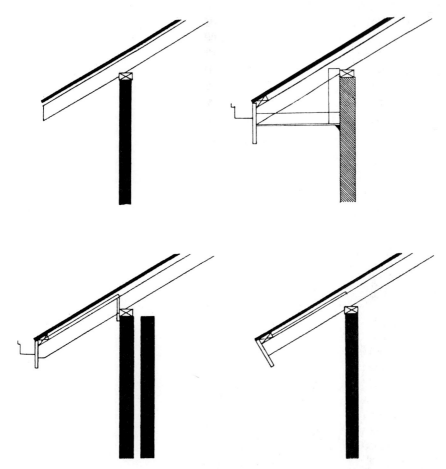

Figure A7.4   Some computer-generated eave details following the set of rules presented in Fig. A7.3. In this implementation, the user is simply asked in turn if each valid rule (one for which the left-hand side has a match in the state of development of the design) is to be accepted or rejected. Either way, the system looks for the next valid rule and repeats the process until there are no more left to apply. *(Written by John Mitchell, Mitchell Walker Wright.)*

which the designer can work. Their domains will for some time be small in scope and lie within well-defined areas, such as through limiting the application (to doors, windows, or eaves, etc.) and/or the variety (to a system building method, to a particular style, to a type of door or window, etc.). There is a need for a solid theoretical basis for their development that will emphasize the accessibility of the knowledge being used, its availability to modification, and the acceptability of the result with respect to an architect's traditional concern with aesthetic as well as functional quality.

Decisions

Chapter

8

Working with Computers

8.1 Introduction

The acquisition of a computer will change the way any organization works; if it doesn't, it's not being used very well. A single microcomputer will not be earthshaking, but a network of microcomputers will cause tremors and a CAD system will cause an earthquake. In this chapter we look at how to make good earthquakes. We first look at the preparation for and implementation of computer systems and then at the particular questions of training users and managing the economics of such systems. In the secondary text we examine the working environment: what computers demand, what humans would like, and an introduction to the options for cabling and power supply and workstation design. All this is addressed to those with the power to make decisions, but it should be read by all (Fig. 8.1).

8.2 Preparation

The very first requirements in computing are *interest, enthusiasm*, and *commitment* among those who have the power to make and implement decisions. These will make the difference between a productive and progressive office and a static and frustrated one. The combination of unskilled directors (power without expertise) and low-level system managers (expertise without power) is usually fatal.

The second requirement is to have a clear *organizational plan*. Large computer systems have been purchased with only the vaguest idea of what they were supposed to do and how they were to fit into an organization. One and all, such installations have been failures. Choosing one system instead of another will not in the end matter as much as using it properly. Further, there is absolutely no point in obtaining a computer in the hope that it will fix up some existing mess. Computers require discipline to use effectively,

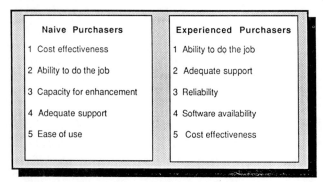

Figure 8.1 People buying computers for the first time have different ideas than experienced purchasers do about what counts as important. Naive purchasers most often mention cost as their primary concern, followed by the system's ability to do the job, but second-time purchasers place its ability first; their experience with cantankerous machines also leads them to emphasize adequate support and reliability. Naive purchasers, worried about their ability to operate a computer, often mention ease of use but this does not figure among experienced purchasers' concerns. *(Diagram by the authors; data from Davies, 1983.)*

and they impose their own methodologies. Far from saving a disorganized office, computers will destroy it.

The third requirement is to have *time*. Both the director and the system manager need some weeks (for a single microcomputer) or some months (for a CAD system) to learn the system, to integrate it into the office, and to sort out the many problems that inevitably arise with any installation. As a rough guide, one partner of a midsize architectural firm estimated that 90 percent of his time was dedicated to his (fairly extensive) CAD system in its first year, and 50 percent thereafter.

The fourth requirement, of course, is to have the *money*. Leighton (1984) suggests that computing should cost around 1 percent of an architectural firm's annual gross income, but surveys in Europe and Australia have noted expenditures commonly in the range of 1 to 3 percent, and a level of 5 percent is probably quite reasonable if the expenditure includes amortized capital costs, operating costs, and specialist staff. Some offices spend much more. It is safe to assume that any system will be useless for the first week to 3 months of its life, so in this period it will be less a benefit than a financial drain.

8.2.1 Getting help

Architects, being rugged individualists, show a perverse pride in doing things themselves. The amount of information on computers readily available is now considerable, but time and again architects decide to go and find out for themselves. And how do they do this? By asking vendors. With a touching, if tragic, naïveté they walk boldly into the arms of beckoning dealers, assured in their own minds of being able to sort out the reality from the hyperbole. On the basis of glossy sales brochures, abrim with photos of attractive young ladies earnestly engaged at drafting stations, architects have been known to buy several hundred thousand dollars worth of CAD system. They would never have dreamed of choosing a building contractor in the same way.

Sales literature is just that: literature designed to sell. Extracting real information out of suppliers is notoriously difficult, even for very popular programs and machines (Cockle, 1983a). The best safeguard is *self-education*, and this book is a good start. Before purchasing anything, we need a sound idea of the overall market and of the functionality of existing products. If a firm does not know what a DBMS is, there is little point in buying one, although many firms will do so because they have been told that DBMS is something they ought to have. Two common mistakes are worth mentioning. The first is to be sold on some feature on the (mis)understanding that it is unique to one product. Vendors will often emphasize quite mundane and expected characteristics of programs, making them out to be especially sophisticated features, like a car dealer claiming that four tires make a unique feature. The second mistake is being impressed by genuinely unusual and powerful abilities that in fact would be rarely used.

There are three general principles in approaching any product selection. First, *talk to someone who has used the program or system* and who is not selling it. One architect was directed by a vendor to the offices of a supposedly satisfied customer. Mistaken for the vendor's representative, she learned with great clarity just what the customer thought of their service and maintenance staff. Second, *read the documentation*. The manuals will tell us everything we need to know about the capabilities of the system, and if they are so poor that they do not answer our questions, we shouldn't be buying the product. Their clarity and comprehensiveness are key guides to the overall quality of the program or system. Third, get an *independent view* from a written review and/or a competent consultant. Most national architectural institutes have substantial informational resources, and the national computer-aided design organizations (e.g., CEPA in the United States, CICA in Britain, and ACADS in Australia) are also available to help. These organizations will make reference to certain key written documents (particularly for CAD systems), which, while not cheap, and heavy reading, are probably the best guides available. In App. 1 we list some architectural journals and books that discuss the selection process in detail.

There are, of course, many dealers and original equipment manufacturers (OEMs) around, although they often advertise themselves as consultants rather than vendors. There is nothing wrong in purchasing a computer through such a firm (indeed, the cost direct from the manufacturer might be substantially more), but at least several OEMs should be contacted to get different biases. Since the competition is as cutthroat in the microcomputer and minicomputer markets as it is in the used-car business, a potential buyer is exposed to a good deal of propaganda, sales talk, and downright lies.

8.2.2 Alternatives to buying a computer

We must begin with the alternatives to acquiring a computer at all: service bureau, timesharing, and reprographics systems. A *service bureau* is a company that runs its own minicomputer or mainframe, assembles a collection of programs, and runs jobs for customers (Fuller, 1983). For example, Masterspec2 (a specification service sponsored by the AIA) in the United States and the National Building Specification in Britain are available in this way. We receive a printed master copy, mark by hand the bits we don't want, and return it to the bureau. A day or two later a neat finished copy arrives. Once upon a time, when computers were very expensive, this was a popular way of doing things for all manner of tasks, but many of these have now been taken over by in-house microcomputers. Using a bureau is all well and good, but it hardly provides real computing experience, and over time it is not particularly cheap when compared to buying a much more versatile microcomputer. A word processing or drafting service will probably charge per page or drawing of output each time it is used, plus an initial subscription fee and an annual user fee (Leighton, 1984). To get computing experience, we need to be operating computers ourselves, and many drafting bureaus do indeed allow outsiders to use them in do-it-yourself drafting shops. This is a very good way (perhaps the best way) to get familiar with a particular CAD system at minimal cost.

With a *timesharing service*, a bought or leased terminal in the office is connected to a remote computer owned and run by another organization, often a service bureau. The company charges for storage of information and for central processor time, and it possibly charges access fees for particular programs. The telephone company also charges for the use of the telephone line and, on most dedicated lines, for the amount of information transmitted. These charges can be significant, perhaps several thousand dollars per month in situations of heavy usage. Drafting and design systems will certainly require very high-speed dedicated lines, and these are much more expensive to use than low-speed lines. While timesharing services have their place, many of their functions can be perfectly well handled by microcomputers, and for less cost in the medium to long run. They are excellent for familiarizing an office with CAD, but the cost over several years is probably more than buying or leasing. Their best use is, again, for learning about CAD (but not about microcomputers) and for gaining access to expensive programs that an office cannot afford to buy or

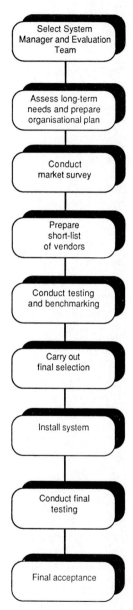

Figure 8.5 A simple flowchart of the selection and acquisition process for computer systems. *(Diagram by the authors.)*

1. A director is appointed to be in overall charge of the firm's computing operations; under the director are a system manager and an evaluation team. In a small practice, of course, the personnel choice is limited.

2. Short- and long-term needs are identified. Just what does the practice want to be doing in 5 or 10 years?

3. Existing office procedures are examined for those which might benefit from computer-based techniques. A management plan is prepared.

4. A performance specification for the computer system is developed, including a list of desired programs or functions. If necessary, a formal request for proposal is written (see Sec. 8.2.4).

5. A market survey of appropriate computer systems is made, and those systems identified as possible choices are investigated. Demonstrations are sought, and existing users are approached for comments.

6. A cost-benefit study is prepared, and the financing is sorted out.

Inevitably, there are some basic issues which always come up and which, although most have been mentioned in earlier chapters of this book, deserve emphasis here. There are seven of them.

The first issue is the dilemma of whether to opt for *state-of-the-art* or *software range*. The rapid development of computer technology sees more powerful machines released regularly. A practice is often faced with the choice of a sophisticated computer that supports little software versus a long-lived but less advanced machine for which a large software base exists. Machines at the leading edge of computer technology will inevitably have less software to offer. The opinion shared by experienced architectural firms is that a firm would do best to opt for a middle-of-the-road system with an established record and with solid but unexciting abilities ("AIA/SC," 1984).

The second issue is the perennial problem of *compatibility*. To ensure a wide selection of software for a machine, it is best if it (1) uses one of the common operating systems, (2) uses a common microprocessor, (3) is selling well, and/or (4) is disk-compatible with a computer that does have a big software base. A CAD system may be selected because it is also used in a sister firm or is widely used by fellow consultants or even by clients. Claims of compatibility with other machines should be treated with a healthy suspicion until personally seen working as required.

The third issue is *vendor support*. Microcomputer manufacturers offer far less support for their machines than do minicomputer makers; given the smaller margins, they cannot afford comparable support. Typically, if a program fails on a microcomputer, it may take days or weeks to get it working again. On the other hand, a wait of hours is more typical for a minicomputer from a major supplier. Good support is important at all levels: hardware maintenance, availability of consumables, range of software, software maintenance, and vendor expertise.

The fourth issue is a decision about *system size*. A large computer installation, such as a drafting or other minicomputer-based system, requires more effort to administer and utilize effectively than does a single microcomputer. Large systems require large resources and cause large changes. The system size that an organization can support depends on how prepared it is to cope with computing, how flexible it is, what expertise is available to it, and how willing it is to allocate resources to system management.

The fifth issue is one of *expansion and change*. Computer installations expand as time goes on and more uses are found for the system (Cockle, 1983b). From the start, an office should plan for this and purchase systems capable of the appropriate expansion in terms of networking, internal memory and mass storage, and additional peripherals, such as printers and even other computers. To think big but start small is good advice, and one should be wary of getting locked into a world of noncompatible, discontinued systems. There is also a matter of moving to a new system when the present one has passed its economic life span. Given the rapid depreciation in computer equipment, 5 years reduces a computer's value to perhaps 5 percent of its purchase price. All the procedures developed and data created under the old installation may have to be thrown out if a significantly different system is introduced. Buying a new machine from the same manufacturer often eases this process, but it locks the firm into that vendor for many years.

Sixth, we need a strategy about *functionality*. The grand aim of computers in architecture is the unification of architectural functions through computers, but we are some distance from this yet. Some observers argue that computer-aided design (not just drafting) systems are the only worthwhile investment (Stoker and Weingarten, 1983) and that architects should aim from the first toward design-integrated systems (Davis, 1984). On the other hand, many firms with full three-dimensional modeling systems find that 80 to 90 percent of their drawings use only the two-dimensional component (Campion, 1984b). Full integration is an ambitious goal and a good long-term objective, but computers offer immediate benefits without such integration.

Finally, we must consider *user sovereignty*. The sharing of computing resources with other firms has not proved to be popular, mainly because the firm that physically has the computer ultimately has supreme control, and partners are reluctant to give this control to others. Sovereignty is diminished by the use of service bureaus or timesharing companies, or when the partners lose touch with the system, as may happen in very large firms. In many commercial organizations with longer histories of computing, the data processing departments have, in the course of years, become bureaucracies unto themselves. With all the computer expertise concentrated in one place, it is difficult for anyone else to determine what the computers can and cannot really do, as distinct from what the computer staff say they can and cannot do.

8.2.4 Evaluation

Having sorted that lot out, we still have to sort out which product to get and how to get it. For large systems, a formal *request for proposal (RFP)* is appropriate. This is a document sent to possible vendors setting out requirements and asking for a definite proposal; Leighton (1984) and Teicholz (1985a) describe the process in detail. An RFP includes a description of the firm and of its objectives in acquiring the system, plus technical details on bidding and deadlines. It should outline the firm's projected growth, its current level of computing expertise, and the functional requirements and projected workloads of the system. As much information as possible should be provided; most RFPs are 10 to 100 pages long. Vendors should be allowed a month or so to respond, but they should be asked to indicate immediately whether they intend to respond at all.

For a sizable system, an *evaluation team* will be constituted, probably including the system manager, one or more directors, middle management, and at least one of the intended users. If a word processor is being purchased, the worst person to carry out an evaluation is a director who cannot type. The users know their jobs best, so they should have a say in how their jobs are best done with a computer. The team will make inquiries among other architects, attend trade shows if appropriate, prepare specifications, evaluate demonstrations, and prepare a management plan and a 5-year plan on how the system will fit into the firm.

A set of *benchmarks* may be useful. For a drafting system, these will be drawings typical of the envisaged workload, so that the effort required to create and store them will provide a rough but very useful guide to the functionality of the system. This will demonstrate the true utility of a system better than canned demonstrations would. Benchmarks should be genuinely representative and useful; the vendor's costs in producing complex examples that are never likely to be required in practice are passed on to consumers in higher prices.

For smaller systems, the least that can be asked is familiarity with the commonly offered features of that sort of product, and this book has dealt with much of the most common software. If the advice given in Sec. 8.2.1 is followed, a firm cannot go too far wrong.

Just as important as the program or system is the nature of the vendor. It must be stable and mature, so that it will still be there over the life of the system. Ideally, its products should be well-established so that a large base of experience exists, but they should also be continuously developing. A program that has remained unchanged for 2 years or more is almost certainly behind the state of the art and about to be superseded. Updates must therefore be available at little cost.

8.2.5 Acquisition and purchase

There are several ways to acquire a computer system. One way is to buy a *turnkey system*, which means that the one vendor sells everything: computer, peripherals, and software. This is sometimes called *bundling*. Although generally more expensive than other methods, it has the advantage that the responsibility for getting the whole assemblage working lies squarely with the one vendor. There is only one number to ring when things go wrong.

A much more common situation is the acquisition of a program for an existing installation; here, the usual approach is to buy a *package (third-party software)*. Commercial off-the-shelf programs are plentiful for both minicomputers and microcomputers. Although they may be less flexible than desired, they do have the advantage of actually working. The program is sold on the basis of nonexclusive *object code* ownership, usually as a nontransferable long-term lease. This means that the vendor does not supply the original source code, thus preventing users from altering the program.

This is not the case with specially written programs, which may be created by *outside consultants, in-house development,* or *vendor customization.* Such programs are supplied on the basis of exclusive ownership of both the source and object codes. Unfortunately, predicting schedules and budgets for program development is notoriously unreliable, much more so than is predicting them in the construction industry. Two-month schedules often stretch out to 6 months or more. Outside consultants are expensive, and internal development consumes a substantial amount of a firm's resources.

A purchase or lease contract must state explicitly just what the vendor is to provide in software, hardware, maintenance, documentation, and training (O'Connor, 1983). One should never buy anything sight unseen (on the vendor's spoken assurance) or on the basis of promised future deliveries of software. Anything not already fully documented, tested, and available may never turn up at all, and almost certainly not at the promised time. Computer contracts have express clauses excluding any verbal promises as well as denying any assurance of the suitability of software or hardware for the buyer's purposes; the vendor may also specify items that are to be provided by the purchasing firm. All contracts should clearly state who is responsible for delivery, setup, cable installation, and testing. More than one architect has arrived at the office one day to find a pile of crates in front of the building and has been stuck with the job of getting them to the right floor.

Quite often the contract specifies that acceptance occurs when the equipment is inspected at the vendor's factory or site and that transfer of title occurs when the equipment leaves the vendor. Clearly, we should have these provisions altered to indicate that acceptance is conditional on passing a mutually agreed-upon acceptance test at our site. Perhaps the equipment should be allowed 30 to 45 days to pass this test, and perhaps penalties should be levied against the vendor if the equipment does not pass it within this period. O'Connor recommends that full transfer of title take place another 30 days or so later, and that the final payment not be made until then.

So at last the boxes arrive; what next?

8.3   Implementation

Some people think that the measure of a system's success is full utilization. This is not so. Quality rather than quantity should be the goal. It is easy to spend long hours at a computer without producing much at all; very easy indeed.

Great expectations are always held for the new baby. Salespeople promise the moon, and buyers, whatever they say, secretly expect it. There is pressure to make the computer productive immediately. Then the anticlimax comes. Perhaps 6 to 12 months elapse before a big computer-aided design or drafting system is functioning anywhere near full efficiency. Implementing even the simplest tasks, such as word processing, takes longer than expected. The early weeks are needed to acquire confidence in the system, to become familiar with its quirks and quibbles, and to learn the language of computing. Like it or not, technical expertise cannot be acquired overnight, and at least one person must learn enough to perform minor maintenance or the whole show will stop when the printer gets jammed — and the computer will end up sitting idle on a desk, in a cupboard, or in the back room. The more sophisticated and extensive the system, the more this expertise is important.

Now this does not mean that every architect has to rush to learn FORTRAN and BASIC and how to rewire a memory board. We don't need to be mechanics to drive cars, but we do need to know something about how cars work. A great many computer systems suffer constant and demoralizing problems; many arise quite simply through what are known as RTBM errors: Read the Bloody Manual. No one ever reads the manuals thoroughly, so no one quite knows what to do when the computer refuses to print or when files mysteriously disappear. True, most computer systems come complete with 6 feet of fat manuals. Too much to read? Then we're in trouble; we shouldn't be running a computer system.

8.3.1   General considerations

Any system, even a single microcomputer, requires a supervisor or manager (Arnold and Senker, 1982). Typically, he or she is responsible for (Heubel, 1982; Leighton, 1984):

1. Making recommendations for long-term planning and budgeting.
2. Training and recruiting operators.
3. Obtaining consumables: paper, disks, tapes, and pens.

4. Organizing the working environment.

5. Controlling time and access.

6. Acquiring technical expertise.

7. Keeping in touch with the vendor and outside user groups.

8. Minor maintenance.

9. Answering questions and helping with problems.

10. Establishing operating procedures, particularly backups.

11. Ensuring compliance with house standards.

12. Obtaining feedback from users.

The manager does not necessarily have to have computer expertise but must be willing to gain it; many firms have committed the error of foisting this job on an unwilling person, who is perhaps afraid of computers, certainly terrified of making mistakes (Smith, 1982). During the early stages, managers must have great patience with themselves and the computer and be prepared to laugh away the most horrifying blunders; a week's work can be destroyed with a few inadvertent keystrokes. By way of becoming competent in computer use, the manager need not be brilliant. More important is a great whack of enthusiasm, and the manager must be able to communicate enthusiasm to the other staff; with enthusiasm and a willingness to learn, half the battle is over.

A host of standards and procedures must be established for matters great and small. Even the manner in which floppy disks are physically labeled and where they are stored can be important in maintaining a smoothly working system. Who can use the computer and when, and which tasks have priority, must be sorted out. Consistent file-naming, drawing-labeling, and layering conventions must be established. Regular data backup must be carried out: CAD system data should be backed up daily, other systems weekly. Ideally, all the standards and procedures should be placed in an *operator's manual.*

The computer must be physically placed where it is needed. Secretaries need word processors on their desks, not in some dim corner. Microcomputers intended for general use by design staff must be placed where all can use them without interfering with someone else's work. A minicomputer may need to be housed in its own air-conditioned room, but CAD workstations should be placed in the drafting studio; otherwise, operators become isolated and reluctant to leave their normal environment (Constantinou, Rathmill, and Leonard, 1982).

8.3.2 Organizing a CAD system

Many approaches have been tried in fitting a drafting system into an office's organizational structure (Heubel, 1982) (Fig. 8.6). In the *service*

Service Bureau Approach

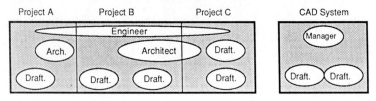

One-Discipline Approach

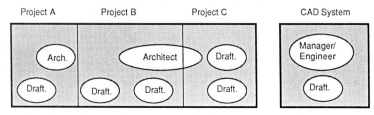

Free Access Approach

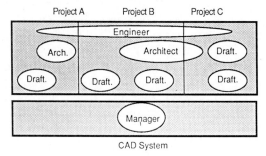

Project Approach

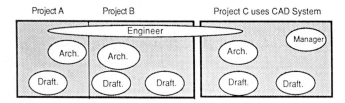

Figure 8.6 Four approaches to organizing a CAD system within a firm. The *service bureau approach* sets the CAD system into its own department, where it acts as an internal drafting service, charging for its services; only a few CAD operators are trained on the system. The *one-discipline approach* is sometimes used in multidisciplinary firms; it allocates the CAD system to one field, usually structural or mechanical engineering. In the *free-access approach* there are no dedicated CAD operators; all drafters in the firm are trained on the system and can use it as needed. This is so for the *project approach* as well, but the system is dedicated to one project at a time. *(Diagram by the authors.)*

bureau approach a separate CAD department is created, staffed by dedicated operators who in effect act as a drafting shop for the rest of the firm. The department charges other sections for its services. In the *one-discipline approach* the system is exclusively used by one discipline within a multidisciplinary firm. The *free-access approach* allows everyone to use the system as they like, with system time being allocated by the system manager. The *project approach* allocates system time to projects, not people. Although the service bureau method is not uncommon in large organizations, most small to medium firms do not find it acceptable (Mileaf, 1983b). The most common solution seems to be a vertical structure in which projects are allocated to the system, and experience indicates that this is the most likely to be successful.

The early establishment of procedures is particularly important. The office must determine: drawing standards for formats, layering, title blocks, dimensioning, and sectioning; system operation procedures for logging in, backups, archiving, and crash recovery; accounting procedures; and operator responsibilities.

When the system is first installed, a *core team* of operators is established to provide a central group of skilled people, and they handle the first project to be implemented on the system (Prince, 1982). Once this first project is out of the way, as many others within the firm as reasonably possible should be trained to use the system. Typical levels are two or three trained operators per workstation (Campion, 1984a; Cockle, 1983b). When this has been accomplished, projects can be allocated to the system at will, knowing that within each project team there will be some individuals capable of using the system.

A very few firms attempt to put virtually every drawing from a project on the system, but most firms find that only certain phases of their drawings are best done by computer drafting (Davis, 1984; "CADD Roundtable," 1984a). If we divide the drawing process into conceptual, graphics, and checking phases, the conceptual phase (accounting for 30 percent of the cost of a drawing) is little helped by a drafting system, the labor-intensive graphics phase (50 percent of the cost) is ideal for computer drafting, and the final phase is often best handled by reprographics methods (Teicholz, 1983a). Hence, each project will have a core team using the computer system and others doing manual drawings. Managing the interaction between the computer draftspeople and the rest of the team can be very trying if the others do not appreciate the limits and abilities of the system, but if everyone within the office has been trained, this problem is eliminated, and there is the further benefit that all have some idea of just what work should be done on the system and what not.

Who should serve as CAD operators is very much an open question. At one extreme, some insist that only low-paid technical-school graduates should be CAD operators, receiving freehand sketches for system entry from the design professionals (Kemper, 1985). The opposite view holds that designers alone should have access to the system, with drafting staff being used only to produce plots and other routine work (Stoker and Weingarten, 1983). This latter position seems to us the more reasonable one. We feel that the imposition of intermediaries between designer and product cannot be beneficial to either and that it discourages the creative use of computers as design tools.

Whether or not to run *multiple shifts* (either two or three per day) is a matter for each firm to decide. In many large American firms a common practice is to dedicate the day shift to designers alone, the second shift to designers and drafting staff, and the third to drafters alone (Mileaf, 1983b; Cockle, 1983b).

For the first 6 months or so, we think it unwise to entrust entire projects to a CAD system. During this period there will be at least one catastrophe of the first magnitude (accidental mass destruction of drawings, nervous breakdowns, that sort of thing), so the practice must be capable of going back to manual backups.

8.3.3 The people

The greatest fears of staff are always about job security (often justified) and competence. Volunteers make better operators; people should be invited, not told, to train, and those who never learn should not become second-class members of the office. Goodwill and good communication are essential to the well-being of any computer installation; passive sabotage is easier than one might think (Allen, 1982; Smith, 1982). Organizations have failed by forcing overawed inductees to operate a system they know nothing about while the rest of the office coldly watches.

Most users look forward to the chance to work with computer drafting. Some see the training as a way to learn more about computers and to acquire new skills, some as a step up in their careers and a way to avoid technological obsolescence, and others as a way of removing drudgery from their work. But some (not necessarily older) professionals feel insecure with the alien equipment and approach their training with trepidation. Fear and doubt can paralyze a professional faced with unfamiliar equipment. Most have absolutely nothing to worry about; the greatest problem is embarrassment over mistakes, which everyone makes. Indeed, keyboard phobia is a very real problem, especially fear of damaging the system. The most common reason for senior management not learning to operate computers themselves is just such a phobia, although they give no consideration to this same fear in their operators. Another fear, sometimes raised by critics of architectural computing in general, is that of the effects of CAD operation on the operators. There is the very real possibility that CAD operators will become captives of the computer rather than masters of it. We postpone discussion of this concern until Chap. 9.

8.3.4   Training for CAD

The CAD education provided by vendors is one of the least satisfactory aspects of the market (Datapro, 1984). A training course on a CAD system must explain the fundamental principles of the hardware involved and some of the theory behind the system, bringing in analogies with existing drawing equipment. This theory is often scoffed at as unnecessary, but continual (albeit minor) problems can arise because the basic theory is not explained to the operators. Training should alternate between hands-on sessions and exposure sessions, in which students are presented with the many ways of using the system in the hope that some will be remembered. Every system has a fundamental core of operations that just have to be mastered and a much larger set that may or may not be immediately useful. Being aware of the existence of these commands is more important than detailed knowledge about them; the manuals can always be referenced later. Introductory courses should aim at the construction of a simple but considerable drawing. All users must acquire a familiarity with the new jargon so they can help each other. A solid introductory course is vastly preferable to one spread over time: 5 or 10 continuous days of training may correspond to 20 days spaced over as many weeks.

Training should, of course, commence before the system arrives. Initial training is always best done away from the firm, where the operators are not distracted by everyday demands and senior management will not be always looking over their shoulders. The operators also get to interact with experienced users of the system. Vendors typically offer a 1-week course, but a 2-week course is better, and 4 to 6 weeks could quite profitably be spent in training (which is best done before the system is installed in the office). Generally, people in training learn the very basics of a drafting system in 3 days and develop adequate proficiency in 3 months. Less than 20 percent fail to develop even marginal skills, mainly through lack of interest or an obstructionist attitude; such people show clear hostility to the system right from the start and are better left to other tasks. Another 20 percent just don't seem to get the hang of it, despite all their efforts. Of the rest, more than half go on to become experts within 9 months.

The vendor should also arrange for a demonstration to the entire firm, showing how CAD works and how it fits into the long-term plans of the office. This is not intended to be a sales pitch, but an instructional session. All management concerned with the system, including the directors, must receive basic training on it. It is crucial that senior management have a sound, realistic expectation about what the system can and cannot do.

After the formal training comes the period when management expects the draftspeople to produce drawings immediately and the trainees find that they get nowhere. This frustrating period requires sympathy from management and perseverance from the drafters. The trainees must be allowed constant access to consolidate their training. Experienced personnel must be around to answer minor questions and provide hints and private tuition. Unfortunately, it is just at this time that the vendor's instructors have disappeared after the contractual training period (Ireland, 1983).

Some managers feel that operators must be producing as soon as possible and should be discouraged from playing and experimenting with the system (Allen, 1982). We believe that operators should be encouraged to be aggressive and inventive, discovering shortcuts and new ways of using the system (Bliss and Hyman, 1980). The first 3 months at least should be considered the experimental, breaking-in period, and no income-producing work should be expected. If it does come in, it is a delightful bonus. This, of course, means that the firm hurriedly installing a CAD system to handle a big new project is handling CAD in precisely the wrong manner. The best time to get into CAD is when there is little work, not a lot.

Staff turnover can be a substantial problem. In one pioneering organization, its CAD experts left after a few months to set up their own partnership (Jones, 1982). A British survey showed that dedicated CAD operators received pay increases, and this is right and sensible (Arnold and Senker, 1982). People realize that after 6 months of training they will be quite fluent in the system's use and be valuable members of the office. If they are denied recognition of this value, then the office has thrown its money away on the training. Few offices really want to act as free CAD training schools.

8.4 Legal Aspects of Computing

The problems of legal liability are a particularly worrisome area for the architect. In this section we briefly present some general considerations, but since we are not legal experts, this is no substitute for professional legal advice. Mathew (1985) has compared the state of liability law in the construction industry to that in the computer industry. The construction industry has a very long history and a mature, well-developed body of procedures established in statute and in common law. The computer industry is young, and its law is undeveloped and imbalanced in favor of vendors. It has so far managed to place the burden of loss on purchasers, its operations are unregulated by licensing or ethical tenets, and there are no standards of minimum required skill. The body of case law on computing is small and fragmentary.

The major problems that may arise over a computer system center on the degree of care owed to users by the computer or program vendor and on the liability that a professional assumes in the event that a program fault leads to a claim by a client. Unlike most other manufacturers, computer vendors expressly disclaim responsibility for the functioning of their equipment, and software houses likewise disclaim responsibility for problems arising through program bugs. Here, for example, is how part of a typical program license agreement might look:

> The program is provided "as is" without warranty of any kind, either ex-
> pressed or implied, including, but not limited to, the implied warranties of
> merchantability and fitness for a particular purpose. The entire risk as to the
> quality and performance of the program is with you. In no event will the
> Company be liable to you for any damages, including any lost profits, lost
> savings, or other incidental or consequential damages. . . .

Vendors are quite keen to protect their own rights, especially concerning
confidentiality. They also expressly decline to fix any bugs. We have to
agree to terms like this:

> I understand that the software will always remain the Company's property:
> even though I have paid a one-time fee for the limited right to use it for up to
> 20 years, if I break any of my promises below, the Company may choose to
> revoke that right without owing me anything and to take other action against
> me. I promise to keep the software confidential, and I agree to keep this
> promise even if our Agreement is broken or ended.

The more you pay for a computer system, the more insistent the dis-
claimers become. Mathew (1985) suggests that the absence of industry
standards indicates that recovery for negligence may not be possible, and
that confusion as to whether a program is a good one might exempt software from products liability law. Even where redress is legally possible, it
may be impractical. In a dynamic industry such as the computer industry,
there are many young companies with limited financial support. There
isn't much point in suing the young contract programmer who wrote that
energy analysis program for you. Lurie (1982) notes that in the United
States the combined effect of all this probably places most of the risk on the
architect, and Cecil (1984) considers that the situation is similar in the
United Kingdom.

On the other side of the coin, it seems that architects must utilize their
normal professional skills and judgment in the use of a computer, as they
would with any other tool of the trade. But just how great is this problem?
How often do mistakes occur in programs and hardware? The answer is,
too often. A voltage spike on the power line can zap part of a disk, and even
static electricity or the background cosmic radiation can alter a bit or two
in the delicate chips of the random-access memory. Programmers readily
admit that no program is completely bug-free. Responsible vendors provide regular bug sheets, notifying users of known problems and providing
updates that (they hope) solve them. These problem sheets can be pages
long.

The field of energy analysis provides an interesting illustration. Lurie
(1982) notes the occurrence of claims against architects made by clients
dissatisfied with the energy-conservative aspects of buildings. Legal liability is determined by the current standards of acceptable professional care,
rather than by results, and it would seem that using an appropriate package would assist in establishing that care. Unfortunately, there is some

difficulty in establishing what constitutes an appropriate package. Different thermal analysis programs can provide quite different results when given identical data.

Clients are becoming more demanding, expecting better and more varied services from their architects. As computer aids proliferate and as extensive databases are established for the construction industry, these clients will expect architects to use them: "If computerized information that would avoid a problem is both available and accessible, the failure to search a database could be professionally unreasonable, resulting in legal culpability. The office that does not have the capacity to search current databases might face legal liability regardless of the professional responsibility evident in its other conduct" (Lurie, 1982, p. 68).

8.5   The Economics of Computer Use

8.5.1   The costs of computer use

Far and away the greatest cost involved in computing is the cost of *people*. Training the staff, education in both general and specific computer use, writing masks for spreadsheets or programs or drafting utilities — these are the major costs that must be borne by an office ("CADD Roundtable," 1984). The next largest cost is the software. Over time, most organizations spend at least as much on software as on hardware, and often a good deal more. Hardware costs are the smallest component, but easier to assess.

Minicomputer software prices are an order of magnitude above microcomputer software prices. Usually, this indeed reflects abilities an order of magnitude greater on the part of the minicomputer-based software, as in such packages as a database manager, a drafting system, and an energy analysis system. The minicomputer-based programs can handle more data much faster than their microcomputer equivalents. A microcomputer database management system (DBMS) might easily handle a file of 500 records but become rather slow with files of 2000 or 10,000 records; searching a long file might take 30 minutes. In contrast, DBMSs mounted on minicomputers can search files of many tens of thousands of records in a second or two. On the other hand, some programs offer much the same abilities no matter what they are mounted on, such as word processors.

Sometimes there are *hidden costs* to programs. A few programs assume that the purchaser already owns some other program or high-level language. We are not talking here about those programs offered specifically as additions to others, but of those which one would reasonably expect to be completely self-contained. In particular, one must check that the program functions under the operating system currently installed on the computer. Remember, too, that the cost of a piece of software may give the user license only to use it on a single, specific machine; thus, other computers owned by the firm may need more copies of the program.

Software also has a *maintenance cost*. Most programs are updated at irregular intervals by the developer. Those programs which are not being updated are probably at the end of their economic life and should not be considered for purchase. To obtain these updates, we must either purchase a maintenance agreement or pay for updates as they appear. An annual charge of 5 to 20 percent of the original price is typical. These updates will enhance the software and correct existing bugs (no program ever works absolutely correctly) (Fanning, 1983). It may seem ridiculous to pay a vendor to make a program work as the vendor said it already did, but that is the way things are in the computer industry, and they are unlikely to change in the near future. Much minicomputer-based software is available for lease only at quite high prices, so of course this would involve substantial ongoing payments.

Maintenance is also required on the hardware. Mainframes require about 10 percent per annum of their capital cost for maintenance, minicomputers about 7.5 percent, and microcomputers about 2 percent (Thomsen and Schappaugh, 1984). For small microcomputers, it is reasonable to opt out of maintenance agreements and pay as needed. However, a really grand catastrophe can cost a substantial percentage of the original price. Most firms do purchase a maintenance agreement, which provides for cheap or free servicing and parts and perhaps for one or two remedial maintenances. The quicker the service, the more expensive the contract. The cheapest contract involves returning the computer to the vendor; the most expensive guarantees an engineer on site in a few hours. One should aim for a contract that guarantees at least 90 percent *uptime;* that is, the computer will be running for at least 90 percent of all the hours it should be running.

A major cost of computing may be the *installation cost.* Some offices require extensive remodeling in order to set up communications systems, a climate-controlled room for a minicomputer and plotter and other peripherals, and suitable furniture and lighting.

Last, but not least, are the *consumables*, items like paper, floppy disks, and printer ribbons. Far from being a step toward the paperless office, a word processing system will double the paper requirements. Continuous stationery is needed as well as floppies, tapes, ribbons, and perhaps plotter paper. Quite often vendors design machines to use only expensive consumables supplied by themselves. Avoid these if at all possible, for the cost of their consumables can be 3 to 5 times higher per annum than for more versatile equivalents. The cost of consumables is far from trivial. Some firms estimate that 25 percent of the first year's cost of running a computer system is in the consumables.

Be sure that your firm knows just what is included in the quoted price. As with many purchases, salespeople will tend to talk about the top-of-the-line models while quoting basic model prices. Manuals, installation, training, additional operating systems and languages, and functional modules (especially with packages such as accounting programs) may all be extra.

8.5.2 Pricing computer services

Stasiowski (1982) has noted that a computer system can be paid for through three elements: tax benefits, such as an investment tax credit and tax savings; cost reductions that the system provides over manual methods; and reimbursement by direct charging of the client. He suggests that a computer system be amortized over 2 years (this is short; 3 to 5 years is often quoted). The firm should expect 20 to 25 percent of the capital cost to come from tax benefits, 20 to 25 percent from cost reductions, and 50 to 60 percent from reimbursement.

Leighton (1984) and Stevens (1984b) note six different forms of pricing possible by a firm that uses its computers to provide project management, design aid, or drafting. We condense them into three strategies:

1. *Incorporation into overhead.* The cost of computerization is borne by the firm as a whole and treated as a normal overhead. All clients are therefore equally and indirectly charged for the computer cost even though its use varies on different projects.

2. *Service charging.* Clients are billed directly for their own costs associated with computing. All explicit costs are charged for, such as consumables, labor of operators, computer time cost, and all other isolatable operating costs. The firm must determine how many other charges to impose; it may impose none at all, an overhead allotment so that the computer runs on a break-even basis, or an overhead plus a profit margin.

3. *Value pricing.* The firm agrees with the client on a mutually acceptable charge reflecting the value, rather than the cost, of the service. This is usually done by charging for the service at the cost of doing it manually. Leighton (1984) notes that this is a disincentive to computer use and is not popular.

Incorporating the system into normal overhead makes the computer into an everyday tool of the practice and avoids the problem of dealing with clients who do not want to pay for computer use. Most firms, happily, find that this is rarely a cause of difficulties and that clients are quite willing to pay directly for computer services. However, one firm that charged computer time internally to projects found that managers avoided the system if prices rose (Mileaf, 1983b; "AIA/SC," 1984).

Service charging carries with it the problem of how much of the costs not directly attributable to a particular job should be included in the charge. The computer carries with it a basic overhead in the attendant administration it requires, as we have discussed above, and in its installation, maintenance, and so on. Beyond these costs are those which the firm bears in general education, staff training, and program and library development. One survey (Witte, 1985b) found that less than 40 percent of firms charging for computers included supplies, operator labor, financing, staff training, and space costs in the calculation. One interesting figure from the survey was that the median billing rate for CAD equipment, not counting operator time, was the same as for a senior or project architect.

8.5.3 Justifying computer use

Teicholz (1985a) mentions three methods for producing measures of CAD system gains:

1. *Productivity ratio.*   The improved productivity over manual methods (the *labor* required on a manual task divided by the labor required using a CAD system), the most common measure.

2. *Turnaround-time ratio.*   The *time* required to do the task manually divided by the time to do it with a CAD system.

3. *Cost ratio.*   The *cost* to accomplish the task manually divided by the cost to accomplish it with a CAD system.

Justifying CAD systems on a cost-benefit basis is notoriously difficult. The traditional method has been to assess benefits on the basis of productivity improvements assessed through productivity ratios. Vendors will quote ratios as high as 10:1 or 20:1, but these are never met in practice (Datapro, 1984). A ratio of about 4:1 seems to be the highest achieved in architectural work (Teicholz, 1983b), as against 6:1 in engineering. Although most firms feel that a CAD system promotes productivity, they have difficulty quantifying it. In one survey, some 25 percent of the respondents were unable to say whether their systems reduced costs, although large majorities felt that they improved accuracy, reduced errors, and shortened cycle times (Datapro, 1984).

We feel that the cost justification of computer systems is not necessarily the best way of assessing their benefits, although it may please the accountants. Charles Thomsen, an architect with 20 years' experience of CAAD, has made some perceptive comments (Thomsen, 1985). He notes, first, that computers do not remove drudgery or reduce labor. Further, firms with CAD systems actually spend marginally more to produce drawings, both in absolute terms and as a percentage of the fee received. However, although the design costs are slightly increased, the product they deliver allows substantial reductions in construction costs. Clients respond by paying higher fees. The result is that firms using CAD systems receive greater profits.

We feel that the cost-benefit analysis of computer systems can be more misleading than useful — and positively dangerous in that it diverts attention from the substantial but unquantifiable benefits, such as improved accuracy and quality of product, that such systems can confer.

8.6   Summary

The material covered in this chapter is too broad and detailed to summarize briefly. Instead, let us echo the theme of Chap. 1: Computers are the most flexible, the most sophisticated, and perhaps the most useful tool that humans have yet devised. Given the possible benefits, it is hardly surprising that a great deal of effort is necessary to achieve the best results. Working with computers needs care, knowledge, determination, experience, and enthusiasm.

Education is crucial to success in managing computers. The more expertise a firm has, the more readily it can adapt to computing—and make computers adapt to it.

SECONDARY TEXT
The Working Environment

A8.1   Computer and Human Needs

The spread of information technology in offices, shops, and factories presents a new set of problems for the architect. Until the early 1980s buildings were designed with telephone and other electrical services in mind, but with little thought for the more complex needs of computers. These needs can no longer be ignored, and clients expect architects to be familiar with the demands imposed by the use of information technology. In this section we discuss some aspects of building design as it is affected by the introduction of computing. It is relevant not only to architects installing a computer system but also to architects providing advice to clients on coping with the new technology.

Atkinson (1983b) and Dietsch (1984) identify four important effects of information technology on building design:

1. *Decentralization and small size of office organizations.*   Physical proximity will become less important, and working from home will become popular.

2. *Less uniformity throughout an office building.*   Individual work spaces will be larger, and record storage spaces and paper documentation and transfer spaces will be smaller (given electronic mail and record keeping rather than mail rooms and filing cabinets). Up to half the space in offices may be committed to meeting and conference areas, activities that are still best done directly in one place rather than via electronic media.

3. *Planning for change.*   There will be more demand for and concern

about facilities planning and managing buildings. For expansion, increased space will not be necessary as increased power and cabling. Flexibility in planning will be important.

4. *Power and cabling.* Vastly increased cabling capacity and emergency power supplies will be required.

We shall look briefly at computer needs, then at human needs. Historically, there is a distressing tendency to care for machines better than for the people who operate them; a good computer installation must take account of the ergonomics of computer use and provide for it.

A8.1.1 Computer needs

Computer installations can be demanding on their environments. Mainframes and minicomputers must be housed in their own rooms where their waste heat can be removed and their noise contained. Manufacturers often provide rigid specifications that cover not only electrical connections but floor structure, ventilation, furniture, and lighting. Ignoring these usually abrogates any warranties or guarantees, so they must be taken seriously.

Any computer is susceptible to *power surges* and *voltage fluctuations*, which are unimportant to most other electrical equipment and undetectable except by monitoring devices. Separate conditioning equipment is usually installed for minicomputers and mainframes, and the power lines from this clean supply are identified to prevent their being used for more mundane purposes. In a large installation the *clean power system* should have its own switchboard connecting to feeders with no other loads. Branch circuits must be protected by circuit breakers. Additional points must be installed for future expansion.

Although usually plugged into the nearest mains socket with no apparent ill effects, microcomputers should best draw power from a central conditioned source or via their own small, cheap *conditioning units* connected in line between the power outlet and the equipment. In an installation in which uninterrupted service is critical, an uninterruptible power supply must be installed. In these systems power is trickled into batteries and the equipment draws from the batteries. The batteries can keep the computers operating for a few hours. In the most expensive systems, a generator is activated if the power fails for more than a few minutes (Cohen and Cohen, 1982).

Computer peripherals, especially disk drives and plotters, can be susceptible to *humidity* extremes. Hard disks must be dimensionally stable to a very fine tolerance, and plotting paper is particularly liable to stretch or shrink. Humidity is best kept to within 40 to 60 percent (Dietsch, 1984). Very dry air can also promote *static electricity*; a static shock may be only a minor irritant to a human, but it can scramble magnetic data and destroy integrated circuits. Installations experiencing inexplicable computer errors have traced these down to static discharges (integrated circuits, in fact, should never be directly handled without grounding; if in doubt, it should be left to a qualified technician or engineer). Antistatic carpet or antistatic mats around individual workstations may be needed. Antistatic sprays are available, but carpeting provides a cheaper and more enduring answer. In very bad situations, metal furniture should be replaced with wooden.

A8.1.2   Human needs

Headaches, fatigue, tenosynovitis, repetition strain injuries (RSI), and nausea are some of the more common complaints made by visual-display unit (VDU) operators. There is little evidence of danger from x-ray, ultraviolet, or infrared radiation, even from damaged or aged VDUs (Myers, 1984), but this is still a relatively unknown area. There is certainly a correlation between a constant environment, monotonous tedious work, and VDU complaints. In those authoritarian systems in which keystrokes are monitored as a measure of work, there is not surprisingly also a correlation between the stress that this generates and operator complaints (Fig. A8.1).

Obviously, part of the solution is a good environment, but there is a further lesson. The operators of any computer should have as much knowledge as they can reasonably digest of the system of which they are a part. Knowing where the information in front of him or her is coming from, what happens to entered information, and how to cope with problems — all such knowledge increases confidence. The computer is an aid to work, not the master of it, and is dependent on the operator, not the operator on it (Myers, 1984).

Of the physical problems, some are related to workstation design. In the wider environment, *lighting* is the most intractable of the problems encountered in installations. Ceiling-mounted fluorescent lighting maintained at a high level has become the orthodox method of lighting offices, but this is quite inappropriate for VDU operators. Reflections and glare on screens are common, and the contrast in illuminance between documents on the working surface and on the screen is too great. Where the density of workstations is low, the problems can be mitigated by shifting the furniture to an appropriate position, but workstations tend to multiply, so this ad hoc solution does not work for long. A common but crude answer is low-level ambient lighting with task lights or illuminated lecterns, but users have found this a most unpleasant arrangement in practice (Evans, 1984).

A more reasonable solution is to shield ceiling luminaires with baffles, diffusers, or lenses that restrict the light to a 90-degree cone. Two major

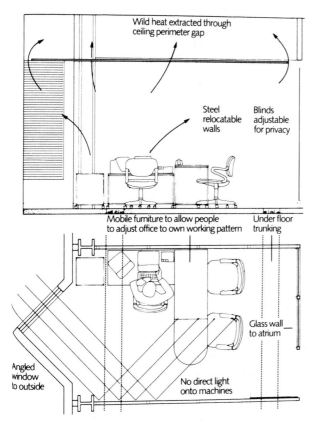

Wild heat extracted through ceiling perimeter gap

Steel relocatable walls

Blinds adjustable for privacy

Mobile furniture to allow people to adjust office to own working pattern

Under floor trunking

Glass wall to atrium

Angled window to outside

No direct light onto machines

Figure A8.1   Elevation (top) and plan (below) of a work environment for automated offices. Glare, cable access, and heat from the equipment are the most pressing problems in such workplaces. *(Used by permission of Rodney Cooper, Building Design Partnership.)*

drawbacks are evident: The ceiling is unnaturally darkened, providing a gothic atmosphere, and the rigidity of the luminaire layout restricts mobility of workstations. The most satisfactory solutions to date use *uplights* (ambient uplighting), which provide a pleasant, almost romantic, ambience. Where power is provided from the floor and uplights are integrated with the furniture, the need for electrical services in the ceiling can be avoided completely. A suspended ceiling may not be necessary at all, and this can be important in building refurbishing (Cooper, 1983). Its major drawback is the higher energy use that goes with reflected instead of direct light and the need for a high-reflectivity (80 to 90 percent) ceiling.

For reasons best known to themselves, architects seem to believe that computer operators have vampirish needs and thus go out of their way to enclose them in windowless rooms. This is not necessary. Reflective film or diffusing blinds seem to provide adequate reduction in daylighting (Dietsch, 1984; Evans, 1984). In general, large surfaces (including the desk surface) should be matte and a neutral pastel or grey. Working surfaces should have about a 30 percent reflectance, the ceiling 80 to 90 percent, lower walls 15 to 20 percent, upper walls (visible behind the VDU) 40 to 70 percent, and the floor 20 to 40 percent. Dark shades of gray, green, blue, red, or brown are inadvisable for ceilings and walls (Swezey and Davis, 1983). Ambient lighting levels should be variable.

Noise is the least problem in computer installations. Large computers, which (with their associated peripherals) generate a lot of white noise, are kept in their own rooms. The only noisy equipment that an office might have in unisolated rooms are printers and plotters. *Acoustic hoods* are readily available for printers, although they are very bulky. European standards lay down a maximum of 55 to 60 dB(A) for printers, rather stricter than the 70 dB(A) or so generated by most daisy-wheel and dot-matrix printers, but easily achieved with these hoods (Cohen and Cohen, 1982). Laser printers will be much quieter, generating about as much noise as a photocopier. Plotters are much too big for acoustic hoods. If noise is a problem, the only solution is to place them in their own room. Generally, 50 dB(A) is regarded as a maximum noise level where work involves concentration or conversation, and 55 dB(A) in other areas.

Heating may be a considerable problem in refurbished buildings. Each workstation generates as much heat as one or two people, and the presence of many stations may overload the ventilation system or, at the least, cause uncomfortable local ventilation problems. Computer rooms give off a substantial amount of heat and must be given special attention; the apparently neat solution of using access floors for heating/ventilating/air-conditioning (HVAC) ducts or to act as a plenum has so far proved difficult to implement (Cooper, 1983).

A8.2 Cabling and Power Supply

Large firms with high densities of computer equipment present the greatest cabling problems. Word processing centers often require that all staff have access to data cables. Some such users require data outlets at $6\frac{1}{2}$-ft (2-m) centers (Parkinson, 1984). Of major concern are the flexibility of the cabling and a provision for substantial expansion. During the lifetime of a building the computer equipment may be completely replaced 3 to 6 times and undergo several expansion phases between each replacement. No organization can predict its cabling requirements through all these changes, so the building shell must be designed to allow as flexible a cabling system as possible. Large organizations will have a data processing or communications manager, and this person should be regarded as the primary client since he or she will have the clearest idea of the organization's future needs.

The total amount of cabling depends on the sort of system implemented. Computer networks were discussed in detail in Chap. 2, and here we need just note that medium to large computer installations come in three forms: ring, bus, or star networks. In a *ring network* each part of the network is connected by a single cable to another piece of computer equipment; the cables are of the thick coaxial or multicore type. A *bus network* snakes a single cable through the building and provides cable drops to each computer or terminal, using similar cable. Since either of these networks can be extended at will, their expansion tends to be unpredictable; however, the total length of cabling is kept to a minimum. The *star network* is typical of installations in which a central computer is connected to a collection of terminals; here, at least the location of the cabling is predictable, but enormous cable congestion is likely at the central computer room (Evans, 1984).

Fiber-optic cables are becoming the preferred method of data transmission, but for the next decade or so copper cables will remain the dominant system. Since these are very susceptible to electrical interference, they should be ducted well out of the way of power cables, preferably at distances of at least 3 ft (1 m). If they must cross power cables, they should do so at right angles. Separate ducting for the data cables is the best means of isolating them from other cables. Cutouts at least 0.3 in^2 (200 mm^2) should be provided for these ducts between stories and in the wall space. Ducts, trunking, and cutouts should be designed with a 100 to 200 percent excess in cross-sectional area to take care of immediate expansion, and additional cutouts should be provided for long-term expansion of the system. The minimum radii of ductwork bends depend on the type of cabling used. Roughly, bends of a 1-in (25-mm) radius are viable for normal coaxial cables, but thick sheathed cables require bends of a 24-in (600-mm) radius (Parkinson, 1984).

Vertical distribution is relatively easy, using the normal service ducts, but horizontal distribution can be quite difficult. Telephone and power cables in poor installations are simply trailed along the floor. Computer equipment requires many more cables, and adopting this prosaic method is dangerous, ugly, and inconvenient. Hall (1984) has identified several methods for handling the horizontal distribution:

1. Poke-through hardwire. This simplest of systems uses cabling installed in conduits in the ceiling void and poked through the slab to the floor above (Fig. A8.2). Outlets stand about 4 in (100 mm) above the slab. This system is the cheapest to install, but it is quite rigid and invariably leads to trailing wires whenever the equipment is rearranged. The number of outlets is limited so as to maintain the fire rating of the slab.

2. Flexible plug-in wiring. This is intended for use in the ceiling void (with poke-through hardwire) or in an access floor. Each component is intended

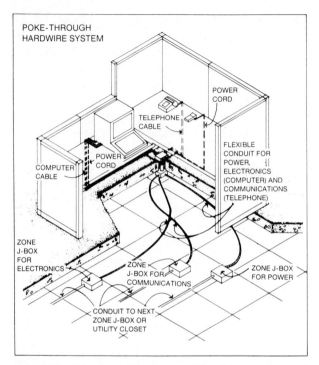

POKE-THROUGH
HARDWIRE SYSTEM

POWER
CORD

TELEPHONE
CABLE

FLEXIBLE
CONDUIT FOR
POWER,
ELECTRONICS
(COMPUTER) AND
COMMUNICATIONS
(TELEPHONE)

POWER
CORD

COMPUTER
CABLE

ZONE
J-BOX
FOR
ELECTRONICS

ZONE
J-BOX FOR
COMMUNICATIONS

ZONE J-BOX
FOR POWER

CONDUIT TO NEXT
ZONE J-BOX OR
UTILITY CLOSET

Figure A8.2   Poke-through hardware cabling. Cables are installed
in the ceiling void and poked through the slab to the floor above.
*(Diagram by Peter Sulerud of Hammel Green and Abrahmson,
used by permission of Architectural Technology.)*

simply to plug into others, rendering an electrician unnecessary. Distribution and junction boxes are supplied with appropriate plugs. Flexible wiring is limited to power and lighting distribution.

3. Modular plug-in ceiling ducting.   In this system, distribution ducts are
placed in the ceiling void to provide services to the floor below (Fig. A8.3).
Cables are sent to the outlets through poles or through wired partitions.
Even when the cost of wiring the partitions is considered, modular ducting
is very cheap.

4. Cellular floor.   Intended for steel frame rather than concrete structures,
this consists of structural steel decking within a concrete slab that also
serves to distribute cabling (Fig. A8.4). Outlets are installed at preset
centers, flush with the top of the slab.

5. Flat cable.   A novel solution is the use of flat cables (ribbon cables) that
are only a millimeter or two thick (Drury, 1984). Carpet tiles can be laid
directly on top of these, and humps only form when cables cross. Flat

cables are very flexible and of average cost. They are often recommended for retrofitting buildings (Dietsch, 1984).

6. Access floor.   Another conventional solution is to install a raised floor (Fig. A8.5). This is fairly expensive (although not as much as often thought) and is generally limited to the special room housing minicomputers or mainframes or to the services core, where cable congestion is likely. Under the tiles, cables can be constrained in ducts or left as a rat's nest of wires. The relocation costs are trivial, though, and when these are taken into account, access floors are only marginally more expensive than other systems. Other advantages include unlimited expansion facility and the freeing of the ceiling plenum for air-conditioning ducts. Access floors are, however, impractical in refurbishing.

7. Underfloor ducting.   Hall found this significantly the most expensive of all systems in terms both of installation and relocation costs. It consists of enclosed ducts laid in the slab.

In his comprehensive analysis, Hall found that each system, except for

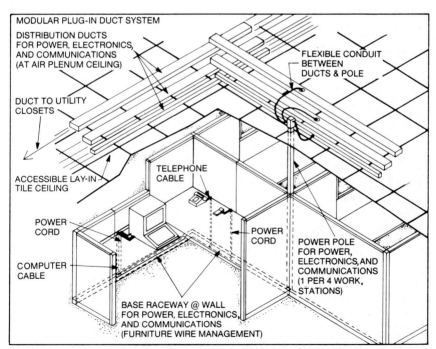

Figure A8.3   Modular plug-in ducting. Cabling is installed in the ceiling void and passed through poles or partitions to the floor below. *(Diagram by Peter Sulerud of Hammel Green and Abrahmson, used by permission of Architectural Technology.)*

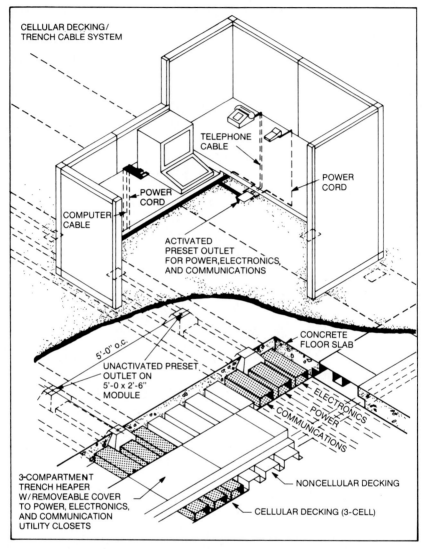

CELLULAR DECKING/
TRENCH CABLE SYSTEM

TELEPHONE
CABLE

POWER
CORD

POWER
CORD

COMPUTER
CABLE

ACTIVATED
PRESET OUTLET
FOR POWER, ELECTRONICS,
AND COMMUNICATIONS

CONCRETE
FLOOR SLAB

5'-0" o.c.

UNACTIVATED PRESET
OUTLET ON
5'-0 x 2'-6"
MODULE

ELECTRONICS

POWER

COMMUNICATIONS

3-COMPARTMENT
TRENCH HEAPER
W/REMOVEABLE COVER
TO POWER, ELECTRONICS,
AND COMMUNICATION
UTILITY CLOSETS

NONCELLULAR DECKING

CELLULAR DECKING (3-CELL)

Figure A8.4 Cellular decking and trench cable. This makes use of the built-in steel decking used in steel frame buildings. *(Diagram by Peter Sulerud of Hammel Green and Abrahmson, used by permission of Architectural Technology.)*

underfloor ducting, was close enough in cost to render other factors more important. However, many firms have used poke-through hardwire only to regret it. We suggest avoiding it unless absolutely impossible. All the systems can use prewired furniture that will eliminate the need for other wiring almost completely.

A8.3   Workstation Design

The requirements for computer workstations are much more stringent than those for simple desks and work surfaces. In the first place, they consume much more space. A microcomputer or terminal has a typical footprint (the area consumed by the machine on the work surface) of $1\frac{1}{3}$ to $2\frac{2}{3}$ ft^2 ($\frac{1}{8}$ to $\frac{1}{4}$ m^2), which may occupy 30 to 40 percent of the available area. Designers must therefore allow individuals perhaps 20 percent more space. A normal desk is not a completely satisfactory surface on which to mount a computer. A great many perfectly good computers lie unused because they

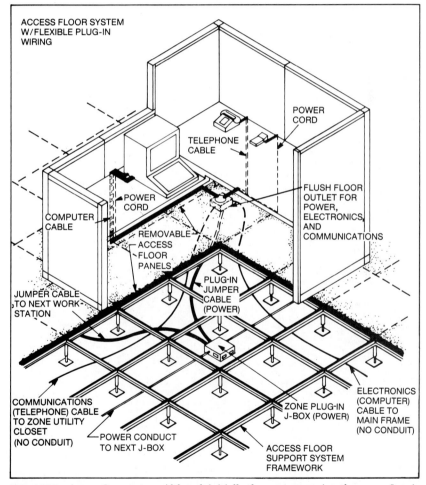

Figure A8.5   Access floor system. Although initially the most expensive, the access floor is unparalled for flexibility. *(Diagram by Peter Sulerud of Hammel Green and Abrahmson, used by permission of Architectural Technology.)*

are mounted on rickety, cramped desks festooned with wires, used computer paper, and the odd floppy or two (Fig. A8.6). There is now a large range of workstation furniture available (Aartsen and Tennenhaus, 1984); although it tends to be expensive, we feel that it is worth the cost and should be used.

Computers accumulate junk. Manuals, boxes of continuous stationery, disk boxes, printer ribbons, and all sorts of other odds and ends gather around workstations and must be kept somewhere. The storage systems these require are often the more expensive part of the furniture, and there is a trend toward mixing costly ergonomic desks with cheaper storage systems for paperwork (Cooper, 1983).

L- and shallow U-shaped desks (Fig. A8.7), with the computer mounted at the apex, are becoming popular, and we will see a trend toward these sorts of forms and away from the standard rectangular desk form in coming years. Ideally, the surface allocated to the computer should consist of two adjustable platforms: one for the screen and one for the keyboard (European standards have obliged manufacturers to produce detachable keyboards). The two surfaces should be adjustable for height, and the screen surface should also be adjustable for tilt. Even the general work surface should be height-adjustable. This is suggested because there is only partial agreement on the desirable dimensions. There is also disagreement on the ideal dimensions of chairs, although the spread of ranges to be accommodated is agreed to be the tallest 95th-percentile man and the shortest 5th-percentile woman. The seat height and tilt and the back height and tilt must be adjustable. A footrest should be provided.

Figure A8.6   More often than not, workstations look like this. Since computer installations and workstations tend to change throughout their lifetimes, it is actually quite difficult to avoid an ever-growing mess. *(Used by permission of Architects Journal.)*

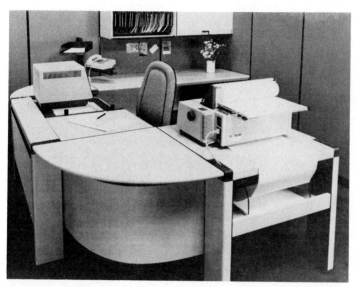

Figure A8.7   This office at Grey Advertising in London shows a U-shaped desk arrangement typical of the automated office. *(Used by permission of the Design Council.)*

Workstation design is aimed at producing a good posture in the operator. Upper arms should be about vertical, elbows close in, forearms about horizontal. The keyboard should be just below elbow height and have a palmrest. The seat should be at a height where the feet relieve underthigh pressure (Myers, 1984). Client and architect have a responsibility to explain ergonomic principles to operators and to ensure that these are understood (Cooper, 1983).

With workstation positioning, the most difficult problem will be in preventing glare and reflections. An operator should neither face nor back onto a window. If there are ceiling luminaires, they should run perpendicularly to the plane of the screen. The maximum horizontal illuminance should be about 500 to 700 lux, declining to 300 to 400 lux where several workstations are grouped together (Atkinson, 1983a; Myers, 1984). Antiglare filters, black nylon meshes, should be affixed to the screens.

Most existing computer installations are environmentally unsatisfactory. This, at least, is one part of computer technology that architects can understand and improve. We should try to do so.

Chapter

9

Speculations

9.1 Introduction

In this last chapter we want to speculate briefly about the role of the architect in the near future (up to the year 2000 or a little beyond), how computers fit into that role, and how the use of computers might affect the form and style of architecture. All this clearly depends on the kind of world in which architects might be operating, and without trespassing too far into the world of science fiction, we need to make some assumptions about the future. We shall assume that the world will continue to survive between crises and will perhaps be a little worse, but hopefully a little better, than the present — not solving all its problems, but at least avoiding catastrophe. We choose this scenario because we find it more believable than a future utopia (in which contented architects develop erudite schemes that miraculously transform themselves into award-winning buildings) and less harrowing than a future postwar or postdisaster world (in which the problem-solving abilities of any surviving architects really will be needed but in which the level of available technology may be rather low). So we assume steady development rather than sudden change and assume that from current trends we can project forward with some assurance.

9.2 The Future

There is no doubt that existing patterns of work, leisure, education, and technology are undergoing change and that computer technology is a major driving force behind this change. Computers are causing a redefinition of work through new methods of communication and finance, robotics, and a change in the relative value of brain and brawn in the job market. Among others, John Brotchie (1980) has argued that whereas the industrial revolution led to formality in space, time, and living (separate zoning of industrial and residential areas, fixed working hours, and a polarization of work and leisure), we are now moving back toward informality in employment, daily activities, and spatial needs. He observed that "We are moving from separate zones to mixed zones; from formal employment to flexitime, from operator telegraph to personal telephone, from the centralised office to decentralised workstations; from mainframe to personal computers; from economies of scale via the microchip to production on demand; from activities tightly coupled through transport links to activities uncoupled because of the neutrality of telecommunications; from uniformity to diversity" (Johnson, Judd, and Le Sueur, 1984, p. 6).

Computers use very little energy or mineral resources and are safe, quiet, and nonpolluting; thus, there appear to be no environmental impediments to utilizing them. They are also a very transportable technology and relatively cheap (in relation to their power); thus, whether directly or through global communications channels, businesses and professionals far from the established commercial centers can get access to the same tools as their urban colleagues. This has led to the notion of the "electronic cottage" (Deken, 1983) in which work and leisure, both using much the same technology, can be combined in the home; consequently, it has also led to predictions of deserted city centers, with office buildings standing empty as personal contact becomes irrelevant to business transactions. Whatever occurs, these technological changes certainly give us many more options about the ways we live and work than we have had in the past. Whether, in turn, this technology helps that majority of the population living in substandard housing probably depends more on politics and on the way the technology is used than on the technology itself.

The theme of our speculations about the future, then, is that there will be greater informality and diversity. Variety in the way that society lives and works requires flexibility in the response of the design professions and construction industries. Rickaby (1979) postulates a future in which architects practice as independent and responsible individuals in multidisciplinary associations rather than as salaried employees in public and private offices. He sees computers as central to this future structure: They will facilitate integrated design by giving design teams expert knowledge and a greater control over the complex process of building, will minimize administrative problems, and will help invert the traditional office hierarchy, in which the really experienced architects spend all their time on administration and paperwork, leaving little time for any involvement in detailed design.

In writing about computer-aided knowledge, we have argued that design knowledge can be represented in computer systems; consequently, an architect's expertise can become partly independent of the person. Mitchell (1986) has suggested a future of franchised architecture in which the expertise of a known master is captured and leased as franchises. At the same time, building construction methods will be affected by computers, robots, and other technological developments. There are also signs, particularly among firms with computer-aided design and drafting systems, that architects are becoming more prepared and more eager to take on problem-solving activities not directly associated with the design of new buildings or building alterations; thus, the nature of the architect's role is changing.

As for building style, our own hope is that the theme of informality and diversity will apply here too. We look forward to a rich, diverse architecture of the future — to buildings which are designed much more completely than most existing ones have been, which are fitted to their local environments because of the computer analysis used in their design, and which are put together accurately and consistently with the aid of robots and numerically controlled machines. It will be an architecture that combines rational responses to performance requirements with that spark of delight and imagination which distinguishes the great from the mundane. And it will be a sculptural architecture, freed from the need to be strictly rectilinear and freed from the pressure to give stock answers to standardized design problems. In short, we hope for a magnificently creative period of architecture, spurred by new tools and techniques, comparable to the creative periods spurred by new ways of looking at the world in the early days of the Renaissance and the early days of the Modern Movement. We might also hope that with increasing leisure, society might become more interested in, and demanding of, quality in the built environment.

Another very active area in which computers are affecting the way people choose to spend much of their lives is that of entertainment, which could, if we are prepared to accept its implications, affect both architecture and the work of architects. Computer imagery and computer games enable people to get out of the real world and live in a pseudo world of the mind and simulated reality, as in the real-time flight simulators of today's pilot training programs. They offer an escape potentially much more satisfying than the previous great escapes of literature, radio, and television because they can be personal, reacting to the actions and desires of the individual rather than only offering a standardized entertainment that individuals can tap but not control. What if this imaginary world becomes more attractive as a way of life than the real world, with all its real problems? We can at least expect a new art form of unbuilt architecture and sculpture which exists only in the databases of computers but which can be interactively explored by both critic and public.

9.3   Now

Given this unashamedly optimistic view of the future (after all, if we are speculating, we may as well be optimistic), why is it that we cannot already begin to see some of these characteristics in the buildings that have been designed with the aid of computers, or at least be able to differentiate such buildings on the ground from the legions of their noncomputer contemporaries? The reasons for this difficulty are, we think, fourfold.

The first and principal reason is simply that we are still only just at the beginning of a very long road and it is too early to expect very much in terms of clear trends and differences. The second reason is a result of this early stage: Architectural firms are presently using computers to mimic manual design methods, so we should not be surprised when they produce buildings that mimic manually designed buildings. Most firms use computers for administration and documentation, not for design. The third reason is that if we concentrate on aesthetics, we are not looking in the right place for what influence there is; right now we should be looking for the results of computer environmental and planning simulations and for the effects of more consistent and coordinated documentation, not for stylistic differences. The fourth reason is that any technological influence on style is necessarily going to work in combination with other influences, so that finding a true relationship may never be easy. We have suggested that computers can be an influence for diversity and decoration rather than for standardization, and there are already signs in much recent architecture of a concern for incident and detail — a concern that is, in a sense, a decorative one.

9.4   On Being a Future Architect

Computers force us to consider the essence of being an architect and whether that role will continue into the future. There are many examples of technology having rendered trades and professions obsolete: blacksmiths, typesetters, locomotive stokers, and lathe operators are examples from different eras of activities now markedly diminished. Architects are defined in dictionaries as "designers of buildings," but that describes what they do rather than what they are. Is the essence of an architect's skill some combination of being an expert, draftsperson, artist, entertainer, and manager, or is it something else?

Expertise has been the traditional basis for the professions, but we have seen that the emerging computer fields of expert systems and knowledge engineering are changing the nature of the knowledge that professionals will need. At least some of the knowledge and experience that is now personal and salable will become more widely available.

Skill in drafting is still the basis for architectural communication, and many newly qualified architects find employment carrying out drafting activities. Computer drafting is much more precise and controllable than manual drawing, can be linked to scheduling and analysis systems, and makes modifications easy. Like pens, computer drafting systems still need an operator, but they greatly increase productivity.

The problem with setting ourselves up as artists is that success depends on other people recognizing our artistic credentials — and that art is, almost by definition, considered by most people to be a dispensable luxury. Anyway, artists traditionally live impoverished in garrets and are only recognized 50 years after their death. This has limited appeal. Computer art is an exciting field, but would we be able to afford the computer?

Perhaps the major problem with being a manager is that few architects enter the profession with a burning ambition to be managers. Architects do, however, want to get buildings constructed, and that implies at least some management of the design process and maybe also the management of an architectural practice as a business. If we can manage aspects of other people's businesses as well (the maintenance of existing buildings, the use of building resources, and the continuing management of a client body's spatial organization and relationships without any necessary decision to build), we shall expect additional fees for the work, and that might overcome our reticence.

Most architects acknowledge elements of these (and other) facets of the profession, but that does not help us focus on the essence of being an architect. It is probably centered around problem-solving skills in the context of space and the built environment, but we do not have an exact answer. Possibly the skills involved are too diverse to expect one individual to have them all. If we are to maintain our usefulness, though, it is our thesis that the essence of an architect's skill must lie in areas where computer technology will extend and not replace his or her function. Further, since computer technology typically increases productivity over the same task carried out without a computer, architects as "designers of buildings" must either find many more buildings to design or change the definition in order for all to remain usefully employed.

Above all, we believe the future architect needs to be imaginative and creative, but by the exercise of imagination and creativity we mean much more than designing aesthetically pleasing one-of-a-kind buildings. We mean an approach to problem solving which understands and exploits technology, which can identify needed knowledge rather than knowing everything, and which can find satisfaction in solving nonvisual as well as visual problems. Some of this problem solving will concern new buildings, but some will concern building management, resource planning, or other problems that are quite outside our present view of architecture. Only the select few will be able to pick their field, to choose to design Architecture with a capital A in the way that architecture schools have tended to interpret Architecture. As for computers: With the promise of faster operation, the reality of high-quality graphics, and the concepts of knowledge engineering, they are showing some real prospect in architecture of finally living up to their awesome reputation.

Information Sources and Bibliography

In section A we list some textbooks on architectural computing up to an intermediate level. We do not provide references for books that teach a specific programming language, since a browse through any technical bookshop will reveal hundreds of titles. Introductory books for all major computer languages are easy to find, but books that proceed beyond the beginner's level are not. We have therefore included some titles that will allow those interested in programming to increase their skills.

Section B lists a selection of journals and magazines that regularly feature articles of interest to architects.

Section C mentions the major regular conferences of interest to students of architectural computing. Their proceedings can be found in university libraries.

Section D, which serves as our bibliography, provides all the references quoted in the text, together with much of the literature published since 1980. We have followed the *5-year rule* of computing information, which is that anything over 5 years old is probably more misleading than useful. Thus, except for references, we list literature no earlier than 1980.

A. Textbooks

Kemper, A. M. (ed.) (1985) *Pioneers of CAD in Architecture,* Hurland/Swenson, Pacifica. (A profusely illustrated directory of activity in computer-aided design in numerous American practices and schools of architecture.)
Laurie, P. (1983) *The Joy of Computers,* Hutchinson, London. (A wonderful, witty examina-

tion of computing today, providing a depth of coverage of the microcomputing field, surprising in what looks like a coffee-table book. Superb diagrams.)

Leighton, N. L. (1984) *Computers in the Architectural Office,* Van Nostrand Rheinhold, New York. (A sound, pragmatic book covering in detail the implementation of a computer system in an office.)

Pulgram, W. L., and R. E. Stonis (1984) *Designing the Automated Office,* Whitney Library of Design (Watson-Guptill), New York. (A comprehensive and superbly illustrated guide for architects in coping with the design problems of modern information technology.)

Some works of a more technical nature:

Bowyer, A., and J. Woodwark (1983) *A Programmer's Geometry,* Butterworths, London. (The first book to collect in one place algorithms and formulas essential to manipulating geometric entities. The code examples are given in FORTRAN 77.)

Foley, J. D., and A. Van Dam (1982) *Fundamentals of Interactive Computer Graphics,* Addison-Wesley, Reading, Mass. (A standard reference for computer graphics work, although hard going in places.)

Harrington, S. (1983) *Computer Graphics: A Programming Approach,* Addison-Wesley, Reading, Mass. (A well-written, clear guide to the software behind computer graphics. Approaches the subject from the point of view of writing a graphics package, similar to the CORE standard. Code is written in a Pascal-like language.)

Kernighan, B. W., and P. J. Plauger (1981) *Software Tools in Pascal,* Addison-Wesley, Reading, Mass. (One of the best books from which to learn good programming.)

Martin, J. (1977) *Computer Database Organization,* Prentice-Hall, Englewood Cliffs, N.J. (A book of outstanding clarity, explaining all aspects of the logical and physical design and theory of databases, with copious, clear diagrams.)

Mitchell, W. J. (1977) *Computer-Aided Architectural Design,* Van Nostrand Rheinhold, New York. (Although first published in 1977, this is still the most comprehensive presentation of the whole field.)

Sedgewick, R. (1983) *Algorithms,* Addison-Wesley, Reading, Mass. (The best easily obtainable, single source for algorithms for most common programming tasks. It includes a good section on algorithms for graphics not covered or poorly treated in other texts. Code in Pascal.)

Teicholz, E. (ed.) (1985) *CAD/CAM Handbook,* McGraw-Hill, New York. (The most comprehensive single reference on all aspects of computer-aided design and drafting systems.)

Tremblay, J. P., and P. G. Sorenson (1976) *An Introduction to Data Structures with Applications,* McGraw-Hill Kogakusha, Tokyo. (An excellent guide to the construction of data structures. Algorithms are written in a language of the authors' own devising.)

B.   Journals and Magazines

Architects Journal (U.K.) continues its tradition of providing detailed technical information, with several series on computing. It is the major source of information on architectural computing among British journals.

Architectural Record (U.S.) provides interesting information on the field not covered elsewhere and provides an excellent source for current topics and the state of the art, particularly on management issues. Regularly publishes comprehensive listings of software of specific interest to architects.

Architectural Technology (U.S.) is the major source of information among American journals and provides good reviews of software.

Architecture and Engineering Systems (U.S.) is a magazine dedicated to the AEC computer-aided drafting system market, with a nontechnical style.

BYTE (U.S.) is the *Scientific American* of microcomputers, an authoritative and comprehensive journal.

CADCAM International (U.S.) is a magazine dedicated to the CAD industry.

Computer-Aided Design (U.K.) is a major source for state-of-the art theory in computer-aided design. Mainly for academics and those in the industry.

Computer Graphics World (U.S.) provides good coverage of the marketplace and the industry for all forms of computer graphics. Quite intelligible to laypersons.

High Technology (U.S.) provides a continuously good source for the current microcomputer industry and the state of the art in computer graphics. Although it covers all modern technology, not just computing, its articles on major developments in computing are detailed and clear.

C. Conferences

A/E/C Systems Conference is a major U.S. conference on computers for the design and construction industry.

CAD is the premier conference on computer-aided design and is organized by the journal *Computer-Aided Design*. It is held biannually in the United Kingdom, and its proceedings are published by Butterworths.

PARC is the international conference on computers in architecture. Its proceedings are published by Online, London.

D. Bibliography

Aartsen, M., and S. Tennenhaus (1984) "Clearing the Decks," *Design,* April.

Abramson, A. B. (1981) "A New Era for Building System Monitoring and Control," *Architectural Record,* May.

"AIA Computer Network on Line" (1983) *Architectural Technology,* vol. 1, no. 1, Fall.

AIA/SC Developing Software Package" (1984) *Architectural Technology,* vol. 2, no. 1, Spring.

"AJ Computing Club" (1983) *Architects Journal,* Dec. 14.

Akin, O. (1978) "How Do Architects Design?" in J. C. Latombe (ed.), *Artificial Intelligence and Pattern Recognition in Computer-Aided Design,* North-Holland, Amsterdam.

Albert, D. (1982) "CAD in the AEC Marketplace," *Computer Graphics World,* December.

Alexander, C. (1964) *Notes on the Synthesis of Form,* Harvard University Press, Cambridge.

———(1979) *The Timeless Way of Building,* Oxford University Press, New York.

———S. Ishikawa, and M. Silverstein (1977) *A Pattern Language: Towns, Buildings, Construction,* Oxford University Press, New York.

Allen, C. W. (1982) "A Case History of Introducing CAD into a Large Aerospace Company," *CAD ED 82,* CAD/CAM Association, Manchester, England.

Arnold, E., and P. Senker (1982) "Computer-Aided Design in the U.K. Engineering Industry," in *CAD 82,* Butterworths, Guildford, England.

Ashley, S. (1985) "A Question of Survival," *Building,* Jan. 25.

Atkins, R. T. (1979) "What Is an Interrupt?" *BYTE,* March.

Atkinson, G. (1983a) "Working with the New Technology," *Building,* Nov. 11.

———(1983b) "The Redundant Office," *Building,* Dec. 9.

———(1984a) "Construction Goes On-line," *Building,* Mar. 9.

———(1984b) "Control Systems in Buildings," *Building,* Mar. 16.

Banham, R. (1984) *The Architecture of the Well-Tempered Environment,* Architectural Press, London.

Barnett, J. (1965) "Will the Computer Change the Practice of Architecture?" *Architectural Record,* January.

Baxter, A. (1984) "The Structural Engineer," *Architects Journal,* Mar. 28.

Bazjanac, V. (1975) "The Promise and Disappointments of CAD," in N. Negroponte (ed.), *Computer Aids to Design and Architecture,* Petrocelli, New York.

Bedford, M., and I. Groak (1983) "Current Issues in U.K. Architectural Education," *Architectural Education,* 3.

Bijl, A. (1980a) "The Revolution Is Here to Stay," *Computer-Aided Design,* May.

———(1980b) *Computing for the Small Architect's Office,* University of Edinburgh.

———(1981) "Progress on Drawing Systems," *Computer-Aided Design,* vol. 13, no. 6.

———(1982) "Dumb Drawing Systems and Knowledge Engineering," in A. Pipes (ed.), *CAD 82,* Butterworths, Guildford, England.

Blecher, R. (1984) "Software Drives System Choice," *Australasian Computerworld,* Sept. 21.

Bliss, F. W., and G. M. Hyman (1980) "Selecting and Successfully Implementing a Turnkey Computer Graphics System," in *Design Automation Conference '80,* Institute of Electrical and Electronics Engineers and Association for Computing Machinery, New York.

Borkin, H. (1983) personal communication with author.

Borkovich, G. (1984) "Off-the-shelf Software: Getting a Quick Payback," *Progressive Architecture,* March.

Borrell, J. (1982a) "Graphics Software Survey," *Computer Graphics World,* no. 8.

———(1982b) "Microcomputer Graphics Software," *Computer Graphics World,* no. 9

———(1982c) "The Solid Modeling Marketplace," *Computer Graphics World,* no. 11.

Braidwood, S. (1981) "Plug-in, Switch-on, Draw-up," *Design,* November.

———(1985) "A Fuzzy Picture at the VDU," *Design,* January.

Brandon, P., and R. Moore (1983) *Microcomputers in Building Appraisal,* Granada, London.

Broadbent, G. (1973) *Design in Architecture,* Wiley, New York.

Brotchie, J. (1980) comments quoted in Johnson, Judd, and Le Sueur (1984).

Burberry, P. (1982) "Microcomputer Aids: Energy Primer Part 8," *Architects Journal,* June 30.

Busick, E. L. (1984) "CAD/CAM Workstation Trends," *Computer Graphics World,* April.

Byers, T. J. (1984) "Electronic Ties That Bind," *Computers and Electronics,* vol. 22, no. 3.

"CAD Methods Probe after Carpark Cracks" (1983) *New Civil Engineer,* Oct. 20.

"CADD Roundtable: 14 CADD Experts Share Information" (1984) *Architectural Technology,* vol. 2, no. 1, Spring.

Cakir, A., D. J. Hart, and T. F. M. Stewart (1980) *Visual Display Terminals,* Wiley-Interscience, New York.

Campion, D. (1968) *Computers in Architectural Design,* Elsevier, Amsterdam.

———(1984a) "Managing a Draughting System 1," *Architects Journal,* Apr. 25.

———(1984b) "Managing a Draughting System 2," *Architects Journal,* May 2.

Capron, H. L., and B. K. Williams (1982) *Computers and Data Processing,* Benjamin/Cummings, Menlo Park, Calif.

Carolin, P. (1983) "Building Services Integration and Intelligence," *Architects Journal,* November.

Carter, J. (1973) "Computers and the Architect 4: Problems of the Future," *Architects Journal,* Oct. 31.

Cassidy, B. (1985) "Read between the Lines," *Building,* Feb. 1.

Cecil, R. (1984) "Microchips with Everything," *RIBA Journal,* January.

Chalmers, J. (1982a) "Guide to Hardware," *Architects Journal,* May 12.

———(1982b) "Guide to Software and Systems," *Architects Journal,* May 19.

CIAD (1981) "The Automation of Draughting Work," *Construction Industry Computing Association,* Cambridge, England.

Clark, J. A. (1978) "A Design-Oriented Thermal Simulation Model," in A. Pipes (ed.), *CAD 78,* IPC Science and Technology Press, Guildford, England.

Cockle, R. (1983a) "Choosing a CAD System," *Architects Journal,* Nov. 9.

———(1983b) "Installing a CAD System," *Architects Journal,* Nov. 16.

Cohen, A., and E. Cohen (1982) "Ergonomics and the Electronic Revolution," *Architectural Record,* September.

Cole, B. C. (1981) "Computer Language Roundup," *Interface Age,* June.

Coleman, B. (1984) "When You Can't Afford Systems Drafting," *Progressive Architecture,* November.

"Computer Capability Inquiry Sought in A/E Procurement" (1980) *AIA Journal,* December.

"Computing Products and Services" (1982) *Architects Journal,* June 30.

"Computing Products and Services 2" (1982) *Architects Journal,* Sept. 29.

Connelly, C., and P. Carolin (1983) "Toward the Electronic Office," *Architects Journal,* Oct. 26.

Constantinou, S., K. Rathmill, and R. Leonard (1982) "Ergonomic Aspects of Installing Graphics CAD Systems," *CAD,* vol. 14, no. 3.

Cooley, M. J. E. (1980) "The Designer in the 1980s: The Deskiller Deskilled," *Design Studies,* April.

Cooper, R. (1983) "Office Refurbishment: Vocabulary of Office Space," *Architects Journal,* Nov. 23.

Cornell, D., A. Sambura, and J. Gero (1984) "Icon-Driven Interfaces for Drafting Systems," *Ausgraph '84,* Australian Computer Graphics Society, Melbourne.

Cortes-Comerer, N. (1983) "Wordprocessing: Tips on How to Choose a System," *Civil Engineering/ASCE,* February.

Coutts, N. (1983a) "Low-Cost Computing 2: Analyzing Your Requirements," *Architects Journal,* Feb. 2.

——(1983b) "Low-Cost Computing 5: Finance," *Architects Journal,* Mar. 2.

——(1983c) "Low-Cost Computing 9: Available Software," *Architects Journal,* May 11.

——(1983d) "Low-Cost Computing 12: Developments," *Architects Journal,* June 1.

——(1983e) "Low-Cost Computing 13: Impacts," *Architects Journal,* June 8.

——(1984) "Low-Cost Computing: Networks and Communications," *Architects Journal,* Apr. 11.

——and J. Greig (1983) "Low-Cost Computing 8: Computer Peripherals," *Architects Journal,* May 4.

Coyne, R. (1986) "A Logical Model of Design Synthesis," Ph.D. thesis, Department of Architectural Science, University of Sydney.

——and J. S. Gero (1986) "Semantics and the Organization of Knowledge in Design," *Design Computing,* vol. 1, no. 1.

Crawford, J. R., J. R. Mitchell, and I. E. Booth (1980) "Application of a Computer Model to the Redevelopment of Royal Canberra Hospital," *CAD/CAM in the Eighties,* Association for Computer-Aided Design, Melbourne.

Cross, N. (1977a) "Problems and Threats of CAD," *RIBA Journal,* vol. 84, no. 10, pp. 438–440.

——(1977b) *The Automated Architect,* Pion, London.

Daratech (1984) *CAD/CAM, CAE: Survey, Review, and Buyer's Guide,* Daratech, Cambridge, Mass.

Datapro Research Organization (1984) "Users and Vendors Evaluate the Current Status and Future Prospects of CAD/CAM," *IEEE CG&A,* February.

Davies, B. J. (1983) *Proceedings of the 6th Annual Conference on Design Engineering,* IFS Publications, Kempston, England.

Davies, N. (1984) "The Australian Small-Business Computer Market," *Australian Computer Bulletin,* March.

Davis, C. F. (1973) "Do We Need the Computer?" *Proceedings of the Environmental Design Research Association Conference,* Virginia, pp. 389–390.

——(1984) "Computers: Their Real Advantage Can Be in Giving a Thorough Grasp of Design," *Architectural Record,* June.

Davis, D. B. (1983) "Super Micros Muscle into Mini Markets," *High Technology,* December.

Davis, R. (1982) "Expert Systems: Where Are We and Where Do We Go from Here?" *AI Memo No. 665,* MIT Artificial Intelligence Laboratory, Cambridge.

Deken, J. (1983) *The Electronic Cottage,* Bantam Books, New York.

Derfler, F. J. (1983) "To LAN or Not to LAN," *PC Magazine,* August.

——and W. Stallings (1983) *A Manager's Guide to Local Networks,* Prentice-Hall, Englewood Cliffs, N.J.

Dietsch, D. (1984) "Minding your VDUs," *Progressive Architecture,* May.

Dill, J. C., and J. H. Pittman (1983) "The Single-User Workstation—A New Concept That Promises to Benefit the Design Profession," *Architectural Record,* August.

Ding, G. D., et al. (1984) "Simulation Studies of Building Energy Performance in Warm and Humid Climates," in H. J. Cowan (ed.), *Energy Conservation in the Design of Multi-Storey Buildings,* Pergamon, Sydney.

Doubilet, S. (1984) "CAD: The Wows and Wherefores," *Progressive Architecture,* May.

"Draughting and Design" (1983) *Architects Journal,* Jan. 19.

Driscoll, P., J. Marzeki, and F. Wilson (1982) "Architecture and the Information Revolution," *AIA Journal,* July.

Drury, J. (1984) "Buildings with Information Technology 4: Industrial Buildings," *Architects Journal,* July 11.

Duffy, F., and J. Worthington (eds.) (1982) "The Architect and Information Technology," *Architects Journal,* Aug. 25.

Dunning, A. (1984) "Systems Drafting in the Small Firm," *Progressive Architecture,* April.

Durinski, A. (1982) "A Graphics Designer Looks at Computer Imagery," *Computer Graphics World,* November.

Eastman, C. M. (1982) "The Computer as a Design Medium," *Eastern Regional ACMS Conference,* Carnegie-Mellon University, Pittsburgh.

Evans, B. (1983) "Low-Cost Computing 6: Implementation," *Architects Journal,* Mar. 19.

———(1984) "Buildings with Information Technology 5: Offices," *Architects Journal,* July 18.

Fabos, J. G. (1983) "Paperless Landscape Architecture: Future Prospects," *Landscape Journal,* vol. 2, no. 1.

Fanning, B. (1983) "Financial Management Options," *Architectural Technology,* vol. 1, no. 1, Fall.

Fawcette, J. (1983) "Mighty Chips," *PC World,* vol. 1, no. 5, August.

Feigenbaum, E., and P. McCorduck (1983) *The Fifth Generation,* Addison-Wesley, Reading, Mass.

Fisher, T. (1984) "Intelligent Architecture," *Progressive Architecture,* May.

Fisk, D. (1983) "Computers and Building Services — Japanese Style," *Building Services,* July.

Fullenwider, D. R. (1984) "Computers: What Some of the Smaller Offices Are Doing," *Architectural Record,* October.

Fuller, D. H. (1983) "The Architect/Service Bureau Connection," *Computer Graphics World,* January.

Garratt, B. (1981) "Facing Up to Change," *Architects Journal,* Oct. 28.

Gero, J. S. (1984) *Optimization in Computer-Aided Design,* North-Holland, Amsterdam.

——— and R. D. Coyne (1984) "The Place of Expert Systems in Architecture," in J. Wexler (ed.), *CAD 84,* Butterworths, Guildford, England.

——————(1985) "Logic Programming as a Means of Representing Semantics in Design Languages," *Environment and Planning B,* vol. 12, pp. 351–369.

Ginzberg, E. (1981) "The Mechanization of Work," *Scientific American,* September.

Giuliano, V. E. (1981) "The Mechanization of Office Work," *Scientific American,* September.

Goldblum, E. (1982) "Computing: Planning for Disaster," *Architects Journal,* Oct. 27.

Goumain, P., and G. Mallen (1980) "Interface Design and the Future Development of Interactive Building Design Systems: A Study Report," *CAD 80,* IPC Press, London.

Green, R. (1982) "File under Future," *Design,* May.

Greenberg, D. (1984) "The Coming Breakthrough of Computers as a True Design Tool," *Architectural Record,* September.

Greig, J. (1983a) "Low-Cost Computing 1: A Strategy for Computing," *Architects Journal,* Jan. 26.

———(1983b) "Low-Cost Computing 4: Choosing Hardware," *Architects Journal,* Feb. 23.

———(1983c) "Low-Cost Computing 7: Microcomputers," *Architects Journal,* Apr. 27.

———(1983d) "Low-Cost Computing 10: Programming," *Architects Journal,* May 18.

———(1983e) "Low-Cost Computing 11: How a Computer Works," *Architects Journal,* May 25.

Gretes, F. C. (1984) "Need Information? You Can Get a Lot with On-line Retrieval Services," *Architectural Record,* March.

"A Guide to Computer Software for Architects and Engineers" (1984) *Architectural Record,* October.

Gunn, T. G. (1981) "The Mechanization of Design and Manufacturing," *Scientific American,* September.

Hall, G. (1984) "Wired for Change," *Architectural Technology,* Spring.

Hamilton, I. (1981) *Computer Draughting for the Building Team,* Construction Industry Computing Association, Cambridge, England.

——— and J. R. F. Burdett (1982) "Computer Drafting Systems in Construction — The Buyers' Problem," in *CAD 82,* Butterworths, Guildford, England.

——— and J. Chalmers (1980) "A Comparison of Draughting Systems," in J. Lansdown (ed.), *Computer Graphics 80,* Online, London.

Hanson, N. (1983) "Computers and Design," unpublished working paper, Department of Architectural Science, University of Sydney.

Harper, G. N. (1968) *Computer Applications in Architecture and Engineering,* McGraw-Hill, New York.

Harrison, S. (1983) "Coordinating A/E/C CAD," *Computer Graphics World,* November.

Hayes-Roth, F., D. Waterman, and D. Lenat (1983) *Building Expert Systems,* Addison-Wesley, Reading, Mass.

Heard, H. (1982) "The Chip Revolutionizes Fire/Security Systems," *RIBA Journal,* April.

Heubel, K. (1982) "Practical Issues of Managing a CAD System," in *ACADS National CAD/CAM Conference,* Association for Computer-Aided Design, Melbourne.

Heuristic Programming Project (1980), Stanford University.

Higgins, M. (1982) "A CAD System for the A-E-C Industry," *Computer Graphics World,* December.

Hittle, D. C. (1979) "Building Loads Analysis and Systems Thermodynamic (BLAST)," U.S. Army Construction Engineering Research Laboratory (CERL), Champaign, Ill.

Hooper, W. D., and D. R. Levy (1983) "The AIA Computer Hotline," *Architectural Technology,* vol. 1, no. 1.

Howe, H. (1980) "Computers for the Future," *Building,* November.

Hoyt, C. K. (1984) "Computers: Their Real Advantage Can Be in Giving a Thorough Grasp of Design," *Architectural Record,* June.

Hubbard, S. W. (1983) *The Computer Graphics Glossary,* Onyx Press, Phoenix, Ariz.

Hunn, B. D. (1979) "The DOE-2 Computer Program for Building Energy Analysis," presented at the *Conservation/Energy Management by Design Conference,* El Paso, Tex.

Hutchinson, P. (1985) "An Expert System for the Design of Earth Retaining Structures," Master of Building Science thesis, Department of Architectural Science, University of Sydney.

Hutzel, I. (ed.) (1984) "Ergonomics Forum," *Computer Graphics World,* April.

Ireland, D. A. (1983) "Ideas in CAD Education," in *Graphics '83, First Australasian Conference on Computer Graphics,* Institution of Engineers, Canberra.

Jadrniczk, R. (1984) "Computer-Aided Design," *BYTE,* January.

Johnson, P. A., B. Judd, and G. Le Sueur (1984) "The Integrated House: An Experiment in Habitability in a Context of Social and Technological Change," in *54th Australian & New Zealand Association for the Advancement of Science Congress* (unpublished), Canberra.

Johnson, R. H. (1982) "Solid Modeling for CAD/CAM," *Computer Graphics World,* no. 11.

Jones, B. (1982) *Sleepers, Wake! Technology and the Future of Work,* Oxford University Press, Melbourne.

Jones, J. C. (1970) *Design Methods,* Wiley-Interscience, New York; also 1980 ed.

Kemper, A. M. (ed.) (1985) *Pioneers of CAD in Architecture,* Hurland/Swenson, Pacifica.

Killpack, C. (1982) "Computer Mapping, Spatial Analysis, and Landscape Architecture," *Landscape Architecture,* vol. 1, no. 1.

Kinnucan, P. (1982) "Solid Modellers Make the Scene," *High Technology,* vol. 2, no. 4.

———(1984) "Computers That Think like Experts," *High Technology,* January.

Klein, S., and P. Kilburn (1985) "Market Projections," in E. Teicholz (ed.), *CAD/CAM Handbook,* McGraw-Hill, New York.

"Know Your Building" (1982) *Architects Journal,* June 23.

Koning, H., and J. Eizenberg (1981) "The Language of the Prairie: Frank Lloyd Wright's Prairie Houses," *Environment and Planning B,* vol. 8, p. 295.

Krawczyk, R. J. (1984) "Computer-Assisted Scheduling for Architects," *Architectural Technology,* vol. 2, no. 1, Spring.

Kusuda, T. (1974) "NBSLD Computer Program for Heating and Cooling Loads in Buildings," NBS report NBSIR 74-574.

Lamb, J. (1984) "Commerce without the Personal Touch," *New Scientist,* July 26.

Land, F. (1984) "IKBS and Expert Systems: Are There Limitations to Their Use in Management Systems," seminar (unpublished), University of Sydney.

Lane, V. P., and P. Loucopoulos (1985) "Knowledge-Based Systems as a Mechanism for Optimization of Conceptual Design in Civil Engineering Projects," in J. Gero (ed.), *Optimization of Computer-Aided Design,* North-Holland, Amsterdam, pp. 81–100.

Lansdown, J. (1980) *Computer Graphics '80,* Online, London.

———(1983) "Dealing with Uncertainty and Imprecision," in J. Chalmers (ed.), *PARC 83,* Online, London.

———(1984a) "Expert Systems 1: Knowledge for Designers," *Architects Journal,* Feb. 8.

———(1984b) "Expert Systems 2: A Prototype for Designers," *Architects Journal,* Feb. 15.

———and T. W. Maver (1984) "CAD in Architecture and Building," *Computer-Aided Design,* vol. 16, no. 3, pp. 148–154.

Laurie, P. (1983) *The Joy of Computers,* Hutchinson, London.

Laver, M. (1983) "The Birth of Computers," *New Scientist,* Sept. 15.

Lawson, B. (1978) "Computer Potential in Design Education," *RIBA Journal,* April.

———(1982) *How Designers Think,* Architectural Press, London.

Le Corbusier (1956) *The Modulor,* English ed. translated by P. De France and A. Bostock, Harvard University Press, Cambridge.

Leighton, N. L. (1984) *Computers in the Architectural Office,* Van Nostrand Rheinhold, New York.

Lickley, J. M., and W. Todd (1982) "Building Communications," *Building Services,* July.

Lipchin, L. (1982) "Managerial and Strategic Planning Aspects of CAD/CAM Technology Implementation," in A. Pipes (ed.), *CAD 82,* Butterworths, Guildford, England.

Lurie, P. M. (1982) "Computer Systems and Professional Liability," *Progressive Architecture,* no. 12.

Lush, B. (1984) "Control Systems in Building: Under Control," *Building,* Mar. 16.

Lyall, D. (1984) "Control Systems in Building: Savings in Store," *Building,* Mar. 16.

MacDougall, E. B. (1983) *Microcomputers in Landscape Architecture,* Elsevier, New York.

Macewen, M. (1973) *Crisis in Architecture,* RIBA Publications, London.

Machover, C. (1985) "CAD/CAM: Where It Was, Where It Is, and Where It Is Going," in E. Teicholz (ed.), *CAD/CAM Handbook,* McGraw-Hill, New York.

——— and R. E. Blauth (eds.) (1980) *The CAD/CAM Handbook,* Computervision, Bedford, Mass.

Malik, R. (1982) "Computers Simplified," *Architects Journal,* Jan. 27.

March, L., and G. Stiny (1985) "Spatial Systems in Architecture and Design," *Environment and Planning B [Planning and Design],* vol. 12, no. 1.

Markus, T. A., et al. (1972) *Building Performance,* Applied Science, London.

Markusz, Z. (1982) "Design in Logic," *Computer-Aided Design,* vol. 14, no. 6.

Martin, J. (1983) "Silent Running," *PC World,* December.

Mathew, P. A. (1985) "Computers: Where You and They Stand with the Law," *Architectural Record,* September.

Maver, T. W. (1977) "Building Appraisal," in J. S. Gero (ed.), *Computer Applications in Architecture,* Applied Science, London.

———(1978) "The Benefits of Using Computer-Aided Design," *RIBA Journal,* March.

McLuhan, M. (1964) *Understanding Media: The Extensions of Man,* Routledge, London.

Meade, B. (1983a) "Using CAD Effectively with Reprographics," *Architectural Record,* September.

———(1983b) "Using Reprographics Effectively with CAD," *Architectural Record,* October.

Mermet, J. (ed.) (1981) *CAD in Medium-Sized and Small Industries,* North-Holland, Amsterdam.

Michie, D. (ed.) (1979) *Expert Systems in the Microelectronic Age,* Edinburgh University Press.

Mileaf, H. (1982a) "Computers: The Evolution Is Over; the Revolution is On," *Architectural Record,* June.

———(1982b) "Computers: How Do You Jump In?" *Architectural Record,* August.

———(1982c) "Computers: The Soft Spot is Software," *Architectural Record,* October.

———(1983a) "Computers: Where Is Your Firm to Get Software?" *Architectural Record,* January.

———(1983b) "Round Table on Computers in Architecture," *Architectural Record,* May.

Miller, N., P. Ngai, and D. Miller (1984) "Computer Graphics in Lighting Design," *International Lighting Review,* vol. 4.

Milne, M. A. (ed.) (1968) *Computer Graphics in Architecture and Design,* Yale University Press, New Haven, Conn.

———(1982) "SOLAR5, A User Friendly Computer-Aided Energy Conserving Design Tool," A. Pipes (ed.), *CAD 82,* Butterworths, Guildford, England.

———(1984) "A Building Energy Design Tool That Draws Pictures of Thermal Performance," *Proceedings CAMP 84,* AMK, Berlin, sec. C4.3.

Mitchell, W. J. (1977) *Computer-Aided Architectural Design,* Van Nostrand Rheinhold, New York.

———(1979) "Synthesis with Style," *Proceedings PARC 79,* Berlin, pp. 119–134.

———(1982) "Computer Graphics in Architectural Practice Today," *Computer Graphics World,* no. 4.

———(1985a) "A Comprehensive Approach to Basic Design," in A. M. Kemper (ed.), *Pioneers of CAD in Architecture,* Hurland/Swenson, Pacifica.

———(1985b) "Facilities Management," seminar, University of Sydney.

—— (1986) "Till Death Do Us Part," *Architecture Australia,* vol. 75, no. 3, pp. 36–37.
Moto-Oka, T. (ed.) (1982) *Fifth-Generation Computer Systems,* North-Holland, New York.
Myers, W. (1984) "The Ergonomics of Visual-Display Terminals," *IEEE Computer Graphics,* January.
Newby, S. (1982) "CAD to Aid and Abet," *Design,* no. 336, December.
Newell, A., and H. A. Simon (1972) *Human Problem Solving,* Prentice-Hall, Englewood Cliffs, N.J.
Nichol, J. (1984) "CAD in Practice—The Architects' View," *Building,* June 29.
Nicholson-Cole, D. (1982) "Microcomputer Case Study: Archilab," *Architects Journal,* May 26.
—— (1983) "Cash Flow Information for the Client," *Architects Journal,* Oct. 15.
Nightingale, M. (1984) "Buildings with Information Technology 2: Hospitals," *Architects Journal,* June 20.
Norton, F. J. (1981) "Interactive Graphics and Personnel Selection," in J. Mermet (ed.), *CAD in Medium-Sized and Small Industries,* North-Holland, Amsterdam.
O'Connor, T. C. (1983) "Computers: The Ins and Outs of the Purchasing Contract," *Civil Engineering/ASCE,* February.
Orr, J. (1985) "Tools: Hardware and Software," in E. Teicholz (ed.), *CAD/CAM Handbook,* McGraw-Hill, New York.
Oughton, D., et al. (1983) "Energy Management Systems," *Building Services,* August.
Page, J. K. (1966) contribution to *Building for People,* Conference Report, Ministry of Public Buildings and Works, London.
Palladio, A. (1738) *The Four Books of Architecture,* Isaac Ware (reprinted by Dover, New York, 1965).
Parkinson, K. (1984) "Buildings with Information Technology 1: Specifying Data Cabling," *Architects Journal,* June 13.
Paterson, J. (1980) "Models and the Microprocessor," *Chartered Quantity Surveyor,* May.
Peled, J. (1981) "The 'Gap' between Users and Designers of CAD/CAM Systems: Search for Solutions," in R. J. Smith (ed.), *18th Design Automation Conference,* Institute of Electrical and Electronics Engineers and Association for Computing Machinery, New York.
Perks, D. (1984) "Sound Intelligence," *Building Services,* July.
"Personal Computers in Market Blitzkrieg" (1983) *Australasian Computerworld,* Aug. 26.
Peters, G. (1984) *Construction Project Management Using Small Computers,* Architectural Press, London.
Pipes, A. (1981) "Why Can't We Manage Computer-Aided Design?" *Design Studies,* vol. 2, no. 2, April.
—— (ed.) (1982) *CAD 82,* Butterworths, Guildford, England.
—— (1984a) "Four Pens for £300,000," *Design,* July.
—— (1984b) "Computer Graphics: A Buyer's Guide," *Design,* November.
Pitman, J. H., and J. C. Dill (1984) "Computers: The Need for Graphics Standards," *Architectural Record,* February.
Poitou, J. P. (1981) "CAD and Working Conditions," in J. Mermet (ed.), *CAD in Medium-Sized and Small Industries,* North-Holland, Amsterdam.
Powell, R. B. (1980) "Justification and Financial Analysis for CAD," *Design Automation Conference 80,* Institute of Electrical and Electronics Engineers and Association for Computing Machinery, New York
Powers, E. (1984) "Advanced Systems Drafting in the Large Firm," *Progressive Architecture,* February.
Preiss, K. (1983) "Future CAD systems," *CAD,* July.
Prince, M. R. (1982) "Introducing CAD into the Design Office," *CAD ED 82,* CAD/CAM Association, Manchester, England.
Pulgram, W. L., and R. E. Stonis (1984) *Designing the Automated Office,* Whitney Library of Design (Watson-Guptill), New York.
Putnam, G. (1984) "Low-Cost Front Office Automation," *Progressive Architecture,* January.
Radford, A. D. (1985) "Approaches to Knowledge-Based Architectural Detailing," *Architectural Science Review,* vol. 28, no. 4, pp. 88–94.
—— and J. S. Gero (1980) "On Optimization in Architectural Design," *Building and Environment,* vol. 15, no. 2, pp. 73–80.
—— —— (1985) "Toward Generative Expert Systems for Architectural Detailing," *Computer-Aided Design,* vol. 17, no. 9, pp. 428–435.

———and G. Stevens (1983) "Design for 1984: Computers and Building Form," in J. Chalmers (ed.), *PARC 83,* Online, London, pp. 131–144.

Ralston, A., and C. L. Meek (1976) *Encyclopedia of Computer Science,* Van Nostrand Rheinhold, New York.

Ranch-Hindin, W. (1984) "Micro-Mainframe Links," *Systems and Software,* November.

Reinecke, I. (1982) *Micro Invaders,* Penguin Books, Melbourne.

Reswick, J. B. (1965) *Prospectus for Engineering Design Center,* Case Institute of Technology, Cleveland, Ohio.

Rickaby, P. (1979) "Speculations on the Future Practice of Architecture," *Design Studies,* vol. 1, no. 2, October.

Rosenman, M. A., and J. S. Gero (1985) "An Expert System for Building Regulations," working paper, Computer Application Research Unit, Department of Architectural Science, University of Sydney.

"Roundtable: Computer Use in the Small Architectural Firm" (1984) *Architectural Record,* May.

Sawzin, S. A. (1981) "The Design of a Computer Graphics Training Program," *IEEE CG&A,* November.

Schuster, K. (1984) "Computers: What Some of the Smaller Offices Are Doing," *Architectural Record,* October.

Scoins, D. (1982) "Trends and Experiences with Cadrafting in Europe," *ACADS National CAD/CAM Conference,* Melbourne.

Scrivener, S. A. R. (1982) "Computer Colors," *CAD/CAM International,* December.

Selkowitz, S. (1984) "New Tools for Analyzing the Thermal and Daylighting Performance of Fenestration in Multistorey Buildings," in H. J. Cowan (ed.), *Energy Conservation in the Design of Multi-storey Buildings,* Pergamon, Sydney.

Sennewald, B. (1986) "Smart Buildings," *Architectural Technology,* March–April.

Shan, R. R., and G. Yan (1978) "A Practical Technique for Benefit-Cost Analysis of CAD Systems," *15th Design Automation Conference,* Institute of Electrical and Electronics Engineers and Association for Computing Machinery, New York.

Shaviv, E. (1978) *"The Determination of the Form of Windows and Sun Shades in a Hot Climate," CAD 78,* IPC Science and Technology Press, Guildford, England.

Shirley, M. (1984) "Buildings with Information Technology 3: Shops," *Architects Journal,* July 4.

Shortliffe, E. H. (1976) *Computer-Based Medical Consultations: MYCIN,* Elsevier, New York.

Smith, D. C. (1982) "A Practical Approach to Training Engineers," *CAD ED 82,* CAD/CAM Association, Manchester, England.

Smith, R. J. (ed.) (1981) *18th Design Automation Conference,* Institute of Electrical and Electronics Engineers and Association for Computing Machinery, New York.

Spence, A., and J. Davy (1985) "Spinning the Web," *Building Services,* September.

Stansfield, K. (1982a) "How to Run a Practice with Energy," *RIBA Journal,* March.

———(1982b) "Throwing Away the Drawing Board," *RIBA Journal,* December.

Stasiowski, F. A. (1982) "T Square of Tomorrow," *Progressive Architecture,* no. 5.

Stevens, T. (1982a) "Bonningtons Release Time for Conceptual Design Work," *RIBA Journal,* February.

———(1982b) "How Two Practices Chose a Computer," *RIBA Journal,* April.

———(1983) "Computers: Prepare for the Future," *RIBA Journal,* April.

———(1984a) "Modernizing the GLC," *RIBA Journal,* January.

———(1984b) "Recovering from Investment," *RIBA Journal,* March.

———(1984c) "Programs for Design," *RIBA Journal,* April.

———(1984d) "Computing for the Saudi Club," *RIBA Journal,* May.

———(1984e) "Avoiding an Expensive Mistake," *RIBA Journal,* September.

Stiny, G. (1980) "Introduction to Shape and Shape Grammars," *Environment and Planning B,* vol. 7, pp. 343–351.

———and W. J. Mitchell (1978) "The Palladian Grammar," *Environment and Planning B,* vol. 5, pp. 5–18.

————(1980) "The Grammar of Paradise: On the Generation of Mughul Gardens," *Environment and Planning B,* vol. 7, pp. 209–226.

Stitt, F. A. (1980) *Systems Drafting*, McGraw-Hill, New York.
——(1982) "Computers for the Smaller Office: A Primer," *Architectural Record*, February.
——(1984) *Systems Graphics*, McGraw-Hill, New York.
Stoker, D. F., and N. H. Weingarten (1983) "CAD versus CAD," *Architectural Record*, December.
Swezey, R. W., and E. G. Davis (1983) "A Case Study of Human Factors Guidelines in Computer Graphics," *IEEE Computer Graphics*, November.
Teicholz, E. (1980) "The Biography of a Remarkable Tool," *AIA Journal*, May.
——(1983a) "Can Computer-Aided Drafting Be Effective and Affordable for the Small Firm," *Architectural Record*, February.
——(1983b) "Selecting the Right CAD System for Your Office," *Architectural Record*, July.
——(1985) "System Selection and Acquisition," in E. Teicholz (ed.), *CAD/CAM Handbook*, McGraw-Hill, New York.
Thomsen, C. (1985) "Architecture '85," *Architectural Technology*, Winter.
——and R. Schappaugh (1984) "Computers: Are Personal Computers Ready for the Big Firms?" *Architectural Record*, July.
Th'ng, R., and M. Davies (1972) "A Program Package for Producing Sketch Layouts," *ABACUS Occasional Paper 23*, Department of Architecture, Strathclyde, Glasgow.
"Trends toward 32-bit Minis in CAD/CAM War" (1982) *Pacific Computer Weekly*, Jan. 29.
Trombley, S. (1982) "Scissors and Paste Challenge the Mighty Micro," *RIBA Journal*, July.
"Universal Anxiety over the New Technology" (1985) *Building*, Jan. 18.
"Use of Computers Accelerates, AIA Firm Survey Concludes" (1982) *AIA Journal*, November.
Varrall, G. J. H. (1983) "Time for Manufacturer-sponsored Software," *Building Services*, December.
Wagner, W. F. (1985) "Results of a Record Survey: How Firms with Computers Are Faring and What the Nonusers Are Waiting For," *Architectural Record*, June.
Waldern J. (1984) "Cad—Clever but Unusable," *Design*, March.
Warren, D. (1982) "A View of the Fifth Generation and Its Impact," *The AI Magazine*, vol. 3, no. 4.
Webster, C. A. G. (1984) "Capitol: A Low-Cost 3-D Modelling System and Visualization System for Interior Designers and Architects," in J. Wexler (ed.), *CAD 84*, Butterworths, Guildford, England.
Wendle, R. W. (1983) "Some Cautions on Computers," *Architecture*, September.
Westlake, B. J., and P. J. Waight (1984) "Computer-Aided Knowledge—Beyond CAD/CAE," *Ausgraph 84*, Australian Computer Graphics Society, Melbourne.
Wexler, J. (1984) *CAD 84: 6th International Conference and Exhibition on Computers in Design Engineering*, Butterworths, Guildford, England.
Whittle, P., and C. Walls (1985) "The Best Way In," *Building Services*, September.
Wingert, B., M. Rader, and U. Riehm (1981) "Changes in the Working Skills in the Field of Design Caused by the Use of Computers," in J. Mermet (ed.), *CAD in Medium-Sized and Small Industries*, North-Holland, Amsterdam.
Winston, P. (1984) *Artificial Intelligence*, 2d ed., Addison-Wesley, Reading, Mass.
Witte, O. R. (1984a) "Affordable CAD," *Architectural Technology*, Fall.
——(1984b) "Advice about Hardware and Peripherals," *Architectural Technology*, Fall.
——(1985a) "Financial Management Software: Spring Update," *Architectural Technology*, Spring.
——(1985b) "The Compensation Crisis," *Architectural Technology*, Winter.
——(1985c) "Affordable CAD: Winter Update," *Architectural Technology*, Winter.
Woods, F. (1984a) "Reprographics Developments 2: Processes and Techniques," *Architects Journal*, Oct. 17.
——(1984b) "Reprographics Developments 3: Techniques," *Architects Journal*, Oct. 24.
——(1984c) "Reprographics Developments 4: Case Studies," *Architects Journal*, Oct. 31.
Yessios, C. I. (1982) "TEKTON: A System for Computer-Aided Architectural Design," in A. Pipes (ed.), *CAD 82*, Butterworths, Guildford, England.
Zorkoczy, P. (1982) *Information Technology*, Pitman, London.

Appendix

2

Glossary

This glossary contains most of the significant terms likely to be encountered in architectural computing.

abnormal termination   The self-termination of a program that occurs because the program recognizes that some sort of corruption or extreme error has occurred.

abort   To terminate some computer process prematurely. Aborting a program can cause data corruption.

absolute address   See **address.**

absolute coordinate   See **coordinates.**

ACADIA   The Association for Computer-Aided Design in Architecture in the United States, an association mainly consisting of those engaged in teaching and research in architectural computing in schools of architecture.

acceleration time   The time taken for one plotting head on a computer pen plotter to achieve optimal speed. Since most drawings consist of a large number of short lines, the acceleration time is a better indication of the plotter's speed than is the maximum speed of the plotting head, which may rarely actually be achieved.

acceptance test   A test which a purchaser of a computer system conducts and which the system must pass before final payment is made. Very common for minicomputer-based systems, but not for microcomputer-based ones.

access   To seek, read, or write data from or into memory or mass storage. The time taken to complete an access *(access time)* is a measure of the speed of the mass storage device and should be as short as possible. Internal memory has the shortest times of all, and tape the longest.

access floor   A method of installing cabling to computer sites, it consists of removable raised flooring beneath which the cables are run.

access time   See **access.**

ACM   Association for Computing Machinery, an international organization for computer professionals.

acoustic coupler   A device for linking a voice telephone to a modem by placing the telephone handset into rubber cups, rather than having a direct connection to the telephone socket.

acoustic hood   A box internally covered with acoustic absorbing materials used to shield the noise from impact printers.

actuator   A device that receives data from a computer and directly controls items of machinery plant, such as the valves, motors, and pumps of a building service system.

Ada   A structured computer language created by the U.S. Department of Defense as its universal language.

A/D converter   Analog-to-digital converter. See **analog data.**

address   (1) The location of an item in a computer memory. (2) An identifier that is given to an input-output device sharing a bus with other devices so that the CPU can recognize it. (3) Any means of identifying the location of data in memory or mass storage. An *absolute address* gives the true physical address of the item. A *relative address* gives the distance of the item from some reference point called the *base address.* The distance from the base address is called the *offset,* or *displacement.*

address bus   See **bus.**

addressable point   An output device such as a screen, being a plane, nominally has an infinite number of points; however, the electronics restricts the usable points to a subset of these — the addressable points.

A/E   Abbreviation for *architecture* and *engineering.*

AEC   *Architecture, engineering,* and *construction.*

aiming circle   A small circle of light projected onto a screen by a light pen to inform the user where the pen is pointing. Performs the same function as a cursor.

ALGOL   Acronym for *algorithmic language,* a programming language in which the statements have a general resemblance to algebraic formulas and English sentences, used for scientific and mathematical purposes. Not a popular language for new work, although the algorithms published by the ACM are written in it. It is the ancestor of Pascal and C.

algorithm   A sequence of steps or instructions for solving a problem. Strictly, the procedure must be guaranteed to terminate in a finite time.

alphanumeric character   Both the letters of the alphabet and the 10 numerical digits: A to Z, a to z, and 0 to 9.

analog computer   See **analog data.**

analog data   Data that can vary along a continuum — as opposed to digital data, which can only assume a discrete number of values. An *analog computer* uses such data, usually but not necessarily employing varying electric currents or voltages. A slide rule is a simple analog computer. Any device that accepts as input or provides as output analog data, such as a speedometer or fuel gage, is an *analog device.* An *analog-to-digital converter* is a unit for translating output signals from an analog device (such as a sound-level meter or temperature probe) into digital form for input into a digital computer system.

analog device   See **analog data.**

analog-to-digital converter   See **analog data.**

analogy   The representation of one phenomenon by a different phenomenon, as in the representation of the passage of time by the rotation of the hands of an analog clock, or the representation of temperature by electric current.

analysis   The process of resolving or separating a problem, process, situation, or object into its component parts and discovering the relationships between those parts, or the results of that process. In particular, *systems analysis* is concerned with the analysis of processes toward achieving greater efficiency in the management of those processes, often with the aid of a computer. A systems *analyst* is an expert analyst.

analyst   See **analysis.**

anchor point   A reference point in a graphics symbol, or macro, used to locate the macro within another drawing.

ANSI   American National Standards Institute. Develops standards for signaling schemes and computer communications, among other things.

answerback   Some terminals communicating with a remote computer do not actually place any characters on the screen but send them directly to the computer. *Answerback* is the echoing of this character by the remote computer to the terminal screen. The operator is thus reassured that the computer has received the character.

antialiasing   The process of removing the jagged edges characteristic of lines drawn on low- and medium-resolution computer screens to make the lines smoother. This jagged effect, called the *staircase effect,* is most apparent in lines that are nearly (but not exactly) horizontal or vertical.

APL   *A programming language.* Developed as an elegant means of expressing mathematical expressions; now a cult language. Characterized by compact expressions and the use of the array as the basic unit of manipulation.

application program   See **program.**

appraisal   (In CAD), the process of judging the success or not of a design proposal and (implicitly) of modifying it accordingly.

architectural computing   The use of computers in architectural design offices.

architecture   The overall manner in which the various components of a computer are integrated to form a single system.

archive   To transfer data from online mass storage devices (such as hard disks) to offline media (such as tapes). Archiving is done to remove old or little-used data and to free room on online media. While online data is limited to the number of mass storage devices available, archived data is limited only by the existing storage facilities for tapes and other offline media.

area fill   Filling a polygon displayed on a computer screen with a pattern or color.

argument   See subprogram.

array   See data structure.

artificial intelligence   The endowing of machines with some of the characteristics of intelligence (learning, recognition, etc.) normally associated with humans.

artificial language   As opposed to the natural languages, a language self-consciously created to serve as a vehicle for communication with humans or machines. Natural languages include English, Russian, and Spanish; artificial languages include all computer languages, mathematics, Esperanto, etc.

ascenders   See descenders.

ASCII character set   Acronym for *A*merican *S*tandard *C*ode for *I*nformation *I*nterchange, the standard association of a pattern of 7 bits with an alphanumeric or control character so that components of a computer system can recognize input and output. An *ASCII file* contains only data encoded in the ASCII code, that is, a normal text file. Carriage-return and line-feed characters are appended to the end of each line. Most data files are ASCII files and can be output without any processing directly to a printer or screen. ASCII tables can be found in many microcomputer books. The *extended ASCII* character set uses all 8 bits in a byte to establish a further 128 characters.

ASCII file   See ASCII character set.

aspect ratio   The ratio of a screen's height to its width.

assembler   See assembly language.

assembly language   A low-level computer language using abbreviations or codes to replace the binary machine code with which computers work, but still generally retaining a 1:1 relationship with the computer's machine language (i.e., one command in the assembly language represents just one command in the machine language). An *assembler* is a program that translates the programmer's assembly language program into machine code. The translation process is called *assembly*.

association matrix   A matrix in which numbers indicate the relative importance of the association between facilities or spaces. Used in facilities planning.

asynchronous transmission   A method of serial data transmission in which characters are transmitted at indeterminate intervals and accompanied by start and stop bits that delimit them. Generally used for human-computer communication, as between a terminal and host computer. *Synchronous transmission* methods do not use the additional bits but rely on timing sychronization to ensure proper transfer; they are used most often for computer-computer transmission.

attribute   In computer graphics, any label or characteristic associated with an entity, such as the width of a line or the cost of the item represented by an object. An attribute occupies one or more fields in a record.

auxiliary storage (or memory)   An old term for mass storage.

back end   See front end.

background processing   Low-priority computer processing over which foreground processing takes precedence, as in the printing of a document by a word processing program while the computer is also being used to edit or create more text.

backspace   See **character.**

backup   A duplicate of existing data and programs, made to safeguard against corruption or loss of the originals.

bandwidth   The range of frequencies that a transmission circuit can carry. A wide bandwidth allows faster and more varied information to be transmitted. In *baseband* transmission, medium signals occupy the entire bandwidth of the circuit. In a *broadband* system, a single signal occupies only part of the bandwidth, leaving space for other signals to be transmitted simultaneously.

bank switching   A technique used in some computers to allow that form of multiuser access in which each user has available a unique bank of memory. The CPU switches rapidly between banks, depending on the demands made on it.

baseband   See **bandwidth.**

BASIC   *B*eginner's *a*ll-purpose *s*ymbolic *i*nstruction *c*ode, a high-level computer language easy to learn and use and very common on microcomputers, but held in disdain by computer professionals.

batch processing   The processing of data in "batches," or groups, usually of programs that are left to run on a computer at a later time, as distinct from current or interactive processing. Few processes in architectural computing are done this way.

baud, or baud rate   A measure of transmission speed: 1 bit per second. One character per second is about 10 baud.

BBS   *B*ulletin *b*oard *s*ervice.

benchmark   A key test of the performance of a program or computer system. CAD systems are often required to produce key drawings provided by a potential purchaser as a means of comparing their performance.

beta testing   The second-stage testing of a program that occurs when it is sent to selected users (beta sites) for examination and discussion. The program will be commercially released when it has passed these tests.

Bezier curve   A mathematical method of encoding a complex curve into a more tractable mathematical form. A *B-spline* is another such method.

binary arithmetic   An arithmetic system with a base (or radix) of 2 (instead of base 10, as in decimal arithmetic), so that it only needs the two digits 0 and 1. Thus, "10" represents 2, and "100" represents 4. It is used by digital computers because the two possible conditions of an electric circuit (current or no current), switch (on or off), magnetic field (north or south), or other bistable device can be used to represent the digits 0 or 1. These two digits are called *binary digits*. A *bit* can hold a single binary digit and is the smallest unit of information used in computing. Any code consisting entirely of binary digits is called a *binary code*. A *byte* is a string of bits whose length is the smallest accessible unit in the computer memory, usually 8 bits. In the ASCII code system, a byte can hold precisely one character.

binary code   See **binary arithmetic.**

binary digit   See **binary arithmetic.**

binary file   A file encoded in binary form rather than in normal ASCII format. Data files are sometimes encoded this way. All machine-code programs are in binary form. A binary file cannot be displayed or output. See **ASCII character set.**

BIOS   *B*asic *i*nput-*o*utput *s*ystem, the inner part of a microcomputer operating system responsible for handling the details of input and output. Highly machine-dependent.

bit   See **binary arithmetic.**

bit-map memory   Computer memory that keeps a description of the pixels in a raster display. The set of bits in each location of the bit map corresponds to the color or intensity of a particular pixel on the display. In a *bit-mapped display* the pixels are also mapped to the computer's working RAM, allowing manipulation under direct program control.

bit-mapped display   See **bit-map memory.**

bit pad   Sometimes used to refer to a small digitizing tablet.

blank   (1) (Noun) See **character.** (2) (Verb) To prevent the display of a graphic line or drawing so as to clear the screen of unnecessary data.

BMS   See **building management system.**

board   A system or subsystem of computer chips and circuitry mounted on a board.

boilerplate   Ability of a word processor to insert pieces of text from one file into certain places in another.

boolean algebra   An algebra of logic in which the value of a proposition can be either true or false and therefore represented by a bit.

boot   To start a computer from scratch. A very simple program called the boot program and stored in a ROM in the computer will order the computer to load in the operating system from disk.

bounding rectangle   The smallest rectangle that will enclose a graphic object; used to optimize certain computer operations on that object. When carried out in three dimensions, it leads to *box geometry,* in which the full geometry of an object is not stored; instead, plans and elevations are mapped onto a box.

box geometry   See **bounding rectangle.**

broadband   See **bandwidth.**

B-spline   See **Bezier curve.**

buffer, or buffer store   A temporary store of data when information is being transferred from one unit to another, as between a computer and screen (screen buffer) or a computer and printer. The buffer partly compensates for differences in the send and receive rates between the two items.

bug   Any error or malfunction in a computer program or system. *Debugging* is the exasperating process of eliminating bugs from a program.

building automation system   Same as **building management system.**

building control system   Same as **building management system.**

building management system (BMS)   A system in which one or more computers are used to control the HVAC system of a building, and possibly other aspects, such as elevators, security, and fire.

bulletin board   A communal place available to all users on a network in which they may put messages for general view.

bundling   The inclusion of several items of hardware or software into a single indivisible package by a vendor. Once a common marketing strategy but now falling into disuse.

bus   A line, usually a set of tracks on a computer circuit board, on which bits are transmitted as electric impulses and into which are plugged several components. The *address bus* of a microcomputer is used to tell the RAM where a word is to be stored or retrieved from. The *data bus* carries the data itself.

bus network   See **network.**

byte   See **binary arithmetic.**

C   A computer language designed to retain the good structuring allowed by Pascal, without its restrictions.

CAAD   *Computer-aided architectural design.* An ugly acronym, for which there is no acceptable alternative.

cable drop   The attachment connecting a computer to the cable that acts as a transmission medium in a network.

CAD   Acronym for *computer-aided-design,* sometimes used for *computer-aided drafting.*

CADAM   Sometimes used as an acronym for *computer-augmented design and manufacturing.* Also a proprietary name.

CAD/CAM   Acronym for *computer-aided design/computer-aided manufacturing.*

CADD   Acronym for *computer-aided drafting and design.*

calligraphic display   See **vector graphics.**

carriage return   See **character.**

cartridge disk.   A hard-disk pack that can be removed from a disk drive, unlike a Winchester disk drive.

catalog   See **directory.**

catenate   (1) The process of joining two or more character strings together end to end to produce a single new string. (2) In a more general sense, refers to any sort of joining or linking process.

cathode-ray tube (CRT)   Visual-display device in which a beam of electrons is directed to produce an image on the surface of an evacuated glass tube.

CCITT   Consultative Committee of International Telephone and Telegraph, a UN committee that publishes data transmission standards. The most likely to be encountered is CCITT V.24, a standard that defines the common RS-232C serial interface.

cell matrix   The rectangular dot matrix from which a character is formed on a screen or on a dot-matrix or laser printer. The more pixels within the matrix, the better the shape of the characters formed.

central processing unit (CPU)   The computer component that interprets and executes program instructions and communicates with storage, input, and output devices; the heart of a computer.

centronics port   See **parallel transmission.**

CEPA   Society of Computer Applications in Engineering, Planning, and Architecture, a U.S. organization.

character   A single digit, letter, or special character, such as $, +, and /. The characters A to Z, a to z, and 0 to 9 are called *alphanumeric characters*. The standard punctuation marks plus some less common ones (e.g., ' { } | \ å <<) are called *special characters*. The blank space, which of course prints as a blank, is also a character. In the ASCII character set there are also some characters, called *control characters,* that are intended to control the operation of a computer system component (usually the screen or printer) rather than to be printed; examples are carriage return (symbolized cr), backspace (bs), and linefeed (lf): respectively, ASCII numbers 8, 13, and 10.

character set   The set of characters that a computer, printer, daisy wheel, etc., is capable of printing or recognizing. They vary enormously from machine to machine.

check bit   It serves as one of the many ways to ensure error-free data communication. Each transmitted character has a bit that is used not to define the character but as a check that the preceding bits have been transmitted correctly. The check bit is set so that the sum of the bits in the character is even *(even parity)*. Some systems set it so that the sum is odd *(odd parity)*. If the check is ignored, the character is said to have *no parity.*

chip   An integrated circuit etched on a semiconductor material and hermetically sealed; usually plugged into a printed circuit on a computer board. Chips can contain processing, memory, input-output, or other circuits. It is a matter of debate whether this is a slang term or a bona fide technical term.

chromaticity diagram   A diagram defined by the Commission Internationale de l'Eclairage (CIE), it sets out the three primary colors and a mechanism by which they may be combined to form any visible color. Used in computer graphics to compare the color characteristics of color screens, among other things.

CICA   Construction Industries Computing Association, a British organization.

clipping   See **window.**

clock chip   The chip that regulates the timing of the CPU.

cluster diagram   Diagram showing the associations between different facilities in facilities planning; usually derived from an association matrix.

coaxial cable   Cabling like that used for color television sets; often used in local-area networks for its shielded nature.

COBOL   *Common business oriented language*, a high-level programming language for business applications that uses English-like statements. The most commonly used language, but very rarely used in CAD applications.

code   (1) (Noun) A written piece of a computer program. (2) (Verb) To encode or translate an algorithm into a specific computer language. What programmers do for a living.

coding   See **code** (2).

color table   A method used in computer graphics to provide a large color palette even though the screen can display few colors at any instant. The value of a pixel is not interpreted directly as a color but as an index into the table, each entry of which is a color.

command   An instruction that tells the computer what to do; usually used for those instructions which a human may issue to the computer. The totality of these commands is called a *command language*. A program in which the user types commands, rather than using a menu or iconic system, is called a *command-driven program,* often preferred by experienced users and touch typists. A *command processor* is that part of the operating system which accepts, interprets, and acts on commands given by the user; it usually involves the computer executing some subsidiary service program.

comment   A note which is included in a computer program (amid its code) to clarify its operation for a human reader but which has no effect on its execution.

compatibility   (1) Two computers are said to be compatible if the same programs will run on both without alteration or with minor alterations. A term used so loosely that it is positively misleading. In the case of microcomputers, compatibility implies that they use the same disk formats, although machines so labeled often do not. (2) Two components of a computer system (e.g., computer and printer) are said to be compatible if they can be used together without an intervening converter.

compilation   The process of translating an algorithm written in a high-level programming language (such as Pascal or C) into machine code for a particular computer. The program that does this is called a *compiler.* Compiled programs run faster than interpreted ones.

compiler   See **compilation.**

composite   That signal accepted by a color display in which the red, blue, and green components are in a combined form.

composition   A term used in computer graphics to refer to the product of all the transformation matrices that result in the net transformation. In simpler terms, the total effect of several manipulations done on a graphic object.

compression   Same as **data compression.**

computer   Any device that can accept data, process it, and produce results. Now generally used only to denote an electronic digital computer.

computer science   The field of computer study and development, involving both hardware and software.

computer system   A computer processor and associated memory, screen, printing, and/or other devices that together make up a viable set of equipment for some purpose. The manner in which these parts are put together is called the computer's *configuration.*

concatenate Same as **catenate.**

concurrent processing Synonym for **multitasking.**

configure To customize a peripheral or program for the computer with which it is intended to be used. Often a difficult process, requiring some technical knowledge.

console The manual control unit for a computer, providing a display of information and a means of communicating with the computer, either via a keyboard or switches.

consumables Items such as paper, ribbons, and disks.

contrast ratio The brightness ratio between a character or graphic and the screen background.

control character See **character.**

control key A key (working like the shift key) that is used in conjunction with any normal key to allow the latter to produce a control character.

controller A piece of hardware that controls some major component of a computer system, such as a disk drive, under the guidance of the CPU.

coordinates An ordered pair or trio of numbers that defines a point in two- or three-dimensional euclidean space. An *absolute coordinate* refers to a fixed origin, as in the normal cartesian system. A *relative coordinate* takes the last drawn point as the origin.

copy protection Any of several schemes to prevent the unauthorized copying (and hence piracy) of microcomputer software. Simple schemes can be broken by dedicated individuals, and complex ones are expensive. One method uses a small microprocessor installed in a box, called a *dongle,* which plugs into one of a microcomputer's serial ports and which must be present for the program to operate. Others include various ways of tampering with the supplied disk so as to render a copy ineffective.

core (1) A computer graphics standard suggested by the ACM but rejected by the ISO in favor of the German GKS standard. (2) An old name for internal memory or RAM.

cost ratio The ratio of the cost of doing a task manually to the cost of doing it with a CAD system.

cps Characters *per second.* A measurement of printer speed.

CPU See **central processing unit.**

cr *Carriage return.* See **character.**

CRT See **cathode-ray tube.**

cursor A special symbol (such as a flashing underscore or a rectangular block) used to specify a particular position on the screen. It usually indicates where the next alphanumeric character will be displayed. In a graphics system, the cursor might be a cross hair or small cross indicating a particular point on a drawing area.

cylinder   When a disk drive contains more than one surface, as in a platter of disks, all the tracks equidistant from the center comprise a cylinder.

daisy-wheel printer   A character printer in which the characters are embossed at the end of the spokes of a wheel. The wheel rotates, and the desired character is impacted against a ribbon when in the print position. Usually the daisy wheel is removable, allowing different fonts (character sets) to be used.

data   General expression used to describe any fact, number, group of characters or symbols, or other value used by but not part of a computer program. In some languages, like LISP, the distinction is clouded.

database   A collection of interrelated data stored together in a way that facilitates the addition, modification, and removal of required data for various applications. The basic unit stored is the *record,* which usually represents a single real-world entity, such as a person, firm, line, or point. A record is typically divided into *fields,* each of which represents a single simple piece of information, such as a surname, street number, or coordinate. Databases are structured into one of three forms: hierarchical, network, or relational. A *hierarchical* (or *tree*) *database* is logically structured into a tree, in which records lower down the tree can only be accessed from a record higher up, which is said to own it. A *network* (or *plex*) *database* allows for any sort of relationship between records. A *relational database* is structured into tables; it is conceptually the simplest and cleanest database, but difficult to implement.

database management system (DBMS)   A computer program or set of programs that organizes and provides access to a database. That part of the package which is used to define the structure of the database is called the *data definition language.* That part which allows the user to interrogate the database is called the *database manipulation language.*

data bus   See **bus.**

data communications   Transmission of data over cables or telephone lines or via satellite.

data compression   Any of various techniques to reduce the space occupied by data; often used when large amounts of information must be stored efficiently.

data definition language   See **database management system.**

data dictionary   A directory of the data items and data types used in a database system or program.

data file   A file of data, as opposed to a file that is a program. Data files may be stored as ASCII files or as binary files.

data integrity   The safeguarding of important data against electronic corruption or human malfeasance. Computers suffer enough mishaps that programmers have found it necessary to contrive various schemes for ensuring that data is stored and accessed correctly.

data item   In a database or data structure, the smallest unit of information that carries meaning, usually representing a single entity from the real world. It is subdivided into fields. Its *fields* can be any one of several *data types* defining the allowable values the field can take; the simplest data types are the integer, floating-point (real), and character types. Since all data is stored ultimately as a bit pattern, the data type tells the computer how to interpret the pattern. Most languages forbid a variable of one type to be used to store data of another type.

data manipulation language   See **database management system.**

data processing   Same as **information processing**

data structure   A programming entity consisting of simple data items that are connected in certain specific ways and viewed as a logical whole; a fundamental concept in programming. The simplest data structure is the *array,* which is a table of related items, each of which must be of the same data type (homogeneous); it is an arrangement of data whereby each item is identified by a variable name, followed by one or more indices or subscripts. The dimension of an array is the number of indices needed to identify an item; a one-dimensional array needs one index, a two-dimensional array two indices, etc. Only linear relationships between items in the array are possible. A *record,* another form of data structure, does not have to have homogeneous subparts. A *linked-list* data structure is much more complex than a record or an array and can provide for more sophisticated (and nonlinear) relationships between data items. One common form is the *tree* (or *hierarchical) structure,* which looks rather like a family tree; the most complex is the network structure.

data type   See **data item.**

DBMS   See **database management system.**

DCE   *D*ata *c*ommunications *e*quipment. Defined by the RS-232C standard, referring to computers and modems; these use a female plug.

debugging   See **bug.**

dedicated   Refers to any computer system component that carries out a single task.

delimiter   A symbol used to show where an expression starts and stops, to distinguish it from the following text. In "word," for example, the double quotes act as delimiters.

depth cuing   Any method used in computer graphics to connote varying depth in a three-dimensional view. A common technique is to make the more distant parts of the object dimmer.

descenders   Those parts of a character which descend below the line, such as the tails of g and q. *Ascenders* are those parts which rise above the body of a character, such as the high parts of t or d.

design grammar   A grammar for manipulating designs according to rules, paralleling a linguistic grammar.

design methods movement   See **design theory**

design theory   The theory of the design process and of approaches to the design process; in architectural computing, particularly the role and implications of computer technology in design. The *design methods movement* developed the idea that design could be a systematic, analytical process.

diagnostic   (1) A program that tests a computer or peripheral to ensure that all is working. (2) A message issued by a program that indicates that an error of fault has occurred and suggests the location and cause of the error.

dialogue   The interaction between human and machine; usually used to refer to preplanned or guided interaction. Much effort is expended to ensure a natural and smooth dialogue.

digital computer   A computer that processes data represented in digital or numerical form, as distinct from an analog computer. Electronic digital computers are now commonly just called computers.

digitizer   A device for converting drawn shapes into digital data, usually by pointing to the vertices of a shape with a special stylus or digitizer pen while the shape lies on a special table or tablet that is able to record the position of the pen.

direct access file   See file access.

direct digital control   The use of a computer to monitor and control the operations of a building's plant or other equipment.

directory   An index giving the addresses of data: for example, the location of files on a floppy disk. More generally, the *catalog* of files maintained on a mass storage medium.

direct view storage tube (DVST)   A cathode-ray tube in which the screen surface is coated with phosphors that are able to retain an image for some time. Changing this image requires erasing the entire screen and redrawing it.

disable   To disconnect, usually electronically rather than physically, a component of a computer system so that it can neither receive nor send data to the rest of the system. *Enabling* is the reverse process.

disk   A magnetic data recording device that rotates within a disk drive and is read by one or more read-write heads. A *floppy disk* (so-called because of its physical characteristics) is single-layered, removable, and housed in a paper sleeve. A *hard disk* is a multilayered device that can either be removable or permanently sealed within the hardware (a Winchester drive).

diskette   Alternative name for a floppy disk.

disk operating system (DOS)   A computer program that controls the way in which information is stored on and accessed from magnetic disks. It usually includes the file management functions required for generating, storing, and modifying programs.

displacement   See address.

display   A visual presentation of a drawing or of data, usually referring to the screen image on a cathode-ray tube.

display buffer   A memory device, or a portion of the main computer memory, used to store the data necessary to generate a display.

display file   A file, held in the display buffer, that can be interpreted directly by a display device to produce an image on the screen.

distributed data processing   A system in which processing is carried out by several different computers linked together in a network rather than by one single computer.

dither   A method used by a computer graphics program or display to simulate a halftone or continuous-tone image.

documentation   The descriptive commentary on a computer system or computer program: for example, the comments in a computer program or in the manuals that accompany software.

dongle   See **copy protection.**

DOS   See **disk operating system.**

dot-matrix printer   A printer in which characters are formed as a matrix of dots; often capable of printing graphics as well as text.

double-precision number   A form of real number offered by some languages, it occupies twice the number of words as a normal real number, providing a greater range and/or greater precision.

down   A computer is "down" if it is not working because of a fault (the opposite of "up"). *Downtime* is the amount of time that a computer is not functional when it should be.

DP   *D*ata *p*rocessing. See **electronic data processing.**

dragging   Moving a drawing element dynamically across a display in response to the movement of a mouse, stylus, or other graphic input device.

drive   General term for a device that physically moves a recording medium, such as a disk drive or a tape drive.

driver   See **subprogram.**

drum plotter   A pen plotter in which the drawing is held on a drum. Lines are drawn by a combination of rotating the drum and moving a pen along its surface parallel to its axis of rotation.

DTE   *D*ata *t*erminal *e*quipment. Part of the RS-232C standard, referring to printers, terminals, and even computers acting as terminals; these use a male plug.

dumb terminal   A computer terminal that cannot do any processing itself, meaning that it must be connected to a computer elsewhere.

dump   A mass output of the state of a computer program; used for debugging purposes.

DVST   See **direct view storage tube.**

dynamic models   Mathematical or symbolic models that include change over time.

dynamic programming   A mathematical optimization technique suitable for some nonlinear problems in which the problem is decomposed into a series of linked stages.

dynamic storage management   The ability to allocate storage space automatically from external to internal memory as and when it is needed, and to return it when finished.

dynamic tracking   When moving a graphic object about a drawing, it is helpful if the operator can see the object move as it is dragged into place. This process is called dynamic tracking.

EBCDIC   A coding scheme serving the same purpose as the ASCII system; traditionally used by mainframes, particularly IBM machines.

eCAADe   *E*ducation in *c*omputer-*a*ided *a*rchitectural *d*esign in *E*urope.

echo   The output of information as soon as it is received; used to verify that the information has been received correctly.

editor   Same as **text editor.**

electronic data processing (EDP)   Data processing by electronic machines. A rather old-fashioned way of referring to computing, usually preferred by older members of the commercial computing community. Younger members prefer the more fashionable term *management information services (MIS).*

electronic mail   The sending of messages via communication lines between computers. The messages are stored on the receiving computer for later retrieval.

electrostatic printer plotter   A printing or plotting device in which parts of the receiving paper are given an electrostatic charge, which then attracts a fine dust that is fused to it by heat.

emulator   A program that allows a computer to function like some other computer. It is often used for programs that make a microcomputer appear to incoming data to be one of a variety of popular terminals for minicomputers or mainframes.

enable   See **disable.**

EPROM   *E*rasable *p*rogrammable *ROM,* a ROM that can be erased by ultraviolet light and reprogrammed.

error message   A message that a program gives to indicate that an error has occurred, which may or may not require user intervention.

escape key   See **escape sequence**

escape sequence   A sequence of characters, preceded by the escape character (ASCII 27, abbreviated esc), that is interpreted by the computer or peripheral (such as a printer or plotter) as a command instead of just text. Different devices understand different sequences. Most computer keyboards have a key called ESCAPE that emits the escape character.

executable file   A file containing a program, as opposed to one containing data.

exhaustive enumeration   Finding an optimal solution to a problem by examining every possible solution, undertaken when all else fails or the number of possibilities is small. Also known as the "bruteforce and ignorance" approach.

expert system   A computer program that will model the performance of human experts within their domains of expertise.

explode   To decompose a complex graphic object into its components.

extended ASCII   See **ASCII character set.**

external memory   That memory which is under the control of a computer but not necessarily permanently connected to it, such as a floppy or hard-disk drive.

facilities management   The management of the planning and continuing operation of buildings and other facilities and the relationship between the facilities and the using organizations.

facilities planning   The process of laying out rooms, spaces, or parts of an organization within an existing building or as part of a new building design.

field   See **database** and **data item.**

file   An organized collection of data, such as a computer program or a piece of text, stored in a computer's internal or external memory. The fundamental unit stored on external memory. Conceptually equivalent to a single document.

file access   The method by which records in a file are accessed. There are basically two means: sequential and random access. In *sequential access,* records can only be accessed by starting from the first and proceeding to the last; this is used for simple processing involving the whole file. *Random access* (or *direct access*) allows a program to read or write any record of a file at any time.

firmware   A term sometimes used to refer to the software encoded in a ROM, denoting that it is halfway between a piece of equipment (hardware) and a program (software).

flatbed plotter   A pen plotter in which the paper is held on a flat surface while the pen moves along both axes.

flat cable   A cable which is flat and ribbonlike rather than round and which can be laid under carpet tiles without humping.

flip-flop   A device or circuit with two stable states. One state is maintained until a signal is received that causes it to change to the other state.

floating-point number   Same as **real number.**

floppy disk   A single flexible magnetic disk, either $3\frac{1}{2}$, $5\frac{1}{4}$, or 8 in. in diameter, used as a medium for storing memory; see **disk.** The smallest size, which is enclosed in a rigid plastic case, is sometimes called a *microfloppy.*

flowchart   A diagram illustrating the sequences of operations in a procedure for solving a particular problem.

font   Typeface.

footprint   The area of a work surface consumed by a computer or peripheral, usually on the order of $5\frac{1}{2}$ ft^2 (0.5 m^2).

foreground processing   See **background processing.**

format   (1) The particular manner in which data is laid out in a file. (2) The layout of text within a single line.

FORTH   A computer language, used largely on microcomputers.

FORTRAN   *For*mula *tran*slation, a widely used high-level computer language for scientific and technical applications.

fourth-generation language   A language that provides sophisticated database manipulation far above and beyond that available from a high-level programming language.

fractal   An unusual type of curve used in computer graphics to simulate the rough, textured surfaces found in reality and thereby to produce realistic images.

front end   Also known as a *preprocessor*. A program that conducts preliminary processing of data for another program or for a later part of the same program. This second program is sometimes called the *back end*.

function   See **subprogram**.

function key   A key on a computer keyboard that has different meanings under program or user control.

garbage   (1) Meaningless data. (2) A first attempt at writing a program.

gateway   A communications device, often a computer, connecting dissimilar communications channels. Applied particularly to the interfaces between local-area networks and large-scale networks.

generation   The synthesis of a solution by a computer program.

geometric modeling   The representation of the geometry and topology of an object. Particularly used in mechanical engineering CAD systems for the design of complex parts, such as propellers and car panels.

geometric representation   The manner in which the geometry of an object is represented inside the computer.

geometric transformation   A translation, scale, or rotation of a graphic object.

GKS   A computer graphics software standard accepted by the International Standards Organization (ISO).

graphic display device   A device that can display shapes and drawings as well as alphanumeric characters.

graphics language   A language designed especially for computer graphics. It usually consists of a set of procedures that must be called from within a host language.

graphics primitive   A fundamental graphics entity, such as a point, line, or filled area.

handshaking   A system to control data transmission between devices, consisting of some agreed-upon set of control codes to be exchanged at appropriate times. The two most common on microcomputers are the XON/XOFF and the ENQ/ACK methods.

hard copy   Printed paper output.

hard disk   A nonflexible magnetic disk for the storage of data (see **disk**), usually either stacked in layers in a removable disk pack or sealed inside the disk drive as a nonremovable Winchester disk.

hardware   Physical equipment, such as a computer, display screen, disk drives, etc., as opposed to software.

heuristic   A rule based on experience rather than on axiom. A heuristic optimization method is likely, based on experience, to produce good results but is not guaranteed to do so.

hexadecimal   The common notation for expressing binary numbers, simply base 16. Hexadecimal digits range from 0 through 9, then A through F. A byte is represented by two hexadecimal digits, 00 to **FF**, where 00 = 0 and **FF** = 255 in decimal notation.

hidden line   See **hidden surface.**

hidden surface   A graphics image or drawing in which all the lines and planes that would be obscured by closer surfaces are removed, to give a realistic image. On those screens incapable of displaying solid areas of color or gray, the equivalent is a *hidden-line* image. When all the lines in a drawing are visible, the image is known as a *wire-frame.* Hidden-line and hidden-surface images are very expensive computationally, often taking many minutes or hours on a microcomputer.

hierarchical database   See **database.**

high-level language   A computer language in which each statement corresponds to a set of machine-code instructions that work together to carry out some desired operation. FORTRAN, Pascal, COBOL, and many others are high-level languages.

home   The upper left-hand corner of a screen.

homogeneous coordinate   An elegant mathematical notation for carrying out geometrical transformations.

host computer   The main computer to which others are attached.

host language   An everyday high-level language from which special procedures may be called, such as those required for database manipulation or graphics.

icon   A symbol used to represent a command or mode of use. Usually the icon depicts some object familiar to a user: for example, an image of a pen in a computer drafting system.

IEEE Standard 488   A standard for interfaces defined by the Institute of Electrical and Electronics Engineers, used mainly for connecting computers to data-logging equipment.

IGES   *I*nitial *G*raphics *E*xchange *S*pecification. A preliminary standard for the storage of graphics data so that it may be transported between different CAD systems.

image processing   The processing of photographic images by computer.

implementation   A version of a program written for many different computers running on a particular computer. Implementations of the same program will usually vary from machine to machine depending on the sophistication of the host.

index   Like its printed equivalent, it allows the rapid retrieval of data from a database without having to search the whole thing.

inference engineers   A mechanism in an expert system that infers new knowledge from existing knowledge.

information processing   The production of information by accessing and processing data on a computer; traditionally called electronic data processing.

information technology (IT)   A term used to describe anything to do with computers and telecommunications.

ink-jet printer   A printer that uses the dot-matrix principle, spraying ink onto the paper through a matrix of controlled jets. Multiple colors are possible by using multiple nozzles.

input   Information or data entered into a computer via keyboard, tape, graphic device, or other means. An *input device* is a device that accepts such information.

instruction   Usually reserved for the vocabulary of the very lowest level of language understood by a computer, machine code, or assembly code.

integer   A subset of the real number system. The whole numbers.

integrated building description system   A description of a building in a computer database to be used for many different design and documentation purposes.

integrated circuits   Complex electronic circuits etched onto a single piece of semiconductor material, such as a silicon chip.

integrated services digital network (ISDN)   A network in which all data (such as voice) is transformed into digital form for transmission.

integrated software   (1) A suite of programs performing the common business functions of word processing, spreadsheet, business graphics, and database management, often using iconic interfaces, in which the links between different components are transparent. (2) Any suite of software in which the components can read data generated by other components.

intelligent building   Common term for a building containing a computer building management system, which controls its response to the environment and the users within it. Also called a "smart" building. See **building management system.**

intelligent terminal   A computer terminal that has some local computer processing capability.

interactive programs   A way of using computers in which the user and computer program interact with each other via commands, questions and answers, graphic input, etc.

interface   A boundary between two computer components or systems, or the specification for the connection between two components or systems. Also the boundary between a computer and a human user.

internal memory, or internal storage   The RAM and ROM memory contained within the main memory of a computer, as distinct from memory on removable or peripheral devices.

internal network   Same as **local-area network.**

interpreter   A program that translates the statements of an interpretive high-level language (such as BASIC or APL) and executes them immediately. If a programming error is found, execution stops at that point but can continue after the error is corrected.

interrupt   A request from a computer component or peripheral for attention (a fundamental means of controlling devices on a common bus). *Interrupt handling* is one way of dealing with the problem of controlling several devices simultaneously. Another way is by *polling*, in which the computer cyclically asks each peripheral whether it wants attention.

ISDN See **integrated services digital network.**

ISO International Standards Organization.

IT See **information technology**

iterate To repeat.

joy stick A lever that can be moved in at least two degrees of freedom to control the movement of a displayed element; often used with computer games.

justification Alignment of text against a margin. Except for special effects, text is always left-justified. Right justification is only done in printed matter and on word processors.

K See **kilobyte.**

Kb See **kilobyte**

key The field used to locate a record.

keyboard A set of alphanumeric and other keys for entering data. A computer keyboard typically has a QWERTY typewriterlike keyboard plus a numeric pad, function keys, arrow keys to move the cursor, and some other special keys.

kilobyte (K, or Kb) 2^{10} (1024) bytes.

knowledge engineering The acquisition and representation in a computer system of knowledge about a domain of expertise.

LAN See **local-area network.**

landscape mode The position to which a computer screen is turned so that it is wider than it is tall. (See **portrait mode.**)

laser printer A printer using laser beams instead of nibs to form an electrostatic image on paper, which then attracts a fine dust that is fused to it by heat, as in an electrostatic printer.

latency The time it takes for a disk to spin under the head of a disk drive.

layer Computer-aided drawings are often subdivided into layers, analogous to overlaid sheets of tracing paper. Different layers may be displayed or hidden at will. One layer might be used for textual annotation, another for dimensions, another for electrical layout, another for plumbing, etc.

layout planning Same as facilities planning.

learning curve A graphic means of depicting the rate at which a person acquires a new skill, plotting productivity against time.

library (1) A collection of subroutines or procedures of general utility kept together for ease of use. (2) Any collection of information: e.g., a library of element images in a drafting system.

light pen A pen with a light-sensitive cell at its end. When it is placed against the screen of its associated computer terminal, it closes a photoelectric circuit, enabling the terminal to identify the x-y coordinates of the point indicated.

linear programming A mathematical process used to solve certain classes of optimization problems in which the functions describing the constraints and the objective are all linear.

line conditioning Treatment of the general power supply to remove voltage fluctuations as a safeguard against damaging equipment drawing from that supply.

line speed The rate of information transfer between computer equipment, usually measured in baud or bits per second.

line style The style of a displayed line (solid, dashed, dot-dashed, etc.).

linked list See **data structure.**

linker A program that transforms object code (produced by a compiler or assembler) into a ready-to-run form. The linking process is invisible to users of minicomputers and mainframes but is often evident to microcomputer programmers.

LISP *List* processing, a language popular in artificial intelligence work; designed especially for the manipulation of lists.

list See **data structure.**

loader That part of an operating system which loads a program from mass storage into internal memory and then executes it. Invisible to users.

local-area network (LAN) A network implemented within a single building or group of buildings, typically connecting microcomputers for intraorganizational use.

lock A mechanism activated by a multiuser system when a record from a file is accessed, temporarily preventing other users from accessing the same record.

logical An adjective applied to the way a system is perceived, often quite different from the physical form. Applied often to databases, files, and input-output devices.

LOGO A language emphasizing graphics derived from LISP and now favored among educationalists over BASIC as a first programming language.

log on/log off The initial identification that a user gives to a multiuser computer is called *logging on.* It usually requires the user to give a password and often some accounting details. *Logging off* is the termination of a computer session.

low-level language A computer language close to the level of the computer's electronic operation. Applied to machine-code and assembly languages.

M See **megabyte.**

machine code The lowest level of computer language, consisting of binary digits; idiosyncratic to different microprocessors. The language directly understood by the microprocessor.

machine dependence See **machine independence.**

machine independence That desirable quality in a program intended for wide distribution of not depending on unusual properties of particular computers. Machine independence is invariably achieved at the expense of efficiency. *Machine dependence* is theoretically frowned upon but often unavoidable; the aim is to localize the machine-dependent features to small areas of the program.

macro   (1) In drafting systems, a macro is an image that can be treated as an entity in repetition, deletion, transformation, and so on. (2) Sometimes used as a synonym for a procedure or subroutine or for any reusable program chunk.

macro language   A language for writing procedures, particularly within drafting systems.

magnetic disk   See **disk.**

magnetic tape   See **tape drive.**

mainframe   (1) The largest, fastest, and most expensive class of computers, capable of supporting many computer terminals. (2) Often applied to any computer, regardless of size, that drives a peripheral.

main memory   Same as **internal memory.**

maintenance   (1) In the normal sense, the physical maintenance of computer equipment. (2) The upkeep of programs by correcting minor bugs, adapting to changing conditions, etc.

management information systems (MIS)   The current term for commercial data processing.

mapping   A mathematical process in which elements of one group of objects are associated with one or more elements of another group of objects.

mass storage   Same as **external memory.**

mathematical model   A mathematical formulation that describes the behavior of some real or proposed system.

matrix dot printer   A printer that produces characters out of a matrix of dots, either by impacting a ribbon or by ink-jet techniques. Usually able to print graphics (out of dots) as well as alphanumeric characters.

Mb   See **megabyte.**

megabyte (M, or Mb)   Roughly 1 million bytes, or precisely 1024 kilobytes.

megaflop   One million floating-point operations per second. A measure of CPU speed.

memory   A device for storing information.

memory mapping   A technique whereby a peripheral device appears to the CPU as a portion of memory, providing a straightforward and elegant means of communicating between the two.

menu   A list of options, usually either displayed on a screen or fixed to a digitizer tablet, from which a program user can select the next program action.

microcomputer   A small and relatively low-cost class of computers.

microfloppy   See **floppy disk.**

microprocessor   A general-purpose computer processor contained within a single chip.

migration   (1) Trends within a field of computing. (2) Moving from one form of computer system to another one, usually more advanced, but hopefully at least partly compatible.

minicomputer A medium-size class of computers, generally capable of supporting several terminals.

Mips *Million instructions per second.* A measurement of CPU speed.

MIS See **management information system.**

modeling system Computer software that models some selected characteristics of reality. Usually refers to the modeling of three-dimensional objects.

modem A device that changes digital data to an analog signal, and vice versa, for sending over communications channels. It allows a computer to connect to the telephone system or to a private long-distance communications line. An RS-232C interface is almost always used for the computer-modem connection.

module A self-contained part of a program, usually consisting of several procedures.

monitor Synonym for **display.**

mouse A device that fits in the palm of the hand and is moved over a flat surface to cause a corresponding relative movement of a pointer on a display screen.

multiplexer A device that transmits several signals simultaneously through the one transmission medium. Usually used to combine the signals from several terminals into the one transmission line.

multiprocessor system A computer system with several CPUs, generally for several users.

multitasking system A system able to carry out several tasks apparently simultaneously.

multiuser system A computer system that can support several users simultaneously.

MUX Abbreviation of **multiplexer.**

native language The language directly understood by a particular microprocessor.

natural language Any human-human language, such as English.

network Two or more computers and their peripheral equipment linked together so that information can be transmitted between them. Each computer, terminal, or peripheral in the network is called a *node*. Networks are usually classified by topology. A *start network* has several terminals or computers all linked directly to a single central computer. In a *ring network* each node is connected by a single cable in a loop. In a *bus network* each node is connected by a nonlooping cable, broadcasts to every other node, and listens to every message.

network database See **database.**

nibble Half a byte, 4 bits.

node See **network.**

normalization   A mathematical process of transforming a database structure into a proper form for a relational system.

object code   The machine-language program produced by a compiler or assembler.

octal   A number written to base 8, used on some mainframes.

office automation   The integrated computerization of business tasks.

offline   Describes those parts of a computer system which are not directly linked to the central processor. Tapes sitting in a cabinet are offline storage. An *online* component is one connected to and under the control of the computer. Disk drives are online storage.

offset   The distance of an entity from some fixed origin. In computer graphics, the entities are points.

online   See offline.

open systems interconnection (OSI)   A standard sponsored by the ISO for long-haul networks.

operating system   A set of programs that controls the management and operation of the computer's components during the running of other programs.

operations research   A branch of applied mathematics that aims to improve decision making by building mathematical models.

operator   (1) A user of a computer. (2) A mathematical object, such as the $/ + -$ operations.

optimization   The process of trying to find the very best solution in terms of efficiency, cost, time, or some other criterion or combination of criteria.

optimum start/stop control   That control of building plant which monitors the weather to start or stop the plant at the earliest or latest time so as to maintain comfortable conditions within the building.

OSI   See open systems interconnection.

output   The results or messages produced by a computer. An *output device* is a device that accepts such information.

overlay   That part of a program kept on disk which is brought into memory by another part of the program when needed — a technique for fitting large programs into restricted memories.

overlay drafting   See systems drafting.

package   A collection of programs forming an integrated whole.

packet   See packet-switched network.

packet assembler dissembler   See packet-switched network.

packet-switched network   Also known as an *X.25 network*, after the standard defining it. A method of implementing a long-haul network in which data is subdivided into discrete bundles called *packets* and stored at switching nodes until a communications channel is free to send the data. Data is sent from users' terminals or computers to a *packet assembler/disassembler (PAD)*, which translates the data into a form suitable for transmission.

paging   See **virtual memory.**

pan   To move across a drawing in order to make portions at the side, top, or bottom come into view.

parallel port   See **parallel transmission.**

parallel processing   Computer processing in which certain operations in a computer program are performed concurrently with other operations. Also applied to the use of several CPUs to accomplish this.

parallel transmission   A data transmission method in which all the bits in a character are sent simultaneously. A *parallel port* is a plug on a computer or peripheral used for parallel data transmission. The most common is the *Centronics port,* often used for microcomputer-to-printer connections; its primary advantage is the lack of any complicated setup protocols.

parameter   Same as **argument.** See **subprogram.**

parameterized shape   A geometric shape in which certain dimensions are free, that is, assigned values when needed.

parametric function   Description of a complex function in which only a single variable is free to be altered.

parametric variation   The study of design possibilities by systematically varying a parameter at intervals within a range.

parity   See **check bit.**

Pascal   An elegant, high-level programming language encouraging good programming practice.

patch   To make minor ad hoc alterations to a program.

pen plotter   A plotter using a wet-ink drawing pen, felt-tip pen, or similar tool as the means of drawing an image.

peripheral equipment.   Those components of a computer system which are operated under computer control but are not part of the computer, such as a printer, disk drive, and digitizer board.

physical   An adjective referring to the implementation of something in hardware, as opposed to the way people look on it logically.

pick device   Logical device in computer graphics. Any device used to pick an item from a screen.

pixel   The smallest area on the screen of a raster display whose characteristics (color and brightness) can differ from those of its neighbors.

PLEC   Acronym for *p*ower, *l*ighting, *e*lectronics, and *c*ommunications.

plex database   See **database.**

plotter   A device that produces an image on a removable medium, such as paper or film.

PL/1   *P*rogramming *l*anguage 1, a language widely used in the data processing community.

pointer   (1) A programming mechanism. A pointer is an address in internal memory at which data is stored. Linked-list data structures are implemented by using pointers. Each element contains a pointer to another element, thus eliminating the need for elements to be physically adjacent. (2) A pick or pointing device.

pointing device   Same as **pick device.**

polling   See **interrupt.**

port   (1) (Verb) To transport a program from one type of computer to another. (2) (Noun) A computer that is used to transfer data.

portability   The degree to which a program may be transported from computer to computer without significant changes having to be made. Facilitated by using standardized high-level languages and structured programming.

portrait mode   The position to which a computer screen is turned so that it is taller than it is wide. (See **landscape mode.**)

preprocessor   See **front end.**

primitive   In computer graphics, a low-level graphics entity; e.g., a point, line, character, or basic volume (such as a dimensionless cube). In a more general sense, any small graphics entity that can be assembled into more complex entities.

print spooler   A means of sending text for printing to a buffer in order to free the computer for other tasks. The spooler may be a program running invisibly in the computer, or an actual device placed on the cable between the computer and printer.

print wheel   See **daisy-wheel printer.**

priority   A computer that is tending to several peripherals or subsidiary processes will often allocate to each a priority for attention. When tending to one peripheral or process, it will attend to a higher-priority one if this higher one so requests.

procedure   (1) Synonym for *subprogram.* (2) Any sequence of actions. (3) As in an algorithm.

productivity ratio   The labor required to accomplish a task manually divided by the labor to accomplish it using a CAD system.

program   A series of statements or instructions that directs a computer to perform a sequence of operations. An *application program* deals with something in the real world outside of the computer. A *utility program* is concerned with the mundane processes of handling files and writing programs (rather than with applications outside the computer), such as programs to print the current date or to list everybody on the system at the time. A *system program* is one that handles very fundamental operations deep inside the computer, such as reading a keystroke, displaying a character on the screen, copying a file from one disk drive to another, and deleting a file.

PROLOG   A computer language based on the declaration of facts and relationships; used in artificial intelligence work.

prompt   The character(s) output by a program to show that it is ready to accept input.

protocol A set of conventions about the way data is transmitted in order that information can be transmitted between computers or between computers and their terminals. Two simple protocols often used for microcomputers are called ENQ/ACK and XON/XOFF.

public-switched telephone network (PSTN) The everyday telephone system.

purge To delete or erase a file from mass storage.

quantity surveyor (QS) A professional, mainly in British Commonwealth countries, who is responsible for preparing the schedule of quantities of a building.

RAM *Random-access memory*. That memory available for the storage of programs and data in which the memory contents can be altered.

random access See **file access.**

random-access memory Same as **internal memory.**

raster A rectangular matrix, or grid, of pixels. A raster screen or printer is one that creates an image as a matrix of pixels, or dots. A *raster line* is one of the horizontal scanning lines painted on television screens.

raster scan Same as **raster line.**

read To retrieve data from mass storage.

real number An integer or fractional number.

real time A simulated process happening in the same time that one would expect in reality.

record See **database** and **data structure.**

refresh screen A screen in which the image is repainted at least 30 times a second, and which therefore permits animation and selective erasure.

relational database See **database.**

relative coordinates See **coordinates.**

relocation Assigning a computer program to a specific place in internal memory, a process performed by that part of the operating system called the loader.

repetitive strain injury (RSI) Strain caused by the repetitive overuse of muscles in the same way, sometimes suffered by skiers, violinists, and keyboard operators, among others.

reproductive fidelity The fidelity with which an image on a screen represents the image as it will be produced by a printer or plotter.

reprographics The various techniques used to edit and reproduce drawings manually (i.e., without a computer drafting system), often using photographic techniques and photocopying.

resolution The number of pixels (dots) contained on a computer screen, a quantity dependent partly on the computer and partly on the screen; expressed as the number of pixels along each axis. A good resolution is 1000 by 1000.

response time The time elapsing between a user's input and the corresponding reaction from the computer. Responses to trivial actions should be less than 0.5 second. In a more general sense, the time elapsing between an event and its effect.

RGB *R*ed *g*reen *b*lue. (1) A system for defining any color as the amount of the three primaries contained within it. (2) A means for electronically transferring the values of the three primaries used to generate a color image on a CRT.

ring network See network.

ring structure A form of linked list. See **data structure.**

ROM *R*ead-*o*nly *m*emory. Memory that can only be read, meaning that its contents cannot be altered. Often used to store critical parts of a computer's operating system.

RSI See repetitive strain injury.

rubberbanding A graphics technique in which one endpoint of a line remains fixed while the other end is moved about the screen by the user.

sampling In computer graphics, to examine a small portion of a photograph and derive a single measure of chromaticity or luminance for encoding into a computer.

scrolling The process of moving lines up and down a computer screen so that the text or pictures appear to scroll off the top and bottom of the screen.

search To examine data for a particular item, one uniquely identified by its key.

sector A pie-shaped portion of a track on a disk.

seek To locate a piece of data on a mass storage device.

seek time The time it takes the head of a disk drive to move to a wanted track.

segment A defined portion of RAM or of a program; often used to facilitate virtual memory techniques.

semiconductor A material which has controllable electrical conductivity, increasing at high and decreasing at low temperature, and which is used in transistors.

sensor An electronic device that monitors conditions in building plant or within a building.

sequential access See file access.

sequential processing The processing of data in a serial fashion, starting at the beginning and moving forward to the end.

serial port See serial transmission.

serial transmission Data transmission in which each bit is sent one at a time. A *serial port* is a plug on the back of a computer terminal into which a cable may be inserted, which then connects to a serial port on a peripheral or another computer. The most common plug is based on the RS-232C or the newer RS-242 standard.

Shannon text rating A standardized method for rating the speed of printers.

shape grammar A grammar for manipulating shapes according to rules, paralleling a linguistic grammar.

signed number A number that is prefixed with a positive or negative sign; it can be the number zero. An *unsigned number* is positive or the number zero.

silicon chip Same as chip.

simulation   The process of using or operating a model (often a mathematical model encoded in a computer program) to learn about the behavior of the reality being modeled.

simulation language   A language, such as SIMULA, designed to facilitate the writing of programs that simulate some real-world process.

single-tasking system   A system in which tasks must be conducted sequentially.

single-user system   A system that can support one user at a time.

slot   A place on a main circuit board in a computer into which other (expansion) boards may be placed.

small talk   A pioneering operating system that now forms the basis for many iconic operating systems.

smart terminal   Same as an **intelligent terminal.**

smoothing   The process of transforming a rough curve into a smoother (and more aesthetically pleasing) version.

software   Computer programs. Now entering the English language to describe analogous forms, such as videotapes.

software house   Any business concerned with the development and provision of software and systems analysis.

solid modelers   Programs that model solid objects; mainly intended for mechanical engineering work.

sort   To rearrange data into some sequence, usually alphabetical.

source code   The text written by programmers when they write programs, that is, the program itself. Often just called code. A compiler will translate this into object code.

spatial synthesis   The generation of spatial layout or organization, as in layout or facilities planning.

special function key   That key on a keyboard which does not emit a given character but is used by applications for particular functions.

spooler   Same as **print spooler.**

spreadsheet   A program that imitates an accounting spreadsheet; used for the construction of simple to moderate mathematical models and processes.

staircase effect   See **antialiasing.**

stand-alone system   A self-contained computer system, with its display, processor, and memory independent of connections to a computer elsewhere.

star network   See **network.**

storage-tube display   Same as **direct view storage tube.**

streaming tape   A tape backup system often used with Winchester disk drives. It differs from other tape systems in that it is designed for the mass dumping of information to and from the disk, instead of for selective data extraction.

string   Same as **text string.**

structured programming   A common methodology of programming and of programming style.

stylus   A hand-held pointer for indicating choices from a menu or positions on a drawing, such as a digitizer pen or a light pen; a kind of pick device.

subprogram   A program complete unto itself except that data is passed into and out of it from some other subprogram or program called the *driver,* or calling program. Variables within a subprogram are isolated from those in the driver. The variables received from the calling program are called *arguments.* If the subprogram outputs (returns) but a single variable, it is known as a *function,* corresponding to the same concept in mathematics.

subroutine   A rough synonym for **subprogram.**

supercomputer   A term used for the very fastest, largest-memory mainframe computers.

synchronous transmission   See **asynchronous transmission.**

system architecture   Physical makeup of a computer system.

system program   See **program.**

systems analysis   See **analysis.**

systems drafting   The systematization of drafting in an office, including the production and use of drawing standards and procedures and coherent methods of drawing organization and storage. Includes the use of reprographics systems and of *overlay drafting,* which is a method of producing drawings on transparent media so that they may be overlaid and photographed or photocopied to produce a composite drawing.

tablet   A small digitizer board, often used with a stylus and a superimposed menu as a means of indicating commands to a drafting system.

tape drive   A device that uses magnetic tapes as a storage medium. Most often used with minicomputers and mainframes.

technical computing   The use of computers in technical and design offices.

Teletype   A corporate name, now commonly used to refer to a terminal consisting of a printer and keyboard.

terminal   Any device, such as screen and keyboard, or printer and keyboard, at which data can be input to and output from a computer. Loose synonyms are *VDU* and *workstation.*

text editor   A simple word processor allowing the entry and editing of text. Used mainly for program editing.

text string   A group of contiguous alphanumeric characters considered as a single unit, such as a word or sentence.

third-party software   Software neither supplied by the vendor of a computer system nor written in-house. The most common way to acquire microcomputer programs.

thumb wheels   Used to locate points on a screen, two wheels are rotated by thumb to cause corresponding horizontal and vertical movements of a screen cursor.

timesharing   An arrangement in which several computer terminals use the same computer processor apparently simultaneously, the processor "sharing" its operating time between the terminals in small time slices. A firm that leases out time (and terminals) to others is a *timesharing service.*

token passing   A method of implementing a local-area network in which a message called the token is sent continuously through the network. A node is only allowed to transmit if it holds the token.

touch screen   A computer screen with infrared sensors placed around the frame (or with a special transparent grid laid on the screen) that allows a user to pick menu items by pointing or touching.

track   A magnetic area on a disk, consisting of a circle of magnetic medium centered on the disk's center.

transaction   A single read, write, or update to a database.

transfer rate   The speed of data transfer between a central processing unit and its peripherals, usually measured in kilobytes or megabytes per second.

transformation   In the mathematical sense, any mathematical operation that transforms data in some way. In computer graphics, a transformation is a geometric manipulation of graphic data, such as scaling or rotation.

transparency   The more a program hides the computer's internal operations from a user, the more transparent it is.

tree   See **data structure** and **database.**

turnkey system   Applied to a computer system in which all the user has to do is "turn the key." Meant to imply ease of use and all-inclusiveness of function.

unsigned number   See **signed number.**

update   To bring a record up to date by erasing its previous contents and replacing them with more recent data.

user   Anyone who uses a computer. A term also used to avoid the reality that these people are mostly customers, which implies more responsibility on the part of vendors than they would like.

user sovereignty   The user's ability to control his or her work.

utility program   See **program.**

value-added network   A long-distance network that offers any of various computer services. Distinguished from passive long-distance networks, which are simply transmission media.

vaporware   Software that will arrive "soon." Promises, promises.

variable   In the everyday mathematical sense, a mathematical object that has a name and a value. Computer programs manipulate data, and data is always stored in variables. A variable is actually a location in RAM.

VDU   See **visual-display unit.**

vector display   See **vector graphics.**

vector graphics   Drawings in which the image is created as direct continuous lines (vectors) between two endpoints, as distinct from the matrix of dots used to create lines in raster graphics and normal television. A *vector display*, or *calligraphic display*, is one that uses vector graphics.

viewing operation   A mathematical operation applied to graphic data by a computer immediately before the data is drawn on the screen; this operation has no effect on the object being modeled. A perspective is a viewing operation.

viewport   A bounded area that is created on the screen to display an image. A screen may contain several viewports. A close synonym to the now common meaning of *window*, with the difference that viewports cannot be overlapped.

virtual memory   The technique or process whereby a user appears to have a very large amount of RAM, when in fact the actual RAM is much smaller. The illusion is achieved by continually moving data and programs between mass storage and RAM, and it relies on fast disk accesses for its utility. *Paging* is a related method whereby programs and data are divided into fixed amounts called pages and brought into main memory as needed.

visual-display unit (VDU)   A computer display cathode-ray tube (or other sort of screen) and keyboard.

VLSI   *Very large-scale integration*. The common process used in the design and manufacture of integrated circuits.

volatile memory   Computer memory that relies on continuous electric power to store data. Normal RAM is volatile; mass storage media are never volatile.

volume   A logical division of a mass storage medium. A hard disk may contain several volumes.

Winchester drive   A relatively small hard-disk drive unit into which the disk is sealed and cannot be removed. Used extensively and almost exclusively with microcomputers.

window   (1) A bounded area created within a computer screen to contain a separate image from the rest of the screen. A screen can contain several windows at the same time, sometimes superimposed, each defined by the software. In this sense, *window* is a partial synonym for *viewport*. When one is drawing within a window on the screen, *clipping* is the procedure carried out by a program to ensure that no part of the drawing goes outside the window. (2) The original sense was that of defining a bounded subarea of a larger drawing.

wire frame   A form of drawing in which every line comprising the drawing is visible, as though made of wire. See **hidden surface.**

word   The fundamental unit of storage manipulated by a computer; a set of bits that occupies one memory storage location and is treated as a unit. Word lengths are typically 8, 16, or 32 bits. Some large computers use 60-bit words. By and large, the longer the word length, the more powerful the computer.

word processor   A computer program, or entire computer system, that facilitates the typing, editing, and printing of documents. See **text editor.**

workstation   In a computer drafting system, a workstation is the combination of display screen, keyboard, and perhaps a tablet and/or stylus or mouse for each draftsperson using the system. In a more general sense, a unit consisting of screen and keyboard plus any other input devices, suitable for use by a single operator.

wraparound   The process whereby a cursor on a computer display automatically moves down to the next line upon reaching the end of the line above.

write   To place data into either internal memory or mass storage.

X.25 network   See **packet-switched network.**

zoom   A term used in computer graphics (analogous to its original use in photography), it refers to examining a drawing from a greater or lesser distance in order to fit either more or less of the drawing on the screen.

Index

ABOUT THE AUTHORS

ANTONY RADFORD is Senior Lecturer in the Department of
Architectural Science, University of Sydney, and is Associate
Director of the Computer Applications Unit within the
department. He holds academic credentials in architecture
and planning and has been involved with computer
applications for the past 15 years. He is the author of more
than 50 articles and book chapters on design and computing
in architecture.

GARRY STEVENS is Senior Tutor in the Department of
Architectural Science, University of Sydney, and principal of
Cadarch, a computer-aided architectural design consulting
firm in Sydney. He holds academic credentials in architecture
and architectural computing.